Betv
II ir
rang
this
the
of h
Nor
chu
stor
Lor
cha
nor
pat

Jud
Edi
is tl
bet
No
No

Forging the Kingdom

Power in English Society, 973–1189

JUDITH A. GREEN

CAMBRIDGE
UNIVERSITY PRESS

CAMBRIDGE
UNIVERSITY PRESS

University Printing House, Cambridge CB2 8BS, United Kingdom

One Liberty Plaza, 20th Floor, New York, NY 10006, USA

477 Williamstown Road, Port Melbourne, VIC 3207, Australia

4843/24, 2nd Floor, Ansari Road, Daryaganj, Delhi – 110002, India

79 Anson Road, #06–04/06, Singapore 079906

Cambridge University Press is part of the University of Cambridge.

It furthers the University's mission by disseminating knowledge in the pursuit of education, learning, and research at the highest international levels of excellence.

www.cambridge.org
Information on this title: www.cambridge.org/9780521193597
DOI: 10.1017/9781139018074

© Judith A. Green 2017

First published 2017

Printed in the United Kingdom by Clays, St Ives plc

A catalogue record for this publication is available from the British Library.

ISBN 978-0-521-19359-7 Hardback
ISBN 978-0-521-15829-9 Paperback

Contents

Acknowledgements

It is a pleasure to be able to thank those whose help has made this book possible. A much valued continuing attachment to the School of History, Classics, and Archaeology at the University of Edinburgh has, amongst other things, enabled access to its library facilities. The National Library of Scotland creates a peaceful and scholarly environment in which to work. Liz Friend-Smith at Cambridge University Press has been an encouraging and patient editor. Finally, Ian Green has as ever provided support on every front, academic and personal.

Abbreviations

ASC	Anglo-Saxon Chronicle MS C: *The Anglo-Saxon Chronicle: A Collaborative Edition. Volume 5*, ed. K. O'B. Keeffe (Cambridge: D. S. Brewer, 2001) MS D: *The Anglo-Saxon Chronicle: A Collaborative Edition. Volume 6*, ed. G. P. Cubbin (Cambridge: D. S. Brewer, 1996) MS E: *The Anglo-Saxon Chronicle: A Collaborative Edition. Volume 7*, ed. S. Irvine (Cambridge: D. S. Brewer, 2004) MS F: *The Anglo-Saxon Chronicle: A Collaborative Edition. Volume 8*, ed. P. S. Baker (Cambridge: D. S. Brewer, 2000)
Bates, *Acta of William I*	*Regesta Regum Anglo-Normannorum. The Acta of William I (1066–1087)*, ed. D. Bates (Oxford: Clarendon Press, 1998)
DB	*Domesday Book, seu liber censualis Willelmi primi Regis Angliae inter archivos regni in domo capitulari Westmonasterii asservatus. Jubente Regi Augustissimo Georgio Tertio praelo mandatus typis*, ed. A. Farley 4 vols. (London, 1783–1816)

Diceto	*Radulfi de Diceto decani Londoniensis opera historica*, ed. W. Stubbs, 2 vols., RS (London: Longman, 1876)
English Historical Documents	*English Historical Documents* I *c. 500–1042*, ed. D. Whitelock, 2nd edn (London, New York: Routledge, 1996); II, *1042–1189*, ed. D. C. Douglas, 2nd edn (London: Eyre Methuen, 1981)
Geoffrey of Monmouth, *HKB*	Geoffrey of Monmouth, *The History of the Kings of Britain*, ed. M. D. Reeve, trans. N. Wright (Woodbridge: Boydell Press, 2007)
Glanvill	*The Treatise on the Laws and Customs of the Realm of England Commonly Called Glanvill*, ed. G. D. G. Hall (Oxford: Clarendon Press, 1993)
HH	Henry of Huntingdon, *Historia Anglorum*, ed. and trans. D. Greenway (Oxford: Clarendon Press, 1996)
Howden	*Chronica Rogeri de Houedene*, ed. W. Stubbs, 4 vols., RS (London: Longmans, Green, Reader and Dyer, 1868–71)
JW	*The Chronicle of John of Worcester*, II, ed. R. R. Darlington and P. McGurk, trans. J. Bray and P. McGurk (Oxford: Clarendon Press, 1995); III, ed. and trans. P. McGurk (Oxford: Clarendon Press, 1998)
Migne, *Patrologia Latina*	*Patrologia Latina*, ed. J.-P. Migne, 221 vols. (Paris: Garnier and J.-P. Migne's successors, 1844–64)
ODNB	*Oxford Dictionary of National Biography*, ed. H. C. G. Matthew and B. Harrison Matthew, 61 vols. (Oxford: Oxford University Press in association with the British Academy, 2004), consulted online at www.oxforddnb.com/

OV	*The Ecclesiastical History of Orderic Vitalis*, ed. M. Chibnall, 6 vols. (Oxford: Clarendon Press, 1969–80)
RRAN	*Regesta Regum Anglo-Normannorum 1066–1154*, 4 vols., I, ed. H. W. C. Davis, II, ed. C. Johnson and H. A. Cronne, III and IV, ed. H. A. Cronne and R. H. C. Davis (Oxford: Clarendon Press, 1923–69)
RS	Rolls Series
S	Electronic Sawyer enumeration of Anglo-Saxon Charters, www.esawyer .org.uk
WM	William of Malmesbury

NOTE ON REFERENCES

References to the Anglo-Saxon Chronicle are by letter symbol for the manuscript and year.

Domesday Book is cited by volume and folio number.

Pipe Rolls are cited by regnal year in the edition published by the Pipe Roll Society. Page references to *Pipe Roll 31 Henry I* are to the 2012 edition, Pipe Roll Society, New Series, 57.

Unless otherwise stated, Anglo-Saxon law codes are usually referred to by the reference system in F. Liebermann, *Die Gesetze der Angelsachsen*, 3 vols. (Halle: Niemayer, 1903–16).

Introduction

This is a book about power and the way it was exercised in English society between the late tenth and late twelfth centuries. Power is broadly defined, ranging from the most immediate, coercive forms to indirect methods such as influence or persuasion, consumption, display, and ritual designed both to impress and to involve. The focus is on the powerful, and as such the king and the political context within which he operated take centre stage. The main themes are the internal consolidation and coherence of the realm and the mechanisms by which it was ruled; the parallel internal developments within the English church, and its much greater involvement with the wider Latin church; the changing relationship between lordship and land; the transformation of the built environment by the spread and grandeur of building in stone; and the rise of London as a capital city.

It is argued here that the two centuries between the coronation of King Edgar in 973 and the death of Henry II in 1189 were critical in shaping English society. Edgar's reign was in many respects the apogee of Old English kingship, in its claims to overkingship of its neighbours in Britain, in the intensification of royal rule over England south of the Tees, in flourishing economic activity, especially in eastern England, and in the revival of Benedictine monasticism. Nevertheless, there were distinct limits to this success story, notably the relative fragility of royal rule outside the heartland of Wessex, and, a related point, the looseness of ties between the king and noble families, the unevenness of economic prosperity, and of monastic reform. Moreover, this wealthy kingdom proved vulnerable to external predation, culminating in conquests by Danes and then Normans. Whilst not minimizing the destructive impact of the first of these conquests, the Norman Conquest proved not only more thoroughgoing in rooting out the existing elite, but fundamentally recalibrated the relationship between the crown and the aristocracy. Not only that, but beginning in the later eleventh and accelerating in the early twelfth century, the new Norman elite was successful in achieving a much greater penetration of northern England, especially the region to the north and west of Yorkshire, than before. Kings, lords, and churchmen worked in tandem, so that by the mid-twelfth century the north was more firmly integrated into the English kingdom than before. It was in the wake of King Stephen's reign that a third period of fundamental importance in the shaping of English society occurred. The need to stabilize possession of land, to restore order, and to crack down on crime led to the development of a centralized legal system resting on the shoulders of justices, sheriffs, and local juries. The desire for precision in defining spheres of jurisdiction brought conflict with Becket and ultimately a slow clarification of procedure and a greater awareness of the dual allegiance of churchmen to pope and to king. Finally, ever-increasing costs of warfare involved in the defence of Angevin territories led to new ways of raising cash which in turn meant a greater reliance on noble support.

Writing the history of these two centuries raises questions about the chronological limits and the conceptual framework. For twelfth-century chroniclers, this was the history of England and her kings. Picking up the master-narrative of Bede, it was the story of Germanic invasions, and of the early kingdoms giving way to one, Wessex, under the pressure of Viking attack, then William the Conqueror succeeding as the heir of Edward the Confessor: conquest could thus be subsumed under continuity.[1] Between the twelfth and twentieth centuries this perspective remained influential, and in some respects became even more so, with an emphasis on the political and cultural achievements of King Alfred and his successors: his promotion of the Old English vernacular, his law codes, the defence of his realm through the army and through the building of *burhs*, and the levying of general oaths of allegiance binding freemen to the king. His successors went from strength to strength.[2] This was a kingdom with centralized institutions, a sophisticated system of coinage, a means of

---

[1] M. Chibnall, *The Debate on the Norman Conquest* (Manchester: Manchester University Press, 1999), chapter 1; J. Campbell, 'Some Twelfth-Century Views of the Anglo-Saxon Past', reprinted version in Campbell, *Essays in Anglo-Saxon History* (London: Hambledon Press, 1986), pp. 209–28.

[2] Patrick Wormald, 'Alfred (848/9–899)', *ODNB* www.oxforddnb.com/view/article/183, accessed 20 May 2016; J. Campbell, 'Was It Infancy in England? Some Questions of Comparison', reprinted in Campbell, *The Anglo-Saxon State* (London: Hambledon Press and London, 2000), pp. 179–99.

mobilizing wealth through taxation, and, by the later tenth century, flourishing Benedictine monasteries. The reality seemed to match the chroniclers' rhetoric, and for some historians this amounted to an Anglo-Saxon state.[3] If not a nation-state, this was a kingdom with relatively settled boundaries, a high level of local participation in courts and assemblies, and capable of absorbing external invaders into an English political community. These views seemed to confirm the idea of the lengthy and basically continuous evolution of the English state which was influential for so long in English historiography.[4]

However, terms such as 'state' and 'nation' are inevitably problematic for our period. The nature of royal authority, especially in marginal zones, differed from that in the core. Not only was control of what became the northern counties of England disputed, but along the borders with Wales autonomous marcher lordships were established in the eleventh and twelfth centuries. Tenth-century English kings took over regions in parts thickly settled by Danes and Norwegians: in terms of the written record there is much less information about their loyalties and identities than about southern England. That division of the kingdom could be contemplated on several occasions in the tenth and eleventh centuries provides a salutary reminder of the fragility of union.[5]

Moreover, the lengthy periods when England was ruled in conjunction first with Denmark, then Normandy, and finally with Ireland and the French territories of Henry II, has led some historians to frame discussion round the idea of empire. As in the case of state, the term empire also has to be used with caution. The view that Cnut ruled a north-sea empire has attracted support, but some have queried whether this was how Cnut himself saw his rule.[6] Contemporaries knew of the Roman empire and its

---

[3] Campbell, 'The Late Anglo-Saxon State: a Maximum View', reprinted in *Anglo-Saxon State*, pp. 1–30.

[4] For an excellent introduction to English constitutional history, see J. Campbell, 'Stubbs, William (1825–1901)', *ODNB* www.oxforddnb.com/view/article/36362, accessed 20 May 2016; more generally, J. W. Burrow, *A Liberal Descent: Victorian Historians and the English Past* (Cambridge: Cambridge University Press, 1981).

[5] After the death of Eadred in 955, he was succeeded by Eadwig in Wessex and Edgar in Mercia, and it was only after Eadwig's death that Edgar became king of the whole realm, ASC, D, 955; B, C, 959. Cnut and Edmund Ironside agreed to divide the realm in 1016, and once again it was a death, in this case Edmund's, that meant Cnut succeeded to the whole, ASC, C, D, E, 1016.

[6] See, for example, L. M. Larson, *Canute the Great (circ.) 995–1035 and the Rise of Danish Imperialism during the Viking Age* (New York: Putnam, 1912), p. 257; more recently T. Bolton, *The Empire of Cnut the Great: Conquest and the Consolidation of Power in Northern Europe in the Early Eleventh Century* (Leiden, Boston: Brill, 2009).

successor, and the term *imperium* could be used of a king's rule over different peoples. An alternative framework would have been that of the British Isles. Again, the history of England in the context of her relations with other kingdoms and principalities in the British Isles offers fresh perspectives on periodization. The late Rees Davies saw the year 1093, when the deaths of Welsh and Scottish kings occurred, as a more decisive date in terms of the history of the British Isles than 1066.[7] The idea of England as part of a Norman empire was raised by Le Patourel, who argued quite correctly that Normandy could not just be viewed as an offshore principality of the English kings.[8] Recently David Bates has returned to the question of empire in relation to the Normans, discussing how useful terms such as 'empire' and 'imperialism' are in this context.[9] Alternative terms for the relationship between England and Normandy have been used such as 'Anglo-Norman state', 'condominium', or *espace*.[10] Finding a term which accurately sums up the larger assemblage of Angevin territories and claims is even more difficult, but 'empire' seems to be the most popular.[11]

Sensitivity to the changing political context of English kingship raises further questions about loyalty to the king and national identity, or about 'Englishness'. How 'English' did the Scandinavian settlers in Yorkshire or Lincolnshire feel in the tenth century? How important was loyalty to the English king in the world view of those who, say, lived in Cornwall? The rise of the papacy within the Latin church was yet another cross-current, for clergy in England now had to recognize another allegiance beyond that to the king (who had often secured preferment for them). At times these loyalties were conflicted, even dangerously so.

Framing the discourse thus helps to determine major themes. In the past, in an age of nationalism and national history, the two conquests of the eleventh century, especially that by the Normans, marked the end of one era, that of Anglo-Saxon England, and the beginning of another, that of Anglo-Norman England. Even today many books either begin or end round about 1066, and historians tend to divide into Anglo-Saxonists or Anglo-Normanists, a divide

[7] *The First English Empire: Power and Identities in the British Isles, 1093–1343* (Oxford: Oxford University Press, 2000), pp. 4–5.
[8] J. Le Patourel, *The Norman Empire* (Oxford: Clarendon Press, 1976).
[9] D. Bates, *The Normans and Empire* (Oxford: Oxford University Press, 2013).
[10] M. Aurell, *L'empire des Plantagenêts 1154–1224* (Paris: Perrin, 2003), p. 11; for the term *Anglo-Norman condominium*, see, for example, D. Crouch, *The Reign of King Stephen 1135–1154* (Harlow: Longman, 2000), p. 22.
[11] J. Gillingham, *The Angevin Empire*, 2nd edn (London: Arnold, 2001).

reflected in the two major specialist journals, *Anglo-Saxon England* and *Anglo-Norman Studies*. Historical debate still tends to work round ideas of continuity and change across 1066. Here the timescale is different, because the focus is not simply about dynastic and political change, but the way the exercise of power, broadly defined, shaped English society. The starting date of the book is what might be regarded as the apogee of the Old English kingdom, the 'imperial' coronation of King Edgar in 973: the pious, peace-loving king crowned by the archbishop of Canterbury at Bath, a place evocative of the Roman past. At the time of Edgar's death royal power was penetrating much of England, and kings were asserting claims not just over England, but over all Britain. They were able to raise contributions of men and money for their armies. Defended *burhs* provided protection for local settlements, and it was within their walls that moneyers issued coins in the king's name.

Yet that coronation was to be the calm before the storm as the renewal and intensification of Danish raids ratcheted up the pressure on the Old English kingdom. Demands for money, armed men, ships, and defences all increased, and the framework of royal governance developed during those decades was taken over subsequently by the Norman kings. It will be argued that 1066 was an important date for two principal reasons. Firstly was the arrival of an alien, French-speaking elite, and secondly was a different relationship between that aristocracy and the crown. Following from these changes was the gradual penetration by king, south-ern aristocracy, and church of England north of the Humber and Mersey in the twelfth century. In fact, in terms of the greater integration of the realm, a further acceleration of developments in law and finance, the emergence of London as a capital city, and the great boom in stone building, this book needs to continue to the death of Henry II in 1189. There is of course an argument for treating the reigns of all the Angevin kings together, and ending this book in 1215, but the counterargument is that the financial demands of Richard and John, coupled with rising price inflation and John's political methods, imposed a greater degree of pres-sure and discontent than experienced under Henry II. However, change was not a story of linear progression towards a medieval state on Weberian lines with central institutions run by a bureaucracy, which claimed a monopoly of the legitimate use of force, and a prior claim on the loyalty of its inhabitants.[12] Rather, cross-currents, compromises, and

---

[12] M. Weber, *Economy and Society. An Outline of Interpretive Sociology*, ed. G. Roth and C. Wittich, I (Berkeley, London: University of California Press, 1978), p. 56.

constraints shaped and restricted developments. The remainder of this chapter considers definitions of power and contemporary sources, and the main themes of this book are introduced.

For much of the time England's fate was tied into events in Scandinavia and northern France. The conquests differed in terms of the origins and numbers of the invaders and therefore in their long-term consequences. The earlier conquest was the culmination of years of raids and, latterly, of large-scale expeditions. Consequences included casualties and infighting in aristocratic families, destruction and pillaging of churches for treasure, and pressure on royal resources to raise men and ships, to renew defences, and to fund tributes. How far the rule of King Cnut and his two sons disrupted English society is not clear. At the apex of English society there were changes, but not the same degree of upheaval that followed 1066.[13] The restoration of peace and the potential strengthening of trading links across the North Sea probably brought a renewal of economic growth.[14] Cnut's empire may not have been bad news in the Danelaw towns. The Norman takeover followed only one invading expedition in 1066, and the widespread building of fortifications in the countryside as well as the towns made it more difficult to oust the newcomers. The newcomers soon dominated the upper levels of the church and of civil society, with far-reaching consequences for language and culture.

Power in this world was vested in men, whether kings, warriors, or churchmen. Patriarchy was enduring, and in certain areas became more pervasive, in the stronger exclusion of women from the ruling hierarchy of the church and from those opportunities for advanced education at cathedral schools which offered the means of social advancement for young men. There are signs apparently pointing in the other direction. Individual high-status women were able to exercise real power, and by the twelfth century there were more opportunities for women as well as men to enter the religious life. Yet both of these were not necessarily signs that social change was favouring women. Opportunity to exercise power depended very much on circumstances and on personality, and could be shut down speedily, as happened to Queen Emma in 1043 and Eleanor of Aquitaine in 1174. Greater opportunity to enter the religious life might reflect, in an

---

[13] See M. K. Lawson, *Cnut: the Danes in England in the Eleventh Century* (Harlow: Longman, 1993); A. Rumble (ed.), *The Reign of Cnut. King of England, Denmark and Norway* (London, New York: Leicester University Press, 1994).

[14] For the wealth of England on the eve of the Conquest, see P. H. Sawyer, *The Wealth of Anglo-Saxon England* (Oxford: Oxford University Press, 2013), pp. 28–9.

age of rising population, that daughters had greater freedom to pursue a religious vocation, but the foundation of nunneries could also be taken as reflecting concerns that religious women be cloistered. The veneration of female saints of the past like Etheldreda of Ely or Edith of Wilton, it could be argued, was fuelled by the agenda of the (male) communities where their relics were housed. The ever rising cult of the Virgin likewise reflected her perceived importance in religious practice and ritual, especially in the monasteries, and with her role as an intercessor for the sins of mankind, not that she had been in any sense representative of female power.

This was an era when the use of documents as instruments of authority vastly expanded, encouraging some historians to write of the 'rise of bureaucracy'.[15] However, documents did not replace older channels for the transmission of power, ritual, and display: they augmented them. Many documents resulted from developments in law, justice, and taxation. Up to a point these developed in tandem in royal and ecclesiastical government. From the perspective of coercive power, kings worked with the aristocracy, the warrior class, which either directly or indirectly provided the muscle and the men to fight wars, and through whose cooperation money could be raised. Success depended on consensus, and this depended on what has been described as assembly politics. Who was summoned, when, and how consent was achieved all evolved. The important point is that by the late twelfth century the exercise of power by Henry II depended on having the elite on board. The limits as well as the potential of royal authority have to be recognized.

The exercise of power was in certain senses a form of theatre. The setting of ritual and ceremony, whether the king's court or a great church, contributed to and was part of the message. One very striking development was the increasing grandeur of that setting. In the eleventh century more churches were being built in stone and, after 1066, on a vast scale and, it would seem, with an eye on the competition. Experimentation and ambition were the order of the day. In terms of style this was the period of a transition from Romanesque to Gothic. Residential accommodation for the great included great halls for feasting and assemblies.

At the apex of earthly society was the king, sanctified and crowned by the rites of the church. He was at the centre of a spider's web of agents and, increasingly, of agencies. A history of royal power is thus centre-outwards,

---

[15] For discussion, see M. T. Clanchy, *From Memory to Written Record*, 3rd edn (Oxford: Wiley-Blackwell, 2013), pp. 19, 69–70, 329.

as well as top-down, of effective kings subordinating and integrating the provinces into the kingdom, although on the furthest periphery royal authority was necessarily attenuated. A core-periphery approach is too simplistic: the boundaries of the kingdom in the north shifted over time. Internally the kingdom was not unified, but a congerie of earlier kingdoms and regions. Historians of later periods have dabbled with the idea of regions, usually in the end to downplay their importance, but in these centuries England remained a patchwork of regions and jurisdictions.

For most people, the most important social bonds were immediate: family and neighbourhood, lords and men, membership of gilds. Their lateral and vertical aspects shifted over time and according to circumstance. In landed families the strengthening of lineage gave preference to eldest sons. The church's emphasis on the sacramental character of marriage led ultimately to the downgrading of other relationships and their offspring. Lordship became increasingly tied to the position of specific estates, often carved out of larger territories, and relationships between lords and peasants evolved. Increasingly peasants were tied to lords, sometimes as free men, otherwise more heavily burdened by labour service. Peasants who cultivated shares in the common fields of a manor, *villani*, were legally tied to the manor and the lord's jurisdiction. Those who were personally unfree were styled serfs, *servi*, the same word used for slaves, but by the twelfth century the practice of buying and selling slaves was dying out.

The pre-eminence of land as the source of wealth and prestige has in some respects led to an underestimate of the social importance of towns and cities as nodes of power. The fortifications newly built or reinforced in the south and in English Mercia provided defended centres for commerce and trade, and places where moneyers could supply the silver coinage. Towns and cities were communities, which included bishops and chapters, monastic houses and hospitals, lay lords and townsmen. They provided a different kind of theatre of power. Physically dominated by new churches and castles, the landscape of towns was transformed by the twelfth century. Towns do not in themselves seem to have acted as a political entity, with the notable exception of London. By far the largest and wealthiest of English cities, London was protected by its walls, able to raise its own militia, and to organize its own affairs. By the end of our period it had developed into a capital city.

This book aims to offer a different perspective on two centuries by focussing on the powerful, on the collaboration between kings, lords, and churchmen, on changes in the way power was exercised with increasing use of courts and documents, on buildings as the visible expression of power, and on the rise of London as a capital city.

POWER TO DO WHAT?

The first issue to be addressed is that of the definition of power. As Steven Lukes wrote, discussions of power rest on hidden assumptions and leave important questions unanswered.[16] Are we to concentrate on the nature of its intended effects, or to include only the actual? Power over other human beings? Power of individuals or of the state? Power in the Middle Ages obviously differed in many ways from that in modern society: individuals had fewer material resources at hand, and could directly affect fewer people. Relatively little is heard about crowd violence. On the other hand, power exercised by God and His saints was an ever-present possibility: the veil separating the physical world from the heavenly cosmos was permeable.

In sketching out the principal characteristics of power in English society between the tenth and twelfth centuries, it is useful therefore to think in terms of function and method, or power to do what, to whom, and by what means? Here the headings are power to compel obedience and ideological and economic power.[17] Power to compel obedience includes physical force either demonstrated or implied, charisma, and tradition. Tradition leads on to a second theme, the power of ideas, especially hierarchy, patriarchy, and gender. Economic power is wealth, mainly in the form of land, crucial to which was lordship, and commerce.

Theoretical discussions about power in historical contexts bring us directly to the concept of the state. Some historians have been ready to use the term in the context of late Anglo-Saxon England, whilst others have argued that the term is unhelpful, not least because it was not employed at the time.[18] It is one of the arguments of this book that

[16] S. Lukes, 'Introduction', *Power*, ed. S. Lukes (New York: New York University Press, 1986), pp. 1–18.

[17] Cf. Michael Mann's four categories: ideological, military, economic, and political, in *The Sources of Social Power*, 4 vols., I (Cambridge: Cambridge University Press, 1986).

[18] Patrick Wormald and James Campbell have been the chief proponents of the idea of an Anglo-Saxon state. For the former's views, see 'Germanic Power Structures: the Early English Experience', L. Scales and O. Zimmer (eds.), *Power and the Nation in European History* (Cambridge: Cambridge University Press, 2005), pp. 105–24. J. Campbell, *The Anglo-Saxon State*, especially 'Introduction', 'The Late Anglo-Saxon State: a Maximum View', and 'The United Kingdom of England: the Anglo-Saxon Achievement'. For a more sceptical view, see R. R. Davies, 'The Medieval State: the

whether or not there was a state in England at the start of our period, in some respects it had become more like a state by the end, if nothing like a nineteenth- or twentieth-century nation-state.

In its most immediate sense, power is coercive, being able to compel someone else by the threat or use of force to obedience and conformity on pain of punishment or death, and to provide labour and payment. Through force or the fear of force people may be enslaved or imprisoned, held to ransom, mutilated, raped, or killed. They may be compelled to provide service or to give money. Violence was not confined to specific social groups, but the mobilization of armed bands, the hiring of professional soldiers, and the building of fortifications was the purview of the social elite. The rationale of the noble class was that they were the warriors. Kings and princes were expected to be warriors, too, and they summoned men to their armies, both on the basis of personal loyalties and in respect of their land. Yet the king did not, could not, exercise a monopoly over the legitimate use of violence. Noble warfare has often had a bad press, but we hear little about how it was justified to contemporaries.

Arms were held widely – indeed, it would have been foolish to go about unarmed – and men expected to avenge wrongs done to them. Often redress took the form of self-help. Kings and lords could not eradicate violent disputes, though they could exert pressure for negotiated settlements. Deaths and injuries not compensated for could lead to feuds, which by the tenth century kings were seeking to regulate. Many forms of homicide remained emendable, though aggravated homicide was another matter.[19]

Self-help was often in fact the most realistic option for securing redress of wrongs: court actions, even if the wronged man had access to court, were lengthy and unlikely to produce a decisive solution. The king had responsibility for dealing with a narrow range of serious offences such as murder and rape, offences against his person, property, and royal rights. Punishments for serious offences were usually death or mutilation, often

Tyranny of a Concept?', *Journal of Historical Sociology*, 16 (2003), 280–300, and for a rejoinder, S. Reynolds, 'There Were States in Medieval Europe: a Response to Rees Davies', *Journal of Historical Sociology*, 16 (2003), 550–5; S. Foot, 'The Historiography of the Anglo-Saxon Nation-State' (ed. Scales and Zimmer), *Power and the Nation*, pp. 125–42. For a recent review, see G. Molyneaux, *The Formation of the English Kingdom in the Tenth Century* (Oxford: Oxford University Press, 2015), pp. 232–3.

[19] J. Hudson, *The Oxford History of the Laws of England*. II, 871–1216 (Oxford: Oxford University Press, 2012), pp. 178–9, 183–4, 409–10, 722–5.

combined with a fine. The overriding ideas were punishment and deterrence. Imprisonment was used less as a punishment than as a form of remand, to ensure that prisoners were held until they faced court.

Power was used to enslave, and slavery was still widespread in England at the start of our period. Domesday Book does not consistently record slaves, but where it does, there were often substantial numbers. Men and women were taken out of the country as slaves, to Ireland, to the Vikings, or to the Scots. Over time chattel slavery declined, partly because of condemnation by church leaders and partly for economic reasons (see later in this chapter). More peasants became unfree and the restrictions on them became more acute. There were proportionately fewer free rent-paying peasants and more who were serfs, tied to the estate, legally unfree to leave, and subject to labour service and other burdens. Lords disciplined their peasants, and could raise their obligations and dues at will, constrained only by peasants' collective action, about which little is reported in English sources. Perhaps there were rent strikes and go slows, but if so they have escaped the written record. Where landlords were oppressive, flight may have been the only remedy.

One of the problems for kings in this era was that of enforcing obedience in their absence. Why should an order be obeyed in a region rarely if ever visited by the king and where the representatives of royal authority could be evaded? The charisma attached to kingship provides one answer. Kings were special people and by our era were transformed by anointing with holy oil and crowning by archbishops. Their duties were to protect the church and people and to administer good laws.

Even more charismatic were the saints who, living and dead, were able to exercise power to assist men, to cure their ills, to prophesy, and to punish wrongdoers. They were often venerated at places where they had lived or died, and where there were relics. Shrines were holy places, protected by their patron saints. Thus St Cuthbert protected those who venerated his shrine at Durham and punished those who scoffed or who infringed his lands and rights. St Cuthbert even punished William the Conqueror for his temerity in expressing doubt whether the saint was buried at Durham. He planned to inspect the body himself, and if it were not found, heads were to roll. On the Feast of All Saints, whilst all were imploring God through St Cuthbert, the king was struck down with a high temperature, and fled, leaving behind a great feast prepared for him.[20]

---

[20] Symeon of Durham, *Libellus de Exordio atque Procursu istius hoc est Dunhelmensis Ecclesie*, ed. and trans. D. Rollason (Oxford: Clarendon Press, 2000), p. 196.

Some Anglo-Saxon kings were venerated; other saints were monks, nuns,
archbishops, or bishops and, above all, the Virgin Mary. Saints had power
over natural events as well as human affairs. St Swithun of Winchester
famously was the saint to pray to for rain.[21] They had visions, could
foresee the future, and were able to help in cases of both physical and
mental illness.

Saints and angels were warriors, too, fighting the Devil and demons
who were waiting in ambush for the unwary.[22] Concern about the
Devil peaked around the year 1000, for it was believed that the term of
1,000 years during which he had been imprisoned by the Archangel
Michael was coming to an end.[23] For many, it must have seemed relatively
unimportant whether a prayer, a spell, or a charm was invoked as long as
it had the desired effect: in that sense the dividing line between magic and
religion was not always clear, though by the twelfth century greater
emphasis was being placed on the distinction.[24] Church leaders condemned the evil arts and their practitioners, but probably to little
effect.[25] Questions arose about natural phenomena such as comets, and
about methods of foretelling the future. Ideas about magic had drawn
heavily on the writing of St Augustine and Isidore of Seville, but anxieties
grew as new discoveries in intellectual disciplines, in medicine and veter-
inary science, and about the natural world were being made.[26] Hence the

---

[21] M. Lapidge, *Anglo-Saxon Minsters of Winchester*, 4 part 2. *The Cult of St Swithun*
(Oxford: Clarendon Press, 2002).

[22] V. I. J. Flint, *The Rise of Magic in Early Medieval Europe* (Oxford: Oxford University
Press, 1991).

[23] *Ibid.*, pp. 168–71; D. F. Callahan, 'The Cult of St Michael the Archangel and the "Terrors
of the Year 1000"', R. Landes, A. Gow, D. C. Van Meter (eds.), *The Apocalyptic Year
1000: Religious Expectation and Social Change, 950–1050* (Oxford: Oxford University
Press, 2003), pp. 181–204. For a recent discussion, see C. Cubitt, 'Apocalyptic and
Eschatological Thought in England around the Year 1000', *Transactions of the Royal
Historical Society*, 6th series, 25 (2015), 27–52.

[24] C. Fanger, 'Christian Ritual Magic in the Middle Ages', *History Compass*, 11/8 (2013),
610–18; C. Watkins, *History and the Supernatural in Medieval England* (Cambridge:
Cambridge University Press, 2007).

[25] The so-called Canons of Edgar 1005 x 1008, cap. 16, *Councils and Synods with Other
Documents Relating to the English Church, I A. D. 871–1204*, ed. D. Whitelock,
M. Brett, and C. N. L. Brooke, Part I, *871–1066* (Oxford: Clarendon Press, 1981), pp.
319–20; V Atr, cap. 28, 2–3, *ibid.*, p. 371; 'The Northumbrian Priests' Law, *c.* 1008
x 1023 cap. 48, *ibid.*, p. 461; II Cn, cap. 4a, 5, *ibid.*, pp. 488–9. Council of London 1075
cap. 8, *Councils and Synods of the English Church*, I Part 2, *1066–1204* (Oxford:
Clarendon Press, 1986), p. 614. Legatine Council of Westminster 1125, cap. 15, *ibid.*,
p. 741.

[26] A. Lawrence-Mathers, *The True History of Merlin the Magician* (New Haven, CT,
London: Yale University Press, 2012), chapters 5, 6.

idea of Merlin as a powerful magus whose father was an incubus fell on fertile ground. Astrology, aided by the study of astronomy, was seen as a legitimate field of inquiry.[27]

The wide range of practitioners at the court in the twelfth century was the subject of extended discussion amongst the 'courtiers' trifles' in the *Policraticus* of John of Salisbury. In general he regarded magic as the work of demons.[28] In Book I chapter 12 he listed enchanters, wizards, sooth-sayers, prophets, those who use images (*vultivoli*) to work on men, those who send images to obtain information (*imaginarii*), dream interpreters, palmists, crystal gazers, astrologers, those who interpreted sudden movements of the body, fortune tellers, and augurs.[29]

Churchmen had a range of sanctions at their disposal. These included cursing, verbally or by means of anathema clauses in charters, and excommunication.[30] Of these there were important changes in the way excommunication was regarded as canon lawyers began to prescribe appropriate procedures to be followed.[31] Perhaps not surprisingly, more is heard of excommunication during Stephen's reign when churches suffered through war and predation. Bishop Henry of Winchester prescribed excommunication as the penalty for those who injured the church in his legatine council of 1143.[32] Miles, earl of Hereford, and Geoffrey, earl of Essex, were both subjected to the penalty, but, whilst Miles was reconciled, Geoffrey died excommunicate.[33] Barons and royal servants were not supposed to be excommunicated without the king's permission, at least after 1066: this was one of the

[27] Watkins, *History and the Supernatural in Medieval England*, pp. 153–60.

[28] *Policraticus*, Book I, caps. 10–11, *I–IV*, ed. K. S. B. Keats-Rohan (Turnhout: Brepols, 1993), pp. 56–7.

[29] *Ibid.*, pp. 57–60.

[30] L. K. Little, *Benedictine Maledictions: Liturgical Cursing in Romanesque France* (Ithaca, NY, London: Cornell University Press, 1993); B. Danelt and B. Bogoch, 'Whoever Alters This, May God Turn His Face from Him on the Day of Judgment', *Journal of American Folklore*, 105 (1992), 132–65.

[31] For an example of a malediction attributed to Ealdred archbishop of York, see William of Malmesbury, *Gesta Pontificum*, ed. and trans. M. Winterbottom (Oxford: Clarendon Press, 2007), I, p. 384; for an excommunication of Ansger the Staller, see *Liber Eliensis*, ed. E. O. Blake, Camden Society, 3rd series, 92 (1962), pp. 165–6; for an English translation, see *Liber Eliensis: a History of the Isle of Ely from the Seventh Century to the Twelfth, Compiled by a Monk of Ely in the Twelfth Century*, trans. J. Fairweather (Woodbridge: Boydell Press, 2005); R. Helmholz, 'Excommunication in Twelfth-Century England', *Journal of Law and Religion*, 11 (1994), 235–53.

[32] *Councils and Synods of the English Church*, I Part 2, pp. 794–800.

[33] *Gesta Stephani*, ed. and trans. K. R. Potter with a new introduction and notes by R. H. C. Davis (Oxford: Clarendon Press, 1976), pp. 158–66.

'new customs' Eadmer reported.[34] However, not all were prepared to ask permission. Thomas Becket in particular used the weapon freely, against tenants-in-chief such as William of Eynsford and without warning, as at Vézelay in 1166.[35] Failing to follow procedure provided grounds for a challenge in the form of an appeal to Rome, and over time the older practices died out.[36]

Abjuration developed as a way of dealing with those who had taken sanctuary after a serious crime. Sanctuaries could obviously be abused and become havens for fugitives from justice. Already in the *Leges Edwardi Confessoris* it had been recognized that murderers and traitors who had been granted their lives by the king had to promise to leave the realm as quickly as possible.[37] Abjuration was used during Henry II's reign for those who, having been accused of serious crimes, were cleared at the ordeal.[38] Abjuration was thus an extension of the punishment of exile seen in early medieval law codes, and in the twelfth century was being used as a mitigation of death or mutilation as the punishment for serious offences.

The exercise of power therefore depended on patterns of belief as well or even more than force. The power of tradition was strong. Men obeyed those in authority because, they believed, that authority was legitimate. Hierarchy was part of the natural order of things. So, too, was patriarchy. Both could be found in the Bible. Children were to obey their parents, who arranged their marriages. Wives were subordinate to their husbands. Churchmen believed that the best solution for widows was that they should become nuns. In practice, women tended to remarry and lengthy widowhoods were rare. Marriage came to be seen as a sacrament, and vows freely taken in the presence of a priest were deemed sacramental and indissoluble.

Ideas about masculinity and femininity did not remain static. One issue was the dividing line between men and women. Men who wore their hair

---

[34] Eadmer, *Historia Novorum*, ed. M. Rule, RS (London: Longman and Co, 1884), p. 10.

[35] William FitzStephen, *Materials for the History of Thomas Becket, Archbishop of Canterbury*, ed. J. C. Robertson and J. B. Sheppard, 7 vols., RS (London: Longman and Co, 1875–85), III, p. 78; Herbert of Bosham, *ibid.*, pp. 391–2.

[36] R. Helmholz, 'Excommunication and the Angevin Leap Forward', *Haskins Society Journal*, 7 (1995), 133–49.

[37] *Leges Edwardi Confessoris*, cap. 18, 2–3; B. R. O'Brien, *God's Peace and King's Peace: the Laws of Edward the Confessor* (Philadelphia, PA: University of Philadelphia Press, 1999), pp. 176–7.

[38] Assize of Clarendon, cap. 14; Assize of Northampton, cap. 1, W. Stubbs, *Select Charters*, 9th edn, revised H. W. C. Davis (Oxford: Clarendon Press, 1913), pp. 172, 179.

long as was the fashion in the late eleventh and early twelfth centuries aroused concern, as the distinction between men and women was blurred.[39] So too did celibate males, who seemed to be renouncing their masculinity, albeit for spiritual motives.[40] Women who behaved like men, leading armies or exercising power, were equally worrying.

The third dimension to be considered is economic power. In the first instance this was about access to and control of resources. Kings, lords, and churchmen held the greatest share by far of land, and controlled the peasant workforce. Many peasants were tied to the estate, owing labour services as well as dues. By the twelfth century lords could use a legal action the writ *de nativis* to recover those who had absconded.[41] The burdens on unfree peasants increased, for landlords could vary rents and services at will.[42] The legal developments of Henry II's reign sharpened the distinction between free and unfree, the latter being excluded from the new forms of action.[43] However precarious their lives through the possibilities of famine, disease, and abduction, the number of peasants nevertheless was growing, and thus helped to cushion lords' incomes.

Economic power could be augmented through warfare and the acquisition of territory. The two great conquests of the eleventh century had winners as well as losers. Earl Godwin and his family stood as a spectacular success story in the first half of the century, holding earldoms and the estates associated with them, together with lands which they had acquired, by one means or another, from the church.[44] The Norman

[39] R. Bartlett, 'Symbolic Meanings of Hair in the Middle Ages', *Transactions of the Royal Historical Society*, 6th series, 4 (1994), 43–60.

[40] J. A. McNamara, 'The *Herrenfrage*: the Restructuring of the Gender System, 1050–1150', C. A. Lees (ed.), *Medieval Masculinities: Regarding Men in the Middle Ages* (Minneapolis: University of Minnesota Press, 1994), pp. 3–29.

[41] R. Faith argued that writs *de nativis* were a post-Conquest development, and were important in shaping ideas about unfreedom; see *The English Peasantry and the Growth of Lordship* (Leicester: Leicester University Press, 1997), pp. 249–51. These writs seem to have been particularly numerous in the early years of Henry II's reign. It may be that earlier disputes about absconding peasants had been resolved by extra-legal action.

[42] S. P. J. Harvey, 'The Extent and Profitability of Demesne Agriculture in England in the Later Eleventh Century', T. H. Aston, P. R. Coss, C. Dyer, and J. Thirsk (eds.), *Social Relations and Ideas: Essays in Honour of R. H. Hilton* (Cambridge: Cambridge University Press, 1983), pp. 45–72.

[43] P. Hyams, *Kings, Lords and Peasants in Medieval England: the Common Law of Villeinage in the Twelfth and Thirteenth Centuries* (Oxford: Oxford University Press, 1980).

[44] R. Fleming, *Kings and Lords in Conquest England* (Cambridge: Cambridge University Press, 1991), chapter 3.

Conquest was followed by a much more extensive replacement of the top layer of English society, dominated by Normans, but including also Flemings and Bretons. Two Norman bishops, Odo of Bayeux and Geoffrey of Coutances, were also granted vast estates. Many of the new-comers had estates in different regions of the country, and resided in only a handful. It was thus more convenient for them to draw their profits in cash, to lease out their demesne manors, and to drive up rents and services from peasants. After 1066 there was plenty of scope for further expansion into Wales, into the north-west of England and, if invited, in Scotland. Most was by members of the elite rather than peasants, though peasants are known to have settled near Carlisle, in Rufus's reign, and in Pembrokeshire in the early twelfth century.[45]

Other than acquisitions of these kinds, lords could only hope to extend their lands by royal grants or by marriage. Given that land at this level was held rather than owned, marriage was of crucial importance as the mechanism for acquiring land and providing for younger sons. The alternative was to increase the yield from existing resources and to market surplus produce. Tenth-century kings protected merchants and laid down laws about sales. Fortified towns or *burhs*, mainly in southern England, were nodal points of trade.[46] Markets and fairs did not have to be regulated, but there were obvious advantages in securing recognition from the king. By the late eleventh century kings were granting licences for markets, probably recognizing their existence *ex post facto*, and giving the grantee a position of strength in the locality.

What was economic power used for? Landlords could invest in their land by clearing waste, constructing mills or fish weirs, and canalizing rivers. Many may have given little thought to investment so long as their wealth was sufficient to sustain their lifestyle. What we do see is the growth of consumption by way of greater display of wealth in dress and lifestyle. Building in stone was much more expensive than timber, and by the twelfth century lords, bishops, and abbots were building in stone and on a very large scale. Finally, those with wealth were expected to give, especially to the church. The duty to give a tenth or tithe of all one's goods

---

[45] For Carlisle, see ASC, E, 1092; HH, p. 416; for Pembroke, see *Brut y Tywysogion or the Chronicle of the Princes. Red Book of Hergest Version*, ed. and trans. T. Jones (Cardiff: University of Wales Press, 1955), p. 53; *Brut. Peniarth MS 20 Version*, ed. and trans. T. Jones (Cardiff: University of Wales Press, 1952), pp. 27–8.

[46] R. Hodges, *Dark Age Economics: the Origins of Towns and Trade A. D. 600–1000* (London: Duckworth, 1982), especially chapter 9, pp. 162–84.

was emphasized. Only a few had the resources to give land on a scale to establish a new Benedictine abbey, but many could give the churches and tithes on their lands to monastic houses. By the twelfth century there were different types of religious community, less expensive to found, and the number of new foundations was to reach its highest point.

In fact, the views of churchmen about wealth were ambivalent, as they always had been. A renunciation of personal wealth was intrinsic to the monastic ideal, and there was a strong vein of teaching that following the life of Christ meant a life of poverty. It was an ideal far removed from the wealth bishops and archbishops enjoyed. An early twelfth-century example was Robert Bloet, bishop of Lincoln, whose way of life was later recalled by Henry the archdeacon of Huntingdon: his knights, his horses, and the vessels of gold and gilt on which elaborate meals were served by richly clad attendants.[47] One of the hallmarks of sanctity was personal austerity, and a sign of sanctity was the adoption of a simple way of life. Ailred of Rievaulx, even at the court of King David of Scots, adopted simple dress.[48] The way of life of Thomas Becket as the king's chancellor was that of a great magnate. He entertained lavishly and dressed splendidly. When he was sent as an emissary to the French court he had a retinue of about 200, dressed in new clothes, whilst he himself had no fewer than twenty-four changes of clothing. All this changed when he became archbishop, when he wore a hair shirt beneath his vestments.[49]

When it comes to the sources of wealth, there are indications of prejudice against those who had made their money in trade. Henry II was outraged by Becket's obduracy, given his humble origins, though William FitzStephen described Becket's parents as citizens of London of the middle order, not making money by usury or engaged in business, but living on rents.[50] William of Canterbury, another of Becket's biographers, commented on the sheriff of Kent, Gervase of Cornhill, also from a London family, that Gervase had too much of an eye on profit.[51] How widespread such prejudice was is not clear, for there was interaction between the city and magnate families.

[47] HH, p. 586.

[48] Walter Daniel, *The Life of Ailred of Rievaulx*, ed. and trans. F. M. Powicke (London: Thomas Nelson, 1950), pp. 4–5.

[49] William FitzStephen, *Materials for the History of Thomas Becket*, III, pp. 22–3, 29–31. For the hair shirt, see William of Canterbury, *ibid.*, I, 10–11.

[50] *Ibid.*, III, p. 14; IV, p. 28.   [51] *Ibid.*, I, p. 100.

PERCEPTIONS OF POWER

The sources relating to the history of social change from the perspective of power are plentiful and various. Written sources include narratives, saints' lives, poems, sermons, homilies, laws, treatises about government, and charters. Manuscripts include illuminated texts of the Bible and of saints' lives. The Bayeux Tapestry provides a unique narrative account of events between 1064 and 1066. In addition there are other material remains, coins, royal and noble palaces and castles, and the cathedrals and priories built after 1066. Illuminated manuscripts and architectural sculpture supply images of God, Jesus, the Virgin and the saints, of angels and demons.

God presided over the cosmos, which was peopled by a heavenly host of saints and angels, and threatened by the Devil and demons. Hierarchy and patriarchy were intrinsic. Kings were subject to God's power. Through consecration they were sanctified and transformed in ways which were hotly debated in the eleventh and early twelfth centuries. Archbishop Wulfstan of York (1002–23) composed his *Institutes of Polity* at a time of repeated Danish invasions. He outlined the roles of different orders in a Christian society.[52] The tract begins with the affirmation that there is one eternal king, 'king and glory of kings'. The duty of a Christian king in a Christian nation was to be 'the people's comfort and a righteous shepherd over the Christian flock'. He must bring peace and reconciliation and punish wrongdoing. Through the king's wisdom the people prosper, and through an unwise king comes the people's wretchedness. 'Seven things befit a righteous king: first, that he have a very great awe of God; and second that he always cherish righteousness; and third that he be humble before God; and fourth that he be resolute against evil; and fifth that he comfort and feed God's poor; and sixth that he advance and protect the Church of God; and seventh that he order correct judgement for friend and stranger alike.' Kings, bishops, earls, generals, reeves, scholars, and lawyers were to be in agreement in the sight of God and the world and cherish God's law. In other words, Wulfstan's response to the challenges facing the kingdom was to reiterate ever more strongly the need for obedience to God's laws and the role of the king as their upholder.

---

[52] *Die 'Institutes of Polity, civil and ecclesiastical': ein Werk Erzbischof Wulfstans von York*, ed. and trans. K. Von Jost (Bern: Francke, 1959), *The Political Writings of Archbishop Wulfstan*, ed. and trans. A. Rabin (Manchester: Manchester University Press, 2015), pp. 101–24. Patrick Wormald, 'Wulfstan (d. 1023)', *ODNB* www .oxforddnb.com/view/article/30098, accessed 20 May 2016.

The essential unity of Christian society was maintained, whether the king was English or Danish, and the king's counsellors were to remain faithful to the same concept. Wulfstan elaborated on the duties of a bishop in *Episcopus*: a bishop ought to teach what belonged to the church and what to laymen; to pursue concord and peace; so to instruct as to prevent injury by oath swearing or ordeal; to ensure correct weights and measures; to forestall sin; and to prevent injustice.[53]

Wulfstan's agenda was to persuade the English people of the need to repent and conform to God's law at a time of heightened anxiety about the first millennium and, it seemed, the punishment of the English through the Danes. As the eleventh century wore on, reformers emphasized the need for clergy to remove themselves from such sins of the world as purchasing preferment or marrying. Then the debate widened in scope, swirling round the figures of Emperor Henry IV and Pope Gregory VII, and centring on the appointment process of bishops and archbishops. For reformers, the process should be completely detached from lay involvement, but for their opponents, this was too extreme, given the importance to lay rulers of bishops and the lands they controlled. The debate centred on the acts of investiture of bishops and abbots and their homage to lay rulers, acts which suggested to reformers that lay rulers were conferring office on ecclesiastics.

In England investiture was not heard of until after 1066. The Norman kings exercised a decisive say in the nomination of bishops and abbots, and the election of popes and counter-popes gave them the opportunity to sidestep the question of investiture until Archbishop Anselm returned to England in 1100, having attended papal councils where lay investiture was explicitly condemned, when he refused to perform homage or to consecrate those bishops and abbots who had been nominated in his absence.[54] A collection of tracts known as the 'Anglo-Norman Anonymous' from their likely provenance either in England or Normandy around the year 1100 includes tracts which give a sense of the arguments used to counter those who condemned lay investiture. Tract 24A in particular had relatively conservative views about sacramental kingship: kings and priests were both anointed, but kings represented the divinity of Christ and priests His humanity; therefore, kings were superior to priests.[55]

---

[53] *Political Writings of Archbishop Wulfstan*, pp. 61–4.
[54] Eadmer, *Historia Novorum*, pp. 119–20.
[55] For an online edition, see http://normananonymous.org/ENAP/ToC.jsp and for translated excerpts, see *English Historical Documents* II, ed. D. C. Douglas and

In England the veneration of past kings, notably Oswald of Northumbria and Edmund of East Anglia, was gaining traction, not least because communities associated with their relics had strong reasons to promote the cults.[56] Oswald and Edmund were venerated as saints for meeting their deaths in battle against the heathen, and Edward the Martyr because he had been murdered at Corfe in 959.[57] Mode of life as well as death was another route to sanctity. Edward the Confessor may have seemed an unlikely candidate to his contemporaries, yet the combination of a patron, his widow, Queen Edith, a hagiographer (probably Goscelin of Saint-Bertin), and, most crucially, the monks of Westminster Abbey, meant that his memory was not forgotten. The anonymous *Life of King Edward* is thought to have been commissioned in the first instance by his widow, Queen Edith, and the community at Westminster he enriched maintained a cult which eventually led to papal recognition of his sanctity.[58]

The courts which surrounded kings were becoming larger and more powerful, and by the twelfth century their operations were being recorded in two treatises, one recording the operation of the exchequer and the

G. W. Greenaway, 2nd edn (London: Eyre and Spottiswoode, 1981), pp. 725–6. The tracts survive only in a single manuscript and included a range of other topics: on ecclesiastical law as an outcome of the law of love which underpins the Christian community, the nature of hierarchy within the church (the author is opposed to the primacy of the archbishopric of Lyon), and the nature of penitential discipline, whose shortcomings fail to reconcile Christians. It has been pointed out that the author is emphasizing the bishops' pastoral duty to bind the Christian community together. J. Ginther, 'Between *Plena Caritas* and *Plenitudo Legis*: the Ecclesiology of the Norman Anonymous', *Haskins Society Journal*, 22 (2010), 141–62.

[56] C. Stancliffe and E. Cambridge (eds.), *Oswald: Northumbrian King to European Saint* (Stamford: Paul Watkins, 1995); D. J. Craig, 'Oswald [St Oswald] (603/4–642)', *ODNB* www.oxforddnb.com/view/article/20916, accessed 20 May 2016; S. Ridyard, *The Royal Saints of Anglo-Saxon England* (Cambridge: Cambridge University Press, 1988). Abbo, *Passio Sancti Eadmundi, Memorials of St Edmund's Abbey*, ed. T. Arnold, 3 vols. (London: HMSO, 1890–6), I, pp. 3–25; Herman the Archdeacon and Goscelin of Saint-Bertin, *Miracles of St Edmund*, ed. T. Licence (Oxford: Clarendon Press, 2014). Most of the information about Oswald's life comes from Bede, *Ecclesiastical History*. A revision does not seem to have been written before Reginald of Durham, *Vita Sancti Oswaldi Regis et Martyris*, in Symeon of Durham, *Opera omnia*, ed. T. Arnold, 2 vols., RS (London: Longman and Co, 1882–5), I, pp. 326–85.

[57] S. Keynes, *The Diplomas of King Æthelred the Unready, 978–1016: a Study in Their Use as Historical Evidence* (Cambridge: Cambridge University Press, 1986), pp. 169–71; L. Keen, *Studies in the Early History of Shaftesbury Abbey* (Dorchester: Dorset County Council, 1999), pp. 99–116, at pp. 109–12.

[58] *The Life of King Edward Who Rests at Westminster*, ed. and trans. F. Barlow, 2nd edn (Oxford: Clarendon Press, 1992), pp. xviii–xxviii; F. Barlow, *Edward the Confessor* (London: Eyre Methuen, 1970), chapter 12.

other the operation of royal justice. Both the *Dialogue of the Exchequer* and the treatise known as 'Glanvill' date from the reign of Henry II and can be seen as reflecting contemporary awareness of change. Richard FitzNigel, the author of the *Dialogue*, was arguably motivated by a recognition that royal revenues were being channelled in new ways to defend what he saw as the traditional form of audit. For the author of 'Glanvill', possibly but not definitely the royal justice of that name, the aim was to set out procedures by writ which lay at the heart of expanding royal justice.[59]

The rise of writing about the royal court in the twelfth century is striking. Already in the early twelfth century there were critical remarks in the *Quadripartitus* and slightly later by the historian Henry of Huntingdon. Criticism became much more vocal in the later twelfth century. John of Salisbury's *Policraticus* is celebrated as the first treatise of political theory since the fall of the Roman Empire, yet, as in the case of the Anglo-Norman Anonymous, the sections dealing with the king and the commonwealth form only one element in a wide-ranging treatise.[60] The work was written in 1159 or 1160 when John was one of Archbishop Theobald's clerks. Its subtitle was 'the courtier's frivolities (*nugae*) and the footsteps of philosophers'. Books one to three deal with the frivolities: hunting, gaming, music, acting and conjuring, omens, astrology, and flattery. Books four to six offer a discussion of the body politic, the prince as its head, its armed hands the soldiery, and its feet the farmers and artisans whom the magistrates should protect. The idea of the commonwealth as a body with the prince as its head was pursued further: an attack on the head affected all the members. More, such an attack was an attack on God Himself. If every man did his own bit, then the body as a whole would flourish. The head would not weigh down the members, nor would the head suffer because of the weakness of the members. Book

---

[59] *Dialogus de Scaccario: the Dialogue of the Exchequer*, ed. and trans. E. Amt; *Constitutio Domus Regis: Disposition of the King's Household*, ed. and trans. S. D. Church (Oxford: Clarendon Press, 2007); *Tractatus de legibus et consuetudinibus regni Anglie qui Glanvilla vocatur: the Treatise on the Laws and Customs of the Realm of England Commonly Called Glanvill* (hereafter Glanvill), ed. G. D. G. Hall with further reading by M. T. Clanchy (Oxford: Clarendon Press, 1993). The latter was drawn up, if not by the justiciar himself, then by someone from his circle, John Hudson, 'Glanville, Ranulf de (1120s?–1190)', *ODNB* www.oxforddnb.com/view/article/10795, accessed 20 May 2016.

[60] For an edition of the whole text, see *Ioannis Saresberiensis Episcopi Carnotensis Policratici sive De Nugis Cvrialium et Vestigiis Philosophorum Libri VIII*, ed. C. C. Webb, 2 vols. (Oxford: Clarendon Press, 1909).

four outlines the difference between a tyrant and a prince. The prince obeys the law, and it is on this basis that his authority over the rest of the community lies. His power is from God. He is a minister of the priests and subordinate to them. In book eight John returns to the subject of kingship and tyranny, and it is here that he defines tyrants, including not only kings, but also private men and priests. Tyrants are those who abuse power, but since all power comes from God, tyrants are there by the will of God. It has always been an honourable thing to kill public tyrants, except those to whom one is bound by fealty, and providing it can be done without loss of religion and honour. Tyrants in any case come to a miserable end, as examples from history demonstrate. The discussion of kingship and tyranny was written in general terms, and the fate of tyrants was left both to God and to citizens. It was intended to display the author's learning at the schools on a subject he knew well, that of a court. However, he was not unique. Not only were there authors like Richard FitzNigel and 'Glanvill', but also Walter Map (*Courtiers' Trifles*), and Gerald of Wales (*Liber de Instructione Principis*).[61]

Much writing about power took the form of history. Rarely did the authors reflect on long-term changes such as population growth, the disappearance of slavery, or the ever-expanding use of documents. Rather, the course of events was understood in terms of the hand of God: the English were punished for their sins by the conquests of the Danes or the Normans. Loyalty was described not as an impersonal state, but as a personal bond to the king. The actions of queens and noblewomen were on the whole of less interest, and the poor appeared usually as victims rather than as active figures.

A good deal of comment about power occurs in works of hagiography and history. Saints' lives follow a certain pattern: saints are born with the marks of sanctity, their struggles to renounce the world are described, and their deaths are examples of a good end. Understanding how and why saints' lives were written and revised helps us to understand how charismatic power was conceived of and, sometimes, they provide illuminating details of individual lives. Had there not been interest in the life of Christina of Markyate, for instance, our knowledge of urban society,

---

[61] Walter Map, *De Nugis Curialium. Courtiers' Trifles*, ed. and trans. M. R. James, revised edn, C. N. L. Brooke and R. A. B. Mynors (Oxford: Clarendon Press, 1983); Gerald of Wales, *De Principis Instructione Liber, Opera*, ed. J. S. Brewer, J. F. Dimock, G. F. Warner, 8 vols., RS (London: Longman, Green, Longman and Roberts, 1861–91), VIII (London: Eyre and Spottiswoode, 1891), pp. 1–329.

and in particular the situation of a bishop's mistress, of a pious daughter who resisted her parents' efforts to see her married, and of her association with a local hermit, would be much impoverished.[62]

There were often specific impulses towards writing or rewriting saints' lives. The Benedictine reform of the late tenth century was one such factor. Another was the post-Conquest building boom, which was often accompanied by the translation of relics to new and splendid shrines. Sometimes the changes were uncomfortable. Paul Hayward has pointed out that at the Old Minster at Winchester the cult of St Swithun was promoted in the late tenth century as at the time Bishop Æthelwold was seeking to reform the community. After the Conquest the cult was used to bolster monasticism there at a time when the bishop, Walkelin, wanted to replace the monks with a secular chapter.[63] At Durham the saint's reburial in the monastic church was celebrated by a rewriting of his life. Later in the twelfth century the life was revised yet again, removing references to Cuthbert's alleged misogyny, to repackage the saint in the face of the sensational cult of Thomas Becket.[64] The life of St Dunstan, archbishop of Canterbury, was written up shortly after his death and then revised by Eadmer at a time when Dunstan's importance to the Canterbury community had been challenged by Archbishop Lanfranc.[65]

History even more than hagiography is illuminating about power. The twelfth century was a golden age of historical writing in England, partly due to the need to explain and justify the past in a changing social context. Benedictine communities wished to record the history of their houses and their benefactors, crucial as documentation for their early history was often lacking. However, a few had their eyes on wider horizons, Eadmer of Christ Church Canterbury on the life and career of St Anselm, Orderic Vitalis of Saint-Evroul in Normandy on an epic ecclesiastical history from the life of Christ to his own day, and William of

---

[62] *The Life of Christina of Markyate*, trans. C. H. Talbot, revised with an introduction and notes by S. Fanous and H. Leyser (Oxford: Oxford University Press, 2008).

[63] P. Hayward, 'Saints and Cults', J. Crick and E. Van Houts (eds.), *A Social History of England 900–1200* (Cambridge: Cambridge University Press, 2011), pp. 309–20 at pp. 313–14.

[64] V. Tudor, 'The Cult of St Cuthbert in the Twelfth Century: the Evidence of Reginald of Durham', G. Bonner, D. Rollason, and C. Stancliffe (eds.), *St Cuthbert, His Cult and Community* (Woodbridge: Boydell, 1989), pp. 447–67.

[65] *The Early Lives of Dunstan*, ed. and trans. M. Winterbottom and M. L. Lapidge (Oxford: Clarendon Press, 2012); Eadmer of Canterbury, *Lives and Miracles of Saints Oda, Dunstan, and Oswald*, ed. and trans. A. J. Turner and B. J. Muir (Oxford: Clarendon Press, 2006), pp. 41–159.

Malmesbury on a history of the English church and its saints in tandem
with a history of its kings. Eadmer was both a hagiographer and
a historian, composing lives of various archbishops of Canterbury as
well as Wilfrid, whose relics were thought to be at Canterbury, and of
Oswald, bishop of Worcester and archbishop of York.

The greatest of this group of monastic historians was William of
Malmesbury. Historical works, *Gesta Regum*, *Gesta Pontificum*, and
Historia Novella formed only one element in a very considerable body of
writing including hagiography, works on the Bible, and digests of the work
of others.[66] William was extraordinarily well read and, even more exceptionally, had made what can only be described as research visits to other
libraries. His view of the purpose of historical writing was framed by
Christian and ethical concerns.[67] His *Gesta Pontificum* was a history-cum-
gazetteer of the English dioceses, successive bishops, and the major shrines,
culminating in a history of St Aldhelm of Malmesbury composed, he
claimed, at the request of Queen Matilda II. The *Gesta Regum* was composed in tandem. His principal source for the pre-Conquest period was the
Anglo-Saxon Chronicle and we can see from his reshaping of his source his
views on the shortcomings of those early kings and queens. Paul Hayward
has drawn attention to William's use of innuendo and gossip, arguing that
this was a rhetorical device designed to prompt reflection on a message
about the need for royal restraint and moderation.[68] For the period after
1066 William presented a series of pen portraits of the Norman kings
modelled on Suetonius's *Lives of the Caesars* where again the message is
about the need for moderation and restraint. William's historical writing
was shaped by his personal experience as a monk of Malmesbury Abbey
whose future as an independent house with an illustrious past had been
thrown into jeopardy by its lack of an abbot. After the death of Abbot

[66] *Gesta Pontificum Anglorum*, I, ed. and trans. M. Winterbottom, II, Introduction and
Commentary, R. M. Thomson (Oxford: Clarendon Press, 2007); *Gesta Regum
Anglorum*, I, ed. and trans. R. A. B. Mynors, R. M. Thomson, and M. Winterbottom
(Oxford: Clarendon Press, 1998); *Historia Novella*, ed. E. King trans. K. R. Potter
(Oxford: Clarendon Press, 1998); R. M. Thomson, 'Malmesbury, William of (*b. c.*
1090, *d.* in or after 1142)', *ODNB* www.oxforddnb.com/view/article/29461, accessed
20 May 2016.
[67] S. O. Sønnesyn, *William of Malmesbury and the Ethics of History* (Woodbridge: Boydell
Press, 2012).
[68] P. Hayward, 'The Importance of Being Ambiguous: Innuendo and Legerdemain in
William of Malmesbury's *Gesta regum* and *Gesta pontificum Anglorum*', *Anglo-
Norman Studies*, 33 (2010), 75–102. Cf. B. Weiler, 'William of Malmesbury on
Kingship', *History*, 90 (2005), 3–22; Weiler, 'William of Malmesbury, King Henry I,
and the *Gesta Regum Anglorum*', *Anglo-Norman Studies*, 31 (2008), 157–76.

Godfrey, Queen Matilda gave the temporalities to a monk of Winchester named Eadwulf, writing to Archbishop Anselm, who had not yet returned to England, that he had the right of disposing of the pastoral staff. Anselm praised her for making this distinction, but refused to confirm the nomination of Eadwulf because he had sent the archbishop a goblet, arousing the suspicion of simony.[69] In 1118 Bishop Roger took over the abbey's temporalities (whether Eadwulf had died or not is not clear).[70] What William wanted above all, therefore, was to persuade King Henry and the bishop to allow a fresh abbatial election to proceed. The *Historia Novella* was composed some years later, continuing the *Gesta Regum*, and addressed once again to a powerful patron who might be able to assist the abbey, Robert earl of Gloucester.[71]

Henry archdeacon of Huntingdon is particularly important in the context of power. His interpretative framework differs from that of William of Malmesbury: he offers a history of the English people, punished for their sins by successive waves of invaders of whom the Normans were only the latest. He was commissioned to write by Bishop Alexander of Lincoln, and his audience is much wider than that of a monastic community. It is even possible that for a time he saw himself as a potential court poet for Henry I.[72] Nevertheless, he was capable of some very acid remarks about Henry I, composed after the latter's death: his three brilliant qualities of wisdom, victory, and wealth were opposed by three vices: greed, cruelty, and debauchery.[73]

There were of course those who chose to write not about the history of peoples, kings, bishops, or saints, but about individuals. One remarkable tract is the Latin praise poem in praise of Queen Emma. This was

[69] Anselm, *Opera omnia*, ed. F. S. Schmitt, 6 vols. (I, Seckau: Office of the Abbot of Seckau, 1938), II–VI, Edinburgh: Thomas Nelson 1938–61), V, pp. 326–8; *The Letters of Saint Anselm of Canterbury*, trans. W. Fröhlich, 3 vols. (Kalamazoo, MI: Cistercian Publications, 1990–4), nos. 384, 385.
[70] Winchester Annals, *Annales Monastici*, ed. H. R. Luard, 5 vols., RS (London: Longman and Co, 1864–9), II, p. 45.
[71] *Historia Novella*, prologue, p. 4. We should note too the *Gesta Stephani*, an account of the events of Stephen's reign. This was less hostile to the king than the *Historia Novella*. Although it is usually seen as a narrative about the king, in fact its focus was about the breakdown of order after the death of Henry I, the different rebel leaders, and, in the second book, the search for peace.
[72] J. Gillingham, 'Henry of Huntingdon in His Time (1135) and Place (Between England and the Royal Court)', K. Stopka (ed.), *Gallus Anonymous and His Chronicle in the Perspective of the Latest Research* (Krakow: Polish Academy of Arts and Sciences, 2010), pp. 157–72.
[73] HH, pp. 698–700.

composed in the reign of her son Harthacnut (1040–2) and was intended
to explain and justify her role in the events of some four decades.[74] It is
a one-sided account of events, but useful for its insights into the fault lines
in English politics between the Danes and the English, and into the position of a twice-married queen.

William of Poitiers's *Gesta Guillelmi* is another example of the actions
of an individual, William the Conqueror. It was written to praise and also
to justify his actions, not least because the invasion and conquest of
a Christian people, resulting in many deaths and destruction, had opened
the Conqueror up to criticism.[75] This author wanted to draw out comparisons between William and an earlier conqueror of Britain, Julius Caesar.

Not surprisingly given the clerical authorship of most hagiographic and
historical writing, many of the archbishops, bishops, and abbots loom
large. Eadmer's account of Anselm's troubles was paralleled at York by
Hugh the Chanter's *History of the Church of York and Its Archbishops*.[76]
At Durham different tracts recorded the history of that church. William of
Malmesbury's *Gesta Pontificum* offers a good deal of (barbed) comment
on bishops of the recent past. Benedictine houses, for example, Abingdon
and Battle, recorded the history of their houses with the acts of successive
abbots.[77] Rather different is Jocelin of Brakelond's chronicle which
focusses on Abbot Samson of Bury (1182–1211), and which comes
much closer to a warts-and-all biography than any of the other texts
mentioned.[78] A shift in emphasis occurred with the rise of the
Cistercians, who composed lives of saintly abbots, such as Ailred of
Rievaulx. Here the author was at once recording a saint's life and pious
death and his spiritual headship of the community at Rievaulx.

---

[74] *Encomium Emmae Reginae*, ed. A. Campbell (reprinted Cambridge: Cambridge
University Press, 1998).

[75] *Gesta Guillelmi*, ed. and trans. R. H. C. Davis and M. Chibnall (Oxford: Clarendon
Press, 1998); D. Bates, 'The Conqueror's Earliest Historians and the Writing of His
Biography', D. Bates, J. Crick, and S. Hamilton (eds.), *Writing Medieval Biography
750–1250: Essays in Honour of Professor Frank Barlow* (Woodbridge: Boydell Press,
2006), pp. 129–41.

[76] Hugh the Chanter, *History of the Church of York, 1066–1127*, ed. and trans. C. Johnson,
new edn, revised M. Brett, C. N. L. Brooke, M. Winterbottom (Oxford: Clarendon Press,
1990).

[77] *Historia Ecclesie Abbendonensis. The History of the Church of Abingdon*, ed. and trans.
J. Hudson, 2 vols. (Oxford: Clarendon Press, 2002, 2007); *The Chronicle of Battle
Abbey*, ed. and trans. E. Searle (Oxford, 1980).

[78] Jocelin of Brakelond, *Chronicle of the Abbey of Bury St Edmunds*, trans. D. Greenway
and J. Sayers (Oxford: Oxford University Press, 1989).

Sermons and homilies are other sources which are rewarding, too. Perhaps the most famous sermon of this period is that of Archbishop Wulfstan of York, 'The Sermon of the Wolf to the English', where men are exhorted to obey God's law or suffer the consequences.[79] One of Wulfstan's contemporaries, Ælfric, the abbot of Eynsham, was a distinguished homilist, and his homilies contain valuable nuggets about contemporary society, as do his colloquies with their famous descriptions of different occupations.[80]

Writing about law and justice changed very considerably during this period. Anglo-Saxon kings had law codes drawn up in their name as ideological programmes, as well as statements of law in force. It has been argued that in this respect, they were conforming to the Old Testament idea of kings as legislators.[81] Archbishop Wulfstan played a critical role in drawing up the legislative codes of Kings Æthelred and Cnut.[82] After the Conquest there were efforts both to preserve texts of Anglo-Saxon laws and to record the legislation of the Norman kings, the *Textus Roffensis* compiled at Rochester being a prime example.[83]

Writing about lay figures in their own terms brings us to an entirely different range of sources, from skaldic poetry, celebration of battles and heroes, to, by the early thirteenth century, the earliest biography of a layman, that of William Marshal. Again the focus is on action and heroic deeds. The *Song of Maldon* commemorated not victory, but courage in defeat as Beorhtnoth's men chose to die with their lord.[84] Skaldic poetry written down long after the event recorded the deeds of Swein, Cnut, and their leading followers.[85] The battle of Hastings generated

---

[79] For a translation, see *English Historical Documents*, I, ed. D. Whitelock, 2nd edn (London: Eyre Methuen, 1979), pp. 928–44.

[80] *Ælfric's Catholic Homilies. The First Series: Text*, ed. P. Clemoes, Early English Text Society (1997); *Aelfric's Catholic Homilies, Second Series*, ed. M. Godden, Early English Text Society (1979). For Wulfstan, see J. T. Lionarons, *The Homiletic Writings of Archbishop Wulfstan: a Critical Study* (Woodbridge: D. S. Brewer, 2010).

[81] P. Wormald, *The Making of English Law: King Alfred to the Twelfth Century*. I, *Legislation and Lawsuits* (Oxford: Blackwell, 1999), chapter 6.

[82] *Ibid.*, pp. 330–66; M. Townend (ed.), *Wulfstan, Archbishop of York. The Proceedings of the Second Alcuin Conference* (Turnhout: Brepols, 2004).

[83] *Textus Roffensis*, ed. T. Hearne (Oxford: e Theatro Sheldoniano, 1720). Online images of the manuscript at http://enriqueta.man.ac.uk/luna/servlet/detail/Man4Medieval VC~4~4~990378~142729.

[84] *English Historical Documents*, I, pp. 330–3.

[85] M. Townend, 'Cnut's Poets: an Old Norse Literary Community in Eleventh-Century England', E. M. Tyler (ed.), *Conceptualizing Multilingualism in Medieval England, 800–1250* (Turnhout: Brepols, 2011), pp. 197–215.

written accounts in prose and poetry, as well as the Bayeux Tapestry. The deeds of Hereward in the fenlands a few years later were remembered as those of an English hero fighting the Normans. By the early twelfth century tales of valour and adventure were being recorded in French. Gaimar's *Lestoire des Engleis*, the first history of the English in French, relates the story of Havelock, a hero of the war against the Danes, as well as that of Hereward.[86] The battle of the Standard in 1138 was also written up as a Norman victory in a religious war.[87] In the 1170s Jordan Fantosme wrote a verse account of the Scottish invasion of Norman England in 1173, and of English resistance.[88] The story told is one of early success of the Young King and his allies, King William of Scots and his brother Earl David, and then how fortune turned against them and Henry II triumphed. The work is both history and romance, and it is in romance that we are brought into the world of kings, lords, knights, their lady loves, and their adventures. Up to a point it could be argued that the story line of the warrior world hardly changed during our period, only language and genre, but by the time of the romances we see violence being used in a different context and for different ends. We learn too of the ties between lords and men, of fidelity and treachery.

Other aspects of lordship were less interesting to these authors, especially the effects of war and the fates of those who suffered from lordly power. It is from narrative sources that we hear about the violence of aristocratic politics in the late tenth and early eleventh centuries, of slaves carried off by the Scots, and of famine in the north following William the Conqueror's harrying. In the Latin chronicles we learn of the northern peasants who fled the harrying campaign of 1069–70 and starved to death by the roadside as they worked their way south.[89] Without Domesday Book we would be left to speculate about the impact on local populations

---

[86] Geffrei Gaimar, *Estoire des Engleis. History of the English*, ed. and trans. I. Short (Oxford: Oxford University Press, 2009), lines 98–818, 5457–5700.

[87] HH, pp. 712–19; Richard of Hexham, *Chronicles of the Reigns of Stephen, Henry II and Richard I*, ed. R. Howlett, 4 vols., RS (London: Longman and Co, 1884–9), III, pp. 139–78; John of Hexham continuation to *Historia Regum*, Symeon of Durham, *Opera omnia*, II, pp. 284–332; Ailred of Rievaulx, *Battle of the Standard, Chronicles of the Reigns of Stephen, Henry II and Richard I*, ed. R. Howlett, 4 vols., RS (London, 1884–9), III, pp. 181–200; *Aelred of Rievaulx: the Historical Works*, translated Jane Patricia Freeland, ed. M. L. Dutton (Kalamazoo, MI: Cistercian Publications, 2005), pp. 247–69.

[88] *Jordan Fantosme's Chronicle*, ed. and trans. R. C. Johnston (Oxford: Clarendon Press, 1981).

[89] OV, II, pp. 230–2; JW, III, p. 10; Symeon of Durham, *Historia Regum, Opera omnia*, II, p. 188.

of new lords with new ways, of freemen subjected to greater dependence, and of raised rents and services. The decades between about 1076 and 1136 may have been relatively peaceful, but the outbreak of conflict after the death of Henry I brought many reports of the seizure of land and property from churches, of the imposition of forced labour on peasants, and of arbitrary exaction of money. It is from the Anglo-Saxon Chronicle we have the famous picture of the nineteen years when Christ and his saints slept.[90] The northern chroniclers, Richard and John of Hexham, reported the atrocities committed by the Scots.[91] Elsewhere there were men like Robert FitzHubert, a freebooting lord who terrorized Wiltshire.[92] So the evidence about lords tends to fall either into the category of deeds of valour on one hand or oppression on the other.

What these genres do not tell us much about is of the economic aspects of lordship, of the relations between lords and peasants. In other words, our sources tell us much more about the powerful and the way power was exercised than about those on the receiving end. We also have little evidence written on behalf of the powerless, the masses of the rural and urban poor, and women, other than a select band of elite and exceptionally holy individuals.

The following chapters begin with the contexts of social change (2): invasions, climate change, population growth, diminution of external attacks, and movements for reform in the Western church. There follow three chapters (3, 4, and 5) devoted to the powerful, kings, lords, churchmen, to the changing ways power was exercised, and to the areas of friction. Chapter 6 tackles power from a different perspective, by considering networks cutting across vertical and horizontal relationships through ties of family, neighbourhood, voluntary associations such as gilds, and shared experience through attending courts and participating in juries. Chapter 7 considers the physical context of power through place, looking at the major themes such as the transition to stone building and, by selected examples, towns and cities as theatres of power. The rise of London is the subject of Chapter 8, whilst the last chapter, 9, returns to the question of identities. Its title, 'Patchwork Kingdom', underscores the limits of political and economic integration and explores overlapping and changing identities.

[90] ASC, E, 1137.   [91] See earlier in this chapter.   [92] WM, *Historia Novella*, pp. 74–6.

2

Contexts

Before considering the exercise and experience of power, it is important to establish the wider geographical, political, and cultural contexts. Without the easing of external pressures from raiders and invaders, without environmental change and population growth, and without the changes in the Western church, social change in England would have been very different. It is conceivable that England would have been partitioned between different polities, north and south, and that the tempo of change, whether economic and social or in the church, would have been different, perhaps more gradual, with less by way of brutal adjustments necessary in the aftermath of conquest.

RISE AND DECLINE OF EXTERNAL INVASIONS

England at the start of our period was rich in raw materials and, with the shelter of a network of fortified towns, commerce and trade were thriving. Scandinavian people had settled in northern and eastern England and cities like York, Chester, and Lincoln were prospering through contacts with the Scandinavian world, whilst London's overseas trade via Flanders and Germany was also growing. From 980 raiders began to arrive: in that year Southampton was sacked, and Thanet in Kent and Cheshire were attacked.[1] These raiders, and those in 981 (Devon and Cornwall), 982 (Dorset), and 988 (Somerset), may have come from the Irish Sea littoral.

Much more serious were the fleets that began to appear in 991, large in size and led by kings and warlords. In that year a fleet of ninety-three ships

---

[1] ASC, C, 980.

arrived, landing in Kent and moving up the coast to Maldon in Essex, where Ealdorman Beorhtnoth of Essex met them, to be defeated and killed in battle.[2] These expeditions were clearly different in size, leadership, and objectives from earlier hit-and-run raids. Their leaders needed to reward their followers to build up their own power against their rivals, and this may have become more difficult as the supply of silver from Russia declined. The development of large and fast ships provided the transport necessary.

After Maldon the decision was taken, on the advice of the archbishop of Canterbury and two ealdormen it was said, to pay tribute to the Vikings 'because of the great terror they inspired along the sea coast'.[3] Yet only a brief respite was gained because the fleet returned in 992. This time the English counterattacked, and the Londoners and men of East Anglia are said to have been victorious.[4] In the following year a fleet attacked in the north: Bamburgh in Northumberland was sacked, and the army did much damage on both shores of the river Humber. The leaders of the English force fled instead of engaging the enemy, 'because they were Danes on the father's side', according to the Worcester chronicler.[5] Then in 994 a fleet of ninety-four ships led by Olaf Tryggvason, king of Norway, and Swein Forkbeard, king of Denmark, arrived. They attacked London, but were beaten off.[6] They then proceeded to raid through the south-east and Æthelred promised tribute and maintenance if they desisted. Accordingly they overwintered at Southampton. Olaf was baptized with the king as his sponsor, and promised not to come again with an army.[7]

Meanwhile Swein Forkbeard became more prominent in the descriptions of attacks on England. Swein had relatives in England: his sister Gunnhilda and her husband were said to have been killed in the St Brice's Day massacre in 1002.[8] He raided in 1003, 1004, and 1006, when a very large tribute was

[2] ASC, A, C, D, E, 991; *English Historical Documents*, I, pp. 319–24; D. Scragg (ed.), *The Battle of Maldon* (Manchester: Manchester University Press, 1981).

[3] ASC, C, D, E, 991; JW, II, p. 438.   [4] ASC, C, D, E, 992; JW, II, pp. 440–2.

[5] *Ibid.*, p. 442.

[6] Niels Lund, 'Óláf Tryggvason (*d.* 999)', *ODNB* www.oxforddnb.com/view/article/49266, accessed 20 May 2016; I. Howard, *Swein Forkbeard's Invasions and the Danish Conquest of England, 991–1007* (Woodbridge: Boydell Press, 2003).

[7] ASC, C, D E, 994; JW, II, pp. 442–4.

[8] ASC, C, D, E, 1002; JW, II, p. 452; for the massacre, see R. Lavelle, *Æthelred II King of the English 978–1016* (Stroud: Tempus, 2002), pp. 99–102; A. Williams, *Æthelred the Unready: the Ill-Counselled King* (London: Hambledon Press and London, 2003), pp. 52–3; S. Wallis, *The Oxford Henge and Late Saxon Massacre with Medieval and Later Occupation at St John's College Oxford*, Thames Valley Archaeological Service Monograph, 17 (2014).

paid.[9] In 1009, however, an even larger force arrived, comprising Danes and Swedes, and this time led by Thorkell the Tall, which ravaged southern England, and in 1012 captured and killed Archbishop Ælfheah of Canterbury.[10] After this Thorkell changed sides and put his fleet at Æthelred's service in return for pay and supplies. Meanwhile Swein returned in 1013. He landed in the mouth of the river Humber in 1013 and gained submissions from all of England north of Watling Street. Leaving his ships in the north in the care of his son Cnut, Swein went south, gaining further submissions, though Æthelred remained at London with Thorkell's fleet until he fled to Normandy, and the Londoners submitted, but Swein died soon afterwards.

The struggle then became even more complex as the contenders vied for power. Initially the Danes chose Swein's son Cnut as his successor, but English magnates negotiated Æthelred's return from Normandy, promising that 'no lord was dearer to them than their rightful lord, if only he would govern his kingdom more justly than he had done in the past'.[11] Cnut meanwhile was based at Gainsborough with support from the men of Lindsey. When Æthelred arrived, Cnut left by sea for Sandwich. In the following year Eadric Streona, earl of Mercia, killed two leading figures from the Danelaw boroughs, and Edmund Ironside, Æthelred's son, married the widow of one of them, gaining support from his wife's kin. At this stage Edmund was in alliance with Eadric, but the two parted company and Eadric went over to Cnut. Æthelred meanwhile sent for levies to assemble, but when they did so, 'it came to nothing, as so often before'.[12] Edmund joined forces with Earl Uhtred of Northumbria and fought on. Æthelred died and Cnut won a great victory at *Assandun* (either Ashdon or Ashingdon in Essex), when several prominent Englishmen died. Soon after an agreement with Edmund to divide the kingdom, Edmund died, leaving Cnut master of the kingdom.[13]

Making sense of these events is not easy, but they highlight the way loyalties shifted under pressure and over time. Danes had kinsmen and potential support, especially in northern England and the east midlands, whilst London resisted and stood firm for Æthelred. There were obviously different views about the wisdom of fighting versus accommodation, the

[9] ASC, C, D, E, 1003, 1004, 1006.
[10] Richard Abels, 'Thorkell the Tall, Earl of East Anglia (*fl.* 1009–1023)', *ODNB* www.oxforddnb.com/view/article/27403, accessed 20 May 2016.
[11] ASC, E, 1014.   [12] ASC, E, 1016.
[13] The principal source for these events is ASC, C, D, E, 1012, 1013, 1014, 1015, 1016, 1017; see also for additional details, JW, II, pp. 470–504.

upshot being that armies were assembled and were then sent away without fighting, and vast sums were handed over to the raiders. The size and timing of fleets was obviously related to the ebb and flow of politics in Scandinavia, as different individuals established themselves for a period but died or were ousted in favour of rivals. Cnut's accession in particular created logistical problems in Denmark and Norway. His sons Swein and Harold Harefoot were ousted from Norway, where a new king, Magnus Olafsson, was able to establish himself. Magnus became king of Denmark and in 1045 threatened to invade England, but was prevented by Swein Estrithson, Cnut's nephew.[14] In Norway, Magnus's son and successor, Harold, 'Hardrada', kept alive Norwegian claims to the English throne, and in 1058 a Norwegian fleet joined forces with Gruffydd ap Llewelyn, king of north Wales, to help Ælfgar recover the earldom of Mercia.[15] In 1066 Harold Hardrada himself came at the head of a fleet and joined forces with Tostig Godwinson, but was killed at Stamford Bridge.[16]

During the next three decades the main threat to the Normans in England came from the Danes. In 1070 Swein arrived with a fleet and was paid off by William.[17] In 1075 another fleet arrived under the command of Cnut IV, Swein's son, to join the Norman rebels, but arrived too late and did not engage.[18] In 1085 Cnut himself was planning to invade England in force. He joined forces with the count of Flanders whose daughter he had married, but was killed before the fleet could set off.[19] His death in retrospect marked a turning point: his crews had mutinied and turned on him, presumably because the risks involved outweighed the possible gains. His successors, lacking the revenues from England, did not have the wealth to hire oarsmen in any number and, by the twelfth century, the borders of Denmark were under attack from the Slavs.

The Norwegians meanwhile continued their westward voyages, and from time to time these impinged on English affairs, either directly or indirectly. The incident which led to the downfall of Robert de Mowbray, earl of Northumbria, was the earl's detention of four Norwegian ships which he refused to surrender or to answer the king's summons to court. The king marched north and after a siege of Bamburgh, Robert was captured and imprisoned.[20] Magnus 'Barelegs', king of Norway (1093–1103), was determined to assert his authority in north-west Britain and the regions surrounding the Irish Sea. He may also have aimed to conquer England, for,

---

[14] ASC, D, 1045.   [15] ASC, D, 1058; JW, II, p. 584.   [16] ASC, C, D, E, 1066.
[17] ASC, D, E, 1069, 1070; JW, III, pp. 8–10.   [18] ASC, D, E, 1075.   [19] ASC, E, 1085.
[20] ASC, E, 1095; JW, III, pp. 76–9; OV, IV, pp. 280–2.

according to William of Malmesbury, he took Harold Godwinson's son Harold with him to England.[21] In 1098 he travelled round the north of Scotland, making his presence felt in Shetland and Orkney, before moving on to the Hebrides and Man.[22] It was said that he made a treaty with King Edgar of Scots that all the islands of the west of Scotland, together with Kintyre, were thenceforth to belong to Norway.[23] He crossed to Anglesey and in north Wales defeated a force of Welsh and Normans. Some years later he returned. He allied with Muirchertach Ua Briain, over-king in Ireland, and a marriage was arranged between his son Sigurd and Muirchertach's daughter.[24] Soon afterwards he was killed in county Down, by the Ulaid.[25] There was one last incursion by a king of Norway, in the early 1150s, when Eysteinn II captured the earl of Orkney, in Caithness, then ravaged Aberdeen, Hartlepool, and Whitby.[26]

Cnut IV's killing in 1085 brought an end to his projected invasion, and his successors in Denmark turned their attention to their power base in Scandinavia. Contacts with Denmark and Norway continued to be important, but they were on the whole commercial and ecclesiastical, rather than predatory. When the Norman earl Robert de Mowbray seized four Norwegian ships at Bamburgh in 1094, William Rufus saw this as sufficient reason to remove him.[27]

Over time, then, the threat to England from Scandinavia slowly diminished, but meanwhile that from northern France had increased. The story again went back to the reign of Æthelred. Viking fleets in the English Channel needed safe havens and markets in which to trade. Normandy could offer both, and possibly bases for attacks on southern England. Æthelred needed to prevent this. He made a treaty with Richard I in 991 that neither the English nor the Normans would shelter each other's enemies. The peace did not last, for the Viking fleet went to Normandy in

[21] WM, *Gesta Regum Anglorum*, I, p. 570.   [22] *Ibid.*
[23] *Annals of Inisfallen*, 1105, www.ucc.ie/celt/published/T100004/.
[24] For the marriage, see *Annals of the Four Masters*, 1002, online www.ucc.ie/celt/published/T100005a/; A. Condon, 'Muirchertach ua Briain, Politics and Naval Activity in the Irish Sea, 1075 to 1119', G. MacNiocaill and P. F. Wallace (eds.), *Keimelia: Studies in Medieval History and Archaeology in Memory of Tom Delaney* (Galway: University of Galway Press, 1979), pp. 397–415.
[25] R. Power, 'Magnus Barelegs' Expeditions to the West', *Scottish Historical Review*, 65 (1986), 107–32.
[26] *Heimskringla*, A. O. Anderson (ed.), *Early Sources of Scottish History*, 2 vols. (Stamford: Paul Watkins, 1990), II, pp. 215–17; S. Marritt, 'Drogo the Sheriff: a Neglected Lost Romance Tradition and Anglo-Norwegian Relations in the Twelfth Century', *Historical Research*, 80 (2007), 157–84.
[27] See previously in this chapter.

1000.[28] Two years later he married Emma of Normandy, but around this time was said to have invaded the Cotentin, presumably because ships based there were a threat to the south of England.[29] King Swein of Denmark also made a treaty with the Norman duke which allowed the Danes to sell their loot in Normandy and to send their wounded there.[30]

However, the flight of Æthelred, Emma, and her sons to Normandy was a further complication. Although Emma herself returned to England after her husband's death and married Cnut, her sons remained at the Norman court. Relations between Cnut and the Normans were not easy, despite – or even because of – his marriage to Emma.[31] Duke Robert I in particular seems to have consistently hoped for the succession of one of Æthelred's sons by Emma. A sister of Cnut was offered to Robert as a bride, but the proposal was soon repudiated. The duke contemplated an invasion of England in 1033 on behalf of the two English princes, who were still at his court at the time he left for the Holy Land, leaving his young son William as his heir. However, Alfred was murdered in England in 1036. His brother Edward finally succeeded to the throne in 1042, allegedly with Norman backing.[32]

Edward's plans for the succession have been endlessly discussed. Did he intend to remain celibate, and possibly hope that his kinsman William of Normandy might succeed him? Did he marry Edith, Godwin's daughter, reluctantly, as the price of the powerful earl's support? When in 1051 Edward freed himself from his wife, her father, and brothers, did he make some kind of promise about the succession to William of Normandy?[33] The duke was said to have travelled to England in 1051, a journey which might well have been made so that he could be presented to leading magnates at court. Strictly speaking, the succession was not Edward's to give, and with a change of dynasty the succession to the throne was by now a remarkably open horse race, with rivalry between Æthelred and his

---

[28] ASC, C, D, E, 1000.

[29] William of Jumièges, *Gesta Normannorum Ducum*, ed. and trans. E. M. C. Van Houts (Oxford: Clarendon Press, 1992, 1995), II, pp. 12–14.

[30] *Ibid.*, pp. 16–19.

[31] It is significant that when Emma fled in 1036 after the murder of her son Alfred, she went to Bruges, not to her kindred in Normandy: *Encomium*, p. xxxiv.

[32] William of Poitiers, *Gesta Guillelmi*, pp. 18–21.

[33] William's claim to England has to be set in the wider context of his territorial ambitions in northern France: his efforts to extend his authority over the march country between Normandy and Maine, to take over Maine itself, and his interventions in Brittany and the Vexin. A kingdom was obviously a much bigger proposition, but fits into the same overall pattern of expansionist lordship.

descendants, Swein and his kindred in Denmark, and Harold Hardrada of Norway. Birth and also acceptance by the elite were critical. Edward's escape from the Godwins was all too brief, as within a year Godwin and his sons had been reinstated and Edith restored. A further twist in the tale occurred in 1055 when Edward the Exile, Edmund Ironside's son, was summoned to England, perhaps at the behest of Harold and his brothers and, though he himself died, his son Edgar and daughters Christina and Margaret remained in England.

After 1066 the Normans were to claim that Harold had sworn an oath to William in Normandy concerning the succession to the English throne: that he would aid William and in the meantime have William's knights garrison Dover castle for him, and would fortify certain castles for the duke. William for his part having accepted Harold's homage but before Harold swore allegiance to him, gave lands and power to Harold. In other words, he indicated what lands Harold might expect to hold.[34] The context of the oath, according to William of Poitiers and the Bayeux Tapestry, was that Harold, sent to William by Edward to confirm the promise of the succession, had fallen into the hands of Guy count of Ponthieu, who had wished to hold him to ransom, but surrendered him to the duke's men. The Normans were to claim that Harold's oath was binding, and thus that he had perjured himself when he took the throne in 1066. Harold was not of royal blood, but he could claim to have been 'elected' after King Edward's death, and was duly crowned king.

William's case for invasion in 1066 was thus that he was claiming the inheritance promised to him by his kinsman. His success at Hastings, the deaths of Harold and his brothers Gyrth and Leofwin and many other nobles, both at that battle and the two earlier battles, at Fulford and Stamford Bridge, left Edgar Ætheling as the only realistic alternative candidate for the throne. However, Edgar could not command enough support. Edwin, earl of Mercia, and his brother Morcar, earl of Northumbria, submitted to William, and William was crowned king on Christmas Day 1066. By the time of his departure for Normandy early in 1067, William had taken charge in Sussex, Hampshire, Kent, and perhaps the counties surrounding London. His lieutenants, Odo, bishop of Bayeux, and William FitzOsbern, were left in charge, Odo in Winchester and William on the borders with Wales.

The Normans had profited in several ways from the Danish conquest. The years of English resistance and heavy taxation as tribute and for the

---

[34] William of Poitiers, *Gesta Guillelmi*, pp. 70–1.

Danish forces, and the destruction of the power of some great aristocratic families, had eaten away at the fabric of Edgar's England. The concentration of power in the hands of Godwin's family, and its downfall at Hastings, left English resistance to coalesce behind Edwin, Morcar, and the young Edgar Ætheling, grandson of Edmund Ironside. The Normans had also benefitted from Harold's decision to go for a speedy resolution on the battlefield. Had he not opted to fight and with the autumn drawing on, William would have found it difficult to hold his army together. His victory, the decision of Ealdred, archbishop of York, to perform a coronation relatively quickly, and his entry into London, gave him and his forces an advantage over their enemies. Yet the story of the Norman Conquest was only just beginning: most of the country still had to be subdued, and there remained the possibility of further Scandinavian interventions, especially in eastern and northern England.

The danger reached a climax in 1069 and 1070 when the Danes arrived in the Humber to ally with the Yorkshiremen and Northumbrians in attacking York. They then overwintered where William, who spent Christmas at York, could not reach them. They moved on to Ely, where Kings William and Swein met, and the Danes were allowed to leave with their loot, some not leaving immediately but proceeding south to the Thames.[35] Again in 1075, during a major revolt, the rebels in England sent to Denmark and, according to the Anglo-Saxon Chronicle, a fleet of 200 ships arrived. They went to York, where they looted the Minster, and then left, without meeting King William in battle.[36] It was by no means certain that the Normans had arrived to stay. Their hold over the north was still precarious, and the revolt of 1075 demonstrated divisions in the ranks of the victors. Earl Ralph, one of the leaders of the revolt of 1075, is said to have gone to Denmark after the collapse of the revolt in England and was planning to return with a fleet.[37] With every year that passed it was harder to remove the Normans.

Thus twice within fifty years England had been conquered, with the result that she was part of a larger polity. The effects, especially the second, long-lasting conquest by the Normans, were wide-ranging and felt in every sphere, political, cultural, and economic. The long years of resistance under Æthelred drove ever greater demands for manpower and money to finance defence by land and sea, and then her foreign rulers were able to deploy the same resources for their wars. Yet the kingdom also had to be defended from its neighbours in Britain, from attacks by the Welsh and the Scots.

[35] ASC, D, E, 1069, 1070.　　[36] ASC, D, 1075.　　[37] OV, II, p. 316.

WALES AND THE WELSH

Offa's Dyke, the great earthwork between England and Wales, had been
overtaken by events in the sense that there were Welsh and English settlers
on both sides of the Dyke.[38] In the tenth century English kings regarded their
power as kings of Albion or Britain as conveying superiority over Welsh and
Scottish kings and when powerful, they sought acknowledgement of their
superior status, as King Edgar had done in 973. When circumstances
permitted, Welsh kings were able to recover lost territory or launch raids,
on occasion in alliance with Vikings, some of whom settled in Wales, or
Irish. Thus in the north Gruffydd ap Llewelyn had come to power in 1039,
and over time he was to make himself the dominant figure in Wales. In 1049
he allied with a fleet from Ireland, sailed up the river Usk and devastated the
surrounding region. The bishop of Worcester with a local force tried to fight
off the Welsh, but failed.[39] In 1052 Gruffydd harried in Herefordshire, and
many English were killed.[40] In the following year the Welsh ravaged round
Westbury.[41] In 1058, Ælfgar, earl of Mercia, who had been exiled for
a second time, returned from Ireland to Wales, allying with Gruffydd, and
marched on Hereford. They were led by Earl Ralph of Mantes, the king's
brother-in-law, and were said to have fled in the face of the enemy because
they were forced to fight on horseback, contrary to custom. As a result
Hereford was burned, and in the following year the bishop and sheriff were
killed.[42] As Domesday Book shows, Gruffydd was able to extend his influence over the north-east, at Rhuddlan, and over Archenfield, in the south-
east.[43] In 1059 Ælfgar died and was succeeded by his son of the same name.
He too sought help from Ireland and from Gruffydd in order to recover his
earldom. Harold Godwinson was more successful. In 1063 he marched
from Gloucester to Rhuddlan, Gruffydd's stronghold, and burned it. Then
he sailed from Bristol round the Welsh coast, taking hostages whilst his
brother Tostig overran the country by land. Later in the same year Gruffydd
was killed by his own men, and his lands passed to his brothers, who were
prepared to swear oaths of loyalty to Edward. Peace did not last long,
however, for in 1065 Gruffydd's son sacked the hunting lodge which
Harold was building at Portskewett in south Wales.[44]

---

[38] R. R. Davies, *The Age of Conquest. Wales 1063–1415* (Oxford: Oxford University Press,
1987), chapter 1.
[39] ASC, D, 1050; JW, II, pp. 550–3.   [40] ASC, D, 1052; JW, II, pp. 566–7.
[41] ASC, C, 1053.   [42] ASC, C, D, E, 1055; JW, II, pp. 576–9.
[43] DB, I, fols. 269r, 179r.   [44] ASC, D, 1065.

The recent history of disturbances along the border with Wales thus explains why William the Conqueror was taking no chances and sent William FitzOsbern to the Welsh border as early as 1067. He established himself at Gloucester, Chepstow, and Hereford, and started the process by which land was parcelled out to Normans. The middle section of the frontier was entrusted to Roger of Montgomery, possibly in 1067 or 1068, and the north to Gerbod the Fleming and, around 1070 or 1071, to Hugh d'Avranches. In this way three great earldoms were intended to form a buffer zone against the Welsh and also, presumably, as a base for forward expansion. For what is clear is that King William's followers did not regard Welsh territory as out of bounds; rather, they moved into Wales as and when they could. For this reason the boundaries between Welsh Wales, Wales under Norman rule, and England were slow to stabilize. In the north, parts of Flintshire and Rhuddlan were controlled by a kinsman of Earl Hugh in 1086, and in the middle section Earl Roger advanced into Montgomeryshire. After the death of FitzOsbern in 1071 he was not replaced, but several lords of the second rank were established in his place. In the south, the Normans' advance was most spectacular along the coast as far west as Pembrokeshire. In their wake came peasant settlers, Flemings in Cantred Rhos, and English elsewhere.

During the century that followed a pattern emerged. Welsh resurgence against the Normans was followed by an expedition by the English king who sought as a minimum submissions and payment of tribute. In the 1090s the Welsh rose up and, in alliance with Magnus Barelegs, killed a force of Normans headed by Earl Hugh of Montgomery, Roger's son, prompting an expedition by William Rufus.[45] In 1101–2 the Welsh allied with Robert de Bellême, brother and successor of Earl Hugh, against Henry I. The latter confiscated Robert's earldom and instead ruled through the sheriff.[46] Henry's approach, broadly speaking, was to establish a *modus vivendi* with the Welsh princes as far as possible, especially with Gruffydd ap Cynan in north Wales, and to enforce his authority by personal appearances in 1114 and 1121 which were sufficient to secure submissions and payment of

[45] OV, V, pp. 222–4; *Brut y Tywysogion. Red Book of Hergest Version*, pp. 36–9; *Brut. Peniarth MS 20 Version*, pp. 20–1.
[46] OV, VI, pp. 20–32. The powers of sheriff seem to have been exercised in succession by Richard de Beaumais, who was appointed bishop of London in 1108, and Payn FitzJohn, J. A. Green, *English Sheriffs to 1154* (London: HMSO, 1990), p. 72.

tribute.[47] He also used his authority as overlord to establish his own
men in border lordships.[48] His death was followed by trouble along the
border, and during Stephen's reign, the Welsh were able to recover
some of their lost territory.[49] Henry II, here as elsewhere, wished to
turn the clock back to his grandfather's day, which had to be achieved
by military expeditions. By that of 1157 he secured the submission of
and hostages from Owain Gwynedd, and in 1163, after a further expedition, further submissions from the Welsh princes.[50] Unsurprisingly
this provoked a further rising in Wales and another expedition, in
1165.[51] This, unlike the first two, achieved nothing, and in the north
and the south the Welsh were able to recover some lost territory.
However, what is clear by the end of our period is the way the balance
of power had swung towards the English. The settlement of Normans
along the borders, defended by their numerous castles, inhibited Welsh
advance and provided a springboard for further expansion into Welsh
territory. Those Marcher lordships had many castles and a higher
degree of militarization than lordships elsewhere; by the end of our
period they had also established a considerable degree of independence
from the crown (see further in Chapter 9).

THE NORTH AND THE SCOTS

Where Offa's Dyke had provided a formal demarcation between English
and Welsh territory, Hadrian's Wall had a similar symbolic role in the
north, but as in the case of Offa's Dyke, the actual border between
England and Scotland was a moveable feast. Power politics in northern
England (in this context, England north of the Humber and Mersey) in the
tenth century were relatively fluid, in the sense that networks and alliances

[47] R. S. Babcock, 'The Irish Sea Province and the Accession of Henry I', D. J. Fleming and J. M. Pope (eds.), *Henry I and the Anglo-Norman World. Studies in Memory of C. Warren Hollister, Haskins Society Journal*, 17 (2007), 39–62.
[48] J. A. Green, *Henry I: King of England and Duke of Normandy* (Cambridge: Cambridge University Press, 2006), pp. 132–3.
[49] D. Crouch, 'The March and the Welsh Kings', E. King (ed.), *The Anarchy of King Stephen's Reign* (Oxford: Oxford University Press, 1994), pp. 255–89.
[50] William of Newburgh, *Historia Rerum Anglicarum, Chronicles of the Reigns of Stephen, Henry II and Richard I* (ed. Howlett), I, pp. 106–9; Robert of Torigny, *ibid.*, IV, p. 193; *Brut y Tywysogion. Hergest*, pp. 134–7, 142–3; *Peniarth*, pp. 60, 137.
[51] *The Historical Works of Gervase of Canterbury*, ed. W. Stubbs, 2 vols., RS (London: Longman and Co, 1879–80), I, p. 197; William of Newburgh, *Historia Rerum Anglicarum, Chronicles*, I, p. 145; P. Latimer, 'Henry II's Campaign against the Welsh in 1165', *Welsh Historical Review*, 14 (1989), 523–52.

formed, broke up, and reformed. The heartland of the English monarchy remained Wessex. Mercia had been added, but not fully incorporated, and its eastern part had been settled by Danes. The old kingdom of Northumbria had fallen to the Vikings, and to judge from place-name evidence it seems they became a substantial presence round York. The city remained the centre of the northern archbishopric, and it was also the headquarters of Eric Bloodaxe, probably a son of Harald Fairhair, king of Norway and the last Scandinavian ruler, who was killed in 954.[52] The situation north of the river Tees is unclear: the clerics who guarded the remains of their beloved saint, Cuthbert, had to move from Lindisfarne because of the dangers of Viking attack, ending up at Durham.[53] At Bamburgh there were local lords or holds whose family are thought to have ruled northern Northumbria at least since Vikings had settled in the region.[54] West of the Pennines, political groupings and allegiances are even less certain. Cumberland and Westmorland were part of the old kingdom of Strathclyde. One of the last of the native kings, Owain, was present at the battle of Carham with King Malcolm of Scots, who defeated Earl Uhtred of Northumbria.[55] Domesday Book provides a little information about the southern Cumbrian fells, and what was to become the county of Lancashire in the reign of Edward the Confessor: Earl Tostig had held several great estates in north Lancashire and south Cumbria, whilst King Edward held 'the land between Ribble and Mersey'.[56]

In the north-east the land north of the river Tees had belonged to the kingdom of Northumbria. Lothian, broadly speaking the region between the Forth and Tweed, passed to the Scots, probably in the later tenth century.[57] The region between Tweed and Tees remained part of the earldom of Northumbria, but was subject to attack by the Scots in 1006

---

[52] Marios Costambeys, 'Erik Bloodaxe (d. 954)', *ODNB* www.oxforddnb.com/view/arti cle/49265, accessed 20 May 2016; A. Smyth, *Scandinavian York and Dublin. The History and Archaeology of Two Related Viking Kingdoms*, 2 vols. (Dublin: Templekieran Press, 1975–9); C. Downham, *Viking Kings of Britain and Ireland. The Dynasty of Ivarr to A. D. 1014* (Edinburgh: Edinburgh University Press, 2007).

[53] Symeon of Durham, *Libellus*, pp. 122, 144–8.

[54] R. Fletcher, *Bloodfeud. Murder and Revenge in Anglo-Saxon England* (London: Allen Lane Penguin, 2002), pp. 38–41; William M. Aird, 'Uhtred, Earl of Bamburgh (d. 1016)', *ODNB* www.oxforddnb.com/view/article/27981, accessed 20 May 2016.

[55] Symeon of Durham, *Historia Regum, Opera omnia*, II, pp. 155–6; *Libellus*, pp. 156–7. C. Phythian Adams, *Land of the Cumbrians: a Study in British Provincial Origins, A. D. 400–1200* (Aldershot, Brookfield: Scolar Press, Ashgate, 1996).

[56] DB, I, fols. 301v, 269v, 332v.

[57] For discussion, see A. Woolf, *From Pictland to Alba 789–1070*, New Edinburgh History of Scotland, 2 (Edinburgh: Edinburgh University Press, 2007), pp. 234–6.

and 1040.[58] Earl Uhtred, having been defeated at Carham, was soon disposed of by murder. Cnut appointed as earls first the Norwegian Eric of Hlathir and then Siward, possibly Danish, who was successful in holding off the Scots.[59] In 1054 he was said to have routed Macbeth and to have replaced him by Malcolm, 'son of the king of the Cumbrians', possibly Malcolm III or, it has been suggested, another son of Malcolm II.[60] Siward's death in 1055 without an adult son opened the way for the appointment of Tostig Godwinson as earl. He lacked any local connection either at York or at Bamburgh, and Malcolm III crossed the border in 1058 or 1059.[61] He was prepared to meet King Edward, and it seems that peace was made between himself and Tostig. The earl was evidently sufficiently confident to go on pilgrimage to Rome with Archbishop Ealdred. Whilst he was away the Scots raided Northumberland, and possibly Lindisfarne.[62] The Scots' raids at this date were probably about slaves, cattle, and tribute rather than permanent occupation.

The frontier zone remained quiescent until 1067, when Copsi, Tostig's deputy who had been appointed earl by William the Conqueror, was murdered by Osulf of Bamburgh.[63] In the following year there was a revolt in the north against the Normans and when it failed the rebels, including Edgar Ætheling, took refuge at Malcolm's court.[64] A more serious revolt broke out in the following year. William's new earl of Northumbria was murdered at Durham with his retinue. The castellan of York was killed. The rebels entered the city and besieged the castle. As in the previous year William marched north, relieved the castle, and built a second there. A force was sent north, but only reached Northallerton before turning back, and in the autumn a large Danish force arrived, joined forces with the rebels, and killed the Normans in the streets of York. William marched north once again, dealt with the Danes by giving them permission to forage provided

---

[58] *Libellus*, pp. 168, 186 n. See also Symeon of Durham, 'De Obsessione Dunelmi', *Opera omnia*, I, pp. 215–20, for an attack which may relate to 1006 rather than the stated date of 969.

[59] William M. Aird, 'Siward, Earl of Northumbria (*d.* 1055)', *ODNB* www.oxforddnb.com /view/article/25652, accessed 20 May 2016.

[60] JW, II, p. 574; Symeon of Durham, *Historia Regum, Opera omnia*, II, p. 17. For discussion, see Woolf, *From Pictland to Alba*, pp. 254–5, 261–3, 270–1.

[61] Geffrei Gaimar, *Estoire des Engleis*, lines 5085–99.

[62] *Chronicle of Melrose, Early Sources of Scottish History*, trans. A. O. Anderson, 2 vols. (Stamford: Paul Watkins, 1990), II, p. 1.

[63] William of Poitiers, *Gesta Guillelmi*, pp. 184–5.

[64] ASC, E, 1068. Edgar had gone there with his mother and two sisters for the first occasion in 1067, ASC, E, 1067.

they returned home in the spring, and then proceeded to ravage the north, reaching the Tyne valley before returning to York.[65]

Meanwhile Malcolm had married Edgar's sister, Margaret, and in 1070 he moved into Cumberland, crossed the Pennines and ravaged Teesdale and Cleveland.[66] He sent booty back into Cumberland, only to find William's new earl of Northumbria, Gospatric, had looted it.[67] In 1072 William decided to assert his authority over Malcolm, and marched north, finally catching Malcolm at Abernethy, where Malcolm submitted.[68] Even so Malcolm was not permanently deterred; he invaded again in 1079, after which William sent his half-brother, Odo of Bayeux, and eldest son, Robert, to secure a renewal of Malcolm's submission.[69] Malcolm invaded again in 1091 and besieged Durham. Rufus marched north and, hearing that Malcolm had an army in Lothian, Duke Robert and Edgar Ætheling brokered a peace. Rufus granted Malcolm twelve vills which he had held under William the Conqueror, and an annual payment.[70] In the following year it was Rufus who was on the offensive, for he marched into Cumberland, drove Dolfin out of Carlisle, and established a castle there.[71] Malcolm went south to see Rufus at Gloucester, but the latter would not receive him. He wanted Malcolm to perform homage at his court, whereas Malcolm claimed this should be performed on the border.[72] Malcolm returned north, collected an army, and crossed into Northumberland one last time in 1093. On this occasion he and his son Edward were killed by the knights of Robert de Mowbray, earl of Northumbria.[73]

The pendulum had now swung towards the Normans, for they were not dislodged from Carlisle, and William Rufus was able to exert influence by supporting claimants to the Scottish throne. Malcolm's son Duncan by his first wife was sent north with an army. Initially he was successful in removing Donald, but then the Scots fought back, killed Duncan, and restored Donald.[74] Three years later, Donald was expelled

---

[65] For the revolt of 1069, see ASC, D, E, 1068, 1069; JW, III, pp. 8–11; Geffrei Gaimar, *Lestoire des Engleis*, lines 5431–52; OV, II, pp. 224–32.

[66] *Chronicle of Melrose, Early Sources of Scottish History*, II, p. 23.

[67] Symeon of Durham, *Historia Regum, Opera omnia*, II, pp. 190–1.

[68] ASC, E, 1072; JW, III, p. 20.

[69] Symeon of Durham, *Historia Regum, Opera omnia*, II, p. 211.

[70] JW, III, p. 60; Symeon of Durham, *Historia Regum, Opera omnia*, II, p. 218.

[71] ASC, E, 1092. [72] JW, III, p. 64.

[73] Ibid., 66–8; ASC, E, 1093; OV, IV, pp. 270–2; Symeon of Durham, *Historia Regum, Opera omnia*, II, pp. 221–2.

[74] JW, III, pp. 66, 72.

and succeeded by Edgar, son of Malcolm III, supported by *his* uncle, Edgar Ætheling.[75] Edgar survived on the throne, but Norman support came at a price, recognition of overkingship. The accession of Henry I strengthened the relationships between the two dynasties, for Henry married Edgar's sister Matilda. Alexander, the next brother, succeeded in 1107 and married Sybil, an illegitimate daughter of Henry, whilst the youngest brother, David, married a great Anglo-Norman heiress, Matilda de Senlis. David was established as lord of south-west Scotland and Tweeddale.[76] Alexander may not have relished this; it appears Henry had to pressure him into allowing David to hold these lands (which he himself probably held before his accession).[77] When Alexander died without a son of legitimate birth in 1124, David succeeded him.

During Henry's lifetime David respected the Solway–Tweed boundary. He took the oath to recognize Matilda, Henry's only surviving legitimate daughter, and it was, he claimed, to secure the castles on her behalf that he entered northern England in 1136, took Carlisle, Norham, and Newcastle, and subsequently made himself master of Cumbria and Lancashire.[78] A central provision of the Treaty of Durham of 1139 which brought several years of conflict to an end was that David's son Henry would receive the earldom of Northumbria (Northumberland) except the castles of Newcastle and Bamburgh.[79] David meanwhile continued to hold Cumbria and the two parts of Lancashire, as far south as the river Mersey. His son held Northumberland, and between 1141 and 1143 he sought, but failed, to secure the bishopric of Durham for his chancellor, William Cumin.[80] The nature of David's rule in northern England has again prompted reflection. Was it any less kingly than his rule north

---

[75] *ibid.*, 84.

[76] A. A. M. Duncan, *Kingship of the Scots 842–1292. Succession and Independence* (Edinburgh: Edinburgh University Press, 2002), pp. 61–5.

[77] Ailred of Rievaulx, *Battle of the Standard, Chronicles of the Reigns of Stephen, Henry II and Richard I*, III, p. 193; *Aelred of Rievaulx: the Historical Works*, p. 262.

[78] Richard of Hexham, *De Gestis Regis Stephani et de Bello Standardo, Chronicles*, III, p. 145; John of Hexham's continuation of Symeon of Durham, *Historia Regum, Opera omnia*, II, p. 287.

[79] Richard of Hexham, *De Gestis Regis Stephani et de Bello Standardo, Chronicles*, III, pp. 167–76; John of Hexham, continuation to *Historia Regum*, Symeon of Durham, *Opera omnia*, II, pp. 297–300.

[80] J. A. Green, 'Anglo–Scottish Relations, 1066–1174', M. Jones and M. Vale (eds.), *England and Her Neighbours 1066–1453: Essays in Honour of Pierre Chaplais* (London: Hambledon Press, 1989), pp. 66–7; A. Young, *William Cumin: Border Politics and the Bishopric of Durham 1141–1144*, University of York Borthwick Paper, 52 (1978).

of the border?[81] David's success had benefited from civil war in England. He hoped to be able to keep the three northern counties, and in 1149, when he knighted Henry FitzEmpress, Henry was said to have promised that he would not take them back. In fact, he did so in 1157, and neither Malcolm IV (1153–65) nor William the Lion (1165–1214) was able to recover them, bar the lordship of North Tynedale. Moreover, Henry only knighted Malcolm after he had participated in the Toulouse campaign.[82] Malcolm performed homage in 1163 and handed over his youngest son as a hostage.[83] William the Lion joined a coalition of rebels against Henry II in 1173 and had the misfortune to be captured outside the castle at Alnwick. Humiliating peace terms followed: a further submission was made at York and castles were surrendered.[84]

By the late twelfth century, the English had fought off efforts by their Welsh and Scottish neighbours. The boundaries of the kingdom, albeit contested, were established more clearly. For two centuries, then, the kingdom had been the object of attack both from seaborne invaders and from the Welsh and Scots, and, as it proved, permanently taken over by the Normans and their allies. The effects of the Norman Conquest in particular cannot be underestimated, on the relationship between the king and the aristocracy, on the spread of castles, and on language and culture. In the short term the effects of warfare were destructive of people, crops, and buildings. A great deal of silver left the country in the form of coin to pay tribute and soldiers' wages, especially under Æthelred and Cnut. What is harder to judge is how far economic growth was retarded as a result. And it is to economic and environmental factors that we now turn.

ECONOMIC AND ENVIRONMENTAL FACTORS

The climate certainly began to improve around the first millennium, and this benefitted crop yields.[85] Whether this was the primary cause of population growth, or whether growth had already begun is not known. There are no firm figures for population either for the late tenth or the late twelfth centuries. Those Domesday Book provided for the halfway point

---

[81] G. W. S. Barrow, 'King David I, Earl Henry and Cumbria', *Transactions of the Cumberland and Westmorland Antiquarian and Archaeological Society*, 99 (1999), 117–27.

[82] Robert of Torigny, *Chronicles*, IV, pp. 202–3.   [83] Howden, I, p. 219.

[84] Robert of Torigny, *Chronicles*, IV, pp. 267–8. Howden, II, pp. 79–82.

[85] H. H. Lamb, *Climate, History and the Modern World* (London: Methuen, 1982), pp. 164–73.

are notoriously problematic.[86] The total may have been something in the region of between 1,800,000 and 2,000,000.[87] The chronology of change is equally hard to chart. It is possible that the population began to expand in the second half of the tenth century, as the climate began to improve. On the other hand, this was the time when Viking attacks began to increase. Reports of famine and disease highlight other setbacks.[88]

In the longer term more land was being brought under the plough, more commodities were being traded in markets, fairs, and towns, and villages and towns were expanding in number and size.[89] Aerial photography can also demonstrate how settlements expanded.[90] Inroads were being made on uplands, marshes, fens, and woodland.[91] Records from the bishopric of Ely and from Peterborough abbey show the monks engaged in draining the fens. At Battle Abbey in Sussex, founded by William the Conqueror on the site of his famous victory, the monks colonized the wooded land which they had been given. As they did so, their revenues increased.[92] Elsewhere fines for ploughing up land in the boundaries of the royal forests recorded on the annual pipe rolls demonstrate land clearance. For example, Bishop Roger de Clinton of Coventry and Lichfield (1129–48) cleared a good deal of land in the royal forests of Staffordshire, and in 1156 he was fined £100.[93] In the north of England new religious houses founded in the twelfth century built up great flocks of sheep, and made profits from the

[86] S. Harvey, 'Domesday England', H. Hallam (ed.), *Agrarian History of England and Wales*, II, *1042–1350* (Cambridge: Cambridge University Press, 1988), II, pp. 46–8.

[87] J. S. Moore, 'Quot homines? The Population of Domesday England', *Anglo-Norman Studies*, 19 (1996), 307–34.

[88] E. g. ASC, C, 976 'the great famine occurred'; C, D, E, 986 'the great murrain first occurred'; C, D, E, 1005 'great famine throughout England'.

[89] There have been different estimates of how far the economy grew between 1086 and 1300, about the time the economy is thought to have entered a period of crisis: see R. Britnell and B. M. S. Campbell (eds.), *A Commercialising Economy: England 1086 to c. 1300* (Manchester: Manchester University Press, 1995), contributions by Snooks, Mayhew, and Dyer.

[90] M. W. Beresford and J. K. S. St Joseph, *Medieval England* (Cambridge: Cambridge University Press, 2009 edn), pp. 94–102.

[91] For the Cumbrian fells, see A. J. L. Winchester, *Landscape and Society in Medieval Cumbria* (Edinburgh: Edinburgh University Press, 1987), chapter 3; E. Miller, *The Abbey and Bishopric of Ely* (Cambridge: Cambridge University Press, 1951), pp. 95–7. E. King, *Peterborough Abbey 1086–1310* (Cambridge: Cambridge University Press, 1973), chapter 4.

[92] E. Searle, *Lordship and Community. Battle Abbey and Its Banlieu* (Toronto: Pontifical Institute of Medieval Studies, 1974), chapter 4.

[93] *Red Book of the Exchequer*, ed. H. Hall, 3 vols., RS (London: HMSO, 1896), II, p. 652; E. Amt, 'The Forest Regard of 1155', *Haskins Society Journal*, 2 (1990), 189–95.

minerals on their lands. The Cistercian houses, such as Fountains and Rievaulx in Yorkshire, were a great success in economic terms.[94]

Secondly, the way resources were being managed was changing. Depending on the type and location of land, more was being devoted to raising food crops, especially corn. Field systems differed.[95] On heavy soil, large open fields were laid out, tilled by teams of ploughs. Often the farmers came to live in consolidated settlements or nucleated villages, each family having strips in the fields.[96] Whether as yet the fields were farmed cooperatively (common fields rather than open fields) is unclear.[97] Environmental factors may have played a part in the rise of nucleated villages, especially in midland England. It has been argued that such soils drained late and needed to be sown quickly so that the labour force needed to be close at hand.[98]

There was considerable variety not only in farms, villages, and farming, but also in rural society. The most economically active region was East Anglia, where many estates were small and becoming smaller through subdivision, where tenants were often legally of free status, and lords primarily rentiers. In midland England with open fields and nucleated villages, the whole village might be held by a single lord. He or his reeve was resident and thus able to keep a close watch on the peasant workforce which, by the end of our period, was largely tied to the estate or manor. Archaeological excavation of late Anglo-Saxon seigneurial residences has confirmed the rise of a new thegnly class.[99] Elsewhere lordship and settlement took different patterns: in some upland, scantily populated areas, older, larger units of lordship survived, with estate centres collecting dues from outlying farms. In other areas there were isolated farms or hamlets where land was farmed on an infield-outfield basis. The management of pasture and woodland also differed: often such resources were located at

---

[94] J. Burton, *The Monastic Order in Yorkshire 1069–1215* (Cambridge: Cambridge University Press, 1999), chapter 11.

[95] D. Hall, *The Open Fields of England* (Oxford: Oxford University Press, 2014).

[96] J. Sheppard, 'Medieval Village Planning in Northern England', *Journal of Historical Geography*, 2 (1976), 3–20; D. Banham and R. Faith, *Anglo-Saxon Farms and Farming* (Oxford: Oxford University Press, 2014), chapter 12.

[97] S. Oosthuizen, 'The Emperor's Old Clothes: the Origins of Medieval Nucleated Settlements and Their Open fields', *Medieval Settlement Research*, 28 (2013), 96–8; Banham and Faith, *Anglo-Saxon Farms and Farming*, chapter 12.

[98] T. Williamson, *Shaping Medieval Landscapes. Settlement, Society, Environment* (Macclesfield: Windgather Press, 2003).

[99] M. Gardiner, 'Late Saxon Settlements', D. A. Hinton, S. Crawford, and H. Hamerow (eds.), *Oxford Handbook of Anglo-Saxon Archaeology* (Oxford: Oxford University Press, 2011), pp. 198–217.

some distance from village centres. The needs of monasteries and cathedral churches shaped land management. Such communities were not itinerant like the households of kings and lay lords, so their estates continued to
produce renders in food rather than cash, and some still had slave work-
forces. The impact of the Norman Conquest has been seen as accelerating
this trend, by enabling lords to enforce stricter discipline on peasant farmers. Where previously they had been relatively lightly burdened, now their
dues and services were increased, and many of those who had been legally
free lost their freedom.[100] There is still a good deal of debate about
these developments and their inter-relationship, and more local studies
by archaeologists and landscape historians are needed. Nevertheless, the
push towards greater crop growing was clearly due to more demand to
sustain a growing population.

Thirdly, more production for the market was reflected in the growing
numbers of markets and fairs.[101] Those who had the right to markets
increasingly sought royal charters as a means of ensuring that theirs were
the profits. Some of the most important fairs had probably come into
being before the first references in royal charters, as, for instance, the grant
of a fair at St Giles's Church Winchester, by William Rufus.[102] Charters
granting or confirming fairs by Henry I include those at King's Lynn,
St Ives, Bury, Ely, Stow, and Rochester.[103] The overall upward trend in
the number of markets is clear.

Finally, and making allowance for internal migration, the growth in the
size of existing towns and the foundation of new ones are signs of population growth. The picture was not one of universal prosperity: the town of
Chester, for instance, prospered because of its trade in the Irish Sea basin,
but it was also vulnerable to attack in the late tenth century and, like other
towns, suffered in the campaigns after 1066.[104] Exeter experienced
attacks in 1001 and 1003, and sieges in 1068 and 1136.[105] Ipswich was
attacked in 991 and 1010.[106] The major construction programmes in
larger centres after 1066 of castles and churches undoubtedly led to the

---

[100] Faith, *English Peasantry and the Growth of Lordship*, chapter 8.
[101] E. Miller and J. Hatcher, *Medieval England. Rural Society and Economic Change 1086–1348* (London: Longman, 1978), pp. 74–9; E. Miller and J. Hatcher, *Medieval England. Towns, Commerce and Crafts* (London: Longman, 1995), pp. 155–66.
[102] *RRAN*, I, no. 377.
[103] *Ibid.*, II, nos. 911, 1853, 953, 1585, 1916, 1599, 1620, 864, 868, 1867.
[104] *Victoria County History, Cheshire*, V, *Chester*, pp. 17–33.
[105] ASC, E, 1001; ASC, C, D, E, 1003; ASC, D, 1067 (*recte* 1068); ASC, E, 1135; *Gesta Stephani*, pp. 36–42.
[106] ASC, A, 991; ASC, C, D, E, 1010.

demolition of houses, as Domesday Book reveals, but they were major providers of employment (boom time for builders). The building of castles led to the development of settlements close by, either planned or unplanned.[107] A castle was founded at Newcastle on Tyne in 1080, and by 1135 a town had grown up there.[108] As a base for royal authority at the gateway to Northumberland it had obvious strategic importance, as well as commercial potential. The town of Richmond which grew up adjacent to the castle is another northern example.[109] Bishops could do a great deal to encourage the growth of towns: the bishop of Norwich founded Lynn, for instance.[110] The population of Witney in Oxfordshire grew up in the late twelfth or early thirteenth century near a residence built by Henry of Blois, bishop of Winchester.[111] Towns similarly grew up round royal residences. Henry I, for example, granted a charter to Dunstable, where he had a residence and where he founded an Augustinian priory.[112] Woodstock in Oxfordshire was a favoured residence of both Henry I and Henry II, and, according to tradition, the latter made a grant of land outside the park so that men could build houses.[113] Examples could be multiplied indefinitely, and although some new towns did not flourish and others suffered damage or decline, there is no doubt that over the period as a whole, there were more, and larger, towns by the end of the period.

REFORM AND RENEWAL IN THE CHURCH

The third set of factors affecting English society were movements for reform and renewal in the Western church. This, of course, should not be seen as entirely or even mainly as an external factor: English churchmen were in touch with continental reform and themselves reformers. English churchmen were responsive to changing views in the Latin church about penitence and renewal of the Christian life, and to debates about how best

---

[107] M. Beresford, *New Towns of the Middle Ages* (London: Lutterworth Press, 1967).

[108] Stubbs, *Select Charters*, pp. 133–4.

[109] Count Alan of Brittany confirmed to the burgesses their customs as in the time of Counts Alan (d. 1093) and Stephen (d. 1135 x 1136), *Early Yorkshire Charters*, IV, ed. C. T. Clay, Yorkshire Archaeological Society, Record Series Extra Series, I (1935), pp. 22–3.

[110] D. Owen, 'Bishop's Lynn: the First Century of a New Town?', *[Proceedings of the Battle Conference on] Anglo-Norman Studies*, 2 (1979), 141–53, at pp. 196–7.

[111] *Victoria County History, Oxfordshire*, XIV, pp. 15–17.

[112] *Victoria County History, Bedfordshire*, II, pp. 349–68; *RRAN*, II, no. 1827.

[113] *Victoria County History, Oxfordshire*, XII, p. 326, citing *Rotuli Hundredorum*, ed. W. Illingworth and J. Caley, 2 vols. (London: Record Commissioners, 1812–18), II, pp. 839–42.

to follow Christ's teaching. At the start of our period King Edgar and Archbishop Dunstan worked together to promote monastic reform. Wulfstan bishop of London, Worcester, and archbishop of York was a central figure in calls for reform at the turn of the first millennium when the troubles overtaking Æthelred's realm seemed to be bringing home the message that God was punishing a sinful people.[114] Only when the English conformed to God's laws would they be spared. Wulfstan's role was central to the formulation of laws issued in Cnut's reign, the last before the Norman Conquest. In the early eleventh century calls for reform of the papacy, for a celibate clergy, and the eradication of the sin of simony were gathering apace. The English church was relatively far from direct influence from Rome – though increasingly pilgrims were travelling there – and there had been no reforming councils in the country, though English ecclesiastics had attended the Council of Rheims in 1049 and Rome in 1050.

All that changed after 1066 as papal legates arrived in 1070, and Lanfranc was appointed as archbishop of Canterbury. Conciliar decrees proscribed clerical marriage, admittedly with little immediate effect, the diocesan church was reorganized, more account was taken by the new elite of the obligation to pay tithes, and there was an almost complete changeover of personnel in the upper echelons, both bishops and abbots. The map of dioceses took its final medieval shape by 1133, and dioceses were subdivided into archdeaconries. The influence of the papacy took longer to establish. William the Conqueror famously refused to swear fealty to Gregory VII. Conflict over the king's right to homage and investiture of bishops and abbots was finally resolved by a formula by which the king retained homage but not investiture. This dispute, and that over primacy between Canterbury and York, opened the way to increasing contact with Rome. By the end of Stephen's reign the volume of appeals to Rome was growing, a trend Henry II found impossible to reverse.

Reform sparked greater desire and greater need for knowledge, knowledge of the Bible, the 'sacred page', of theology, and of law. Monasteries had traditionally been principal centres of study and learning, but the closing of monastic schools to outside students and the rise of other masters drew students to different centres. As the schools of northern France, especially Paris, boomed, clerks from England crossed the Channel to spend time there, and returned to pursue careers in church and state.

[114] C. Cubitt, 'The Politics of Remorse: Penance and Royal Piety in the Reign of Æthelred the Unready', *Historical Research*, 85 (2012), 179–92.

English intellectual interests were enriched by such experiences, but the old view, that England was essentially a passive recipient of continental scholarship, has been shown to have been wide of the mark: in certain areas such as computation and political philosophy English scholars such as John of Worcester and John of Salisbury were breaking new ground.[115]

Greater contact with northern France impacted lay culture too. Over time Christian thinking permeated the ethos of the lay aristocracy. It came to be thought unacceptable to kill or maim defeated enemies: instead they were imprisoned or ransomed.[116] The ends and context of violence mattered. Crusading ideals reached England, but without royal backing participation from the Anglo-Norman aristocracy was initially limited.[117] Greater prestige was given to fighting on horseback than on foot, and young knights from England participated in the craze for tournaments.[118] Cultural tastes, already a mix of English, Celtic, and Scandinavian strands, were further enriched from France.[119] In various ways England was becoming less cut off from continental developments.

Young aristocratic males may have been more eager to acquire the skills of fighting on horseback rather than on foot, but fighting on foot was far from being discredited, as was seen at Tinchebray in 1106 and Lincoln in 1141. The English preference for long hair was taken up at the court of William Rufus, displacing short hair seen on the Bayeux Tapestry. Tales of Roland and Oliver, Rou (Rolf) and the Normans, Arthur and his knights were part of a shared cultural currency in England and France. The fashion for tournaments engaged young knights on both sides of the Channel. By language, dress, and occupation, the elite distanced itself from the hewers of wood and drawers of water, as indeed, did the princes of the church from the rank and file.

---

[115] For John of Worcester, see A. Lawrence-Mathers, 'John of Worcester and the Science of History', *Journal of Medieval History*, 39 (2013), 255–74; for John of Salisbury's *Policraticus*, see most recently, C. Grellard and F. Lachaud (eds.), *A Companion to John of Salisbury* (Leiden, Boston: Brill, 2015).

[116] J. Gillingham, '1066 and the Introduction of Chivalry into England', G. Garnett and J. Hudson (eds.), *Law and Government in Medieval England and Normandy. Essays in Honour of Sir James Holt* (Cambridge: Cambridge University Press, 1994), pp. 31–55.

[117] C. Tyerman, *England and the Crusades 1095–1588* (Chicago, London: University of Chicago Press, 1988).

[118] D. Crouch, *Tournament* (London: Hambledon Press and London, 2005).

[119] M. Godden and M. Lapidge (eds.), *Cambridge Companion to Old English Literature* (Cambridge: Cambridge University Press, 2013); A. Galloway (ed.), *Cambridge Companion to Medieval English Culture* (Cambridge: Cambridge University Press, 2011); I. Short, 'Patrons and Polyglots: French Literature in Twelfth- and Thirteenth-Century England', *Anglo-Norman Studies*, 14 (1991), 229–49.

3

Kings

Our exploration of power in English society begins with kings. How did their powers change and grow over time, and how far were changes reflected in shifts in thinking about them? The central duties of kings were repeatedly outlined by clerical commentators, that of wielding the sword to protect their people and to punish wrongdoers. Consecrated and anointed with holy oil, they were subject to God alone. How these duties translated into practice altered considerably over time. By the end of our period the range of royal power, and the number of its agents, had been transformed, by the characters and aims of individual rulers, by the challenges they confronted, and by the contexts within which they operated. Between the tenth and twelfth centuries their claims to rule the whole of England south of the Solway and the Tweed became a reality, and so too that of over- or high kingship over other rulers in the British Isles. Key to the power of successful kings was, firstly, their influence over the nobility, the power to raise up, to reward, and, if need be, to destroy. Secondly, the extension of infrastructure in the form of hundreds, wapentakes, and shires provided a framework which could be built on for a range of purposes, from peacekeeping, to military obligation and financial exaction. Thirdly, a related point, the rise of sheriffs, the increasing use of writs and courts, were the indispensable channels through which royal authority penetrated the localities. The processes of integration and penetration depended greatly on active participation by the lay and ecclesiastical elites, but this came at a price: although there were few formal restraints on royal power, in practice kings were constrained by the need for sufficient support, as Æthelred, Stephen, and, later, King John, were to find. Finally, royal and ecclesiastical power were usually mutually supportive. The intellectual challenges to royal power posed by some movements of reform in the church could not be evaded indefinitely as the English church was opened up to external influences. Although Henry I was pressured into surrendering the ritual of investing bishops and abbots, he and his successors continued to enjoy a considerable influence over the choice of prelates. His grandson Henry II sought to retain oversight of judicial appeals to Rome, and to be able to bring clerks accused of crime within the purview of his courts, the two issues at the heart of his quarrel with Thomas Becket. These were technical issues which came to stand for the 'liberty of the English church' in both its external relations and internal governance, and neither king nor church achieved a clear-cut victory.

OVERKINGSHIP

The royal titles used in charters are evidence of claims to rule. In the tenth century the charters of Æthelstan and Edgar particularly articulated claims to be kings of Britain or of Albion rather than *rex Anglorum*, kings of the English.[1] Edgar's coronation at Bath in 973 was designed, it has been suggested, to display his kingship in an imperial context.[2] The occasion when Edgar had been rowed by kings on the river Dee was political theatre designed to demonstrate Edgar's superior authority.[3] Edgar's successors tended to revert to the style 'kings of the English' and then, from 1172, 'king of England'. The term Britain did not fall out of use, and was most famously employed by Geoffrey of Monmouth in his *History of the Kings of Britain*. This was composed around the time Henry I died, and offered an historical narrative that competed with that of Bede and his twelfth-century followers. Instead of the history of England from the fall of Rome and the arrival of the Angles, Saxons, and Jutes, Geoffrey offered an alternative narrative: that the British descended from Brutus, a follower of Aeneas. After the Romans came Vortigern, and then Arthur. After the latter's death followed a time of civil war, famine, and disease. The Britons became known as the Welsh, and because they

---

[1] G. Molyneaux, 'Why Were Some Tenth-Century English Kings Presented as Rulers of Britain?', *Transactions of the Royal Historical Society*, 6th series, 21 (2011), 59–91.
[2] J. L. Nelson, 'Inauguration Rituals', *Politics and Ritual in Early Medieval Europe* (London: Hambledon Press, 1986), pp. 283–307, at p. 302.
[3] J. Barrow, 'Chester's Earliest Regatta? Edgar's Dee-Rowing Revisited', *Early Medieval Europe*, 10 (2001), 81–93.

were so divided they could not keep their enemies at bay.[4] It was the Saxons who were to conquer the whole land.

Edward the Confessor was keen on the idea of imperial rule, and one group of his charters does use the style 'king of Britain'.[5] Edward's seal was modelled on that of Emperor Otto III, and the legend is *basileus Anglorum*.[6] Although Edward was not a particularly effective king of the English, he continued to assert his authority over the Welsh and Scots. The see of Durham in this period was caught between the Scots, the earls of Northumbria, and the southern kings. After the death of Edmund, two brothers, Benedictine monks from Peterborough, held the see in succession.

William the Conqueror too was conscious of the legacy of empire, demonstrated again by retaining the majesty image on his seal, and by the construction of stone castles at London and Colchester.[7] Both William and his followers regarded Welsh territory as being within their sphere of influence, and the king himself is said to have visited St Davids in 1081.[8] Three great lordships were set up along the border, centred on Hereford, Shrewsbury, and Chester. William also marched into Scotland, and Malcolm III submitted to him in 1072 (see earlier in this volume for relations with the Welsh and Scots). Secular claims to a superior kingship were paralleled in the ecclesiastical sphere. Archbishop Lanfranc wrote to the pope in 1072 to relate the proofs that the primacy extended 'over the church of York and the whole island which men called Britain and over Ireland as well'.[9] Canterbury subsequently sought to sustain its wider primacy, though by the early twelfth century primacies had less support at Rome.[10]

---

[4] Geoffrey of Monmouth, *HKB, passim*; H. Pryce, 'British or Welsh? National Identity in Twelfth-Century Wales', *English Historical Review*, 106 (2001), 775–801.

[5] Barlow, *Edward the Confessor*, p. 136.

[6] *Anglo-Saxon Writs*, ed. F. E. Harmer (reprinted edition, Stamford: Paul Watkins, 1989), pp. 94–101, plate 2.

[7] For the use of his seal, see Bates, *Acta of William I*, pp. 102–5; for a comparison with Julius Caesar, see William of Poitiers, *Gesta Guillelmi*, pp. 168–75.

[8] For St Davids, *Brut y Tywysogion. Red Book of Hergest Version*, p. 31; C. P. Lewis, 'The Norman Settlement of Hereford under William I', *Anglo-Norman Studies*, 7 (1985), 195–213; Davies, *Age of Conquest*, pp. 27–34.

[9] *Letters of Lanfranc, Archbishop of Canterbury*, ed. and trans. H. Clover and M. Gibson (Oxford: Clarendon Press, 1979), no. 4. For the primacy, see M. Gibson, *Lanfranc of Bec* (Oxford: Clarendon Press, 1978), pp. 116–31.

[10] M. T. Flanagan, *Irish Society, Anglo-Norman Settlers, Angevin Kingship: Interactions in Ireland in the Late Twelfth Century* (Oxford: Clarendon Press, 1989), chapter 1.

CROWN AND NOBILITY

Kings could only gain their thrones and keep them with noble backing, a simple fact which remained as true at the end of our period as at the start. There were only a few great noble clans dominating court politics in middle and later years of the tenth century whose lands and interests spread across the country. Successive kings had to work with these powerful families and to advance their allies when the opportunity arose.[11] King Edgar promoted monastic reform, and the leading ecclesiastics, Archbishop Dunstan and Bishop Æthelwold, Edgar's third wife, Ælfthryth, and Ælfhere ealdorman of Mercia, jostled for power with other kindreds like those of Æthelwine, ealdorman of East Anglia, and Beortnoth, ealdorman of Essex.[12] In the early years of Æthelred's reign there was a good deal of continuity, then the deaths of Æthelwold (984), Dunstan (988), Beohrtnoth (991), Æthelwine (992), and Queen Ælfthryth around the year 1000 paved the way for others to rise, notably Eadric Streona.[13] A decisive change came in 1006, with the murder of Ealdorman Ælfhelm, the blinding of his sons, the appointment of Uhtred as earl of Northumbria, and the promotion of Eadric Streona.[14] Cnut proved ruthless in dealing with powerful native families. Uhtred was murdered, probably with Cnut's connivance, and Eadric Streona was put to death.[15] Cnut appointed a few of his allies and followers as earls, such as the Norwegian Eric of Lade as earl of Northumbria and Thorkell the Tall in East Anglia, but the former died in 1023 and the latter was exiled in 1021.[16] There were new men, like Siward, earl of Northumbria, Tovi the Proud, and Osgod Clapa, and Cnut also relied on those Englishmen prepared to work with him like Leofwine and Leofric his son, the latter appointed earl of Mercia, and

---

[11] C. Hart, 'Athelstan "Half King" and His Family', *Anglo-Saxon England*, 2 (1973), 115–44; A. Williams, '*Princeps Merciorum Gentis*: the Family, Career and Connections of Ælfhere, ealdorman of Mercia', *Anglo-Saxon England*, 10 (1981), 143–72.

[12] See especially the essays in D. Scragg (ed.), *Edgar King of the English, 959–975: New Interpretations* (Woodbridge: Boydell Press, 2008).

[13] R. Lavelle, *Aethelred II*, chapter 2.

[14] Keynes, *Diplomas of Æthelred 'the Unready'*, pp. 210–12; P. Stafford, 'The Reign of Æthelred II: a Study in the Limitations on Royal Policy and Action', D. Hill (ed.), *Ethelred the Unready*, British Archaeological Reports, British Series, 59 (1978), pp. 15–46, at p. 33.

[15] ASC, C, D, E, 1016, 1017; JW, II, p. 504; Symeon of Durham, '*De Obsessione Dunelmi*', *Opera omnia*, I, p. 218.

[16] Bolton, *Empire of Cnut the Great*, chapter 2; Pauline Stafford, 'Erik of Hlathir, earl of Northumbria (*fl.* 995–1023)', *ODNB* www.oxforddnb.com/view/article/39234, accessed 20 May 2016; Richard Abels, 'Thorkell the Tall, Earl of East Anglia (*fl.* 1009–1023)', *ODNB* www.oxforddnb.com/view/article/27403, accessed 20 May 2016.

Godwin, initially in command in eastern Wessex, but then in charge of the whole.[17] When Edward the Confessor became king he had little option but to ally himself with the three powerful earls, Godwin, Leofric, and Siward. He was able to dispense with a few of the Danes still present: Cnut's niece Gunnhildr was dismissed in 1043, and Osgot Clapa in the following year. He also introduced a few Normans, and by 1051, when an opportunity arose, and with the backing of Leofric and Siward, challenged the power of Godwin and his sons, and put his wife, Godwin's daughter, into a nunnery. In the following year, when Godwin returned in force, the king was forced to come to terms with the family, and to bring Edith back to court.[18]

The year 1066 saw the downfall of the house of Godwin. William received the allegiance of Edwin and Morcar, and kept Edgar Ætheling in his household. Edwin was promised a Norman bride, but she did not materialize. Both he and Morcar found that Normans and castles were appearing in their earldoms. Edwin was killed by one of his men, Morcar was imprisoned, and Waltheof executed.[19] Meanwhile a new elite was being established, whose most important members were related to the ducal house.[20] Some compact lordships were created, especially in border zones, but the great lords in general were granted land across the country in tranches.[21] Older landed estates were destroyed, but even more important than this disruption was the recalibration of the political relationship between crown and lay nobility, and crown and bishops and abbots. All had to submit to the king and became tenants-in-chief holding their land by dependent tenure. Each change of personnel on either side, king or tenant-in-chief, necessitated a renewal of the bond, acknowledged in the form of homage and, usually, a succession payment, by the tenant-in-chief. The tenant-in-chief took on responsibility for the geld and service owing. At some point quotas of service were assigned. Whatever had been the

---

[17] William M. Aird, 'Siward, Earl of Northumbria (*d.* 1055)', *ODNB* www.oxforddnb.com /view/article/25652, accessed 20 May 2016; Ann Williams, 'Tovi the Proud (*fl.* 1018–1042)', *ODNB* www.oxforddnb.com/view/article/52355, accessed 20 May 2016; Ann Williams, 'Osgod Clapa (*d.* 1054)', *ODNB* www.oxforddnb.com/view/article/20890, accessed 20 May 2016; S. Baxter, *The Earls of Mercia: Lordship and Power in Anglo-Saxon England* (Oxford: Oxford University Press, 2007), pp. 17–23, 32–43; Bolton, *Empire of Cnut the Great*, p. 47.

[18] Barlow, *Edward the Confessor*, chapters 3, 4, 5.

[19] ASC, D, E, 1071, 1075, 1076; Baxter, *Earls of Mercia*, chapter 7.

[20] C. W. Hollister, 'The Greater Domesday Tenants-in-Chief', J. C. Holt (ed.), *Domesday Studies* (Woodbridge: Boydell Press, 1987), pp. 219–48.

[21] J. A. Green, *The Aristocracy of Norman England* (Cambridge: Cambridge University Press, 1997), chapter 2.

basis of landed estates before 1066, tenure, by knight service or some other form of ministerial service, was henceforth pervasive. Domesday Book was the record of that new bargain, recording tenants-in-chief, their estates, and their assessments, in hides or plough lands.

It was imperative from the king's perspective that he did not lose touch with the wider community of arms-bearing freemen, and it was here that the Oath of Salisbury came in. The famous account in the Anglo-Saxon Chronicle, slightly expanded in the Worcester Chronicle, reported that at Lammas in 1086 'all the landholding men over all England, no matter whose men they were (*landsittende men ... wæron ofer eall England wæron þæs mannes men þe hi wæron*), bowed to him and were his men, and swore hold oaths that they would be loyal to him against all other men (*7 ealle hi bugon to him 7 weron his menn 7 him holdaðas sworon þet hi woldon ongean ealle oðre men him holde beon*)'.[22] In the Worcester version this was altered: the king ordered 'his archbishops, bishops, abbots, earls, barons, and sheriffs with their knights (*militibus*) to meet him on 1 August at Salisbury. On that day he made their knights swear allegiance (*fidelitatem*) to him no matter whose vassals they were'.[23] Oaths of loyalty had not been unknown in England, though historians are divided about their significance.[24] In 1086 the Salisbury Oath was of critical importance in reinforcing political loyalties, and that the obligation of loyalty to the king took precedence over and beyond that to the lord.[25]

This recalibration of the relationship between the king and the aristocracy transformed both political relations and land law. The tenants-in-chief had a duty and a right to offer counsel, as noted previously; they expected 'good lordship', and in return they owed service, usually knight service, in their own person and for the land they held, and financial obligations such as payment in lieu of service, 'aids' to assist their lord king in time of need, and, most critically of all, they accepted his right of intervention in their affairs in the same way they as lords had the right to

---

[22] *The Anglo-Saxon Chronicle. A Collaborative Edition, 7 MS E*, ed. S. Irvine (Cambridge: D. S. Brewer, 2004), p. 94.

[23] JW, III, p. 44.

[24] For the view that the oaths of loyalty prescribed in the first clause of Alfred's laws 'hold the key to early English law and order', see Wormald, *Making of English Law*, p. 283; Wormald, 'Oaths', M. Lapidge, J. Blair, S. Keynes, and D. Scragg (eds.), *Blackwell Encyclopaedia of Anglo-Saxon England* (Oxford: Blackwell, 1999), pp. 338–9; cf. L. Roach, *Kingship and Consent in Anglo-Saxon England 871–978: Assemblies and the State in the Early Middle Ages* (Cambridge: Cambridge University Press, 2013), pp. 113–14.

[25] J. C. Holt, '1086', reprinted in Holt, *Colonial England* (London: Hambledon Press, 1997), pp. 31–57 at pp. 31–5, 53–4.

intervene in the affairs of their men. A new bargain had been struck, and the Norman kings used their power to install their men on land, to intervene in their family arrangements, and to remove them should they prove disloyal. Over time rights of inheritance strengthened, but this did not diminish the king's 'feudal incidents', though it was beginning to prove harder for tenants who were also lords (mesne tenants) to secure their rights from *their* under-tenants. All tenants-in-chief had to negotiate succession payments for their lands, for the marriage of daughters and widows, and for the custody of any underage children. At the heart of their relationship with the king was the obligation to provide service and aid. If, when the summons came, they provided personal service, then a money payment was made for themselves and for the quota of knights they owed. At other times the king could ask them for financial aid, an obligation which became heavier in the late twelfth century.

The king's clout made his intervention in the affairs of great families likely throughout our period, but after 1066 it became both pervasive and visible because of the bargains struck with tenants-in-chief, who held their land in return for service, rather than owned it outright. There has been a great deal of debate over the centuries about the degree of novelty in these arrangements. The individual elements were certainly not new: leasing land in return for service was known; an obligation to provide military service had been assessed against land; and pre-Conquest kings had intervened in the affairs of great families. A contrast between 'ownership' before 1066 and 'tenure' afterwards is almost certainly overdrawn. However, the bringing together of the different elements in a relationship that was ubiquitous certainly was new. Tenure did not convey an absolute right of inheritance, and land could be confiscated for involvement in revolt, though on the whole it was usually re-granted.[26] The kings' rights over marriage, especially the marriage of heiresses and widows, and the wardship of minors, were of key importance as a way of transferring land to someone whose loyalty was being rewarded or sought. Under Rufus and Henry I at least, it was possible for the king to make a handsome profit in the process.[27] After Henry's death there is a gap in the evidence, and when the sequence of pipe rolls resumes in 1155 there is still little to suggest that Henry II was exploiting his rights to the same degree via the

---

[26] J. C. Holt, 'Politics and Property in Early Medieval England', *Past and Present*, 57 (1972), 3–52, reprinted in Holt, *Colonial England 1066–1215*, pp. 113–59.

[27] J. A. Green, *The Government of England under Henry I* (Cambridge: Cambridge University Press, 1986), pp. 83–7.

exchequer, even if a close watch was kept on the stock of heiresses and widows.[28] They were of course highly sensitive politically: the supply of heiresses and widows was restricted. It may be, too, that the younger Henry was careful about potentially alienating baronial families, choosing instead to intervene in a wider range of land disputes, and then, in 1176, to strengthen the position of heirs against lords.[29]

Royal power, then, rested with the king, but he was supposed to take counsel from the great men. In the past there was much discussion about the constitutional significance of counsel, and the extent to which it limited the power of the king. The idea of a long pedigree for limited monarchy proved very attractive in England between the seventeenth and the twentieth centuries. Anglo-Saxon kings were bound by the witan, it was argued, and the accession of William the Conqueror made no difference in this respect. The witan thus evolved seamlessly into the great council of the Norman kings, and that developed in turn, via the Magna Carta crisis, into parliament. Shorn of the weight of historiography, the essential need for tenth- and eleventh-century kings to govern by consensus and in the company of the great men is clear enough: kings did not command a standing army to enable them to force through contentious decisions. As the frontiers of their realm expanded, so did the numbers of those called to court, to assemblies known as the witans 'of the English people'.[30] Consensus politics came under severe strain under King Æthelred, as demands for men and money to fight the invaders became incessant, and accusations of treachery poisoned the atmosphere. The accusations in the Anglo-Saxon Chronicle about the treachery of Eadric Streona tell their own story.[31] It is clear that Cnut was only accepted after protracted negotiation. He promised to abide by the laws of King Edgar made at Oxford, and followed this up by a letter in English addressed to 'his archbishops, bishops, Earl Thorkell and all his earls and all his people'.[32] Edward the Confessor probably had to agree to

---

[28] *Rotuli de Dominabus et Pueris et Puellis de XII Comitatibus 1185*, ed. J. H. Round, Pipe Roll Society, 35 (1913). For discussion, see S. M. Johns, *Noblewomen, Aristocracy and Power in the Twelfth-Century Anglo-Norman Realm* (Manchester: Manchester University Press, 2003).

[29] Hudson, *Oxford History of the Laws of England*, II, pp. 645–53.

[30] J. R. Maddicott, *The Origins of the English Parliament 924–1327* (Oxford: Oxford University Press, 2010), p. 49.

[31] ASC, C, D, E, 992; A, 1001; C, D, E, 1003, 1009, 1011, 1015, 1016.

[32] ASC, D, 1018; JW II, pp. 504–5; for texts of the letters and discussion, see E. Treharne, *Living through Conquest. The Politics of Early English 1020–1220* (Oxford: Oxford University Press, 2012), pp. 17–43.

conditions before being accepted as king in 1042, and the power of Earl
Godwin and his family curtailed his freedom of manoeuvre. When he did
move against them in 1051 he had support, but in the following year they
were able to pressurize the king into restoring them.[33]

Moreover, the idea that kings made specific commitments at their
coronations was another trend which fed into the idea of contractual
kingship.[34] The promises Cnut made at Oxford, it has been suggested,
fed into his second law code.[35] It may have been these promises that set
a precedent for William Rufus, who made several promises in 1093 when
he thought he was dying, and sent letters throughout the country. This in
turn formed the precedent for Henry I's charter, issued at his coronation.[36]
Henry's was a mix of general statements, 'By God's grace and the counsel
of the barons I have been crowned', and statements of intent on specific
'evil customs', reliefs, marriage, widows, the money tax, debts owed to
his brother, testamentary disposition, judicial penalties, murder fines,
and geld exemption for serving knights. He stated he was going to keep
the forests in his own hand 'by the common consent of my barons'.
The last two clauses promised to maintain a 'firm peace throughout his
realm', and to 'give back the law of King Edward with those emendations
his father had made by the counsel of his barons'.

This charter was to set an important precedent by committing the king
to abolish evil customs (usually his brother's) and by its references to
baronial counsel. Stephen's first charter confirmed 'to all barons and all
my men of England' in general terms the liberties and laws granted by
Henry, those they had held under King Edward. This brief document, in
the normative language of contemporary charters, was amplified at
Oxford in 1136.[37] This spelled out that he had been elected king with
the consent of the clergy and people, made a range of promises mainly
concerning the church, but also promised disafforestation of those forests
added by Henry I, abolition of 'exactions, injustices and miskennings',
and promised a general confirmation of 'good laws and customs'.
The emphasis on church matters evidently reflected Stephen's need to
conciliate his brother, the bishop of Winchester. Unlike his first charter,

[33] ASC, C, D, 1052.
[34] M. Clayton, 'The Old English *Promissio Regis*', *Anglo-Saxon England*, 37 (2008),
91–150.
[35] P. Stafford, 'The Laws of Cnut and the History of Anglo-Saxon Royal Promises', *Anglo-Saxon England*, 10 (1981), 173–90.
[36] Stubbs, *Select Charters*, pp. 117–19 and see also article cited below, note 227.
[37] *RRAN*, III, no. 271.

which had a single witness and that of Henry I, with a relatively brief witness list, Stephen's second charter had a very full witness list. Henry II's was more like Stephen's first charter.[38] It was generally addressed, confirmed those good customs granted by his grandfather, and those evil ones abolished by his grandfather he himself abolished for himself and his heirs. There was a sole witness, Richard de Lucy. The new developments here were the complete omission of Stephen's reign and the promise made not just on his own behalf, but for his heirs too.

So far then, whilst it was becoming normative to issue a written confirmation of promises, there was as yet no set format, and, most significantly, no machinery for ensuring that promises were carried out. The two significant developments under Henry II were the requests for financial aid, which necessitated consent, and the great expansion of legal activity. It was prudent if not compulsory to have major new initiatives, such as greater intervention in matters of land inheritance, aired at meetings of the king's council. There was as yet no strict requirement about its composition, but once again it was sensible to have major matters agreed in a large assembly, and the term *great council* (*magnum concilium*) came to be attached to such assemblies.[39]

INFRASTRUCTURE

At the start of our period the term *ealdorman*, literally *elder man*, was used for men appointed by kings.[40] The greatest ealdormen of the tenth century were often of royal descent, had widely scattered estates, and held sway over great regions, sometimes comprising lesser ealdormanries. In the north the term *hold* or *high reeve* was used of the lords of Bamburgh.[41] Under Cnut the ealdormen gave way to 'eorls' or 'earls', once again appointed by the king.[42] The term was Latinized as *comes*, which continued in use after 1066. After 1066 the term *eorl* was equated with the Latin *comes*, though the powers of the English earl and the Norman count were not identical.[43]

---

[38] Stubbs, *Select Charters*, p. 158.
[39] For the usage of Roger of Howden, see Maddicott, *Origins of the English Parliament*, p. 75.
[40] A. Williams, *Kingship and Government in Pre-Conquest England, c. 500–1066* (Houndmills: Macmillan, 1999), pp. 89–90.
[41] W. E. Kapelle, *The Norman Conquest of the North: the Region and Its Transformation, 1000–1135* (London: Croom Helm, 1979), pp. 15–26.
[42] S. Keynes, 'Cnut's Earls', Rumble (ed.), *Reign of Cnut*, pp. 43–88.
[43] D. Crouch, *The Image of Aristocracy in Britain 1000–1300* (London: Routledge, 1992), chapter 1.

Those counts who received land in England retained their title, Count Alan
of the Bretons and Count Eustace of Boulogne, but after the early years
there was a certain reluctance to appoint additional earls. Only a handful of
men were granted the title by Rufus and Henry I, and they were not put in
charge of all the land owing knight service in the county.[44] Under Stephen
the number of earldoms rose dramatically as both he and the empress vied
for support in the shires, and in some cases the earls aggregated powers to
themselves.[45] Henry II in contrast halted this trend, by allowing some
earldoms to die with their holders, and by not creating new titles. Not
only that, but the title became a mark of rank, rather than a substantive
office: the real power lay with the king's sheriffs and justices.[46]

One of the key developments which buttressed royal power between the
tenth and twelfth centuries was the progressive establishment of hundreds,
shires, wapentakes, and their courts, and of sheriffs.[47] Hundreds were
territorial units for peacekeeping, for pledging, and for dispute resolution.
Some were already old units by the tenth century, probably representing the
territory of an early people, or that of a royal vill. Although hundreds are
first mentioned by name in the Hundred Ordinance, the laws of Edward the
Elder refer to a court which met every four weeks.[48] They were extended
across the East Midlands, probably in the reign of King Edgar.[49] Groups of
hundreds were united into shires, or shires were subdivided into hundreds.
Again, some shires were much older than others. In the Danelaw, hundreds
were grouped into wapentakes, and in Lindsey and Yorkshire there were
ridings as an additional layer.[50] Both hundreds and shires had reeves, and
then shire-reeves had a supervisory role over the smaller units. The creation
of these units was a protracted process, beginning in the tenth and continuing into the eleventh century, and their roles changed over time. Hundreds
were subdivided into hides and wapentakes into carucates; it was on these

[44] Green, *Aristocracy of Norman England*, p. 268.   [45] *Ibid.*, pp. 298–305.
[46] N. Vincent, 'Did Henry II have a Policy towards the Earls?', C. Given-Wilson, A. Kettle,
    and L. Scales (eds.), *War, Government and Aristocracy in the British Isles, c. 1150–1500:
    Essays in Honour of Michael Prestwich* (Woodbridge: Boydell Press, 2008), pp. 1–25.
[47] Molyneaux, *Formation of the English Kingdom in the Tenth Century*, pp. 141–72.
[48] Liebermann, *Die Gesetze der Angelsachsen*, I, pp. 144–5 (II Edward, cap. 4); *ibid.*,
    pp. 192–5 (Hundred Ordinance).
[49] Molyneaux, *Formation of the English Kingdom*, chapter 4.
[50] D. Roffe, 'The Lincolnshire Hundred', *Landscape History*, 3 (1981), 27–36; Roffe,
    'Nottinghamshire and the Five Boroughs', S. N. Mastoris (ed.), *History in the Making,
    1986: Papers from a Seminar of Recent Historical Research on Nottingham and
    Nottinghamshire 6 September 1986* (Nottingham: Nottingham Museums, 1987),
    pp. 7–11; D. M. Hadley, *Vikings in England: Settlement, Society and Culture*
    (Manchester: Manchester University Press, 2006), pp. 89–92.

smaller units that military service and geld was calculated in most parts of the country. Both were obviously critical to the military effort needed under King Æthelred. An ever-expanding army of agents was needed to watch over the king's rights and to ensure they were not neglected, and a growing volume of documentation resulted. Reeves were proliferating in Anglo-Saxon England, in the shires, boroughs, and hundreds. The fact that there were courts at every level provided kings with a channel through which their authority could reach local communities. The shire-reeves or sheriffs had responsibilities for organizing military service, geld, revenue collection, policing, and frankpledge, and for providing information, the last function displayed above all in the Domesday Inquest. Many must have been functionally multilingual, as the links between rulers and ruled. Were they also able to read, and possibly even to write, as the agents responsible for carrying out written instructions?

Literacy in tenth- and eleventh-century England was clearly extensive, though how far it penetrated lay society is unclear. Relatively few vernacular documents survived. One argument is that they had been numerous, but were discarded after 1066 when the language in which administrative documents were issued changed to Latin.[51] What is clear is that from the later eleventh century the volume of documentation began to increase.

By and large royal agents were unsalaried: they profited from their office, so a balance had to be struck between what was regarded as acceptable by the king and by themselves, and what went beyond the pale. Complaints about unjust reeves go back to Wulfstan's day.[52] A sheriff named Ævic was said to have seized land belonging to the church of Worcester after the death of King Æthelred and during the struggle between Edmund Ironside and Cnut.[53] An imposition of a severe geld by Harthacnut in 1041 was forcibly resisted in Worcester. Two of the king's housecarls who were collecting the geld were killed by the inhabitants, and in reprisal the king harried the county.[54] A few of the sheriffs of William the Conqueror achieved notoriety for their spoliation of the church.[55] At one level, kings like the Conqueror or

[51] Clanchy, *From Memory to Written Record*, chapter 1.
[52] Institutes of Polity, cap. x, *Political Writings of Wulfstan* (ed. Rabin), p. 111.
[53] *Hemingi Chartularium Ecclesiae Wigorniensis*, ed. T. Hearne, 2 vols. (Oxford: e Theatro Sheldoniano, 1723) I, pp. 277, 278.
[54] JW, II, p. 532.
[55] W. A. Morris, *The Medieval English Sheriff to 1300* (Manchester: Manchester University Press, 1927), p. 70–1; J. A. Green, 'The Sheriffs of William the Conqueror', *Anglo-Norman Studies*, 5 (1982), 129–45.

his son William Rufus were not going to be too exercised by unjust reeves and officials, so long as what was owed was collected. The monastic chroniclers fulminated against Ranulf Flambard's exploitation of vacant churches, but nothing was done during Rufus's lifetime. The problem for kings came if they returned to England after an absence and found the coffers empty.

One option was to take direct action. Henry I immediately on his accession imprisoned Ranulf Flambard in the Tower of London.[56] When the quality of the coinage deteriorated so much that his soldiers in Normandy protested about the poor quality of the coins in which they were paid, Henry sent orders that the moneyers be mutilated.[57] Sheriffs were not usually allowed to run up arrears indefinitely, and from time to time their numbers were purged.[58] In 1129 Henry I went further and appointed custodian sheriffs who had to pay surcharges in addition to the shire farms.[59] In 1130 the powerful sheriff and justice Geoffrey de Clinton was indicted in the king's court for treason.[60] Another option was to use other agents to check on the first. Sally Harvey has argued that a primary motive behind both the Domesday Inquest and its follow-up was the difficulty of getting in the geld because both leading members of the elite and sheriffs had profited too much from beneficial ratings and exemptions.[61] The exchequer grew out of this need to audit sheriffs' accounts. First mentioned in 1110, it developed into a twice-annual court under the chief justiciar.

Shires, hundreds, and wapentakes were the agencies through which kings could reach out to the wider body of freemen using sheriffs, reeves, and justices, making ever-increasing use of documents, especially writs and notifications, and calling on groups of freemen to pronounce on disputes, to act as pledges, and to produce wrongdoers in court.

MILITARY OBLIGATION

At the start of our period armies comprised royal and noble retinues, and also men raised from each county, who owed service in return for the

---

[56] ASC, E, 1100.   [57] *Gesta Normannorum Ducum*, II, pp. 236–8.
[58] Green, *Government of England under Henry I*, pp. 201–5.   [59] *Ibid.*, pp. 65–6.
[60] HH, p. 486; David Crouch, 'Clinton, Geoffrey of (d. c.1133)', *ODNB* www.oxforddnb.com/view/article/5680, accessed 20 May 2016.
[61] S. Harvey, *Domesday: Book of Judgement* (Oxford: Oxford University Press, 2014), pp. 239–64.

land they held, assessed on land through the counties, hundreds, and wapentakes.[62] The local levies were sometimes commanded by the ealdormen and their successors, the earls.[63] As well as land forces, obligations based on land could be used to finance warships.[64] A major and sustained effort was needed in the later tenth and early eleventh centuries to combat Danish attacks. Armies and fleets were raised not simply on a basis of obligation, but also through the use of cash. Cnut in particular is known to have had fleets of warriors paid with cash, the lithsmen.[65] The obligation organized through hundreds remained in place after 1066, but the king now assigned quotas of service on his tenants-in-chief.[66] By the twelfth century tenants-in-chief were passing this on to lands held by their under tenants, and the expectation was that the service due was that of a knight, mounted as well as armed. The old obligation evolved into the duty of all freemen to maintain arms, in the Assize of Arms.[67] Kings continued to raise armies on the basis of their own and their lords' retinues, and soldiers they could hire for cash, whether cavalry, archers, or foot soldiers. From the mid-twelfth century Henry was taking financial contribution from knights and, on two occasions, danegeld. The ability to raise armies thus involved not just the king but the whole of the elite, who would need to be convinced of the rightness of the cause for which troops were being raised. Military expertise, loyalty, and preparedness, and cash all came into play. After 1066 there may have been a brief period when the Conqueror had great wealth at his disposal for knights and castles, but by the twelfth century the regular sources of finance were relatively inelastic, and growth had to come from elsewhere.

[62] N. Hooper, 'The Housecarls in England in the Eleventh Century', *Anglo-Norman Studies*, 7 (1985), 161–76; R. P. Abels, *Lordship and Military Obligation in Anglo-Saxon England* (Berkeley, Los Angeles, London: University of California Press, 1988); C. W. Hollister, *Anglo-Saxon Military Institutions on the Eve of the Norman Conquest* (Oxford: Clarendon Press, 1962).

[63] For a discussion of the earls' role as military leaders, see Baxter, *Earls of Mercia*, pp. 85–9.

[64] N. Hooper, 'Some Observations on the Navy in Late Anglo-Saxon England', C. Harper-Bill, C. Holdsworth, and J. L. Nelson (eds.), *Studies in Medieval History Presented to R. Allen Brown* (Woodbridge: Boydell Press, 1989), pp. 203–13.

[65] N. Hooper, 'Military Developments in the Reign of Cnut', Rumble (ed.), *Reign of Cnut*, pp. 89–100.

[66] J. C. Holt, 'The Introduction of Knight Service into England', *Anglo-Norman Studies*, 6 (1983), 89–106; S. Morillo, *Warfare under the Anglo-Norman Kings 1066–1135* (Woodbridge: Boydell Press, 1994).

[67] Stubbs, *Select Charters*, pp. 183–4.

WEALTH

Land

At the start of our period, the resources of English kings came mainly from their estates, their revenues from tolls, from judicial fines, from their monopoly of coinage, and from gifts. Thanks to Domesday Book, we have a very good idea of the distribution of royal estates in 1066. The king was particularly rich in land in counties that had been the heartland of the kingdom of Wessex (Berkshire, Hampshire, Dorset, Somerset, and Wiltshire), Gloucestershire, and Devon. Elsewhere in the country they were distributed unevenly, as Robert Bartlett has pointed out.[68] They were valuable in Norfolk, Suffolk, Essex, and Oxfordshire, and relatively few and far between in Kent and Sussex.[69] They were swollen in the aftermath of the conquest by the addition of the lands of the Godwin family, making King William immeasurably richer than Edward the Confessor had been.[70] Yet there were pressures on William and his successors to continue granting land out and, had it not been for the confiscations bringing land back under direct control, the stock of land would have continued to diminish. Even so, studying twelfth-century pipe roll evidence demonstrates that land, though the most important element in royal revenue in our period, was not a readily expandable source of revenue. Mostly it was let out at fixed sums to sheriffs or other officials, which made it difficult for revenues to be increased. Under Stephen there were many grants from the royal demesne (*terrae datae*), and it was an urgent priority for Henry II to recover as many of these as possible. Similarly the king's rights in towns were subsumed into the borough farms paid by the sheriffs or, in a few cases, by the citizens. What could be done was to ask for an aid from the peasants of rural manors and from the townsmen. The king in that sense was like other lords. The first we hear of what came to be known as royal tallage was in 1130 in the form of aids of boroughs and a gift from the burgesses and men of the soke of Grantham.[71]

---

[68] R. Bartlett, *England under the Norman and Angevin Kings 1075–1225* (Oxford: Clarendon Press, 2000), pp. 160–1.

[69] J. A. Green, 'William Rufus, Henry I and the Royal Demesne', *History*, 64 (1979), p. 351 table.

[70] Fleming, *Kings and Lords in Conquest England*, chapter 7.

[71] *Pipe Roll 31 Henry I*, p. 90.

Profits of Jurisdiction

There was greater potential for profit from royal jurisdiction. Before the era of pipe rolls this remains invisible, though there is no reason why pre-Conquest kings did not receive voluntary offerings for favours of various kinds. What we do see by the twelfth century is the profitability of the king's role as lord over the richest laymen: the payments agreed for inheritances, marriages, and wardships. Also after the Conquest may have come the practice of taking the revenue from vacant bishoprics and abbeys, regalian rights. The assertion of forest law over great expanses of the country led to a considerable income from fines for poaching and for ploughing up forest land (*assarting*). As the scope of royal justice expanded, so did the revenue. Spikes in the annual revenues recorded on the pipe rolls are found following the introduction of the Assizes of Clarendon and Northampton. Apart from land and borough income, however, all of these depend on negotiation and management. They could not be depended on year by year, and there was an element of political judgement as to which could be squeezed, and when.

War Finance

The king's ever-growing demands for finance to pay for men, fortifications, fleets, subsidies, and tributes are a *leitmotif* of our period. As the demand for cash increased, kings experimented with different ways of raising funds. In addition to the gelds paid as tribute, a further onerous impost known as *heregeld* was introduced in 1012, apparently to pay for hired fleets of lithsmen.[72] Edward the Confessor had done away with the tax in 1051, though he may have continued to take other kinds of gelds.[73] At some stage William the Conqueror began to take geld. The best-known, and possibly the first levy, was the triple geld of 1084 ordered in anticipation of an invasion from Denmark.[74] The levy brought into focus the plus and minus points of this form of taxation. On the one hand it was based on customary assessments, which must have been well known, and it applied to all land.[75] On the other it had become customary apparently for the demesne or inland parts of manors to be exempted, presumably because the lord was expected to serve himself. The new tenants-in-chief were going to be expected to provide service and, in addition, to house knights the Conqueror had

---

[72] Hooper, 'Some Observations on the Navy in Late Anglo-Saxon England', pp. 205–6.
[73] ASC, D, 1051.   [74] ASC, E, 1084.
[75] D. Pratt, 'Demesne Exemptions from Royal Taxation in Anglo-Norman England', *English Historical Review*, 128 (2013), 1–34.

brought from abroad. Low yields may have led to an experiment in reassessment.[76] The issue must certainly have fed into discussions at Christmas 1085 at Gloucester. It appears that those parts of manors held in demesne, that is, in direct lordship, were to be exempt from geld, presumably in recognition of personal service, as shown in the geld rolls. In other words, there was a mix of old and new in the response to crisis, a mix that was to continue as kings tried to capitalize in different ways on military obligations. The idea of a reassessment of geld was abandoned, possibly by Rufus in 1088 when faced with an uprising.[77]

One of the factors which changed, of course, was the kind of wars fought. The proclamation of the first crusade and Duke Robert's mortgaging of his duchy in return for funds to his brother resulted in an unprecedented drive to raise money, part of which at least was another geld raised, it was claimed later, without customary exemptions.[78] In 1100 Henry I promised to allow exemptions for the demesne lands of serving knights.[79] Danegeld in the 1130 pipe roll occurs as an annual levy of two shillings per hide. The under-assessment of some counties was compensated for by taking annual 'aids' from counties. Annual aids were also being taken from boroughs.[80] The term *aid* was a useful omnibus term encapsulating the spirit of assistance rather than obligation. It was used of contributions from tenants of royal manors, a payment which came to be known as *tallage*.[81] An aid on knights' fees came to be known as *scutage*.[82] Payments were taken from knights on vacant bishoprics, from lay lords (when there was a new lord), from Crowland Abbey, and from lands in Wales.[83] Not all of these were annual or taken at the same time,

[76] S. Harvey, 'Domesday Book and Anglo-Norman Governance', *Transactions of the Royal Historical Society*, 5th series, 25 (1975), 175–93; J. A. Green, 'The Last Century of Danegeld', *English Historical Review*, 96 (1981), 241–58, at p. 243.
[77] ASC, E, 1088. Rufus promised the English 'the best law that ever there was in this land' and forbade *unriht geold*.
[78] *Leges Edwardi Confessoris*, cap. 11, *Die Gesetze der Angelsachsen*, ed. F. Liebermann, 3 vols. in 4 (Halle, 1898–1916), I, pp. 634–7; O'Brien, *God's Peace and King's Peace: the Laws of Edward the Confessor*, pp. 168–9.
[79] Stubbs, *Select Charters*, p. 119.
[80] For the position in 1130, see Green, 'Last Century of Danegeld', pp. 247–50.
[81] S. K. Mitchell, *Taxation in Medieval England* (New Haven, CT: Yale University Press, 1971 reprint), chapter 5.
[82] *Pipe Roll 31 Henry I*, p. 90 (Grantham).
[83] *Ibid.*, pp. 101, 104 (Durham); for past years, see pp. 46 (fee of Waleran), 66 (Crowland Abbey), 71 (Carmarthen), 90 (bishop of Lincoln), 121 (bishop of Exeter, Baldwin de Redvers), 126 (Baldwin son of Hamelin).

but clearly the obligation to contribute to the king's coffers was already widespread.

Geld continued to be too financially important to be abolished. Moreover, benefactors who gave land to the church were trying to give it free of geld, 'in free alms'. Henry I seems to have promised to remit the levy for seven years in 1131, a promise which Stephen renewed and pledged to remain permanent, though, it was said, he broke his word.[84] In 1156 when Henry II revived the tax, there was a good deal of resistance, recorded on the pipe rolls in the form of claims to exemption and 'waste'.[85] The younger Henry was very short of money at the start of his reign and was seeking to recover as many of the lost rights of the crown as he could. In pursuit of this aim, we can trace the results on the early pipe rolls. They included one levy of danegeld, in 1155–6, payments of aids and gifts from knights, boroughs, counties, and the Jews. Danegeld was taken again in 1161–2, and a levy was ordered but not carried out in 1174.[86] At the council of Woodstock in 1174 Henry had floated the idea of taking an annual aid usually paid to sheriffs at two shillings a hide, only to be met with resistance from Thomas Becket, who as archbishop had a hefty liability to geld.[87] The king thereafter preferred to take aids, especially levied on knights' fees.

However, the needs of the crusading kingdom of Jerusalem prompted an important new development in taxation. In 1166 King Louis of France took an aid on property and goods for the relief of the Holy Land, and Henry II followed suit both in France and in England.[88] The underlying principle was that of tithe, a duty to pay ten per cent of all one's property and income to the church. In effect what these kings were doing was adding an extra tithe for what could be construed as a holy war. Little is heard in the English sources about the levy of 1166. All laymen and clergy

---

[84] JW, III, p. 202; HH, p. 704.

[85] Green, 'Last Century of Danegeld', pp. 251–2; E. Amt, *The Accession of Henry II in England. Royal Government Restored 1149–1159* (Woodbridge: Boydell Press, 1993), pp. 137–41.

[86] T. Madox, *The History and Antiquities of the Exchequer of England*, 2nd edn (London: W. Owen and B. White, 1769), I, p. 692; *Pipe Roll 20 Henry II*, p. 115; *Pipe Roll 21 Henry II*, p. 15.

[87] Edward Grim, 'Life of St Thomas', in *Materials for the History of Thomas Becket*, ed. J. C. Robertson and J. B. Sheppard, 7 vols., RS (London: Longman and Co, 1875–85), II, pp. 373–4. Cf. Garnier de Pont-Sainte-Maxence, *La Vie de Thomas Becket*, ed. E. Walberg (Lund: C. W. K. Gleerup, 1952), pp. 27–8; Anonymous I, *Materials for the History of Thomas Becket*, IV, p. 23.

[88] Gervase of Canterbury, *Opera historica*, I, pp. 198–9.

were to promise to give sixpence in the pound from their annual income and goods.[89] A much greater impression was made by the Saladin Tithe of 1188: all laymen and clergy who had not taken the cross were commanded to give a tenth of their income and goods, to be collected in each parish in the presence of the priest, the rural dean, one Templar, and one Hospitaller. Bishops were to send out letters to each parish, and those who did not pay were to be excommunicated.[90] This tax, like its predecessor in 1166, used the tithe, an obligation well understood, and it taxed wealth more effectively than a land tax. As yet it had not been used as a tax for a secular war. That was to come in 1207. Taxation, driven by the costs of war, developed in ways fundamental to the rise of the modern state.

Coinage

One striking symbol of royal power was the high-quality coinage issued in the king's name. Only briefly in Stephen's reign was the king's monopoly broken as coins were issued in the name of great magnates. The contrast between the situation in England and that in France, where there were many private coinages in circulation, is striking. For the first three-quarters of the tenth century, the coinage of King Alfred technically remained in circulation, but was being struck to a much lower weight standard, and with regional variations. Hence a strong motive for Edgar to set in hand a reform *c.* 973 was to reassert central control.[91] A new design was issued, and it was produced at mints throughout the kingdom, probably as an echo of Edgar's aspiration to be seen as king over all England.[92] The coins were more than 96 per cent silver in content, and to maintain this high quality the issues had to be replaced at relatively frequent intervals, when the design and sometimes the weight was

[89] *Chronicon Petroburgense*, ed. T. Stapleton, Camden Society, 48 (1849), p. 3; Diceto, I, p. 329.

[90] *English Historical Documents*, II, pp. 453–4.

[91] K. Jonsson, 'The Post-Reform Coinage of Edgar – the Legacy of the Anglo-Saxon Kingdoms', B. Cook and G. Williams (eds.), *Coinage and History in the North Sea World c. 500–1250. Essays in Honour of Marion Archibald* (Leiden, Boston: Brill, 2005), pp. 325–46.

[92] R. H. M. Dolley and D. M. Metcalf, 'The Reform of the English Coinage under Eadgar', R. H. M. Dolley (ed.), *Anglo-Saxon Coins: Studies Presented to F. M. Stenton on the Occasion of His 80th Birthday* (London: Methuen, 1961), pp. 136–68; cf. K. Jonsson, *The New Era: the Reformation of the Late Anglo-Saxon Coinage* (Stockholm, London: Kungl. Myntkabinett, Kungl. Vitterhets, historie och Antikvitets Akademien, Spink and Sons, 1987); M. Blackburn, 'Æthelred's Coinage and the Payment of Tribute' (ed. Scragg), *Battle of Maldon*, pp. 156–69.

adjusted.[93] As the supply of silver from English sources was not great, the new coins were made from the old, plus silver coming in from abroad, from traders from Scandinavia and Flanders. Those responsible for minting the coins, the moneyers, are thought to have made a profit from taking in silver and coins and issuing coins, and the king took his cut.[94] Some moneyers made an annual payment, whilst others may have been directly employed, and the king also gained from new issues.[95]

Edgar's system survived the Norman Conquest. The Conqueror stabilized the weight of the English penny, perhaps to reduce the degree of overvalue of English coins, which may have discouraged people from exchanging old coins, or possibly to harmonize with the weight in common use in northern France.[96] He also exacted a new payment called the money tax from the moneyers, possibly in recognition that the issue was not to be changed.[97] Henry I reversed this by abolishing the taxes and returning to periodic re-coinages. However, there were serious concerns about both debasement and counterfeiting. Debasement in part reflected shortage of silver. Counterfeiting was another matter. In 1125 he ordered the mutilation of all the moneyers (the loss of the right hand and castration), the closure of some of the smaller mints, and the introduction of a new issue with a higher-quality design.[98] This issue lasted into the first

---

[93] There has been a good deal of discussion about the dating of the issues. Dolley's original view was that these occurred at regular six-year intervals. Cf. I. Stewart, 'Coinage and Recoinage after Edgar's Reforms', *Studies in Anglo-Saxon Coinage*, ed. K. Jonsson, Numismatiska Meddelanden, 35 (Stockholm 1990), 455–85.

[94] P. Nightingale, '"The King's Profit": Trends in English Mint and Monetary Policy in the Eleventh and Twelfth Centuries', reprinted in Nightingale, *Trade, Money and Power in Medieval England* (Aldershot: Ashgate, 2007), VII, 61–75.

[95] Exactly from what source and how much profit the king derived from the coinage is not altogether clear. P. Nightingale has argued that some moneyers were royal *ministri* who either supplied the dies for mints or had an oversight over the moneyers, and of these some were directly employed by the king, whilst others held the mints at farm, 'Some London Moneyers and Reflections on the Organization of English Mints in the Eleventh and Twelfth Centuries', reprinted in *Trade, Money and Power in Medieval England*, V, pp. 34–50; cf. M. Allen, 'Henry II and the English Coinage', C. Harper-Bill and N. Vincent (eds.), *Henry II. New Interpretations* (Woodbridge: Boydell Press, 2007), pp. 257–77, at p. 264.

[96] P. Nightingale, 'The Ora, the Mark, and the Mancus: Weight Standards and the Coinage in Eleventh-Century England', parts 1 and 2, reprinted in Nightingale, *Trade, Money and Power in Medieval England*, II, pp. 248–57; III, pp. 234–48; M. Blackburn, 'Coinage and Currency under Henry I: a Review', *Anglo-Norman Studies*, 13 (1990), 49–81, at p. 75.

[97] P. Grierson, 'Domesday Book: the Geld *de moneta* and *monetagium*: a Forgotten Minting Reform', *British Numismatic Journal*, 55 (1985), 84–94; D. M. Metcalf, 'The Taxation of Moneyers under Edward the Confessor and in 1086', J. C. Holt (ed.), *Domesday Studies* (Woodbridge: Boydell Press, 1987), pp. 279–93.

[98] M. Blackburn, 'Coinage and Currency under Henry I'.

years of Stephen's reign, when it was succeeded by an issue in the name of
that king. The real problem came in the 1140s, when Stephen's monopoly
was broken and coins were issued in the names of barons and, it would
seem, of the empress.[99]

One of the provisions of the Treaty of 1153 was that there should be
one coinage.[100] Stephen's last issue lasted until 1158, when many moneyers were replaced, the number of mints reduced, and a new issue, the cross-
and-crosslets type, was introduced.[101] As it was not changed, the quality
in circulation declined. There were concerns, too, about forgery, and in
1180 there was a far-reaching reform. The number of mints was again
reduced, and moneyers were dismissed. The new moneyers simply took
charge of the process of production of coins, and salaried exchangers
collected the profits. By the late twelfth century, therefore, the royal
monopoly had been maintained, the practice of frequent re-coinages had
been shelved, and production was concentrated in fewer centres.

Justice

Key to royal authority was the notion of the king as the upholder of
justice. What that entailed, and how it was to be administered, changed
radically during our period. The idea of the peace extended by the king to
those under his protection was central to early medieval law. It extended
over his court and household, and to those who would otherwise have
little protection, travelling merchants, widows, monks, and priests.[102]
Violating that protection incurred penalties more severe than that of
other protectors like ealdormen or earls. Then there was a narrow range
of offences deemed offences against society, secret slaying (murder), rape,
robbery with violence, or housebreaking, literally destroying homes by
breaking them up.[103] By the tenth century kings were also reaching out to
try to limit feud, not to stop it, but to try to ensure that compensation was

[99] M. Blackburn, 'Coinage and Currency', E. King (ed.), *The Anarchy of King Stephen's Reign* (Oxford: Oxford University Press, 1994), pp. 145–205.
[100] Diceto, I, pp. 296–7.
[101] Allen, 'Henry II and the English Coinage', Harper-Bill and Vincent (eds.), *Henry II*, p. 260.
[102] Hudson, *Oxford History of the Laws of England*, II, pp. 19–21, 386–8.
[103] For murder, see B. O'Brien, 'From *Morðor* to *Murdrum*: the Preconquest Origin and Norman Revival of the Murder Fine', *Speculum*, 71 (1996), 321–57. For rape, see C. J. Saunders, *Rape and Ravishment in the Literature of Medieval England* (Cambridge: Cambridge University Press, 2001), chapter 1. For robbery and house-breaking (*hamsocn*), see Hudson, *Oxford History of the Laws of England*, II, pp. 165–6.

paid.[104] Theft, especially of cattle, was another preoccupation, and efforts were made to see that sales took place in front of witnesses.[105]

What made something a crime to be dealt with by the king came up against the church's ideas about sin. There was an overlap here, or even a symbiosis, most visible under Archbishop Wulfstan, and leading to friction in the twelfth century. Concerns with protecting churchmen and church property, and issues such as marriage, wills, and debt, crossed jurisdictional boundaries. Beyond these, though, was a wide range of matters which were in effect civil matters, to be dealt with by those wronged or by their families.

Changing social patterns and preoccupations necessitated the making of new law, and in the surviving records of royal laws we can see a balance between old and new, encapsulated again in the coronation promise to uphold good laws and to root out iniquity. Kings made new laws, and these were promulgated in assemblies to ensure publicity and support. As yet, though, there was no requirement for conciliar consent, formal record, or, with the possible exception of coronation charters, of dissemination.[106] Theoretically this gave the king, subject only to the laws of God, the upper hand when it came to lawmaking. In practice there were severe practical constraints on what could be achieved. The most crucial growth points arguably reflected not the king's interests, but pressure from below.

The king thus had sole cognisance of a range of offences which by the time of Glanvill were defined as felonies.[107] Initially these had to be brought to court by personal accusation, or appeal, with the obvious possibility of intimidation, or by *fama*, public notoriety.[108] An alternative was community liability, prescribed for instance in Æthelred's Wantage code and then in the procedure for murder laid down by William the Conqueror.[109] The threat of a hefty fine for non-compliance focussed the minds of members of local communities. A third possibility was *ex officio* prosecution, and it seems that in the early twelfth century this was beginning to

---

[104] *Ibid.*, pp. 178–9. [105] *Ibid.*, pp. 161–99.

[106] For a recent discussion of Anglo-Saxon legal culture, see L. Roach, 'Law Codes and Legal Norms in Later Anglo-Saxon England', *Historical Research*, 86 (2013), 465–86.

[107] Glanvill, pp. 83, 91.

[108] Hudson, *Oxford History of the Laws of England*, II, 721–40; R. C. Van Caenegem, 'Public Prosecution in Twelfth-Century England', C. N. L. Brooke, D. E. Luscombe, G. H. Martin, and D. Owen (eds.), *Church and Government in the Middle Ages: Essays Presented to C. R. Cheney on His Seventieth Birthday* (Cambridge: Cambridge University Press, 1976), pp. 41–76.

[109] IIIAtr, 3,1–2; Wl art, 3; Liebermann, *Die Gesetze der Angelsachsen*, I, pp. 228, 487.

happen.[110] There were problems with unsupported accusations, and in 1166 Henry II ordered that those suspected of robbery, murder, theft, or those who harboured them, were to be formally accused by juries, handed over to sheriffs, and held in custody until the arrival of justices.[111]

Proving guilt or innocence presented further challenges. Barring confession, oaths might be allowable, but credibility depended on social status or trustworthiness, and, after 1066, the possibility that Englishmen would swear against a Norman opponent that black was white.[112] Otherwise proof could only be determined by the use of the ordeals, in effect calling on God to judge. Cold water and hot iron were the two most commonly used in Anglo-Saxon England.[113] These had to take place in the presence of a priest. After 1066 – for it seems that trial by battle was not used in England earlier – battle was used in serious cases against the person or movable goods, or in land cases.[114] Punishment for the most serious offences was usually death or mutilation, exile, or possibly restitution to the victim. The king could pardon offenders, and it seems that by the reign of Henry I pardons could be used to acquit killers from prosecution but leave them open to prosecution by the kin.[115]

In the early Middle Ages sometimes compensation was paid, with a fine to the king on top, but by the early twelfth century those convicted were said to be in the king's mercy for their life and land, or for their land. Instead of a graded range of penalties, therefore, the man convicted had to come to an agreement about the scale of the penalty.[116] One offence specially affected by this change was homicide.[117] As noted earlier, at the start of our period feud was still a possibility for homicides of various kinds and for wounding unless compensation could be arranged. Compensation still features in the *Leges Henrici Primi*, but it seems to

[110] R. C. Van Caenegem, 'Public Prosecution of Crime'.

[111] Howden, II, p. 248; Assize of Clarendon, *English Historical Documents*, II, pp. 440–3.

[112] Hudson, *Oxford History of the Laws of England*, II, pp. 81–4, 322–5, 829–30.

[113] R. Bartlett, *Trial by Fire and Water: the Medieval Judicial Ordeal* (Oxford: Clarendon Press, 1986).

[114] Hudson, *Oxford History of the Laws of England*, II, p. 327.

[115] *Leges Edwardi Confessoris*, cap.18 – 18.3, Liebermann, *Die Gesetze der Angelsachsen*, I, p. 644; O'Brien, *God's Peace and King's Peace*, p. 176; Hudson, *Oxford History of the Laws of England*, II, pp. 412–14.

[116] J. Goebel, *Felony and Misdemeanor: a Study in the History of English Criminal Procedure* (New York: Commonwealth Fund, 1937); cf. Hudson, *Oxford History of the Laws of England*, II, pp. 403–4, for the view that the change may not have been as stark as Goebel thought.

[117] Hudson, *Oxford History of the Laws of England*, II, pp. 178–9, 409–10, 514–15.

have been declining.[118] The sources remain silent about the reasons. There may have been several: one was that the expanding role of the king meant that capital punishment was used more, and payment due to him which would come before compensation due to the kin would in practice have left little over. The decline of slavery may have removed another option, for enslavement until compensation was paid had been an option.[119] Royal officials may have discouraged out-of-court settlements and insisted that permission had to be sought.[120] By the time of Glanvill, homicide was listed as one of the crimes belonging to the king.[121]

At the start of our period the king's role in land law was fairly restricted. His presence is recorded where his own lands or the affairs of great men were affected, and we must assume that his court was one of last resort for those who had been denied justice elsewhere. It must always have been possible to request the king's aid, and he may have sent orders to this effect. What changed dramatically in the twelfth century was the explosion of written orders in the form of writs.[122] These could take the form of a simple order to a court holder to 'do right', the breach of which technically brought an action into the king's court for contempt of his writ.[123] Much more significant, however, was the rise of returnable writs. These were important in two ways: firstly, their reliance on juries of neighbours called to give evidence about the case at issue, and, secondly, the writs were returnable to the sheriff, who had to report the verdict of the inquest to royal justices. Initially the aim was to restore possession to someone who had been ejected recently and without a court judgement. It was developed in the aftermath of the civil war of Stephen's reign, in order to limit self-help. The rights and wrongs of the matter were not prejudged.[124] By the early years of Henry II's reign it had become the case that no-one need answer unless his adversary had obtained a royal writ.[125]

---

[118] *Ibid.*, pp. 409–10.   [119] *Ibid.*, pp. 194–5.

[120] *Leges Henrici Primi*, ed. L. J. Downer (Oxford: Clarendon Press, 1972), cap. 59, 27.

[121] Glanvill, p. 3.

[122] For the different writs, see R. C. Van Caenegem, *Royal Writs in England from the Conquest to Glanvill*, Selden Society, 77 (1959).

[123] For the writ of right, see *ibid.*, pp. 206–34; Hudson, *Oxford History of the Laws of England*, II, pp. 580–603.

[124] P. Brand, '"Multis vigiliis excogitatam et inventam": Henry II and the Creation of the English Common Law', reprinted in *Making of the Common Law* (London, 1992), pp. 77–102.

[125] Glanvill, p. 148. For discussion, see Van Caenegem, *Royal Writs*, pp. 212–34, where the constitutional significance of this development is underlined. Compare, however, Hudson, *Oxford History of the Laws of England*, II, pp. 556–61.

The king was not shutting off the possibility that an action of right would be held, but was taking oversight of the stage when possession was determined. A hearing of the issue of right could follow before a jury of knights, a procedure known as the *grand assize*. Different writs were developed to deal with different types of problem: *novel disseisin* dealt with recent dispossession; *utrum* 'whether' determined the type of tenure by which disputed land was held, by lay fee or free alms; and *darrein presentment* was to decide who had made the last presentation to a particular church living. Different views have been expressed about the degree of novelty of these developments. Clearly the essentials, writs, juries, and sheriffs, existed before the 1160s. What was different was the way the elements were brought together and filled a real need for both tenants and lords. They were of the greatest significance in bringing many more litigants to royal courts, in offering a relatively speedy remedy for those who had been dispossessed, and, by putting them back in seisin, in fact intervened in the working of seigneurial justice in a significant way.

Another result of the enlarged scope of royal intervention in land law was a fuller integration of the shire courts into royal justice. Technically the courts of shire and hundred in which the sheriff sat as the king's representative were public, not royal courts. In the tenth- and eleventh-century shire courts the bishop and earl as well as the sheriff presided, and judgment was given by all present. Land actions concerning division or land or encroachments between the tenants of different lords were to be heard in the shire court according to a writ of Henry I, but other kinds of actions were heard in lords' courts.[126] If that was problematic – if, for example, a tenant was litigating against his lord – he could secure a writ (*tolt*) which transferred the action from the lord's court to the shire court. If there were problems either in the lord's court or the shire court, a litigant could obtain a writ (*pone*) transferring the action to the king's court, a form of action which seems to belong to the reign of Henry II. The rise of common-law actions was thus one way in which the role of the county courts and the sheriffs was being transformed. The county courts were being more closely integrated into royal justice. The sheriff was on the receiving end of many more writs on an ever widening range of matters, but his role was changing as he became much more than previously an executive of the king's orders.

Much would depend on the active prosecution of wrongdoers by the king or, more probably, by royal justices. It seems that by the late eleventh

---

[126] Henry I's writ, Stubbs, *Select Charters*, pp. 121–2.

century there were locally based men who could serve as royal justices.[127] There may have been justices sent by the king into the localities, on the lines of the Carolingian *missi dominici*.[128] How far back in time these went is not clear. By the 1120s, we know from the pipe roll, there were justices, whose wide remit included pleas of the crown.[129] It was only in 1176, however, that the whole country was divided into areas to be visited by justices within a relatively short period of time, the general eyre.[130]

Ideology of Kingship

Ideas which underpinned royal power were very simple, as noted at the start of this chapter: the king wielded the sword as defender of his people and promoter of justice. Simplicity permitted flexibility to take account of changing circumstances. The idea that a king could rule over different peoples lay behind the expansion of England into other parts of the British Isles (see earlier). In the remainder of this chapter key developments are explored: the implications of coronation, the scope of royal justice, and the office and the individual.

Kingship and Sacrality

King Edgar's relationship with Archbishop Dunstan as described in Dunstan's *Life* epitomized right order in Christian society: a king who served peace was the protector of the church and patron of Benedictine houses.[131] There are signs that Edgar had claims to sanctity, for when his tomb was opened in 1052 his body was found to be incorrupt.[132] Moreover, his son and successor, Edward 'the Martyr', was assassinated at Corfe. Archbishop Dunstan transferred his relics to Shaftesbury in 980, and by the early eleventh century his cult was widespread.[133] The ideas swirling around holiness, royalty, and martyrdom remained influential. The murdered aetheling Alfred, brother of Edward the Confessor, was

---

[127] H. A. Cronne, 'The Office of Local Justiciar in England under the Norman Kings', *University of Birmingham Historical Journal*, 6 (1958), 18–38; Hudson, *Oxford History of the Laws of England*, II, pp. 266–9.

[128] *Ibid.*, p. 40.

[129] W. T. Reedy, 'The Origin of the General Eyre in the Reign of Henry I', *Speculum*, 41 (1966), 688–724; Hudson, *Oxford History of the Laws of England*, II, pp. 269–70.

[130] Diceto, I, p. 404; Howden, I, pp. 106–8, 238–9.

[131] B, *Vita S. Dvnstani, The Early Lives of St Dunstan*, pp. 74–9.

[132] WM, *Gesta Regum Anglorum*, I, pp. 260–3.

[133] *Ibid.*, I, pp. 266–9; C. Fell, *Edward King and Martyr* (Leeds: University of Leeds, School of English, 1971).

venerated at Ely.[134] Edward the Confessor's life was written up, apparently round about 1066 under the patronage of his widow, Queen Edith.

The Confessor proved the last of the sainted kings and queens, and it
has been suggested that by the twelfth century the English monarchy had
in effect been desacralized: the reality of royal power was such that there
was no need to emphasize the power of anointed kings.[135] This view
overlooks the importance of context in the promotion of sainted kings:
overwhelmingly their cults were promoted by Benedictine houses, the
resting places of past kings and their relics. A new Benedictine foundation
such as Westminster was seemingly slow to capitalize on the tomb of
its founder, King Edward, but by the twelfth century his cult was being
promoted by members of the community like Osbert of Clare. Of his
successors, William Rufus, Henry I, and Stephen were buried in England,
and there are no indications of cults developing around their tombs. Of the
kings of our period, only Edward the Martyr and Edward the Confessor
were candidates, the one as a martyr, the other as a celibate. Any cult that
might have grown up at the tomb of Harold Godwinson at Waltham was
evidently firmly scotched. The official view was that he was a faithless
perjurer who had died in battle through the judgement of God. There is
no indication in the Waltham Chronicle that there was a cult at his tomb,
which the canons would doubtless have discouraged.[136]

The Norman and Angevin kings continued to engage with the rituals
associated with kingship. William the Conqueror famously wore his crown
three times in state each year when he was in England. The regularity of
crownwearings only broke down during Henry I's long absences abroad,
and they were still held from time to time. Moreover, the Conqueror and his
successors, the unmarried Rufus apart, made sure that their wives were
anointed and crowned as queens, and Stephen and Henry II sought to have
their eldest sons crowned in their lifetimes.

There were potentially conflicting ideas about the sacredness or otherwise of the king's person. There was support for the idea that to attack
the king's person was *lèse majesté*.[137] The rituals surrounding the death
and burial of kings might in themselves have promoted incipient cults,

---

[134] *Liber Eliensis*, pp. 158–60.
[135] G. Koziol, 'England, France, and the Problem of Sacrality in Twelfth-Century Ritual',
T. N. Bisson (ed.), *Cultures of Power: Lordship, Status, and Process in Twelfth-Century
Europe* (Philadelphia: University of Pennsylvania Press, 1995), pp. 124–48.
[136] *The Waltham Chronicle*, ed. and trans. L. Watkiss and M. Chibnall (Oxford: Clarendon
Press, 1994), pp. xliii–xlvi, 44–56.
[137] OV, VI, p. 238.

concretized in grand tombs. We see in the Bayeux Tapestry the body of the dead King Edward being taken through the streets on a bier, shrouded, with small figures ringing bells alongside. Henry II's body, in contrast, was taken from Chinon to Fontevraud dressed in royal fashion and wearing a crown.[138] The presence of Stephen of Blois at his uncle's funeral at Reading Abbey in January 1136 was a very visible symbol that he was heir to the throne.[139] In England there was as yet no single royal mausoleum. Edgar and Edmund Ironside were buried at Glastonbury, Edward the Martyr at Shaftesbury, Æthelred at St Paul's London, Cnut, Harthacnut, and William Rufus at the Old Minster, Winchester, Henry I at Reading, Stephen at Faversham. Henry I's body was the first to be divided, with his heart being buried at Notre-Dame du Pré just outside Rouen. Four kings were buried abroad, Swein at Roskilde in Denmark, William the Conqueror at Caen, the Young King in the cathedral at Rouen, and Henry II at the abbey of Fontevraud.

In some cases the corpses of dead kings were subjected to indignities. Harold Harefoot's body was reportedly thrown into a ditch after his death in 1040, before being reburied, it was said, in the Danish cemetery in London.[140] William the Conqueror's corpse was robbed by his servants, and at his funeral, a man claimed he had been robbed of the plot of land intended for his burial.[141] After Rufus's death in the New Forest whilst hunting, his body was carried on a makeshift hurdle to Winchester.[142] Henry I's body was not embalmed satisfactorily, and whilst it lay in the abbey church of St Stephen's Caen over Christmas waiting for transit to England, fluid ran out, terrifying the attendant who had to mop it up.[143] Commentators wanted to underscore the point that death was a great leveller. These of course were 'ordinary' kings. When the body of Edward the Confessor was exhumed in 1102, wearing a crown, his body was incorrupt, a sign of sanctity.[144]

Moreover, the post-Conquest kings, with the possible exception of William Rufus, were evidently aware of the importance of associating themselves with their sainted predecessors, especially St Edmund at Bury. There are signs of a particular awareness on the part of Henry I, especially

---

[138] *Gesta Regis Henrici Secundi*, ed. W. Stubbs, RS, 2 vols. (London: Longman, 1867), II, p. 71.
[139] WM, *Historia Novella*, p. 30.   [140] ASC, C, D, 1040; JW, II, p. 530.
[141] OV, IV, pp. 100–6.   [142] WM, *Gesta Regum Anglorum*, I, pp. 574–5.
[143] HH, p. 702.
[144] M. Bloch, 'La vie de S. Edouard le Confesseur par Osbert de Clare', *Analecta Bollandiana*, 41 (1923), 121; Barlow, *Edward the Confessor*, p. 254.

after 1120, of a desire to associate himself with the shrines of English sainted kings.[145] He ordered that his first wife should be buried in Westminster Abbey, and there are signs of an incipient cult at her tomb, but this did not really get off the ground, and the monks perhaps were more interested in promoting Edward's cult.[146] This finally received papal sanction in 1161, at a time when Henry II was keen to have a sainted predecessor and the pope was prepared to accept the claim.[147] So whilst it is true that contemporaries did not seek to promote any of the Norman or Angevin kings as saints, the kings themselves were not indifferent to the value of association with sainted predecessors.

Coronation: Rites and Regalia

The ceremony of anointing and coronation was the most potent symbol of royal rule. For details of the various elements and their order, we are largely dependent on surviving liturgical manuscripts. There is general agreement about the form of the ceremony performed by Archbishop Dunstan in 973, for which the second recension provides details.[148] It began with the king processing from the place where he and the ealdormen who had elected him were assembled into church, where he prostrated himself. He made a threefold promise, to maintain peace, to root out iniquities, and to uphold justice and mercy. He was anointed with chrism, the holy oil with which priests were anointed, invested with regalia, and enthroned. The queen's coronation followed, and the proceedings closed with mass. Every stage of the ceremony was freighted with symbolism, spelled out in prayers and anthems. The king's promises summed up the key components of his role, subsequently spelled out in coronation charters. The use of chrism heightened the idea that the king was 'king and priest'. The coronation of the queen marked a further stage

---

[145] For Nostell (Oswald) see J. A. Frost, *The Foundation of Nostell Priory 1109–1153*, University of York Borthwick Paper, no. 111 (2007); for Bury (Edmund), see *RRAN*, II, nos. 644, 653, 655, 656, 657, 658, 672, 694, 759, 760, 761, 777, 861, 1079, 1139, 1227, 1278, 1321, 1340, 1430, 1443, 1444, 1597, 1598, 1599, 1605, 1613, 1614, 1642, 1733, 1812, 1813, 1913, 1914; for Shaftesbury (Edward the Martyr), *ibid.*, nos. 1165, 1347; and for Westminster Abbey, *Westminster Abbey Charters*, ed. E. Mason, London Record Society, 25 (1988), nos. 57–96.

[146] WM, *Gesta Regum Anglorum*, I, p. 758. The monks may have had to be ordered to have Queen Edith buried beside her husband. According to the same author, it was the king who arranged her funeral, *ibid.*, 502.

[147] Barlow, *Edward the Confessor*, chapter 12, pp. 279–85.

[148] For the text, see L. G. Wickham Legg (ed.), *English Coronation Records* (Westminster: Constable, 1901), pp. 15–29.

in her elevation from king's wife to king's partner in the kingdom, with a role that complemented his.[149] At every stage the ceremony was presided over by bishops, who invested the king with regalia and led him to the throne. After mass there was a great feast in which, it seems, the custom was for king and queen to preside over separate banquets.[150]

Over time details of the rite changed, and items of regalia multiplied. The third recension is first known to have been used for the coronation of Richard I in 1189. The key developments were the change from the use of chrism to holy oil, to downplay the idea of 'king and priest', the addition of new items of regalia including spurs, and the further elaboration of prayers for the queen.[151] The timing of the changeover has been the subject of some discussion. On the one hand it has been argued that the third recension might well have been introduced by Archbishop Ealdred in 1066 either for Harold or William the Conqueror.[152] On the other hand the case for continuity for coronations of kings keen to underscore their legitimacy has been pointed out.[153] All we know is that the third recension was known at Canterbury by 1120.

Until 1066 there was no fixed location for the ceremony: Edgar's coronation was at Bath, Æthelred's at Kingston, and Edward the Confessor's at Winchester.[154] There is no direct evidence about coronation for Swein, Harold Harefoot, or Harthacnut, or indeed, Cnut himself, though he and Queen Emma (here styled Ælfgifu) were depicted in the *Liber Vitae* of the New Minster at Winchester being crowned by angels,

---

[149] P. Stafford, *Queen Emma and Queen Edith: Queenship and Women's Power in Eleventh-Century England* (Oxford: Blackwell, 1997), chapter 6.

[150] Byrhtferth of Ramsey, *Vita Oswaldi, The Lives of St Oswald and St Egwine*, ed. and trans. M. Lapidge (Oxford: Clarendon Press, 2012), pp. 436–8; Geoffrey of Monmouth, *HKB*, book IX, paras. 156–8 (ed. Reeve, pp. 208–15).

[151] Wickham Legg, *English Coronation Records*, pp. 30–42; R. Strong, *Coronation. From the 8th to the 21st Century* (London: Harper Perennial, 2006), pp. 44–5, for a brief summary. It is not clear when spurs were added to the coronation regalia. J. H. Round suggested that their introduction may have derived from Carolingian practice, *King's Serjeants and Officers of State with Their Coronation Services* (London: Nisbet and Co, 1911), pp. 348–9. Henry I gave Geoffrey of Anjou spurs when he knighted him, so possibly it was at the coronation of Geoffrey's son Henry II that they were first used.

[152] J. L. Nelson, 'The Rites of the Conqueror', *Anglo-Norman Studies*, 4 (1981), 117–32, 220–1.

[153] G. Garnett, 'The Third Recension of the English Coronation *ordo*: the Manuscripts', *Haskins Society Journal*, 11 (1998), 43–71. G. Garnett, 'Coronation and Propaganda: Some Implications of the Norman Claim to the Throne in 1066', *Transactions of the Royal Historical Society*, 5th Series, 36 (1986), 91–116.

[154] ASC, C, 973, 979; C, D, E, 1043.

commemorating their gift of a gold cross.[155] The king and queen are
depicted below, respectively, St Peter and the Virgin, between whom is
Christ enthroned in a mandorla holding the Book of Life. The manuscript
dates from Cnut's lifetime. The drawing of the king and queen precedes
that of the Last Judgement and, it has been suggested, relates the royal pair
to the day of judgement to come. Cnut is depicted with a sword, possibly
as the protector of the community, whilst Ælfgifu receives a veil, possibly
to identify her with the Virgin.[156]

Of the regalia, nothing survives from our period save only a late
twelfth-century spoon which came to be used for the anointing.[157]
Edward the Confessor apparently commissioned a new crown from
Spearhavoc, abbot of Abingdon, in 1051.[158] When his tomb was opened
in 1102, he was found to have been buried wearing a crown, with a sceptre
and a ring.[159] In the twelfth century his regalia had passed into the custody
of the monks of Westminster.[160] According to the *Song of the Battle of
Hastings*, the Conqueror had a splendid new crown made, allegedly by
a Greek craftsman, with twelve great gemstones, and a sceptre and rod.[161]

Solemn crownwearings recreated and reaffirmed the rite of coronation.
These may have been held at regular intervals before 1066, and they
certainly were continued regularly under William I and William II.[162]
The practice was for the king to wear his crown in state at three of the
great festivals of the Christian year, Christmas at Gloucester, Easter at
Winchester, and Whitsun at Westminster.[163] The grandeur of the king's
appearance was striking. According to the biographer of Archbishop
Lanfranc, the king's jester cried out 'Behold I see God' of William the
Conqueror wearing a crown and robes, to be reproved by the archbishop.[164]
At such solemn festivals royal acclamations were sung to the king, and then

---

[155] London, British Library MS Stowe, 944, fol. 6r.
[156] For discussion, see C. E. Karkov, *The Ruler Portraits of Anglo-Saxon England*
(Woodbridge: Boydell Press, 2004), pp. 119–45.
[157] For a photograph, see Strong, *Coronation*, p. 78.
[158] *Historia Ecclesie Abbendonensis*, i, 196.
[159] 'La Vie de S. Edouard le Confesseur', p. 121.
[160] *Papsturkunden*, no. 24 as cited, Barlow, *Edward the Confessor*, p. 277.
[161] *Carmen de Hastingae Proelio*, ed. and trans. F. Barlow, 2nd edn (Oxford: Clarendon
Press, 1999), pp. 44–7.
[162] M. Biddle, 'Seasonal Festivals and Residence: Winchester, Westminster and Gloucester
in the Tenth to Twelfth Centuries', *Anglo-Norman Studies*, 8 (1985), 51–72.
[163] ASC, E, 1086.
[164] Miles Crispin, 'Life of Lanfranc', Migne, *Patrologiae Latina*, cl, col. 53; translated by
S. Vaughn, *The Abbey of Bec and the Anglo-Norman State 1034–1136* (Woodbridge:
Boydell Press, 1981), p. 107.

the queen, in the hierarchy of heaven with the angels and archangels.[165] Under Henry I the regular succession of these occasions was broken, but they were still held from time to time, as on the occasion of his second marriage in 1121.[166] It may be, too, that chroniclers became less interested in reporting crownwearings. Stephen was crowned in December 1135 and then in the following March his wife, Matilda, was crowned at Westminster.[167] Precisely when and where thereafter he wore his crown is not usually recorded, but he is likely to have continued the practice to shore up his position, and certainly after his release from captivity in 1141 he and the queen solemnly underwent coronation at Canterbury.[168] For the same reason Henry II held crownwearings at the start of his reign. He was crowned in December 1154. Eleanor was present, though it is not clear if she was crowned too. Between 1157 and 1158 there were three important crownwearings, on 10 May at Bury, at Christmas at Lincoln, and at the following Easter at Worcester.[169]

Henry may have avoided crownwearings during the period of his quarrel with Thomas Becket, though they may simply have been unrecorded. There is no doubt that he recognized the importance of coronation, hence pushed ahead with the coronation of his heir, the Young King, in 1170. The custom was established in Capetian France, and King Stephen had tried and failed to persuade Archbishop Theobald to crown his son Eustace.[170] David of Scotland had associated his son with his rule.[171] Hence, although the custom had not been practised in England, it was a way of easing the transition from one king to the next. The experiment failed because of the breakdown of relations between father and son. Whether Henry continued to wear his crown in state is unknown. Thus it is from a pipe roll reference in 1188 that we learn of payment to a clerk for the singing of the '*Christus Vincit*',

[165] H. E. J. Cowdrey, 'The Anglo-Norman Laudes Regiae', *Viator*, 12 (1981), 37–78.
[166] Eadmer, *Historia Novorum*, pp. 292–3. For the decline of triannual crownwearings under Henry, see WM, *GRA*, I, p. 508.
[167] For Stephen's coronation, see WM, *Historia Novella*, p. 28; Annals of St Augustine's Canterbury, *Ungedruckte Anglo-Normannische Geschichtsquellen*, ed. F. Liebermann (Strassburg: K. J. Trübner, 1879), pp. 79–80; Crouch, *Reign of King Stephen*, p. 42.
[168] Gervase of Canterbury, *Opera omnia*, I, pp. 123–4.
[169] *Chronicle of Battle Abbey*, pp. 174–6 (Bury); Howden, I, p. 282 (Lincoln); Diceto, I, p. 302 (Worcester).
[170] HH, p. 758.
[171] *The Charters of King David I: the Written Acts of David I, King of Scots, 1124–1153 and of His Son Henry Earl of Northumberland, 1139–1152*, ed. G. W. S. Barrow (Woodbridge: Boydell Press, 1999), pp. 5–8.

the acclamations sung at crownwearings, at London on the feast of Pentecost.[172]

Crownwearing entailed ritual and expense, and there was also the potential for disputes over precedence. That of 1121 was disturbed by the archbishop of Canterbury. Henry first placed the crown on his own head. When rebuked by the archbishop, he removed the crown and allowed the archbishop to replace it.[173] At Christmas 1126 the king had to warn the archbishop of York to stay in his lodging because Canterbury had said he would refuse to attend the court if York had his cross carried in front of him or played any part in the coronation.[174] At Lincoln in 1157 there was a disturbance involving the two archbishops.[175] It has been suggested that this may have been one of the reasons Henry and Eleanor left their crowns on the high altar following the crownwearing at Worcester, at Easter 1158.[176] Yet the countervailing arguments, that Henry may have been particularly conscious of the need to emphasize his authority after the civil war and, later, after the revolt of 1173–4, especially because he was not the son of a king but of a count, are surely even more persuasive.

Piety, Penance, and Patronage

The piety of the king of a Christian people was not only personal, but also reflected the piety of the nation. Edgar's patronage of Benedictine monasteries was thus an essential dimension of his rule as the peace-loving king. Æthelred's reaction to the severe challenges posed by Danish fleets was to restore and make further donations of land to churches. By 1009 the scale of the invasions was such as to lead to a call for penance from the whole nation.[177]

Demonstrable piety was a marked feature of Cnut's reign. He had a church built at the site of his great victory at *Assandun*.[178] He oversaw the conversion of the church at Bury, centre of the cult of the martyred King Edmund, into a Benedictine monastery. There may have been an element of reparation, for, according to legend, his father, Sweyn, had tried to take tribute and been repulsed by the saint.[179] Cnut showered gifts on a range

---

[172] *Pipe Roll 34 Henry II*, p. 19.   [173] Eadmer, *Historia Novorum*, pp. 292–3.

[174] Hugh the Chanter, *History of the Church of York*, p. 216.

[175] Vincent, *Acta*, no. 501 as cited N. Vincent, 'The Court of Henry II', Harper-Bill and Vincent (eds.), *Henry II New Interpretations*, pp. 278–334 at p. 326.

[176] *Ibid.*   [177] Cubitt, 'The Politics of Remorse'.   [178] ASC, D, 1020.

[179] *Memorials of St Edmund's Abbey*, ed. T. Arnold, 3 vols., RS (London: HMSO, 1890–6), I, pp. 32–4.

of churches.[180] He made a pilgrimage to Rome at least once, possibly twice.[181] The famous story about his inability to hold back the waves was a demonstration of the frailty of royal power before that of God. Afterwards he placed his crown on a crucifix and never wore it again.[182]

Edward the Confessor was the next king whose personal piety was manifested in generosity to the church, in his case the restoration of a decayed minster at Westminster, for love of St Peter.[183] His wife, Edith, was a major benefactor of Wilton Abbey.[184] Their association with particular projects rather than a range was something of a change of direction, followed by William the Conqueror with his foundation of Battle. According to house tradition, William had promised before Hastings to found an abbey to commemorate the fallen.[185] He himself was said to have been personally pious, attending mass before the battle and wearing relics round his neck on the day.[186] The papal legates in 1070 prescribed penances for those who had taken part in the campaign.[187] Henry I's foundation of Reading Abbey, in the aftermath of the Wreck of the White Ship and the death of his heir, is thought to have been motivated by a mood of penitence.[188] Henry was said to have made a pilgrimage to Bury in 1132 because of escape from shipwreck.[189] Stephen and Matilda founded Cluniac Faversham, and both were generous to the Templars.[190] Henry II was a generous patron, especially to Le Mans (the burial place

---

[180] For a survey, see Lawson, *Cnut. The Danes in England in the Early Eleventh Century*, chapter 4.

[181] A visit in *c.* 1030 is mentioned, ASC, D, E, F 1031. For discussion of this and a possible visit in 1027, see Lawson, *Cnut*, pp. 102–4.

[182] HH, pp. 366–9; cf. Goscelin, *Translatio Sancte Mildrethe Virginis*, ed. D. Rollason, *Medieval Studies*, 48 (1986), 139–210, at p. 163.

[183] *Life of King Edward*, pp. 66–8.

[184] Stafford, *Queen Edith and Queen Emma*, pp. 269–70.

[185] *Chronicle of Battle Abbey*, p. 36.

[186] William of Poitiers, *Gesta Guillelmi*, p. 124. For his gifts to churches, *ibid.*, pp. 152–4, 176–8.

[187] H. E. J. Cowdrey, 'Bishop Ermenfrid of Sion and the Penitential Ordinance Following the Battle of Hastings', *Journal of Ecclesiastical History*, 20 (1969), 225–42.

[188] R. W. Southern, 'The Place of Henry I in English History', *Proceedings of the British Academy*, 47 (1962), 127–69, at pp. 162–3 reprinted in R. W. Southern, *Medieval Humanism and Other Studies* (Oxford: Blackwell Press, 1970), pp. 206–33; P. Stafford, 'Cherchez la Femme: Queens, Queens' Lands and Nunneries: Missing Links in the Foundation of Reading Abbey', *History*, 85 (2000), 4–27.

[189] Henry may have been at Bury in 1132, *RRAN*, II, no. 1733. For his vow to visit Bury, see JW, III, p. 202.

[190] *RRAN*, III, nos. 300–2. Their fathers had both been crusaders. For their gifts, see *ibid.*, nos. 843–66.

of his father), Fontevraud, Bec (the burial place of his mother), Poitiers, Reading (the burial place of his grandfather), to Mortemer in Normandy and Stoneleigh in England. Waltham Abbey was reorganized as an Augustinian house, Amesbury as Fontevraudine, and Witham as a Charterhouse.[191] The developing practice of private penance did not preclude public displays of penitence.[192] Henry II became a frequent visitor to the shrine of Becket at Canterbury.[193]

Few of the kings in this period appear not to have been at least conventionally pious: only for Swein and Harold Harefoot is evidence lacking. William Rufus clearly was a Christian, to judge from his words of penitence in 1093 when he thought he was dying.[194] He was not an ungenerous benefactor, especially to Rochester, St Peter's Gloucester, and Bermondsey, where he was co-founder, but his treatment of abbeys during vacancies meant that contemporaries condemned him for his oppression of the church.[195] Throughout our period, then, kings as individuals and as sanctified rulers embodied their people. Disasters such as invasions by the Vikings, the Normans, or the Scots represented the judgement of God on the sins of the people and of their kings. The English defeat at Hastings was God's verdict on Harold's perjury and a reflection of the decay of religion amongst the English, according to William of Malmesbury.[196]

Kings and Clerics

Little is known about kings' role in the appointment of bishops and abbots before the later eleventh century, by which time there is not only more information, but also more debate. From the patchy surviving evidence it seems that the king's wishes were decisive in the case of bishoprics, but

[191] J. A. Green, preface to revised edn of W. L. Warren, *Henry II* (New Haven, CT, and London: Yale University Press, 2000), pp. xx–xxi.

[192] D. Crouch, 'The Troubled Deathbeds of Henry I's Servants: Death, Confession, and Secular Conduct in the Twelfth Century', *Albion*, 34 (2002), 24–36.

[193] T. K. Keefe, 'Shrine Time: King Henry II's Visits to Thomas Becket's Tomb', *Haskins Society Journal*, 11 (1998), 115–22. For context, see N. Vincent, 'The Pilgrimages of the Angevin Kings of England', C. Morris and P. Roberts (eds.), *Pilgrimage: the English Experience from Becket to Bunyan* (Cambridge: Cambridge University Press, 2002), pp. 12–45.

[194] Eadmer, *Historia Novorum*, pp. 30–9. Eadmer described how, once recovered, the king promptly reversed his promises of good behaviour.

[195] F. Barlow, *William Rufus* (London: Methuen, 1983), pp. 113–15.

[196] WM, *Gesta Regum Anglorum*, I, pp. 422, 456–60.

that there may have been free election for abbacies.[197] What came into question was how 'free canonical election' was to be defined, and whether the king had the right to take homage from bishops or abbots, or to invest them with sceptre and mitre. English churchmen could not evade these issues. It was Archbishop Anselm who, attending papal council at Rome in 1098, was confronted by a clear papal condemnation of lay investiture and of homage.[198] When he returned to England following the accession of Henry I, he refused to bless those who had been nominated and invested by the king. A crisis blew up. Anselm refused to disobey a papal diktat; Henry refused to budge. The issue of homage was particularly tricky given that, at least since 1066, bishops and abbots were tenants-in-chief of the king. They owed service and the 'incidents' arising from their tenure. Eventually a compromise was reached, not least because the archbishop threatened the king with excommunication at a critical moment in his contest for Normandy with his brother. Henry conceded investiture but retained homage.[199] It seems too that elections to office were usually held under the king's eye, at least until Stephen's reign.[200]

During the Civil War, royal control over the choice of bishops diminished and there was a growing degree of contact with Rome.[201] Closer to home, the rise of bishops' courts, and their attractiveness to litigants, was another development that was less than welcome to the new king, Henry II. The mantra Henry and his advisors used was that the king's rights in every respect should be returned to the situation at his grandfather's death. The problem so far as the king's position with regard to bishops and abbots, relations with Rome, and the jurisdictions, respectively, of the king and the church were concerned, was that it was by no means straightforward to turn the clock back.[202] Moreover, the king's decision to have the customs recorded in writing made it harder to resolve

---

[197] F. Barlow, *The English Church 1000–1066*, 2nd edn (London: Longman, 1979), pp. 99–108.

[198] Eadmer, *Historia Novorum*, p. 114.

[199] Eadmer provides the most detailed account of the quarrel, *ibid.*, pp. 118–86.

[200] F. Barlow, *The English Church 1066–1154* (London, New York: Longman, 1979), pp. 91–103, for a review of Stephen's dealings with the church.

[201] C. Duggan, 'Papal Judges Delegate and the Making of the "New Law" in the Twelfth Century', *Cultures of Power. Lordship, Status and Process in Twelfth-Century Europe* (ed. Bisson), pp. 172–99; A. Duggan, 'Roman, Canon and Common Law in Twelfth-Century England: the Council of Northampton (1164) Re-examined,' *Historical Research*, 83 (2010), 379–408.

[202] For the situation at Henry's accession, see A. J. Duggan, 'Henry II, the English Church and the Papacy, 1154–76', Harper-Bill and Vincent (eds.), *Henry II. New Interpretations*, pp. 154–83, at pp. 154–72. For a brief account, see H. Mayr-Harting,

differences. Finally, add in the personal quarrel between the king and the archbishop of Canterbury, Thomas Becket, formerly the king's friend, and the result was an incendiary brew.[203]

The question of the royal customs surfaced at the Council of Westminster in 1163, which rapidly became a battle of wills between the king and the archbishop, who said he would only recognize the customs 'saving his order', leaving the bishops alarmed because, as they saw it, they were left between a rock and a hard place.[204] By the time the king's council reconvened at Clarendon in 1164, the archbishop declared that he and the bishops would give their verbal assent. The king had them written down in the form of a chirograph, and although Becket and the bishops refused to append their seals, they had agreed to recognize the Constitutions.[205]

The Constitutions purported to record the royal customs enjoyed by Henry I, but their formulation opened a Pandora's box. In some instances they did accurately represent custom, and remained uncontroversial.[206] In others they were a record of past custom, but in a form that was no longer acceptable to the papacy.[207] Others offered precision in circumstances where there had probably been a degree of flexibility.[208] In these clauses the king was claiming exclusivity for his courts of lawsuits which may have gone to church courts.[209] The pope in practice found all the Constitutions unacceptable, though some more than others. Particularly offensive was the king's demand to oversee appeals to Rome (clause eight), which were only to be allowed as a last resort after English courts had been exhausted.

The most problematic clause was the third, because it encroached on clerical immunity from secular justice. In the first place, it laid down that clerks accused of serious offences had to establish their exempt status in the king's court. If they succeeded, then were tried in the church court and either found guilty or confessed, they were to lose their clerical status, and were to be handed over to the secular court for punishment. In this way the

Religion, Politics and Society in Britain 1066–1272 (Harlow: Pearson Education, 2011), chapter 4.

[203] F. Barlow, *Thomas Becket* (London: Weidenfeld and Nicolson, 1986); A. Duggan, *Thomas Becket (Reputations)* (London: Arnold, 2004).

[204] 'Summa Causae Inter Regem et Thomam', *Materials for the History of Thomas Becket*, IV, pp. 201–5.

[205] For the Constitutions, see *Materials for the History of Thomas Becket*, I, pp. 18–33; for pressure on Thomas and the bishops, see 'Roger of Pontigny', *Materials for the History of Thomas Becket*, IV, pp. 27–37.

[206] Clauses 2, 7, 10, 11, 13, 16.   [207] Clause 8, on appeals to Rome.

[208] Clauses 1, 6, 9, 14, 15.   [209] Barlow, *English Church 1066–1154*, pp. 157–8.

king hoped to curtail abuses of benefit of clergy by many who were in minor orders.

The quarrel between Henry and Thomas lasted for six years. The king particularly proved intransigent over the Constitutions and only finally made a patched-up peace because he had pushed the pope too far. The quarrel ended in Becket's murder, and although Henry was duly shocked and penitent, he remained obdurate over the Constitutions. He reached a form of agreement with the pope's representatives at Avranches in Normandy, when he renounced all evil customs (though he did not think he had introduced many). He was prepared to allow appeals to Rome (unless they damaged his interests), and promised to allow every church its liberties.[210] The knotty issue of 'criminous clerks' was dealt with by the pope's legate only in 1175–6.[211] Henry promised that clerks were not to be indicted before secular judges except for forest trespasses. Wilful murderers of clerks were to be disinherited as well as punished according to secular law, and clerks were not to be forced to fight duels. He also promised to fill ecclesiastical vacancies within a year.[212]

Even at the time Becket was a divisive figure, arousing suspicions about his motives and his sincerity, and in the following centuries there has been debate about his commitment to the 'English church', to the power sought by the papacy, and to Henry II's aims. Was Becket deliberately courting martyrdom? Was the Roman church seeking to control the English church? Would Henry II have proved accommodating if his archbishop had been less intransigent?[213] As Anne Duggan has argued, what Henry intended for the church was part of a wider aim of a 'centrally managed legal process, both as an instrument of control and as a source of regular income'.[214] She maintains, too, that had the Constitutions remained in place unaltered, more and more ecclesiastical suits would have ended up before the king's courts, and that what he lost was systematic jurisdiction over clerical crimes and misdemeanours.[215] The modern citizen might have little trouble with the idea that whilst clerical immunity and the existence of church courts should be respected, their privileges were not to be abused, but this was not how it seemed at the time.

---

[210] 'Lansdowne Anonymous', *Materials for the History of Thomas Becket*, IV, pp. 173–4.
[211] *Ibid.*   [212] Duggan, 'Henry II, the English Church and the Papacy', pp. 178–80.
[213] Warren, *Henry II*, chapters 13 and 14.
[214] 'Henry II, the English Church and the Papacy', p. 172.
[215] *Ibid.*, pp. 181–2, discussed Warren, *Henry II*, pp. 537–8.

At issue in the 1160s was not particularly the appointment process of bishops and abbots, given that the king had surrendered investiture, but where the line between secular and ecclesiastical jurisdiction was to be drawn. The ground had shifted, a reflection of the importance of courts and legal procedures. Whose law? Whose courts? Who decided? By the mid-twelfth century the pope was a much less distant figure than he had been at the start of our period. The fact that Alexander III had problems of his own and could not afford to lose the support of Henry II did not mean he approved of the Constitutions, far from it. In the end, Becket's murder wrong-footed the king and gave the pope the moral high ground. The Constitutions were condemned, with only a few exceptions. Compromises over jurisdiction had to be worked out over time, and in a less highly charged atmosphere.[216]

By the end of our period, ideas about the respective roles of kings and bishops had changed fundamentally. The growing precision of law and legal process on all sides sharpened distinctions. Litigants had some freedom of choice over courts and forms of action, and continuing horse-trading about which courts dealt with which kinds of cases was perhaps inevitable. Yet if we can talk about differences, we must also keep in mind that the relationship between kings and the church remained close, and kings continued to benefit from the potency conferred by coronation, and from their association with sainted kings of the past.

Office and Individual

Undying King

In the long term monarchy developed into an institution over and beyond the individual kings, the development of what Kantorowicz called 'the king's two bodies'.[217] How far did royal power die with the individual, and when did a new reign start? From 1272, according to Richardson and Sayles, a new reign was deemed to have started at the death of the preceding ruler.[218] A new seal with which to authenticate documents, coins issued in his name, and a coronation could not be conjured up overnight. In our

---

[216] C. R. Cheney, *From Becket to Langton: English Church Government 1170–1213* (Manchester: Manchester University Press, 1956).

[217] E. Kantorowicz, *The King's Two Bodies. A Study in Medieval Political Theology* (Princeton, NJ: Princeton University Press, 1957).

[218] H. G. Richardson and G. O. Sayles, *The Governance of Mediaeval England* (Edinburgh: Edinburgh University Press, 1963), p. 151.

period, however, the question of continuity at the death of a king is by no means so clear.

In a close analysis of succession from the tenth century to the Norman Conquest, Ann Williams demonstrated the twists and turns of royal succession to take account of adult siblings within the royal family, the consequences of second marriages, and the changes of dynasty in the first half of the eleventh century.[219] Descent by blood remained important, but so too – and increasingly so in the eleventh century – were the wishes of the previous king. Coronation until 1066 was not of itself constitutive, and there does not seem to have been any thought that between the death of one king and the succession of another there was an interregnum.

What changed in 1066 was the speed with which a new king was crowned. Harold Godwinson was crowned within days of the death of Edward the Confessor, presumably because all in England would have been aware of likely challenges from Scandinavia and Normandy.[220] William the Conqueror was crowned on Christmas Day 1066, his victory at Hastings having taken place on 14 October. Rufus was crowned just as soon as he had crossed from Normandy carrying news of his father's death and wishes over the succession to Archbishop Lanfranc. Henry I was crowned in London three days after his brother's death in the New Forest, and Stephen some three weeks after his uncle's death on 1 December 1135. Only in 1154 was there any delay, Henry II taking his time about his return to England after Stephen's death on 25 October, and being crowned on 19 December 1154.

It has been argued that between 1066 and 1154 coronations were constitutive, and that between one ruler's death and the coronation of the next there was an interregnum.[221] The Conquest, it is argued, changed the relationship between the king and the great men fundamentally so that, whatever had been the situation before, there was now a contractual relationship. On the death of the king, homage had to be renewed, which could only be done when the next king had been crowned. There is no doubt that the period following the death of a king was highly dangerous. Any uncertainty about who was king could tempt men to self-help, or might engender reluctance to seek confirmation of lands and privileges.

---

[219] A. Williams, 'Some Notes and Considerations Connected with the English Royal Succession, 860–1066', [*Proceedings of the Battle Conference on*] *Anglo-Norman Studies*, 1 (1978), 144–67, 225–33.

[220] ASC, E, 1066.

[221] G. Garnett, *Conquered England: Kingship, Succession, and Tenure 1066–1166* (Oxford: Oxford University Press, 2007), chapter 3.

Yet the fact was that every succession in our period was contested, and those who in the event proved on the losing side could try for retrospective legitimation, even if they were not always successful.[222] In 1016 Æthelred was living, but Swein and then Cnut were described as kings in the Anglo-Saxon Chronicle. Similarly, if Harold had not been killed at Hastings, William would have had to argue that his coronation was invalid as a usurper, or persuade the pope to depose him. As Garnett's own argument based on the Penitential Ordinance showed, the Conqueror was regarded as having been king from the date of his victory at Hastings on 14 October 1066, not his coronation on 25 December. It did not mean that no challenge would materialize. Lanfranc's supporters in the dispute over primacy warned William that the archbishop of York might crown a Danish or Scottish king in the north.[223] In 1088 and 1100 Duke Robert's supporters were not deterred by the coronations of Rufus and Henry, respectively, from challenging for the throne, but it is hard to see that either Lanfranc or Anselm would have been prepared to crown Robert in the lifetime of a crowned king.

In the aftermath of the Battle of Lincoln in 1141 with Stephen, the crowned king, in captivity, and the empress angling to take over England, the situation was far from clear. The queen was at liberty, and so too was her son Eustace. The empress was receiving homage and making grants (as empress, daughter of King Henry), and at the Council of Winchester the king's brother, the bishop of Winchester, now papal legate, was preparing the way for her. He made a speech in which he said that King Henry had confirmed by an oath of all the bishops and barons the kingdom of England and the duchy of Normandy to his daughter. Because she delayed in coming to England when her father died, Stephen was 'allowed to reign'. He failed to keep order. God had judged Stephen by allowing him to be captured. He, Henry, had discussed with the clergy 'whose special prerogative it is to choose and consecrate a prince' and they now chose as lady (*domina*) in England and Normandy the daughter of a king who was a peacemaker.[224] Historians have tended to assume that the Council was paving the way for the empress to rule in her own right, and that the title *domina* was leading up to her own coronation in Westminster

[222] This was the case of Brand, who was elected abbot of Peterborough after the death of the previous abbot on the eve of All Saints, that is, 31 October, after the Battle of Hastings on 14 October 1066. Brand was sent to Edgar Ætheling, and this angered William the Conqueror, who had to be placated with forty gold marks (£240), ASC, E, 1066.

[223] Hugh the Chanter, *History of the Church of York 1066–1127*, p. 4.

[224] WM, *Historia Novella*, pp. 92–3.

Abbey. It is possible that she was planning a ceremony there. Perhaps she intended to send for her husband, Geoffrey count of Anjou, and her son, by now some eight years of age, who could have been presented to the magnates. She could have worn an imperial crown, or been crowned as a queen regnant. At the heart of the issue was whether the throne could be held by a woman. Female inheritance to land was possible, though often contested, but office was a different matter, and there were no precedents.

As events turned out, the empress's presence in London proved fleeting. She fled, her half-brother Robert was captured at Winchester, and by the end of the year he had been exchanged for the king. Stephen of course wanted to be succeeded by his son Eustace but, try as he might, he was unable to secure Eustace's coronation by Archbishop Theobald, and, to cut a long story short, he came to terms with Henry FitzEmpress in 1153. According to their treaty, Stephen was to retain the throne for the rest of his of life and 'constituted' Henry successor after him of the kingdom of England. No reference was made to Normandy, of which Henry was by this time duke. Henry did homage and was recognized by the king as his adopted son and was to be succeeded by Henry, to whom the barons had performed liege homage. It would still have been possible for the treaty to unravel if Eustace had lived, but he died, and Stephen's second son did not challenge for the throne, so that Henry was able to accede peacefully.[225] In other words, whilst Garnett is surely right to emphasize the insecurity added by the freshly contractual relationship between the king and the great men after 1066 – the idea that the king was the lord king – the urgency prompting a new king to speedy coronation was surely as much pragmatic as theoretical. Moreover, Henry II clearly felt that insecurities surrounding succession had not been 'solved', to use Garnett's word, hence his keenness to have his son Henry crowned, even by the archbishop of York rather than Canterbury, who was in exile.

The idea that grants by each king needed to be confirmed in a charter by his successor may have been one factor in the perceived need for each king to have his own seal. The Conqueror's like Edward's, was a double-sided seal of majesty, but the reverse showed William mounted as a knight. The legend read 'By this know William patron (*patronus*) of the Normans' and on the other 'By this seal acknowledge the same king of the English'. William Rufus's seal was a double-sided seal of majesty with the legend

---

[225] George Garnett has argued that these oaths 'solved' the problem of an interregnum, *Conquered England*, pp. 262–99.

'William by the grace of God king of the English'.[226] We do not know how long it would have taken to have new seal matrices made. This is not an academic issue when it comes to Henry I's Coronation Charter, which was said to have been 'given' on the day of his coronation, only three days after his brother's unexpected death.[227]

Related to each king's personal responsibility for grants is the idea that agreements and debts did not outlive him. A sense of this is gained from Henry I's Charter of Liberties where the new king promises 'to forgive all pleas and debts owed to my brother, except my own proper dues, and except those things which were agreed to belong to the inheritance of others, or to concern the property which justly belonged to others'.[228] From this we may infer that other debts carried over from reign to reign.

There was then a tension between the individual king and kingship, an office with duties which was evolving into an institution. There are some signs of an awareness of the idea of the kingdom, as opposed to kings. One early example is from Exon Domesday, a draft of the inquest returns in the south-west, where we find the heading, 'The king's demesne belonging to the kingdom in Devon'.[229] Then there are references in the twelfth century to pleas of the crown (impersonal), rather than royal pleas. These occur in the 1130 pipe roll and in the French version of the laws of the Conqueror.[230] The term recurs in the alleged charter of Henry I to the Londoners, possibly an early forgery (see later).[231] Robert of Torigny used the phrase in describing Henry II's revocation of grants of cities and castles 'which belonged to the crown of the realm'.[232] More significant perhaps is the reference to pleas of the crown in clause seven of the Assize of Northampton.[233]

Delegation

A further step away from all royal power being wrapped up in the person of the king was taken with the beginnings of delegation. Queens had

---

[226] Barlow, *William Rufus*, p. 59.

[227] J. A. Green, 'The Charter of Liberties of Henry I', M. T. Flanagan and J. A. Green (eds.), *Charters and Charter Scholarship in Britain and Ireland* (Houndmills: Palgrave, 2005), pp. 53–69. This too bears on the question of the beginning of a reign.

[228] Stubbs, *Select Charters*, p. 118.   [229] Exon DB, DB, IV, fol. 63.

[230] *Pipe Roll 31 Henry I*, p. 72: Benjamin accounted to keep the pleas of the crown; *Leis Willelme* 2, 1: 'plai afierent a la curune le rei', Liebermann, *Die Gesetze der Angelsachsen*, I, 492.

[231] *RRAN*, II, no. 1645; C. N. L. Brooke, G. Keir, and S. Reynolds, 'Henry I's Charter for the City of London', *Journal of the Society of Archivists*, 4 (1972), 558–78.

[232] *Chronicles of the Reigns of Stephen, Henry II and Richard I*, IV, p. 183.

[233] Stubbs, *Select Charters*, p. 180 (from Roger of Howden).

a potentially important role to play here. As with kings, there were expectations of their role: first and foremost they were expected to bear children, to set an example of personal piety, and to oversee the royal household. Depending on their personalities and on circumstances, they could be significant political figures in their own right. Nevertheless they were ultimately vulnerable as the brisk dismissals of Queen Emma and then Queen Edith by Edward the Confessor and the imprisonment of Eleanor of Aquitaine by Henry II showed. If the mother of sons, and if trusted, they could act as regents. Matilda I, wife of William the Conqueror, and Matilda II, wife of Henry I, and Eleanor of Aquitaine each seem to have had this role for a time.[234] Matilda III, wife of King Stephen, assumed an even more important role when her husband was imprisoned at the Battle of Lincoln in 1141, for she took command of his army and carried on the fight against the empress's forces.[235]

It has been argued that by the tenth century queenly coronation, and the elevation of the king's wife to his consecrated consort and mother of his heir, gave them the potential for political agency.[236] Much depended on circumstances as well as personality. Ælfthryth came under suspicion for the death of her stepson Edward the Martyr at Corfe. Her young son Æthelred succeeded to the throne and she remained a dominant figure for the first years of his reign. For William of Malmesbury, writing in the early twelfth century, she was the classic wicked stepmother.[237] Emma, second wife of both Æthelred and Cnut, seems to have been more powerful during her second marriage than her first, presumably because Cnut's absences made her presence all the more important.[238] Cnut's first wife, Ælfgifu, the mother of his son Harold Harefoot, is less well documented, but even so she was able to secure the succession of Harold when Cnut died.[239] On this occasion Emma, who was working for the interests of her son Harthacnut, was outflanked because Harthacnut was in Denmark. She may have been involved in the murder of her son Alfred, though she denied complicity. Harthacnut succeeded in 1040 and invited

[234] For Matilda I, see *Historia Ecclesie Abbendonensis*, II, pp. 14–16; for Matilda II, see L. L. Huneycutt, *Matilda of Scotland. A Study in Medieval Queenship* (Woodbridge: Boydell Press, 2003), pp. 78–94; for Eleanor, see R. V. Turner, *Eleanor of Aquitaine* (New Haven, CT, and London: Yale University Press, 2009), pp. 150–5.

[235] *Gesta Stephani*, pp. 128–30.   [236] Stafford, *Queen Emma and Queen Edith, passim*.

[237] *Gesta Regum Anglorum*, I, pp. 262–6.

[238] Stafford, *Queen Emma and Queen Edith*, pp. 229–36.

[239] Pauline Stafford, 'Ælfgifu (*fl.* 1006–1036)', *ODNB* www.oxforddnb.com/view/article /180, accessed 20 May 2016.

Edward (the Confessor) to England in 1041.[240] However, her relationship with Edward was not repaired, and after his accession he took away her treasure.[241]

The coupling of England and Normandy was a further stimulus to a growing need for a king's deputy. William the Conqueror's wife, Matilda, was formally crowned in 1068, and it seems that on occasion she was able to act on her husband's behalf on either side of the Channel.[242] Matilda II, first wife of Henry I, acted for the first time on her husband's behalf in 1104 in England after the birth of her son. She seems to have overseen negotiations for her daughter's marriage, and perhaps the geld collected for her dowry, and she seems to have continued as a deputy until her last illness.[243] Matilda III, wife of King Stephen, was countess of Boulogne in her own right, and as such lady of a great estate in England. She was mother of three sons, one of whom died young. After Stephen was imprisoned in 1141, she took command of his army, and sent representatives to the Legate's council to argue for his release. Her troops ravaged the south bank of the Thames, causing the citizens of London to rise up against the empress, and she continued in pursuit to Winchester.[244] After 1154 Eleanor of Aquitaine, again, significantly, the mother of sons, acted as regent when her husband, Henry II, was abroad, but her involvement in the revolt of her sons against their father in 1173–4 led to her imprisonment.[245] The ups and downs of queenly power demonstrate very clearly the potential of the position through nearness to the king and to the heir, but also its fragility. Queens who were dangerous could simply be dispatched to nunnery or castle.

The fact that England was only one of the territories of the Danish and the Norman kings was obviously an important reason for making arrangements for viceroys: none of these kings was sufficiently secure to be absent safely for long periods. If not the queen, than an archbishop or bishop could be nominated as viceroy. Lanfranc seems to have held this role during the revolt of 1075 when William the Conqueror was out of the

[240] J. R. Maddicott, 'Edward the Confessor's Return to England in 1041', *English Historical Review*, 119 (2004), 650–66.

[241] ASC, D, 1043.   [242] William of Poitiers, *Gesta Guillelmi*, p. 148.

[243] Huneycutt, *Matilda of Scotland*, pp. 78–9, 85, 91, 93; J. A. Green, 'Duchesses of Normandy in the Eleventh and Twelfth Centuries', D. Crouch and K. Thompson (eds.), *Normandy and Its Neighbours 900–1250: Essays for David Bates* (Turnhout: Brepols, 2011), pp. 43–59, at pp. 50–1.

[244] Marjorie Chibnall, 'Matilda (c.1103–1152)', *ODNB* www.oxforddnb.com/view/article/18337, accessed 20 May 2016.

[245] Turner, *Eleanor of Aquitaine*, chapter 6.

country.[246] Roger bishop of Salisbury also seems to have acted as viceroy between 1123 and 1126 during the absence of the king and the queen in Normandy.[247]

Another consideration was the growing complexity of government. Some decisions could be postponed until the king's return, but the pressing need for money by Rufus's reign led to an alternative arrangement of a small subcommittee of royal officials: Ranulf Flambard, then a royal chaplain, king's chief *exactor* and *placitator*, together with the stewards Eudo and Haimo, Urse d'Abitôt a constable and sheriff, and Walkelin royal treasurer and bishop of Winchester.[248] These men were experienced in working together, probably since the 1080s, and it has been pointed out that they filled the role of the later barons of the exchequer, and perhaps had the same privilege of exemption of their demesnes from geld.[249] There may perhaps have been comparable figures before the Conquest, to mobilize the supplies of coined money needed for tribute and wages. It has been suggested that Bishop Walkelin's role may have been held by Archbishop Stigand before 1066. Whether they were ad hoc groups or in regular session is impossible to say. What comes into sharper focus in the reign of Henry I is the presidency of Roger of Salisbury over a group now called the exchequer.[250] He had oversight of justice and finance, and he presided over the annual meetings of the exchequer and issued writs to execute the king's orders.[251] During one period when the king left for Normandy in 1123, he was said to have been left in charge in England, the king's second wife, Adeliza, being with the king and in any case young (and childless).[252] After 1126 the bishop remained in charge of the exchequer, possibly until

---

[246] D. Bates, 'The Origins of the Justiciarship', [*Transactions of the Battle Conference on*] *Anglo-Norman Studies*, 4 (1981), 1–12, at pp. 5–6.

[247] ASC, E, 1123; Green, *Henry I*, p. 182.

[248] *RRAN*, I, nos. 337, 387, 416, 418, 422, 424. R. W. Southern, 'Ranulf Flambard', Alexander Prize Essay, first published in *Transactions of the Royal Historical Society*, 4th series, 16 (1933), 95–128, reprinted in Southern, *Medieval Humanism* (Oxford: Blackwell, 1970), pp. 183–205; J. F. A. Mason, 'Flambard, Ranulf (*c.*1060–1128)', *ODNB* www.oxforddnb.com/view/article/9667, accessed 20 May 2016.

[249] Harvey, *Domesday*, p. 266.

[250] According to the certificate of his election as bishop of Salisbury, Roger was a priest of Avranches, E. J. Kealey, *Roger of Salisbury. Viceroy of England* (Berkeley, Los Angeles: University of California Press, 1972), pp. 3–5. Cf. William of Newburgh for the (later) statement that Roger was a priest in the suburbs of Caen who was taken into Henry's household and managed his affairs, *Historia Rerum Anglicarum, Chronicles of the Reigns of Stephen, Henry II and Richard I*, ed. R. Howlett, 4 vols., RS (London: Longman and Co, 1884–9), I, 35–6.

[251] *Ibid.*, chapter 2.   [252] ASC, E, 1123.

the time of his arrest in 1139.[253] It was Bishop Roger's position which
seems to have been the template for the justiciars appointed under Henry
II, first Robert earl of Leicester and Richard de Lucy jointly, then the latter
as sole justiciar, finally being succeeded by Ranulf de Glanvill.[254]
The roles of these men obviously changed according to circumstance.
The great growth in common law writs gave increasing prominence to
their role as chief justice. Over time too their position evolved into
a formal office, that of chief justiciar.

CHANGE OVER TIME: THE KEY PERIODS

The first key period is King Edgar's reign when royal government inten-
sified. Hundreds, wapentakes, and shires were being established, the
system of coinage was reorganized, and English rule south of the Tees
was being strengthened over a period of years, probably in the context of
royal peacekeeping.[255] Under Æthelred the pressure came from the need
to raise men and money, and shires and sheriffs were an invaluable
infrastructure.

Secondly, 1066 proved a date of fundamental importance. Relations
between the crown and the aristocracy were reordered. In the first place,
King William was insisting that all land was held by dependent tenure.
If the king or the tenant-in-chief died, homage had to be performed, and
tenants-in-chief were supposed to deal with their tenants likewise. Only
rarely were nobles put to death.[256] On the other hand, security of tenure
became less assured, especially at the highest level.[257] Greater security of
inheritance took time to establish: the assize of *mort d'ancestor* of 1176
was an important step forward in this respect.[258] Finally, there was
perhaps greater emphasis on the right as well as the duty of great men to
proffer counsel, an idea which fed into the composition and frequency of
councils. The potential for erosion of bonds between the king, under-
tenants, and freemen was countered by the use of general oaths of loyalty,

---

[253] WM, *Historia Novella*, pp. 44–9.
[254] F. J. West, *The Justiciarship in England 1066–1232* (Cambridge: Cambridge University
Press, 1966), pp. 35–54.
[255] Molyneaux, *Formation of the English Kingdom in the Tenth Century*, pp. 182–94.
[256] J. Hudson, 'The Fate of Waltheof and the Idea of Personal Law in England after 1066',
D. Crouch and K. Thompson (eds.), *Normandy and England 900–1250: Essays for
David Bates* (Turnhout: Brepols, 2013), pp. 223–35.
[257] Holt, 'Politics and Property in Early Medieval England'.
[258] J. Biancalana, 'For Want of Justice: Legal Reforms of Henry II', *Columbia Law Review*,
88 (1988), 433–536, at pp. 484–7.

most famously at Salisbury in 1086. Such general oaths of loyalty had not been unknown in England, but at this particular time they were of critical importance in reinforcing political loyalties, and the obligation of loyalty to the king over and beyond that to the lord.[259] In other respects, too, the Norman kings brought in change, most obviously in the extension of forest law, in their control over ecclesiastical vacancies and appointments, and of the coinage. Sheriffs were the key agents and writs increasingly the medium through which orders could be transmitted and recorded.

Thirdly, the reign of Henry II saw a further incremental extension in the range of activities of royal government, and in the numbers of officials. Developments in law and justice were of fundamental importance. Building on earlier foundations, the proliferation of writ-based actions using juries and administered by sheriffs provided new remedies for land disputes which offered the opportunity for resolution in court rather than through self-help. A drive against crime used local juries to bring suspects to court, though efforts to bring clerks accused of crime before secular courts, and to regulate appeals to Rome, brought conflict with Becket. The taxation of movable goods, as yet for a holy war, pointed the way to a new form of taxation. The system of coinage was reorganized with fewer mints and exchanges staffed by officials. In all there was a great increase in the number of officials and in reliance on documents, used for record and instruction. The potential for unfettered and aggressive power exercised in the king's name was fast becoming reality. The king's chief forester, Alan de Neville, attracted opprobrium as he went about the country imposing fines for forest offences.[260] As yet opposition was couched in the traditional form of an aristocratic revolt, in support of the Young King in 1173–4. It took time and decades of exploitative rule under Richard and John to bring the crisis of 1215.

---

[259] J. C. Holt, '1086', pp. 31–5, 53–4; for general oaths in Anglo-Saxon England, see previously in this chapter.
[260] David Crook, 'Neville, Alan de (d. c.1176)', *ODNB* [www.oxforddnb.com/view/article /19921, accessed 20 May 2016].

4

Lay Lords: an Age of Aristocracy?

The warrior elite was at the heart of power struggles in the English kingdom between the tenth and twelfth centuries. It was an era of dizzying change as individuals and families rose to power and wealth and then fell. The language and culture of the dominant elite changed from Old English to Old Norse and then to Old French. Modes of fighting changed: the greatest prestige came to be given to fighting on horseback. New theatres of war opened up on the frontiers of the English kingdom, in the Near East, and, lastly, in Ireland. Status and wealth was reflected in the rise of the stone castle, which by the twelfth century was associated with a noble's principal residence. The relationship between lordship and land altered. Lordship became increasingly attached to tenure of particular land: lineage and rights of inheritance were strengthened. Centres of major lordships came to be characterized by the building of stone castles, often close to monastic houses favoured by the lords. A lesser aristocracy was embedded in the countryside, often locally resident in order to supervise a peasant workforce. Finally, the relationship between lords and kings changed. Lords had increasingly to take royal power into account. Royal courts provided the context and the clout to buttress claims to land, and royal patronage the opportunity to acquire land and wealth, so lords increasingly had to work within a framework of royal governance.

COMPOSITION

The term 'aristocracy' rather than 'nobility' is used in this chapter to encompass lay lords ranging from the greatest ealdormen to manorial lords. Birth did of course matter, and the greatest could often claim royal descent or, in the case of the Normans, kinship with the duke. Yet these centuries were a time when fortunes could be made and lost in a relatively short period through the fortunes of war and politics, or through lack of an adult male heir. Excellence in war could bring great rewards. The career of William Marshal, rising from tournament knight to regent of England, is often cited in this respect, though it is worth pointing out that he was a son of a royal official.[1] Moreover, by the twelfth century men were also rising through their indispensability to the king as sheriffs and justices. Many of these were clerks, but there were also laymen, the famous 'new men' of Henry I.[2] They were not unique to England, and they represented a symptom of the need of kings and princes for collectors of dues and enforcers of rights.[3] As such they inevitably attracted criticism as intruders into the social elite. By the later twelfth century their power and prominence was once again the subject of comment.[4]

So far as the distribution of landed wealth within the aristocracy is concerned, our knowledge of the situation before 1066 is patchy. There were clearly ealdormen and great thegns with widely scattered estates, and others with smaller, more compact holdings. Andrew Wareham has argued that East Anglian society around the first millennium witnessed a restructuring as great families fell from power and lesser local men were established.[5] In other words, he believes that developments in this region of England paralleled those on the continent as power became more localized, concentrated in the hands of local lords, much as was happening in France in the same period. Whilst it is useful to keep in mind the contemporary localization of power in France, more work is needed on other English regions to see how far the situation in East Anglia was typical.

---

[1] D. Crouch, *William Marshal: Court, Career and Chivalry in the Angevin Empire, 1147–1219* (Harlow: Longman, 1990); *History of William Marshal*, ed. A. J. Holden, trans. S. Gregory, notes D. Crouch, 3 vols., Anglo-Norman Text Society, Occasional Publications Series, 4–6 (London, 2002, 2004, 2006).

[2] OV, VI, p. 16; Green, *Government of England under Henry I*, pp. 139–40.

[3] For the Erembalds in Flanders, see Galbert of Bruges, *The Murder of Charles the Good Count of Flanders*, trans. and edited J. B. Ross (New York: Harper, 1967), pp. 96–100; for the Capetian court, see E. Hallam, *Capetian France 987–1328* (Harlow: Longman, 1980), pp. 159–60.

[4] R. V. Turner, *Men Raised from the Dust: Administrative Service and Upward Mobility in Angevin England* (Philadelphia: University of Pennsylvania Press, 1988), chapter 1.

[5] A. Wareham, 'The "Feudal Revolution" in Eleventh-Century East Anglia', *Anglo-Norman Studies*, 22 (1999), 293–321.

Other great families succeeded those who fell. The Godwinsons most of all accumulated a vast amount of landed wealth, and when Tostig was appointed earl of Northumbria in 1055 they were positioned to the north and south of the only family of comparable wealth, the Leofricsons, represented by Edwin earl of Mercia.[6] Morcar, Edwin's brother, became earl of Northumbria in 1065, and for a year the Leofricsons' earldoms and lands were to the north and south of the Godwinsons. These two families in particular had profited, firstly from Cnut's need for loyal viceroys as he pursued his ambitions in Scandinavia, secondly from Edward's lack of his own political following at the time of his accession, and thirdly from the failure of his attempt to break free from Godwin and his family in 1051 and 1052.

The destruction of the old order after 1066 was followed by the creation of a new elite. At the top was a handful of super-magnates with estates distributed throughout the country, then a body of tenants-in-chief, more numerous than the leading English thegns. The most important magnates were mostly related to the duke, and were already magnates in Normandy. Most of the newcomers were Normans, but there were also contingents of Bretons and Flemings. This revolution was critically important for three reasons. The first was that it was predicated on a new bargain between the king and his leading followers (see earlier in this volume). Secondly, many of the newcomers held lands throughout much of the country. The establishment of a framework of lordships across the midlands and in Yorkshire provided a springboard for the final incorporation of the north-west and north-east into the English kingdom. Thirdly, the new elite was French speaking, and in many cases had estates and family ties across the Channel in Normandy. Their history was and remained closely bound up with that of France until after the end of our period. Many of the English who had survived long enough to be included in the Domesday Inquest were holding only a few of their former estates, or were king's thegns who had presumably submitted to William, or were still there, but as tenants. Disputed successions to the throne continued to be the occasion of and spur to rivalries in families already settled in England, as they had been before 1066. Not only that, but there were prospects elsewhere in the British Isles for further gains.

Throughout our period there was an important group of lesser lords. Some historians have described them as gentry; others prefer to limit this term to the

---

[6] F. Barlow, *The Godwins: the Rise and Fall of a Noble Dynasty* (Harlow, 2002); Baxter, *Earls of Mercia*, p. 129.

thirteenth century on when the leading local families in each shire were linked through the county courts to parliament.[7] The term 'class' is also problematic: how far were such lords united by a common outlook? What evidence there is suggests they imitated the great men in the way they lived and in their patronage of churches. Continuity across the eleventh-century conquests is likely to have been greater than at the highest social levels. After 1066 Englishmen leased manors, and perhaps intermarried with incoming Normans. There is no evidence that the numbers of lesser lords declined, and they may have increased as more land was brought into cultivation. From such lesser thegns were recruited local officers, hundred and manorial reeves and huntsmen, whose successors appear in Domesday Book and, as royal government extended into the localities, were able to prosper in a modest way.

RANK AND TITLE

As we saw in the preceding chapter, ealdormen and earls were strictly speaking offices to which English kings appointed at pleasure. Individuals were moved from region to region and the counties that made up their ealdormanries could be altered. At first William the Conqueror does not seem to have envisaged changing the position of such earls as he appointed. However, two important changes did occur over time. The first was that earls tended to hold their titles in relation to single counties, and unless they were disloyal, they held for life. Secondly, after Stephen's reign the title increasingly became a mark of status rather than a substantive office. The key office in the shires had become that of sheriff.

Most of the Old English aristocracy came into the category of thegn, which encompassed a wide variety of men from king's thegns, thegns who held of greater lords, and lesser thegns.[8] The dividing line between lesser

---

[7] For the argument that eleventh-century thegns were in effect a lesser aristocracy, see J. Gillingham, 'Thegns and Knights in Eleventh-Century England: Who Was then the Gentleman?', *Transactions of the Royal Historical Society*, 6th series, 5 (1995), 129–53, reprinted in Gillingham, *The English in the Twelfth Century. Imperialism, National Identity and Political Values* (Woodbridge: Boydell Press, 2000), pp. 163–85. Amongst those who would argue that the gentry appeared in the later twelfth century, see H. M. Thomas, *Vassals, Heiresses, Crusaders and Thugs: the Knightly Class of Angevin Yorkshire, 1154–1216* (Philadelphia: University of Pennsylvania Press, 1993), p. 3; P. Coss, *The Origins of the English Gentry* (Cambridge: Cambridge University Press, 2003), pp. 1–19. Cf. D. Crouch, *The English Aristocracy 1070–1272: a Social Transformation* (New Haven, CT, and London: Yale University Press, 2011), pp. 247–50.

[8] N. P. Brooks, 'Arms, Status and Warfare in Late-Saxon England', Hill (ed.), *Ethelred the Unready*, pp. 81–103.

thegns and free peasant farmers is unclear. According to the 'Rights and Ranks of People' (Geþyncðo), probably composed by Archbishop Wulfstan, a ceorl needed five hides of land (about 600 acres), a bell (possibly for a church), and a *burh* gate plus a seat in the king's hall to be considered a thegn.[9] As always, much depended on an individual's way of life. If he trained as a warrior and lived as an aristocrat, he would probably be accepted as such by his neighbours. The payments made on a thegn's death, heriots, give a sense of what thegns were expected to have by way of equipment. The arms of a noble warrior were helmet, spear, shield, sword, and hauberk, whereas those of the ordinary free-man were spear and shield. In Cnut's second law code, clause seventy-one, the heriots of different social groups are spelled out. For the earl, it was four horses saddled and four unsaddled, four each of helmets, byrnies, and swords, and eight each of spears and shields, plus 200 gold mancuses (a unit of account equivalent to thirty pence). For the king's thegn, it was two horses saddled and two unsaddled, one helmet, one byrnie, two swords, four spears, and four shields plus fifty gold mancuses. For a lesser thegn, it was one horse saddled, one each of helmet, byrnie, sword, spear, and shield, or a payment in lieu. In the Danelaw the heriot of a king's thegn was four pounds, of a lesser thegn two pounds. The thegn 'closer to the king' owed one horse saddled and one unsaddled, a sword, two spears, and two shields plus fifty gold mancuses. Heriots seem to have been increased under Æthelred and Cnut, possibly because of the need to ensure retinues of fully equipped men.[10] Thegns were members of the shire court, they owed military service, and they were entitled to hold land granted by charter, book-land, the advantage of which was that they could dispose of it freely.[11] A word to describe a military retainer, a member of a lord's household, was *cniht*, from which the later word 'knight' was derived. It was used of the sons of nobles at the Battle of Maldon, for instance.[12] There was also the word *ridere*, one who rode. Noble warriors in Anglo-Saxon England had horses and used them on campaign.[13] What is not clear is whether they had already begun to fight using the techniques and equipment of heavily-armed cavalrymen.

[9] *English Historical Documents*, I, no. 51, p. 431.

[10] R. Lavelle, *Alfred's Wars: Sources and Interpretation of Anglo-Saxon Warfare in the Viking Age* (Woodbridge: Boydell Press, 2010), pp. 114–28.

[11] A. Williams, *The World before Domesday: the English Aristocracy 871–1066* (London: Hambledon Press Continuum, 2008), pp. 25–37.

[12] Lavelle, *Alfred's Wars*, pp. 129–39.   [13] *Ibid.*

Under the Danish kings new terms appeared. As well as earls there were stallers, those who had a seat or a stall in the king's hall. One of the best known was Ansger the Staller, who seems to have had overall charge of the defences of London in 1066.[14] Then there were housecarls, members of the military households of the Danish kings. The Normans had their own terminology for the duchy's elite. A handful of men, related to the duke, were counts, *comites*.[15] Those who were close to the duke were usually described as his *baruns* (barons) or, on one occasion, his *fideles* (sworn men).[16] The 'ordinary' warrior was usually described as a *miles* or soldier, equivalent to the Old English *cniht*.

After the Conquest Norman terms were transferred. Thus the title *comes* or count was used as the equivalent of earl, and *baro* of the king's men.[17] By the twelfth century the term *baronia* was applied to the lands held by a baron. In dealings with the king they were deemed a collective, an honour in other words, and the reliefs barons owed were not set at a fixed amount, but were negotiable.[18] In Domesday Book and in charters the term *miles* was used of men who did not hold a great deal of land.[19] In 1086 the Anglo-Saxon Chronicle reported that the Conqueror dubbed his son Henry *ridere*.[20] The combination of a version of the French word *dub* with the English *ridere* is significant, and the likelihood is that as the king's son was initiated into the ranks of riders, that this was already thought to be the most prestigious form of warfare. In the annal for 1091 the author of the Anglo-Saxon Chronicle reported that William Rufus in Normandy stationed *cnihts* in some castles and *rideres* in others.[21] The French version of *ridere* was *chevaler*, and it is clear by the way Gaimar used it in the 1130s that *chevalers* were the elite warriors.[22] These were the *cnihtas* who by the

---

[14] Abels, *Lordship and Military Obligation in Anglo-Saxon England*, pp. 160–70.

[15] C. P. Lewis, 'The Early Earls of Norman England', *Anglo-Norman Studies*, 13 (1991), 207–23.

[16] *Recueil des Actes des ducs de Normandie 911 à 1066*, ed. M. Fauroux (Caen: Caron, 1961), nos. 106, 129, 142, 195, 203 (barons), 209 (sworn men).

[17] For the king's barons in Domesday Book, see DB, I, fols. 2r (Kent), 100r (Devon) 377r (Lincs), 175v (Worcs), 238 (Warw); II, fols. 367v, 377 (Suffolk); IV (Exon), fol. 114 (Som).

[18] I. J. Sanders, *English Baronies* (Oxford: Oxford University Press, 1960), pp. v–viii.

[19] S. P. J. Harvey, 'The Knight and the Knight's Fee in England', *Past and Present*, 49 (1970), 1–43.

[20] ASC, E, 1086. M. Lieberman, 'A New Approach to the Knighting Ritual', *Speculum*, 90 (2015), 391–423.

[21] ASC, E, 1091; Gillingham, 'Thegns and Knights in Eleventh-Century England: Who Was then the Gentleman?' in Gillingham, *English in the Twelfth Century*, at p. 172.

[22] For discussion, see J. Gillingham, 'Kingship, Chivalry and Love. Political and Cultural Values in the Earliest History Written in French: Geoffrey Gaimar's *Estoire des Engleis*', C. Warren Hollister (ed.), *Anglo-Norman Political Culture and the Twelfth-Century Renaissance* (Woodbridge: Boydell Press, 1997), pp. 37–8.

later twelfth century were consolidating into a lesser aristocracy.[23] King's thegns occur in Domesday Book, but their holdings either seem to have disappeared or were held in return for ministerial services in the household or the forests, tenancies ultimately known as 'serjeanties'.

ETHOS

The core values of a warrior elite were courage, skill in war, loyalty, and generosity. These remained constant throughout our period, though the changing character of warfare was reflected in debates about the justification for war against Christians and non-Christians, about the treatment of vanquished enemies, death, or ransom, and about the customs relating to sieges, which became more prevalent as the number of castles spread. In England before 1066 soldiers are thought to have engaged the enemy on foot, though horses were used in moving from place to place. Anglo-Saxon and Scandinavian warriors used axes as well as swords, and axes in particular were used by soldiers on foot. Fighting on horseback with lances, whether used overarm as javelins or underarm, couched, was used by the Normans at Hastings, and it soon became the most prestigious method of fighting. Fighting on horseback in squadrons required different techniques, lengthy training, horses of different kinds, and servants to take care of them, reinforcing the need for wealth and contacts.

POWER OF COMMAND

At the heart of lordly power was the ability to command loyalty and obedience freely given. At its simplest this meant going to war and, if necessary, dying in battle alongside one's lord, as the members of Beortnoth's hearth-troop at the battle of Maldon were urged to do.[24] It is mainly to literary sources that we should look for depictions of the relationship between lords and men, as there was little reason to record the relationship. In Anglo-Saxon England men 'bowed down' to lords and swore oaths of loyalty. In England this was by swearing oaths and placing one's hands between the lords' hands, an act of commendation.[25] It was

---

[23] D. Crouch, *The Birth of Nobility: Constructing Aristocracy in England and France: 900–1300* (Harlow: Pearson Longman, 2005), pp. 243–8; Coss, *Origins of the English Gentry*, pp. 1–19.

[24] *Song of Maldon, English Historical Documents*, I, no. 10, pp. 319–24.

[25] Baxter, *Earls of Mercia*, pp. 204–8.

a relationship that was often exclusive but, as we see from Domesday Book, it was possible to be commended to more than one lord.[26] There was also of course the prospect of tangible rewards: men followed lords in the hope of booty and reward. The Viking *liðs* were recruited on this basis.[27] Arm rings of gold or silver were rewards and symbols of prowess.[28] Betrayal of a lord was a most serious offence. However, life was complicated and so too were loyalties, especially if loyalty to a lord clashed with that to the king. Law codes deemed treachery to the king a crime that could not be redeemed.[29] It overrode all other loyalties. By the twelfth century this was made explicit: loyalty was sworn to a lord saving loyalty to the king.[30]

Great lords with established reputations would of course be able to attract more men into their retinues. William the Conqueror attracted men from all over in 1066, according to his biographer, William of Poitiers.[31] Nevertheless, retinues were likely to break up and reform as needed: William paid off many of his knights at the end of the initial campaign in England.[32] Settling followers on land either as a reward for past service or in the expectation of future service in the longer term potentially attenuated personal ties. The scale of land distribution after 1066 in particular fundamentally changed the relationship between William the Conqueror and the secular aristocracy (see previously in this volume). The period when lords recruited their retinues from tenant families is likely to have been relatively short-lived; thereafter, as before,

[26] *Ibid.*, pp. 205–6.
[27] N. Lund, 'The Armies of Swein Forkbeard and Cnut: *leding* or *lið*?', *Anglo-Saxon England*, 15 (1986), 105–18.
[28] A. Pedersen, 'Power and Aristocracy', G. Williams, P. Pentz, and M. Wemhoff (eds.), *Vikings. Life and Legend* (London: British Museum Press, 2014), pp. 122–55, at pp. 128–9.
[29] V Atr cap. 28: anyone who deserted an army under the king's personal command was at risk of losing his wergeld; *ibid.*, cap. 30: anyone who plotted against the king was to forfeit his life. VI Atr cap. 36: desertion of the army under the king's personal command carried the risk of loss of property; *ibid.*, 37: anyone convicted of plotting against the king's life was to lose his own and all he possessed; II Cnut cap. 57: loss of life and forfeiture for those found guilty of plotting against the king or his own lord; *ibid.*, cap. 77: desertion of a lord was punished likewise. The lord was to take back land and property given to the coward, and any bookland was to pass to the king. *Ibid.*, cap. 78: the heriots of him who fell on campaign were to be pardoned. Again, Wulfstan's 'Sermon of the Wolf to the English' declared that it was a great betrayal that a man should betray his lord or drive him into exile, *English Historical Documents*, I, pp. 930–1.
[30] Glanvill began his discussion of crime with that of *lèse majesté*, book xiv, p. 171; Hudson, *Oxford History of the Laws of England*, II, p. 432.
[31] *Gesta Guillelmi*, p. 102.   [32] OV, II, p. 196.

remuneration probably took the form of cash and allowances, with new grants of land being relatively small, even if it would have been natural for lords to recruit suitable men from tenant families.

In the conflict of Stephen's reign the great magnates with their retinues formed the hard core of armies: Robert earl of Gloucester, for instance, chief commander of the empress's forces, was said to have brought more than 300 knights to England in 1142.[33] Funding such large forces was not easy: King Stephen, for instance, paid off the knights of his young rival Henry FitzEmpress in 1147.[34] The stock of disposable land and cash revenues were finite, and lords might have to seek credit from merchants or the Jews. Keeping the troops supplied during campaigns was another problem. The Anglo-Saxon Chronicler's famous description of the Anarchy in 1137 reported the torture 'castlemen' used on any suspected of having wealth.[35] Geoffrey de Mandeville's career epitomized lordly violence, as he and his men went on the rampage after his release from custody in 1143.[36] With the proliferation of charters by the 1140s, it is possible to gain an impression of the size and identity of the inner core of such retinues. William Marshal, for instance, is thought to have had a retinue of some eighteen knights, of whom twelve were not his tenants by knight service.[37]

VIOLENCE AND WAR

It is not always easy to distinguish between different levels of violence, and to distinguish them from war. Those with the power to achieve their ends by armed force could simply do so; often the threat of violence would have been sufficient. Contests for the throne were obviously a major occasion for outbreaks of violence, especially under the Danes and the Normans. Men took up arms for self-protection and also to be on the winning side in contests for power, and force was also used to settle local quarrels. The murder of Edward the Martyr was the outcome of noble factions at court. Ætheling Alfred in 1036 was blinded and died of his wounds, an act attributed to Earl Godwin and his men.[38] Archbishop Wulfstan's sermon

---

[33] *Historia Novella*, p. 128.   [34] *Gesta Stephani*, pp. 206–8.   [35] ASC, E, 1137.

[36] The classic study is J. H. Round, *Geoffrey de Mandeville* (London: Longmans, Green, 1892). For a reappraisal, see J. A. Green, 'The Charters of Geoffrey de Mandeville', P. Dalton and D. Luscombe (eds.), *Rulership and Rebellion in the Anglo-Norman World, c. 1066–c. 1216* (Farnham: Ashgate, 2015), pp. 91–110.

[37] Crouch, *William Marshal*, p. 138.

[38] ASC, C, D, 1036. The D version of the Chronicle involves Harold Godwinson; see also *Encomium Emmae Reginae*, pp. 40–7.

'The Wolf to the English' referred to the violation of churches, widows forced into marriage, men and women enslaved, stealing, and killing.[39] Even allowing for hyperbole, a dismal picture was painted of violent social dislocation. The skaldic poetry enjoyed at Cnut's court was full of martial deeds.[40] The history of the estates granted by Bishop Ealdhun of Durham with his daughter was that of a succession of tit-for-tat killings at the highest level.[41] Violence followed the arrival of the Normans at Durham: the killing of Earl Robert de Commines, of the thegn Liulf who was living at Durham with his retinue, and then those of the bishop and his two lieutenants.[42] Another story of the use of violence comes in the miracles of St Modwenna in a story that is supposed to date between 1085 and 1094. Two villeins that belonged to Burton Abbey put themselves under the protection of Roger the Poitevin, who held land in England at the time of Domesday Book. Roger's retainers fought those of the abbot. The two villeins died, but did not remain at rest, and so were exhumed and their bodies burned. Finally the rest of the villagers of Stapenhill moved to nearby Gresley.[43] The *Liber Eliensis* commented on the powerful *Ricardi* and *Gifardi* (the Clares and the Giffards) at the court of Henry I, who were responsible for many murders, but who could not be touched.[44] The 1130 pipe roll for Cornwall includes five entries relating debts in connection with the killing of the sons of Tochi. This is thought to have been the killing of six brothers mentioned by the 'house of Corineus' (the legendary founder of Cornwall) in the roughly contemporary text 'the Prophecies of Merlin'.[45]

It is impossible to know how widespread such violence was. John Hudson has argued that a powerful crown stood in the background, and that kings were able to use either force or the threat of it to maintain order

[39] *English Historical Documents*, I, pp. 929–34.
[40] R. Frank, 'King Cnut in the Verse of His Skalds', (ed. Rumble), *Reign of Cnut*, pp. 106–24; M. Townend, 'Contextualizing the Knútsdrápur: Skaldic Praise-Poetry at the Court of Cnut', *Anglo-Saxon England*, 30 (2001), 145–79, at pp. 145–6.
[41] Symeon of Durham, *De Obsessione Dunelmi*, *Opera omnia*, I, pp. 215–20; C. J. Morris, *Marriage and Murder in Eleventh-Century Northumbria: a Study of the 'De Obsessione Dunelmi'*, Borthwick Paper, 72 (1992); Fletcher, *Bloodfeud*.
[42] JW, III, pp. 32–7.
[43] Geoffrey of Burton, *Life and Miracles of St Modwenna*, ed. R. Bartlett (Oxford: Clarendon Press, 2002), pp. 192–5.
[44] *Liber Eliensis*, p. 226.
[45] *Pipe Roll 31 Henry I*, p. 126; 'Prophecies of Merlin', Geoffrey of Monmouth, *History of the Kings of Britain*, book VII, para. 113 (ed. Reeve, pp. 146–9): 'the house of Corineus will slaughter six brothers'; O. Padel, 'Geoffrey of Monmouth and Cornwall', *Cambridge Medieval Celtic Studies*, 8 (1984), 1–27.

or to provide remedies for wrongs, and that in this respect the situation in England was different from that on the continent.[46] This is true, but that does not mean that the king's authority was used in a neutral way. The misdemeanours of the Clares, for instance, must have been tolerated by Henry I. The flight of peasants before the arrival of Rufus's court is a graphic indication of the fear aroused by a swarm of rapacious courtiers.[47]

Much better documented is the violence of the 1130s and 1140s, as the Civil War was more fully reported than resistance to the Danes or to the Normans. It was not universal or continuous, but it was widespread and at times severe. There has been some attempt to downplay the level of violence, pointing to continuity in government, and the fact that only a minority of churches reported violence. Yet the signs of an escalation in violence are clear enough.[48] Castles proliferated, and were used as bases from which to pillage the surrounding areas for supplies.[49] Men were kidnapped and held to ransom.[50] There were protection rackets.[51] The chief protagonists threw their weight around. Robert of Bampton's men plundered around the castle of Bampton seizing supplies.[52] Baldwin de Redvers entered the city of Exeter in 1136 accompanied by armed soldiers, and made the local people bow down to his lordship. He based himself in the castle, which technically belonged to the king.[53]

Some castles were besieged, with attendant casualties, as at Shrewsbury in 1138.[54] There was warfare in the northern counties, chiefly before 1139, as a result of Scots' expeditions. In 1138 there was a great battle 'of the Standard' just outside Northallerton, one of the two major engagements of the reign, the other at Lincoln in 1141.[55] In 1139 the knights of Bishops Roger of Salisbury, Alexander of Lincoln, and Nigel of Ely clashed, with deaths and casualties.[56] Parts of eastern England were

[46] *Oxford History of English Laws*, II, p. 199.   [47] Eadmer, *Historia Novorum*, p. 192.
[48] See especially H. M. Thomas, 'Violent Disorder in England: a Maximum Argument', P. Dalton and G. J. White (eds.), *King Stephen's Reign 1135–1154* (Woodbridge: Boydell Press, 2008), pp. 139–70; T. N. Bisson, 'The Lure of Stephen's England: *Tenserie*, Flemings and a Crisis of Circumstance', *ibid.*, pp. 171–81.
[49] C. Coulson, 'Castles of the Anarchy' (ed. King), *Anarchy of King Stephen's Reign*, pp. 67–92.
[50] As, for instance, round Bristol, *Gesta Stephani*, p. 62.
[51] ASC, E, 1137; Robert of Bampton: *Gesta Stephani*, pp. 28–30; for Geoffrey de Mandeville, see earlier in this volume.
[52] *Gesta Stephani*, p. 30.   [53] *Ibid.*, p. 32.   [54] JW, III, p. 250.
[55] E. King, *King Stephen* (New Haven, CT, and London: Yale University Press, 2010), pp. 93, 151–2.
[56] *Gesta Stephani*, p. 76.

affected, as Bishop Nigel fortified the Isle of Ely against the king's men,[57] and then, in 1143, Geoffrey de Mandeville rebelled and pursued a violent campaign until he was fatally wounded. Miles of Gloucester assembled a great company at Gloucester of those whose lands King Stephen had ravaged.[58] By 1143 the earl of Gloucester's men were riding high, and were said from their base at Bristol to put almost half of England from sea to sea under their own ordinances.[59] This was the point in his chronicle that the author of the *Gesta Stephani* wrote of encampments near churches for protection, of famine, and of villages emptied of inhabitants with crops left in the fields. Stipendiary knights whose masters had run out of funds simply exacted money by whatever means possible.[60] For this author, attacks on churches and by churchmen were particularly regrettable. He was also clear about the way some of the combatants, like Ranulf earl of Chester, usurped royal lands and rights.[61] William of Malmesbury, like the authors of the *Gesta Stephani* and the Anglo-Saxon Chronicle, painted a graphic picture of the 'brutalities of war': castles filled with plundering knights, kidnappings, and attacks on churches.[62] So too did Henry of Huntingdon.[63]

The conclusion of a peace treaty and the accession of Henry II was not followed by an immediate cessation of conflict. However, over time the balance slowly tilted away from the more extreme episodes seen in the war. Some of the leading combatants died in 1152 and 1153, like King David, Ranulf, earl of Chester, and, above all, Stephen's son Eustace. The determination of Archbishop Theobald that Eustace should not be crowned in his father's lifetime made it difficult for Stephen's party to look to the future, whereas Henry FitzEmpress, by now master of Normandy and his wife's great inheritance of Aquitaine, was a better prospect. Finally, the terms of the peace treaty had laid down a clear principle about tenure: that the clock was to be turned back to the time of King Henry. Henry was determined, further, to offer remedies against forcible disseisin without legal procedure. Those who had been thrown off their land could now purchase a royal writ to determine the answers to key questions. A further stage came when Henry strengthened the position of heirs against lords who wished to deny them possession. The popularity of the new legal procedures did not remove feud and self-help, as Paul Hyams has shown, though feud is harder to detect within the framework

[57] *Ibid.*, p. 98.   [58] *Ibid.*, p. 94.   [59] *Ibid.*, pp. 148–50.   [60] *Ibid.*, pp. 152–4.
[61] *Ibid.*, pp. 184, 192.   [62] *Historia Novella*, pp. 70–2.
[63] HH, pp. 710, 724, 730–2, 742.

of the new procedures.[64] This may reflect the state of affairs, but there are other points to bear in mind, such as the lack of much contemporary writing, and the fact that as yet we know little about the detailed politics of the reign.

POLITICAL CONTEXT: VIOLENCE AGAINST THE KING

Given disputed successions, it was usually possible to frame an argument that the occupant of the throne was not the rightful king, thus implicitly making armed opposition lawful. In 1066 the Normans claimed that Harold Godwinson had perjured himself by taking the throne, whereas William the Conqueror was the Confessor's rightful heir.[65] In 1087 William Rufus succeeded his father, though not the eldest son, because his father had bequeathed the throne to him.[66] This argument could not be used for the accession of Henry I in 1100. Here the argument seems to have been that Henry alone of the Conqueror's sons had been 'born in the purple' after his father had become king.[67] In 1135 Stephen's supporters claimed that Henry I had bequeathed the throne to Stephen despite having had the magnates earlier swear an oath of allegiance to his daughter, the empress.[68] In 1154 Henry II succeeded because he had been adopted as Stephen's heir in the peace treaty of 1153.[69] The coronation of Henry's eldest son, the Young King, in 1170 in his father's lifetime placed the magnates of England in unprecedented circumstances. The Young King claimed the reality as well as the promise of power, and it seemed that many English magnates were prepared to accept this premise and went to war against Henry II in 1173–4.[70]

---

[64] P. R. Hyams, *Rancor and Reconciliation in Medieval England* (Ithaca, NY, and London: Cornell University Press, 2003), chapter 6.

[65] The clearest statement of the Norman position is in William of Poitiers, *Gesta Guillelmi*, pp. 18–20, 68–70, 102, 118–22.

[66] R. Sharpe, '1088: William II and the Rebels', *Anglo-Norman Studies*, 26 (2003), 139–57; N. Strevett, 'The Anglo-Norman Civil War of 1101 Reconsidered', *Ibid.*, 159–75.

[67] OV, V, pp. 290–3.

[68] John of Salisbury claimed that Henry had nominated Stephen on his deathbed, *Historia Pontificalis*, ed. M. Chibnall (London, Edinburgh, Paris, Melbourne, and Toronto: Thomas Nelson, 1956), pp. 83–6; cf. *Liber Eliensis*, p. 285. For discussion, Crouch, *Reign of King Stephen*, pp. 30–7.

[69] J. C. Holt, '1153', King (ed.), *Anarchy of King Stephen's Reign*, pp. 291–316; reprinted in Holt, *Colonial England*, pp. 161–78; Garnett, *Conquered England*, chapter 4.

[70] A. Heslin, 'The Coronation of the Young King', G. J. Cuming (ed.), *Studies in Church History*, II (1965), pp. 165–78; M. Strickland, 'On the Instruction of a Prince: the

There were other situations where opposition could not be so easily justified. On what basis in 1013 did Earl Uhtred and the Northumbrians submit to Swein of Denmark, followed by all the men north of Watling Street, then Ealdorman Æthelmaer and the western thegns, and, finally, the Londoners, given that Æthelred was living?[71] Then after Swein's death his son Cnut was chosen king 'by the fleet', and Æthelred was recalled 'by the counsellors'. Tensions between Æthelred and his son Edmund Ironside resulted in a three-cornered struggle, in which Eadric Streona changed sides, supporting Edmund (his brother-in-law), then Cnut, then Edmund, and finally the successful claimant to the throne, Cnut.[72] For the Anglo-Saxon Chronicler, Eadric was the arch traitor. His changes of side were doubtless made simply to survive, given that he had made powerful enemies, including the kin of Ælfgifu, Cnut's first wife, and that of Edmund's wife. How he rationalized his actions is unknown, and of course he was eventually put to death on Cnut's orders.

Fast-moving events between 1013 and 1016 presented magnates with difficult choices. By comparison with the early eleventh century there is more information about the way changes of allegiance could be justified in Stephen's reign. Earl Robert of Gloucester commissioned William of Malmesbury to write the *Historia Novella*, a text which reflects the kind of arguments used to present the earl's conduct in the best light. Robert swore the oath of allegiance to the empress in 1126, but (according to William) performed homage to Stephen on condition the king maintained his rank and kept the agreement between them.[73] By 1138 things had come to such a pass that the earl had renounced his homage.[74] A second occasion when the succession to the throne was not straightforward was in 1141, when Stephen, to whom allegiance had been sworn, was in prison and the empress and her supporters were agitating for the recognition of her claim to succeed her father. Once again it is in the *Historia Novella* that the grounds for a transfer of loyalty are laid out. Bishop Henry of Winchester, King Stephen's brother, called a legatine council. He announced that when the old king had died, it was important for a successor to be chosen, hence Stephen succeeded.[75] Stephen broke the promises he had made to the church and through the judgement of God had been delivered to his enemies. Bishop Henry in his capacity as papal

Upbringing of Henry, the Young King', in Harper-Bill and Vincent (eds.), *Henry II. New Interpretations*, pp. 184–214, at pp. 205–7.
[71] ASC, C, D, E, 1013.   [72] *Ibid.*, 1015.   [73] WM, *Historia Novella*, pp. 8, 30–2.
[74] *Ibid.*, p. 40.   [75] *Ibid.*, pp. 90–6.

legate had called a council. The clergy, 'whose special prerogative it is to choose and consecrate a prince', had chosen the empress as lady of England. What William could not disguise was that dissenting voices, those of the Londoners and the queen's representative, were heard. Judgement of excommunication was passed on some of the wrongdoers, but the council broke up without, it seems, coming to a clear conclusion.

The view we have of political society and the role of the aristocracy tends to be conditioned by the ecclesiastical perspective of most commentators. Kings were depicted as peace-loving, and when they used force it was supposed to be to punish wrongdoers. Lords who took action against kings were thus shown as disruptive and rebels, though this was clearly not how they saw themselves. A glimpse of an alternative perspective is gained by the late twelfth-century Battle Abbey Chronicle, when the author placed in the mouth of Richard de Lucy, the abbot's brother, a speech addressed to the king about the history of the abbey 'elevated to the highest rank by you and by all us Normans. Robert earl of Leicester and others then called out that the king should preserve the abbey as if it were his crown, and all the property of their kinsmen.'[76] On a later occasion Richard made a similar appeal to the king, referring to the Battle of Hastings by which William the Conqueror had gained the crown and had given estates and riches to the magnates, whose successors now asked Henry to maintain the abbey's privileges.[77] The speeches were obviously devised for a particular situation, but the link made there between the importance of Hastings for both the crown and the magnates is significant.

JUSTICE AND POLICE

There is much less evidence about lords' powers of justice and police than about royal justice. Kings and their advisers throughout this period were vocal about their role in peacekeeping and punishing crime, so we tend to see lords' powers through a distorting prism. Many disputes, especially those which did not involve land, are likely to have gone unreported. There has been scepticism about how commonly lords had their own courts before 1066, though they certainly received fines from those of their men who were punished for serious offences.[78] Rights of sake and soke, toll, team, and infangthief included in grants of land involved the

---

[76] *Chronicle of Battle Abbey*, pp. 178–80.   [77] *Ibid.*, pp. 180–2.
[78] Hudson, *Oxford History of English Laws*, II, p. 61.

right to hold courts, to take tolls, and to supervise sales. These were enjoyed by men of high status on the eve of the Norman Conquest, but later those who granted land could grant the rights in turn to their men.[79] The creation of local tithing groups to act as pledges and guarantors for producing their fellows in court interlocked with lords' duties to discipline their men, and in many tithings members must have all been men of the same lord. By the twelfth century sheriffs had the duty of inspecting such groups twice each year.

The rise of royal justice in the twelfth century meant a certain amount of retrospective justification where seigneurial justice was concerned, so that it was represented as delegated or franchisal. In practice lords' powers had existed before the creation of hundreds or before outlying areas had been subjected to royal authority. Thus, for instance, estates held by bishops and abbeys with attached hundreds in Domesday Book in some cases had been in their possession probably before the creation of hundreds. There were no hundreds or their northern equivalent, wapentakes, in large parts of northern England, and here local lords had wide-ranging responsibilities for justice and policing.[80]

The overall trend in our period seems to be that whilst the crown asserted greater power over serious offences and more important land disputes, at the local level more hundred courts passed into private hands. From the king's point of view, it made sense anyway to allow lords to deal with misdemeanours and local land disputes, even if this meant lords arrogated powers over freemen as well as their own tenants in a hundred. Lords retained key powers in the twelfth century over granting land. For instance, they could distrain land for non-performance of service, and they could challenge title on the death of a tenant, but the introduction of assizes of novel disseisin and *mort d'ancestor* provided remedies against their arbitrary use of these powers. Ultimately they worked towards greater security for tenants, though pipe roll evidence indicates that in the early years they were used by lords against tenants as well as tenants against lords.

LORDS AND LAND

Some of the most important changes in lordship during this period were in the relationship between lords and land, not just in the way great fortunes

[79] D. Roffe, 'From Thegnage to Barony: Sake and Soke, Title and Tenants-in-Chief', *Anglo-Norman Studies*, 12 (1990), 157–76.
[80] For a summary, see Hudson, *Oxford History of English Laws*, II, pp. 562–5.

were made and dissipated through war and conflict, but in the way land was managed. One long-term trend was the breaking up of relatively large territories, sometimes known as shires, into smaller units, often with resident manorial lords. This process in turn was often associated with the laying out of open fields and nucleated villages. The impulse may have come from peasants rather than lords, but lords obviously stood to benefit from rising agrarian yields and by investment, for instance, in mills and drainage. The different aspects of what was a lengthy and complex process lie outside this chapter, but we should note that, in many ways, what was happening was in effect a territorialization of lordship: a lord's rights and obligations were increasingly tied to a specific piece of land.

Secondly, family strategies towards land evolved. The need to preserve the landed resources of the family across the generations led to one son, usually the eldest, being prioritized over younger sons and daughters who thus had smaller shares in the inheritance. Again this is likely to have been a long-term trend: unless families had ample resources, or other ways of providing for all their children, there was an obvious impulse towards restricting the pool of heirs. The fact that all the English land granted out by William the Conqueror was defined as fiefs in which the king retained a paramount interest strengthened what might have been thought of as a natural tendency towards male primogeniture. Strengthening lineage was reflected in turn in the adoption of hereditary surnames, and some of these were derived from place names, again linking lordship and place. What is striking about England after 1066 is the way such toponyms were derived from places in northern France, especially Normandy.[81]

Another such restriction was the consequence of the church's emphasis on the sacramental character of marriage. True marriages could only be made between partners who were free to marry and gave their consent freely, and increasingly only children born of legitimate marriages were thought to have had rights of inheritance.[82] This obviously raised a question mark over the succession of William the Conqueror in Normandy. The degrees of kinship and affinity within which marriage was prohibited were tightened up in the later eleventh century by reformers keen to eradicate any suspicion that marriage partners were too closely related. The sons of clerical wives or concubines were marginalized.

---

[81] J. C. Holt, *What's in a Name? Family Nomenclature and the Norman Conquest*, Stenton Lecture 1981 (Reading, 1982).

[82] G. Duby, *Medieval Marriage: Two Models from Twelfth-Century France* (Baltimore, MD, and London: Johns Hopkins University Press, 1978), pp. 25–81.

The establishment of church courts meant that the validity of contested unions where lands were concerned could be challenged, as the famous lawsuit of Richard of Anstey was to show. In 1158 Richard claimed the inheritance of his maternal uncle William de Sackville against William's daughter Mabel. He argued that Mabel was illegitimate because her parents' marriage had been annulled on the grounds of her father's pre-contract to someone else. Details of the case survive, including an account of Richard's expenses as the case proceeded, eventually reaching the pope, who ruled in Richard's favour.[83]

Title to land, who could inherit, what, and on what terms were critical questions for landed families, and views about how they were to be answered and disputes resolved changed over time. Title to land could be disputed: churches were particularly tenacious in pursuing claims to lands and churches which they had been given, and in the process documentation and the recourse to courts proved increasingly important. Donations might be recorded in wills, but wills were predicated on the idea that lands could be so given, which was not the case after 1066.[84] Grants of land by the king might be made verbally or reinforced by the issue of writs, but these might be challenged.[85] Lords found that charters particularly were useful as evidence of title, terms, and conditions, although not strictly essential as proof.

Over time the broad outlines of customs in relation to land and inheritance clarified. The position of women as heiresses, wives, and widows was of critical importance. Daughters were provided for both by their own families and those of their husbands, but the possibility that they would be able to transmit much more as heiresses meant that they could make their husbands millionaires. The second marriage of William Marshal in 1189 was a classic case in point, and when he was granted permission to marry Isabel, his first act was to rush to secure her lands, and then her person.[86] The possibility of an heiress meant that the king could use her marriage to reward one of his own men, which in turn might mean that lands would pass to an outsider. This concern lay behind the clauses

---

[83] In fact, Richard's mother had a sister, and in the next generation her descendant successfully claimed a half share in the inheritance, Paul Brand, 'Anstey, Richard of (c.1137–1194/5)', *ODNB* www.oxforddnb.com/view/article/92468, accessed 20 May 2016.

[84] L. Tollerton, *Wills and Will-Making in Anglo-Saxon England* (York: York Medieval Press, 2005).

[85] R. Fleming, *Domesday Book and the Law: Society and Legal Custom in Early Medieval England* (Cambridge: Cambridge University Press, 1998), pp. 53–67.

[86] *History of William Marshal*, lines 9364–9539.

in Henry I's Charter of Liberties that when there was an heiress, the king would act on the advice of his barons before disposing of her in marriage.[87] Henry was prepared to accept extremely large proffers for permission to marry some heiresses, as entries in the 1130 pipe roll show.[88] By the third decade of the reign the idea that daughters should share the inheritance, rather than one being sole heiress, had gained ground. Thereafter this became the norm in English law, though the shares were not necessarily equal.[89]

If an heiress died childless, then in practice her land reverted to her natal family: only if there were children did her lands remain in the custody of their guardian. What happened in the case of children surviving from different marriages? Cnut had two sons by his marriage to Ælfgifu of Northampton (Swein and Harold Harefoot), and a son (Harthacnut) and a daughter (Gunnhildr) by Emma, who had had two sons (Alfred and Edward) and a daughter (Godgifu) by her first marriage, to Æthelred. It is not clear whether Cnut's first marriage was ever formally recognized by the church or set aside at the time of his second marriage, but Cnut evidently recognized Swein as his son and he was sent to rule Norway with his mother. Harold Harefoot succeeded him in England, and it was only when Harold died that Harthacnut succeeded in his turn. In 1035 Emma seems to have rated Harthacnut's chances of success higher than those of Alfred, who was dispatched when he arrived in England. By 1042, however, the decks had been cleared for the succession of Edward. Cnut's daughter Gunnhildr married outside the kingdom, as did Emma's daughter. What determined the succession in turn of Harold Harefoot, Harthacnut, and Edward arguably had more to do with the support of the great men they could command than the church's view of lawful marriage, or any agreement made with Emma at the time of her second marriage.[90]

Marriages of course rarely lasted long because of (by modern standards) high death rates. The position of widows was particularly important in an era of high casualty rates of lay lords. Marriage to a wealthy widow was one obvious way of acquiring land, and around the first millennium Archbishop Wulfstan's writings show concern about their

---

[87] Stubbs, *Select Charters*, p. 118.

[88] E.g. Robert de Vere accounted for £135 for his wife and her land, and Hugh of Eu owed 300 marks of silver to marry the daughter of Richard Engaine with Richard's land and forest office, *Pipe Roll 31 Henry I*, pp. 50, 67.

[89] Green, *Aristocracy of Norman England*, pp. 377–82.

[90] For Emma's view that her son by Cnut was to inherit, see *Encomium Emmae Reginae*, pp. 32–3.

situation. From the church's point of view, it was preferable that men and women should only marry once, but if they were widowed and remarried, it was to be on certain conditions. Widows were to remain unmarried for a year and then could remarry according to their own choice.[91] If they did remarry within the year, they were to lose their morning-gifts (given by their husbands on the morning after) and chattels, and their second husband had to pay a *wergeld*, the sum equivalent to their value.[92] Wulfstan's concern may, as has been suggested, reflect the immediate circumstances of his day as widows were vulnerable to being pressurized into speedy remarriages.[93] The stipulation about no remarriage for a widow within a year, on pain of losing one's land, then freedom to remarry and then take the marriage portion and dower from the first marriage to the second, was stated in Henry I's Charter of Liberties.[94] In the *Leges Henrici Primi* once again widows were allowed to remarry freely after a year, but if they remarried within the year, they were to lose their marriage portions and chattels.[95] Husbands either had to specify the provision they were prepared to make for their wives at the church door, or if widowed a woman could claim up to a third.[96] Given that women were so important in family strategies, but also in some respects wild cards, the question of the extent of their rights over their lands was crucial. Did they have the right to dispose of land, or did they need to secure the consent of their relatives? By the twelfth century it seems that grants by women were usually made with the consent of the heir, presumably to prevent reckless alienation.[97] Moreover, kings had considerable latitude over arrangements for the marriages and guardianship of the womenfolk of their tenants-in-chief, but they did not have to exact large sums. In this respect the apparent restraint of Henry II compared with Henry I and King John is striking.

LORDS AND PEASANTS

Relationships between lords and peasants were as diverse as their geographical location and settlement histories. At one end of the spectrum was

[91] Wulfstan, *Institutes of Polity* 189–95 (ed. Jost), pp. 132–5; *Political Writings of Archbishop Wulfstan of York* (trans. Rabin), p. 121; VI Atr 26.
[92] II Cnut, cap. 73.
[93] S. Hollis, '"The Protection of God and the King": Wulfstan's Legislation on Widows' (ed. Townend), *Wulfstan of York* (Turnhout: Brepols, 2004), pp. 443–60.
[94] Stubbs, *Select Charters*, p. 118.   [95] *Leges Henrici Primi*, cap. 11, 13; 11, 13a.
[96] Green, *Aristocracy of Norman England*, pp. 367–70.
[97] Hudson, *Oxford History of the Laws of England*, II, p. 447.

a substantial slave population, seen especially on estates with large demesnes. At the other were legally free, rent-paying peasants, particularly numerous in East Anglia. Between was a mass of peasantry, many of whom owed labour services, that is, they provided labour for the lord's share of the estate as well as farming their own. Local conditions obviously determined the amount of land devoted to crop growing and pasture, and geography and environmental conditions played a part in determining village and field forms. With such variety in mind, is it possible to detect any general trends which affected relationships between lords and peasants?

One trend noted previously was the breakup of many large territories into smaller units. Another was the laying out of open fields, often associated with nucleated villages, the classic manor of much of midland England. Rising population, too, was reflected in the expansion of settlements with more land being brought under the plough. These trends in theory should have benefited peasants as well as lords: more children were likely to have survived to adulthood, more crops were being grown and animals reared. Cutting across these developments, however, were different ways of life and customary ways of managing resources. The greatest lords like the king had widely dispersed estates and an itinerant way of life. Food renders were needed near their principal residences, but elsewhere cash was probably more convenient. At times substantial sums of money were needed, in their dealings with the king, or, in the twelfth century, for participation in a crusade, or for building new and expensive castles. For the most part such lords are thought to have been *rentiers*, that is, they rented out their estates to middlemen who paid fixed farms, either in food or cash or both. This suited lords in settled times for their income was fixed, but any profit obviously went to the lessee. Minor lords with only one or two estates were clearly more likely to manage them directly and to live on the spot.

Peasants were on the receiving end of war and violence, as well as of famine and disease, usually recorded only laconically in the Anglo-Saxon Chronicle. There is relatively little detailed information there about casualties during the Danish attacks of the late tenth and early eleventh centuries, or about the effects of Æthelred's ravaging of Cumberland in 1000.[98] By contrast chroniclers had much more to say about the victims of the Normans and the Scots, and of the conflicts of Stephen's reign. The harrying of the north by William the Conqueror resulted in death

[98] ASC, E, 1000.

and flight of peasants, whose bodies were found at the roadside as they tried to escape.[99] For the chronicler Orderic Vitalis, the Conqueror's actions in the north were shameful.[100] When Scots raided northern England they carried off women and children as slaves, as well as cattle.[101] The local conflicts of Stephen's reign involved peasants, as Hugh Thomas noted.[102]

A second trend was the change in status of the most unfree peasants, usually known as the transition from slavery to serfdom. Slavery was still very much a feature of English society at the start of our period. The most common word for a slave was the Old English word *þeow*, but in Æthelred's reign the Scandinavian word *þrael* and the word *wealh* are also found.[103] The legal status of the slave may have differed from that of his counterpart in the late Roman Empire, for the Old English evidence suggests that although lords had very extensive rights over their slaves, those rights were not absolute.[104] John Hudson has pointed out that the question of freedom in relation to whom, the king or the lord, has to be addressed, and that rather than trying to establish a clear distinction between the slave and the serf, it might be more accurate to think in terms of evolutionary change.[105] It is worth keeping in mind a distinction between slaves as an element in estate personnel and those who were captured or sold into slavery. Domesday Book reveals a substantial number of *servi*, a word usually translated as *slaves*, probably even more than reported.[106] Their numbers may already have been declining, as Christians were encouraged to free their slaves as a pious deathbed act.

Moreover, there was opposition to the sale of Christian slaves outside the country.[107] Archbishop Wulfstan's 'Sermon of the Wolf to the English' condemned the sale of poor people out of the country and the

[99] Symeon of Durham, *Historia Regum, Opera omnia*, II, p. 188.

[100] OV, II, pp. 230–2.

[101] Richard of Hexham, *Chronicles of the Reigns of Stephen, Henry II and Richard I*, III, pp. 156–7; John of Hexham continuation to *Historia Regum*, Symeon of Durham, *Opera omnia*, II, pp. 290–1.

[102] Thomas, 'Violent Disorder in King Stephen's England: a Maximum Argument', Dalton and White (eds.), *King Stephen's Reign 1135–1154*, p. 155.

[103] Hudson, *Oxford History of the Laws of England*, II, p. 213.   [104] *Ibid.*, p. 215.

[105] *Oxford History of the Laws of England*, II, pp. 425–8. For the Anglo-Saxon period, see *ibid.*, pp. 212–18.

[106] H. B. Clarke, 'Domesday Slavery (Adjusted for Slaves)', *Midland History*, 1 (1972), 37–46; J. S. Moore, 'Domesday Slavery', *Anglo-Norman Studies*, 11 (1988), 191–220.

[107] 7 Atr, 2, 3; 5; 2 Cn, 3; Liebermann, *Die Gesetze der Angelsachen*, I, pp. 260–1, 310–11.

enslavement of children for petty theft.[108] Yet the slave trade continued in the early eleventh century. The Vikings were still heavily involved. Gytha, wife of Earl Godwin, was said to have bought slaves in England and sent them off to her native Denmark.[109] The source of the story is William of Malmesbury, who was hostile to Godwin's family, but perhaps credible on this point. Some of the companions of the Ætheling Alfred, who was killed in 1036, were said to have been sold into slavery.[110] Bishop Wulfstan of Worcester went to Bristol to preach against the slave trade to Ireland.[111] The sale of slaves outside the country was condemned at the Ecclesiastical Council at Westminster.[112] Nevertheless, Welsh and Scots raiders continued to carry off captives. For instance, many were said to have been enslaved in the disorder in Wales in 1136.[113] Queen Margaret of Scotland was said to have deplored the practice and to have paid to free slaves when she could.[114]

The sale of slaves seems gradually to have died away in the twelfth century.[115] Various factors seem to have been at work. One may well have been the church's disapproval. Another was economic pragmatism: it may have been more practicable to settle slaves on parcels of land on the manor than to feed and house them. It has also been argued that the Normans regarded the capture and ownership of female slaves in particular differently from the warrior elite, both English and Scandinavian, of pre-Conquest England.[116] For whatever reason, the term *servus* came to mean not slave in the older sense, but a serf, one who was personally unfree.[117]

Those who owed labour services in return for shares in the open fields of the village, the *villani*, fell into the jurisdiction of their lords' courts, outside the king's courts and those of shire and hundred, unless charged with crime. They paid succession payments, heriots, to the lord and merchet, a fine for the marriage of their daughters. Historians are divided about the speed and timing of this change. Some would argue that the

---

[108] *English Historical Documents*, I, pp. 928–44.
[109] WM, *Gesta Regum Anglorum*, I, pp. 362–3.   [110] ASC, C, 1036.
[111] WM, *Saints' Lives: Lives of Saints Wulfstan, Dunstan, Patrick, Benignus and Indract*, ed. and trans. M. Winterbottom and R. M. Thomson (Oxford: Clarendon Press, 2002), pp. 100–2.
[112] *Councils and Synods*, I part 2, p. 678.   [113] JW, III, p. 220.
[114] *Life of St Margaret*, Huneycutt, *Margaret of Scotland*, p. 172.
[115] *Vita S. Brigide Abbatissae Kildariensis*, cited J. Gillingham, *Conquest, Catastrophe and Recovery: Britain and Ireland 1066–1485* (London: Vintage, 2014), p. 1.
[116] D. Wyatt, *Slaves and Warriors in Medieval Britain and Ireland, 800–1200* (Leiden, Boston: Brill, 2009).
[117] Hudson, *Oxford History of English Laws*, II, pp. 424–8.

Norman Conquest facilitated the tightening of lords' controls over peasants on their land.[118] Others see the development of classic villein tenure as a much more gradual process.[119] By the early twelfth century lords could obtain a royal writ of naifty (from the French form of *nativus*, a native) for the return of absconding peasants.[120] Common law procedures were to make the distinction between the free and the unfree man critical: only the former had access to the new forms of action. The power of lords of the land, whether the king, lay, or ecclesiastical lords, meant that the legal system worked against peasants. Nevertheless the opening up of new land for settlement and the possibility of migration to towns, and with it the prospect of freedom, cannot be discounted. Peasants were not simply victims.

This then was an age of aristocracy, when fortunes could be made and lost in a generation. Families might find themselves with too many children, or not enough. Wealth streamed into and out of their households: it was accrued, displayed, and spent. How far lords grew *proportionately* richer in this period is not clear, nor indeed whether this would have been an issue. Some lords clearly did keep a close watch on the profitability of their lands. Ernulf de Hesdin is a well-known example of a Domesday lord of this kind. However, it has been argued from Domesday evidence that most lords of that era were rentiers, preferring to lease out their estates and, where possible, squeezing their free tenants for higher rents and services.[121] It has been pointed out that rents (*firmae*) tended to remain stable in the twelfth century.[122] Lords might have little incentive to renegotiate farms if their incomes were greatly in excess of their needs. Yet if they were not getting a greater share of available wealth, we are entitled to wonder if the lessees were.

CONCLUSION

Lordship was pervasive in English society throughout our period. It formed the basis of relations between the more and less powerful,

[118] Faith, *English Peasantry and the Growth of Lordship*, chapter 8.
[119] *Ibid.*, chapter 10; P. Vinogradoff, *Villainage in England: Essays in English Medieval History* (Oxford: Clarendon Press, 1892); Hyams, *Kings, Lords and Peasants in Medieval England*.
[120] Van Caenegem, *Royal Writs in England*, pp. 336–44.
[121] Harvey, 'The Extent and Profitability of Demesne Agriculture in England in the later Eleventh Century', Aston, Coss, Dyer, and Thirsk (eds.), *Social Relations and Ideas: Essays in Honour of R. H. Hilton*, pp. 45–72.
[122] C. Dyer, *Making a Living in the Middle Ages. The People of Britain 850–1520* (London: Penguin, 2003), p. 121.

both warriors and peasants. A lord's relations with his followers were created and sustained by oaths. Loyalty and service were freely given to lords. Personal worth was judged by honour and shame. The relationship was created by rituals involving bowing and oath swearing. It was sustained by comradeship and the hope of glory and gain. However, lordship was also exercised over peasants, the slaves, serfs, and *villani* who tilled and were tied to the land. Although the essentials of lordship remained unchanged, we have seen major shifts in the composition of the lordly class in terms of people, ethnicity, and language. Lords were *par excellence* warriors, yet the most prestigious mode of fighting, as a mounted warrior, led to different equipment and training. The legitimacy of war against different enemies, unbelievers and Christians, for and against the king, affected the way the use of force was justified. We have seen important changes in relation to lordship and land: ownership gave way to tenure, which came to be more precisely defined, as did rights of inheritance. Above all the relationship between the aristocracy and the crown evolved. Lords had to accept the intervention of the king in their affairs, as they in turn had rights over the lands of their men. Lords increasingly had to take account of the king's power as the dispenser of patronage. Lords could operate independently of the crown, but it was increasingly dangerous to do so.

5

Archbishops, Bishops, and Abbots

The role of archbishops and bishops in English society was and remained seminal in our period, but their functions, the range of powers at their disposal, and the way they were exercised changed considerably. So too did the kind of men appointed, for by the twelfth century there were few monks or representatives of royal or noble families. Successful diocesans were by this time administrators and managers, capable of overseeing great building works, as well as fulfilling their pastoral missions. The role of abbots of the richer houses, for example, Bury St Edmunds, was not entirely dissimilar: though their primary function was as heads of the monastic community, landed wealth and private hundreds gave them important responsibilities in the locality. By contrast the powers of abbesses, even of richer houses, went largely unrecorded.

Evidence about ecclesiastics is plentiful, both in terms of the way archbishops and bishops should and actually did behave. Abundant hagiographical texts, about both contemporary and past figures, are more than collections of clichés and indicate authorial concerns about the church in their own day. The writings of Ælfric and Wulfstan, homilies, treatises, and law codes offer further insights, as do the tracts *Episcopus* and those in the Anglo-Norman Anonymous collection, Anglo-Saxon law codes, and the records of ecclesiastical councils. For the second half of the period there are growing numbers of charters and mandates and letter collections, notably those of successive popes, Herbert Losinga bishop of Norwich, Gilbert Foliot abbot of Gloucester and successively bishop of Hereford and London, Archbishops Lanfranc, Anselm, and Becket, and John of Salisbury. Charters and mandates reflect a growing reliance on documents to record transactions to do with land, tithes, and the induction of local

125

priests. Letters are texts chosen for preservation, but are nevertheless illuminating about their authors' agenda.

Two preliminary points need to be made. The power churchmen exercised was different from that of laymen. Ordained and consecrated churchmen were thought to be the channels of God's power on earth. By the twelfth century contemporary chroniclers wrote of the all too human frailties of individual bishops, but did not deny the authority vested in their office. Many bishops and abbots exemplified Christian ideals in their way of life, and as living symbols of sanctity they could convey the Christian message. Those who came to be venerated as saints very often were charismatic personalities who made strong impressions on those with whom they came into contact. They were living points of contact between Christians and the heavenly hierarchy, especially those saints whose mantles they had inherited. Bishops were supposed to travel round their dioceses, conducting confirmations, dedicating churches, and preaching to the faithful. By the eleventh century there was a complication in that some – almost all by the late eleventh century – bishops were not native English speakers. The biography of Wulfstan bishop of Worcester by William of Malmesbury (based on a lost text by Coleman) emphasizes his pastoral work, especially his preaching, perhaps having in mind that he was the last surviving Englishman who was a bishop and could speak to the mass of the people in their own language.[1] Bishops and abbots who preached to monastic communities may have preached in French or Latin, and their sermons would have been written down in Latin, but sermons delivered in cathedrals were presumably in English, though we cannot know for certain.[2]

Secondly, the context within which they operated was different: bishops and abbots had an allegiance to the pope as well as to the king. At the start of our period papal authority was venerated, but the papacy was relatively distant. Contacts were chiefly through visits to Rome by archbishops for their *pallia*, by pilgrims, and by requests for the payment known as Peter's Pence. However, when Leo IX summoned a synod at Rome in 1050, representatives were sent from England.[3] William the Conqueror, having solicited papal acquiescence for his invasion of 1066,

---

[1] WM, *Saints' Lives: Lives of SS Dunstan, Patrick, Benignus and Indract, Wulfstan*, pp. 1–155.
[2] E.g. when Becket preached in Canterbury Cathedral on Christmas Day 1170, Herbert of Bosham, *Materials for the History of Thomas Becket*, III, p. 484.
[3] ASC, C, D, E, 1050.

allowed papal legates into the country in 1070 to impose penances and to deal with Archbishop Stigand.[4] Relations between the English church and the papacy subsequently grew more problematic. Disputed papal elections and the strength of the king's hold over the English church made it possible for a time to evade recognizing a pope.[5] That situation could not last. The disputes over the Canterbury primacy, and claims of exempt status by monasteries, brought more appeals to Rome. In 1125 Henry I was obliged to allow a papal legate to hold a council in England, something which he had avoided until that point.[6]

A way round the issue of legates was for the pope to appoint English prelates as legate rather than sending someone from Rome.[7] The growth of appeals to Rome made it necessary to delegate papal jurisdiction to judges delegate.[8] Bishops, chapters, and monasteries sought papal privileges to confirm their churches and possessions. The upsurge in activity meant that English churchmen needed expertise in the law of the church. Archbishop Lanfranc led the way with his collection of canon law, based on Pseudo-Isidore.[9] Other early collections, such as those by Burchard of Worms, Ivo of Chartres, and Gratian, were known in England.[10] Englishmen went abroad to study Roman and canon law and brought back their expertise. To talk of the pope's power over the English church is a misnomer: popes had to work with kings, and, so far as the first three Norman kings were concerned, they faced powerful territorial rulers. Alexander III had to be very careful not to push Henry II too far over the Becket dispute, because of his difficulties vis-à-vis the emperor. On the whole kings found popes useful allies who usually did not obstruct their own rights of patronage. There were of course two major sticking points: Henry I's resistance to the demand he surrender homage and investiture,

[4] *Councils and Synods*, I, Part 2, pp. 563–84.   [5] *Ibid.*, pp. 730–41.
[6] M. Brett, *The English Church under Henry I* (Oxford: Oxford University Press, 1975), pp. 34–50.
[7] H. Tillmann, *Die Päpstlichen Legaten in England bis zur beendigung der Legation Gualas (1218)* (Bonn: H. Ludwig, 1926).
[8] Duggan, 'Papal Judges Delegate and the Making of the "New Law" in the Twelfth Century', T. N. Bisson (ed.), *Cultures of Power*, pp. 172–99.
[9] M. Gullick, 'Lanfranc and the Oldest Manuscript of the Collectio Lanfranci', B. C. Brasington and K. G. Cushing (eds.), *Bishops, Texts and the Use of Canon Law around 1100: Essays in Honour of Martin Brett* (Aldershot: Ashgate, 2008), pp. 79–90.
[10] R. H. Helmholz, *Oxford History of the Laws of England. I. The Canon Law and Ecclesiastical Jurisdiction from 597 to the 1640s* (Oxford: Oxford University Press, 2004), chapter 2; S. Kuttner and E. Rathbone, 'Anglo-Norman Canonists of the Twelfth Century: an Introductory Study', *Traditio*, 7 (1949–51), 279–358; Duggan, 'Roman, Canon and Common Law in Twelfth-Century England'.

and his grandson's attempts to roll back an increasing tide of appeals to Rome. In both cases personalities complicated the issues: Anselm's strict adherence to the papal decrees on homage and investiture, and Becket's refusal to bend to the wishes of Henry II.

STRUCTURE

At the start of our period two archbishoprics existed, Canterbury in the south and York in the north. Henry of Winchester had plans for a third province based at Winchester, with as many as seven bishoprics attached.[11] Pope Lucius II (1144–5) may even have sent a *pallium*, but after his death the plan bit the dust. Gradually the map of territorial dioceses took shape. That in the south-west took in Cornwall (St Germans) and moved from Crediton to Exeter in 1050. Others, East Anglia, Dorchester, Lichfield, Bath, and Ramsbury were relocated after 1066. Ely was created in 1109 by carving off part of Lincoln, and Carlisle in 1133 from the southern portion of the old kingdom of Strathclyde. In some cases there were difficulties as bishops sought to relocate their headquarters to Benedictine abbeys, changes which the communities concerned, notably Bury, Coventry, and Chester, resisted. Some abbeys successfully claimed exemption from episcopal authority. Their success, and what this actually meant in practice, changed over time.[12]

Dioceses were subdivided into territorial archdeaconries, often based on counties.[13] The office of archdeacon was sometimes held by a relative of the bishop.[14] He deputized for the bishop, collected his dues, monitored the local clergy, and probably administered the ordeals.[15] If archdeacons were roughly equivalent to sheriffs, then rural deans were on a par with hundred reeves.[16] In the early twelfth century archdeacons were acting

---

[11] John of Salisbury, *Historia Pontificalis*, ed. M. Chibnall (London, Edinburgh, Paris, Melbourne, and Toronto: Thomas Nelson, 1956), p. 78.

[12] D. Knowles, *The Monastic Order in England. From the Times of St Dunstan to the Fourth Lateran Council*, 2nd edn (Cambridge: Cambridge University Press, 1963), chapter 33.

[13] Barlow, *English Church 1066–1154*, pp. 48–9.

[14] For example, Roger of Salisbury had four archdeacons, two for Wiltshire and one each for Berkshire and Dorset. Roger of Ramsbury and Azo may have been brothers of Roger's wife; Adelelm, the bishop's nephew or son, was archdeacon of Dorset. Roger archdeacon of Berkshire may have been another relative, Kealey, *Roger of Salisbury*, pp. 272–4, and see later in this chapter.

[15] *Twelfth-Century English Archidiaconal and Vice-archidiaconal Acta*, ed. B. R. Kemp, Canterbury and York Society, 92 (2001).

[16] Barlow, *English Church 1066–1154*, pp. 49–50; Brett, *English Church under Henry I*, pp. 211–15; B. Kemp, 'The Acta of English Rural Deans in the Later Twelfth and Early

generally as bishops' deputies, but by Stephen's reign they were dealing with legal business in their own courts. Archdeacons and deans were also increasingly acting as prosecutors rather than relying on individuals or communities, a development which not unsurprisingly made them unpopular. In 1158 Henry II forbade such *ex officio* prosecutions, and in 1164 at Clarendon further laid down (clause six) that if no accusers were to come forward, sheriffs were to provide juries to do so.[17] Brian Kemp has analysed archdeacons' work and demonstrates how they were the people notified of gifts of churches and of developments in churches within their archdeaconries. He suggests that the twelfth century was the golden age of the English archdeacon, before he came under the supervision of a bishop's 'official'.[18]

PRIMACY

Within this structure there were recurrent power struggles between Canterbury and York over primacy, over attempts to establish a third archbishopric, and by some Benedictine abbeys' efforts to establish exemption from episcopal authority. Archbishop Lanfranc fought to secure a written profession of obedience from Thomas of Bayeux archbishop of York. The archbishops were briefed by their own communities, and York resisted. When the matter was raised at Rome, the pope referred it back for settlement to a royal council in England. The case was heard at Winchester before the king in 1072, but Thomas refused to do more than make a profession which bound only himself.[19] The matter recurred under each archbishop's successors. Canterbury profited from the Norman kings' backing for a Canterbury primacy, not only over York, but over all the British Isles, which fitted in well with their imperial ambitions. However, Archbishop Gerard of York was able to evade making a profession as archbishop as he had been translated from the bishopric of Hereford, and Thurstan, his successor, outwitted Canterbury by securing consecration from the pope. This enraged Henry I, who threatened not

---

Thirteenth Centuries', P. Hoskin, C. Brooke, and B. Dobson (eds.), *The Foundations of Medieval Ecclesiastical History. Studies Presented to David Smith* (Woodbridge: Boydell Press, 2005), pp. 139–58.

[17] *English Historical Documents*, II, p. 768.

[18] B. Kemp, 'Informing the Archdeacon on Ecclesiastical Matters in Twelfth-Century England', M. J. Franklin and C. Harper-Bill (eds.), *Medieval Ecclesiastical Studies in Honour of Dorothy M. Owen* (Woodbridge: Boydell Press, 1995), pp. 131–49.

[19] Hugh the Chanter, *History of the Church of York 1066–1127*, p. 6.

to allow Thurstan to enter England until he had made a profession, until a reconciliation was effected.[20] By 1120 the wind had gone out of the sails of the Canterbury primacy, and archbishops could no longer hope for backing from the papacy. This did not stop Gilbert Foliot as bishop of London asserting a primacy for his see on the ground that London, not Canterbury, had been the intended headquarters of the southern archdiocese in Pope Gregory the Great's original plan.[21] Canterbury had to watch out for bids for archiepiscopal status from Scotland (St Andrews), Wales (St Davids), and Ireland (Armagh), and for an attempt by Henry of Blois, bishop of Winchester, to subdivide the southern archdiocese.[22] These struggles were sporadic rather than continuous, but prelates had to be armed with full knowledge of history and precedents and with long pockets before taking their cases to Rome.

COUNCILS

Legates, letters, and privileges were ways through which papal authority reached out to local churches. It was two-way traffic as a growing stream of monks and clergy visited Rome to secure privileges. Councils were likewise key to bringing ecclesiastics together to discuss the issues of the day and to attest papal rulings. As in the case of appeals, kings were not prepared to allow unsupervised access to Rome: ecclesiastics were expected to obtain permission to leave the country, and kings, if they could not stop appeals out of the country completely, wanted to ensure that their own interests were protected. English bishops did not attend the Council of Clermont in 1095, at which the first crusade was preached, for instance. Anselm in exile attended Bari (1097) and Rome (1098), and Thurstan, with the bishops of Durham and Exeter and the archdeacon of Canterbury, was present at Rheims (1119).[23] Both archbishops were summoned to the first Lateran council in 1123, but arrived late. There may have been bishops from England at Rheims (1131).[24] Theobald and four bishops attended Lateran II in 1138.[25] King Stephen was said to have expelled

---

[20] *Ibid.*, pp. 120–60.

[21] A. Morey and C. N. L. Brooke, *Gilbert Foliot and His Letters* (Cambridge: Cambridge University Press, 1965), pp. 152–62.

[22] For the wider ramifications of Canterbury supremacy, see Flanagan, *Irish Society, Anglo-Norman Settlers, Angevin Kingship*, chapter 1.

[23] *Councils and Synods*, I, Part 2, pp. 648 (Clermont), 650–2 (Bari and Rome); Hugh the Chanter, *History of the Church of York*, pp. 118–23.

[24] *Councils and Synods*, I, Part 2, pp. 718–19.   [25] *Ibid.*, 779–81.

the papal legate who came with the invitations for English prelates to attend the papal council at Rheims in 1148 and allowed only three English bishops to attend.[26] The Council of Tours (1163) was particularly well attended, the king having given English prelates permission to attend provided no new customs were brought into the country or its dignity was in any way diminished.[27] Lateran III in 1179 was attended by four bishops from England, plus Peter of Blois, then archdeacon of Bath, and Walter Map.[28]

Councils, whether held by papal legates, archbishops, bishops, or archdeacons, were a crucial means of cascading messages from the top to the bottom. The papal legates in 1070 dealt with the position of Stigand and other irregular appointments in the English church, and imposed penances on those who had taken part in the conflict of 1066. Then there was a gap until 1126, when Henry I allowed John of Crema to enter the country and to hold a legatine council. In 1138 a papal legate was allowed to enter the country and hold a council, and three years later 1141 Henry of Winchester used the occasion of a legatine council to seek to transfer royal authority from his brother, the imprisoned king, to the empress. Henry held a second council in 1143, and in 1151 Theobald held a council. After 1066 church councils are not easy to distinguish from royal councils at which the king presided. For Lanfranc, they were central to his reforming programme. There were recurring concerns, with simony and clerical marriage, the payment of tithes, and the prohibition on marriage within seven degrees. The conduct of bishops, archdeacons, monks, and nuns also cropped up regularly. Bishops and clergy were not to hold pleas where the penalty involved the shedding of blood. Bishops were to call Christians to penitence, to hold annual synods, to consecrate churches, and to ordain and institute clergy. A good deal was also said about the use of excommunication. Other issues were addressed: superstitious practices, irregularities in the sacraments, and the slave trade. In 1151 there was a marked concern with those who took illegal exactions from churches, and those who took illegal tolls were to be excommunicated.

At the diocesan level synods brought together clergy. It was at such a meeting in 1144 that an accusation of murder was brought against the Norwich Jews. The sheriff initially resisted their summons, then produced the Jews, but whisked them away to the safety of the royal castle. Within dioceses archdeacons and rural deans held synods, though evidence of

---

[26] *Historia Pontificalis*, pp. 6–8.   [27] *Councils and Synods*, I, Part 2, p. 846.
[28] *Ibid.*, p. 1012.

their proceedings is elusive. The language question has to be borne in mind, too, for the language of bishops and archdeacons was likely to have been French, and the local clergy, English.[29]

How far archbishops were able to intervene directly in the running of dioceses was not altogether clear. Lanfranc's letters reveal an archbishop determined to exercise a managerial oversight over bishops and abbots, but his successors did not apparently do so, and the archbishops of York do not seem to have intervened in the affairs of Durham. The sacramental functions uniquely attached to archbishops and bishops were relatively few: they consecrated other bishops, kings, and queens, ordained priests, supplied chrism (consecrated oil), confirmed laypeople, and dedicated churches.[30] Beyond these duties they had a general oversight of Christian society within the diocese, that is, they were to regulate the clergy, conduct visitations of religious houses, and safeguard the lands and property of their sees. They were to bring the laity into conformity with God's law, hearing confessions and imposing penances, and reconciling the faithful each year on Maundy Thursday.[31] Many bishops were present in their dioceses only at irregular intervals, if at all, often being absent at court, on journeys to Rome, or in exile.

One of the chief aims of the eleventh-century reform movement was to rid the church of married clergy, but this proved remarkably difficult to achieve. Bishops had sons (sometimes) and nephews (often) to provide for. Prebends and archdeaconries in the eleventh and twelfth centuries were stiff with clerical families. The families of Ranulf Flambard at Durham and Richard of Beaumais at London were two noteworthy examples. The historian Henry archdeacon of Huntingdon was the son of a previous archdeacon.[32] At Lincoln, Dean Simon Bloet was the son of Robert Bloet, fathered before the latter became bishop.[33] In the eleventh century kings increasingly tended to bestow bishoprics on clerks from their chapel. After 1066 the number of Normans appointed as bishops and abbots increased dramatically, but they too had families to provide for.

---

[29] The example usually cited in this context is that of Brictric, the priest of Hazelbury in Wiltshire, who complained that Wulfric the holy man had not taught him to speak French and so he was mute in the presence of the bishop, *The Cistercian World. Monastic Writings of the Twelfth Century*, ed. and trans. P. Matarasso (London: Penguin, 1993), pp. 243–4.

[30] Gilbert of Limerick, 'De Statu Ecclesiae', in Migne, *Patrologia Latina*, clix, col. 1002, as cited Barlow, *English Church 1066–1154*, p. 134.

[31] See, for example, William of Malmesbury on Wulfstan's practice in Lent, *Saints' Lives: Lives of SS Dunstan, Patrick, Indract, Wulfstan*, p. 155.

[32] HH, pp. xxiii–xxviii.   [33] *Ibid.*, p. 596.

Bishops did not have it all their own way in exercising supervision and visitation over the clergy in their dioceses. Churches on the king's own estates were exempt, and became known as 'royal free chapels'.[34] Cistercian houses were relatively self-sufficient, and were exempt from episcopal visitation.[35] A few communities claimed privileged status on the basis of royal and papal grants: Ripon and Beverley in the archdiocese of York, and the abbeys of Ramsey and Bury St Edmunds. Their cases were helped by the antiquity of their claims, even if the charters on which they were described were not above suspicion, to put it mildly.[36] Westminster Abbey did not have old royal charters, but established a privileged status over time by securing bulls from successive popes.[37] Battle Abbey was the only house founded after the Conquest in this category.[38] Bishop Hilary of Chichester, a renowned canon lawyer, sought to establish visitation rights over Battle, but came up against a powerful coalition between the abbot, Walter de Lacy, and his brother Richard, one of the chief justiciars. They persuaded the king, at odds with the bishops over his rights over the English church, to back the abbey.[39]

BISHOPS AND CHAPTERS

Most dioceses were communities of clerks, later canons. The number of canons greatly increased, and it was in this period that they came to be organized under deans, treasurers, precentors, and chancellors. A few, such as Christchurch Canterbury and the Old Minster at Winchester, were communities of monks, not canons, over whom a prior presided. The endowment of the see was divided between the bishop and the canons or monks, so that after 1066 when the bishop died his lands alone were taken into royal control, and subsequently formally restored to his successor.[40] As the number of canons grew, so too did the endowments apportioned to them.

---

[34] J. H. Denton, *English Royal Free Chapels 1100–1300: a Constitutional Study* (Manchester: Manchester University Press, 1970). It is likely that some had been minster churches. Those in south Staffordshire were in the heartland of the early kingdom of Mercia, J. Blair, *The Church in Anglo-Saxon Society* (Oxford: Oxford University Press, 2005), p. 309.

[35] Knowles, *Monastic Order in England*, pp. 633–4.   [36] *Ibid.*, chapter 33.

[37] *Ibid.*, pp. 579–80.   [38] *Ibid.*, pp. 582, 588–9.

[39] *Chronicle of Battle Abbey*, pp. 152–210; N. Vincent, 'Henry II and the Monks of Battle: the Battle Chronicle Unmasked', R. Gameson and H. Leyser (eds.), *Belief and Culture in the Middle Ages: Studies Presented to Henry Mayr-Harting* (Oxford: Oxford University Press, 2001), pp. 264–86.

[40] E. U. Crosby, *Bishop and Chapter in Twelfth-Century England, a Study of the Mensa Episcopalis* (Cambridge: Cambridge University Press, 1994).

LOCAL CLERGY

A major dimension of the bishops' work in this period was their oversight of local clergy by seeking to regularize procedure for appointments, to ensure financial provision for local clergy, and to watch over the creation of new parishes. At the start of the period local churches were being built and priests provided with relative freedom.[41] The faithful were exhorted to pay tithes on all their produce. There was a certain degree of flexibility in practice about the church to which they were paid, as in practice the building of new churches often led to tithes being diverted away from the older minster churches.[42] Not only that, but lay patrons often controlled appointments, and hereditary succession was common. Payment for preferment was the sin of simony and this, together with clerical marriage, was firmly in the sights of eleventh-century reformers who wished to see the clergy as a separate order free from worldly entanglements. It was only over a protracted period that bishops were able to supervise the creation of parishes, and to ensure that financial provision was made for local clergy.[43] By the end of our period a map of parishes and their boundaries could be drawn. Bishops probably could do little to scrutinize the standard of education of local clergy or their marital status, but they did intervene by adjudicating disputes over presentation. Through the appointment of archdeacons and rural deans and the holding of synods, a chain of command was established, and channels through which the church's teaching could be communicated. Many churches had been given to religious houses from the late eleventh century, but often the rights being conveyed had not been precisely stipulated at the time, and were open to challenges, which were brought to the bishop's court and there resolved, with episcopal charters recording the outcome.

By the twelfth century justice and jurisdiction loomed ever larger for bishops, and one of the developments of the time was a greater precision about law and procedure. Litigants had considerable freedom to choose their courts, and certain types of actions, as noted in the previous chapter, lay at the interface: wills, debts, disputes over the status of land given to the church and about rights of presentation.[44] Central to church courts was the issue of discipline over the personnel and property of the church. Barlow argued that churchmen on the whole preferred to settle disputes

---

[41] Blair, *Church in Anglo-Saxon Society*, chapter 7.   [42] *Ibid.*, pp. 440–7.

[43] Cheney, *From Becket to Langton*, pp. 122–39.

[44] Helmholz, *Oxford History of the Laws of England*, I, chapter 2.

between clergy in house.[45] In fact, as he pointed out, there seems to have been a degree of flexibility before the mid-twelfth century about the courts where such cases were heard. Less clear was what was to happen when clergy were suspected of serious crimes, or when laymen attacked churches. As we saw in the previous chapter, Henry II was loath to see 'criminous clerks' escape the penalties of death or mutilation that would be imposed in lay courts, and wanted disputes about the tenure by which land was held by the church or about rights of presentation to be the subject of royal writs empanelling juries.

RELIGIOUS HOUSES

Bishops had a general authority over religious houses in their dioceses. In Edgar's reign monk bishops Dunstan, Æthelwold, and Oswald were the leaders of reform. By the eleventh century some Benedictine houses jibbed against episcopal authority and appealed directly to the papacy for exempt status: St Augustine Canterbury's claim for exemption against the archbishop is one example.[46] Newer communities looked to bishops to confirm their endowments, and indeed individual bishops took a major role in new foundations. One inspiration was that of regularizing communities, for example, by converting communities of hermits into Augustinian priories, or by making provision for religious women by organizing them into convents.[47] Bishops were also prominent in the foundation of hospitals. Again there was a practical concern to do something about the sick who flocked to greater churches and shrines looking for charity. Monasteries had obligations to visitors, but their hospitals were essentially intended for members of their own community, so separate hospitals, sometimes established on the edges of towns and cities, could provide for laypeople. In each wave of new foundations bishops took a prominent role, and again their benefactions were recorded in charters.

[45] *English Church 1066–1154*, p. 171.
[46] E. John, 'The Litigation of an Exempt House, St Augustine's, Canterbury, 1182–1237', *Bulletin of the John Rylands Library*, 39 (1957), 390–415.
[47] J. Herbert, 'The Transformation of Hermitages into Augustinian Priories in Twelfth-Century England', in W. Sheils (ed.), *Monks, Hermits and the Ascetic Tradition: Papers Read at the 1984 Summer Meeting and 1985 Winter Meeting at the Ecclesiastical History Society*, Studies in Church History, 22 (1985), 131–45; T. Licence, *Hermits and Recluses in English Society 950–1200* (Oxford: Oxford University Press, 2011); for women, see S. Elkins, *Holy Women of Twelfth-Century England* (Chapel Hill: University of North Carolina Press, 1988), especially chapters 4 and 5.

PIETY AND PRACTICE

The pastoral duties of medieval bishops included confirmation, confession, and penance, as noted previously, but they also involved the responsibility to ensure orthodoxy of belief and practice and conformability with the sacraments. This was a wide remit. Church councils condemned magic and witchcraft, but how these were to be rooted out was not spelled out: cases would have to be brought to the bishop's attention. Marriage was another growing area of litigation in the church courts (see earlier in this volume). Defining the criteria for valid marriages proved a happy hunting ground for canonists and thinkers. It suited lay families to cooperate with the church's teaching, out of religious conviction, but also the knowledge that, however binding marriage was, its bonds could be loosed if the criteria for validity had not been met.[48] Offences were reported to archdeacons, who brought the accused before church courts. This outraged Henry II, and clause six of the Constitutions of Clarendon, laying down that laymen ought to be accused before lawful accusers, was an attempt to address the problem.[49] It must have been particularly galling for the king given that some archdeacons were themselves married. Many disputes centring on marriage became the subject of appeals to Rome, and were dealt with by bishops as judges delegate.[50]

TEMPORALITIES

Bishops and heads of monastic houses were often in charge of substantial resources of wealth, and could hope for more through pious donations. Managing resources was therefore an important aspect of their work.[51] Estates were often leased out for renders paid in cash or kind. This means that incomes were relatively stable, unless more land was brought into cultivation or acquired. Funding major building projects therefore needed a range of sources: donations by the bishop and chapters, or by lay benefactors, by offerings at the shrines of saints, by charging fees, or by using the profits of fairs.[52] Translating saints to new and more elaborate

---

[48] Barlow, *English Church 1066–1154*, pp. 167–71.

[49] *English Historical Documents*, II, p. 768.

[50] Duggan, 'Papal Judges Delegate and the Making of the "New Law" in the Twelfth Century', Bisson (ed.), *Cultures of Power*, pp. 172–99.

[51] M. Giandrea, *Episcopal Culture in Late Anglo-Saxon England* (Woodbridge: Boydell Press, 2007), chapter 5; Crosby, *Bishop and Chapter*, pp. 369–70.

[52] W. Vroom, *Financing Cathedral Building in the Middle Ages: the Generosity of the Faithful* (Amsterdam: Amsterdam University Press, paperback edn, 2010).

shrines was expensive, and, it must have been hoped, self-funding. The pattern for bishoprics and Benedictine houses was to take income from existing estates. The new orders of the twelfth century adopted a different approach, by developing granges, which were new entities. In theory Cistercian granges were supposed to be situated in remote areas, which were opened up to cultivation for the first time, using their own workforce of lay brothers plus wage labourers. In practice granges were sometimes created on land already cultivated, and meant that local people had to be relocated. Exemption from tithes together with their own work-force meant that Cistercian houses soon became very wealthy. The Gilbertines, closely modelled on the Cistercians, also used lay brothers, unlike the Augustinians, who used either hired labour or peasants with their own holdings.[53]

BISHOPS IN ENGLISH SOCIETY

The sources say relatively little about the way English archbishops and bishops before the Conquest were appointed. It is fairly clear that they were approved and probably in most cases nominated by the king, albeit formally elected by cathedral communities. Monks were particularly important in the later tenth and early eleventh centuries. Archbishop Dunstan at Canterbury, Æthelwold at Winchester, and Oswald at Worcester were key to the promotion of reformed Benedictine monasticism under King Edgar.[54] For appointments to Durham, for instance, we have to rely on Symeon, who may have been seeking to point up the role of the community in the election of Edmund (bishop between 1022 and 1042). Edmund then presented himself to Cnut and returned north in the company of Æthelric, a monk of Peterborough, who instructed him in monasticism. Æthelric then succeeded Edmund, though he was expelled for a time by the community and only restored, according to Symeon, by bribing Earl Siward. He returned to Peterborough having sent ahead

[53] T. A. M. Bishop, 'Monastic Granges in Yorkshire', *English Historical Review*, 51 (1936), 193–214 at pp. 202–8; B. Golding, *Gilbert of Sempringham and the Gilbertine Order* (Oxford: Clarendon Press, 1995), pp. 392–419.

[54] N. Ramsay, M. Sparks, and T. Tatton Brown (eds.), *St Dunstan: His Life, Times and Cult* (Woodbridge: Boydell Press, 1992); N. Brooks and C. Cubitt (eds.), *St Oswald of Worcester: Life and Influence* (London: Leicester University Press, 1996); C. Cubitt, 'The Tenth-Century Benedictine Reform in England', *Early Medieval Europe*, 6 (1997), 77–94.

money he had found at Chester-le-Street, leaving his brother Æthelwine in his place.[55]

In this later account, King Edward's wishes did not figure, and there are other indications that this king did not always get his own way over episcopal nominations. The nomination of Robert of Jumièges to London in 1044 was doubtless his, but when Robert was translated to Canterbury in 1051, he refused to consecrate as his successor Spearhafoc, abbot of Abingdon, the king's goldsmith. Spearhafoc then left the country, taking with him the gems intended for King Edward's crown.[56] An increasing tendency to appoint royal clerks to bishoprics has plausibly been associated with the king's personal preference. It was under Edward, too, that Stigand rose from being bishop of Elmham to Winchester and then archbishop of Canterbury.

At Canterbury the tradition of monk-archbishops continued longer than elsewhere: Lanfranc, Anselm, and Ralph d'Escures were monks. Then after William of Corbeil, an Augustinian canon, another monk of Bec, Theobald, was chosen. Thus the choice by Henry II of his chancellor, Thomas Becket, to succeed Theobald was a clear break with tradition and not one that either the Canterbury monks or the bishops approved.[57] Canterbury was a special case: the archbishop was such an important figure in English society that it was crucial the office be held by someone who could work with the king. Lanfranc's relationship with William the Conqueror is the best example of a successful partnership, that of Anselm and Rufus and Becket and Henry II the worst.

It was not surprising that kings would nominate to bishoprics men who had served them as clerks in their chapel or court, nor that they would promote kinsmen, like Henry of Blois, brother of King Stephen, to Winchester, Roger of Gloucester, cousin of Henry II, to Worcester or Geoffrey Plantagenet, son of Henry II, to Lincoln and then York. The proportion of bishops recruited from noble families declined over our period. More came from clerical families, and had often been archdeacon before bishop. The other noticeable trend by the twelfth century was the appointment of bishops learned in law, having studied in Italy or France.

As time went on, and as more information survives, the strength of royal influence over appointments is clear, as are other interests which

---

[55] *Libellus*, pp. 156–60.   [56] ASC, E, 1048; C, 1050, D, 1051; JW, II, pp. 552–4.
[57] For discussion, see Duggan, *Thomas Becket*, pp. 23–4. Two biographers of Becket refer to the opposition to Becket's election.

were coming to the fore: in the case of Canterbury the concerns of the bishops of the archdiocese and the monks, the influence of Canterbury over episcopal appointments, the interests of cathedral chapters and of the pope. Appointment procedures were tightened up. Money was not supposed to change hands – this was the sin of simony – and from 1107 kings did not invest bishops with their mitres and staffs. In the Constitutions of Clarendon it was prescribed that the king was to summon the more important clergy and the election was to take place in the king's chapel.[58] Kings quite clearly wished to reward clerks in their service, but this did not mean that they were unwilling to recognize other claims, such as expertise in canon law, family ties, or an irreproachable life, such as that of the Carthusian Hugh of Avalon at Lincoln, appointed in 1186. Royal influence clearly slipped under Stephen: the elections at London (1141, 1152), Norwich (1146), Chichester (1147), Hereford and Lincoln (both 1148), Lichfield (1149), Worcester (1151), York (1140), and Durham (1141) were all contested. The king's influence over appointments before 1066 seems not to have been all pervasive, though details are patchy. Although Henry II was more successful in securing appointments for men of his choice, on occasion he took account of the wishes of the cathedral communities concerned. For the most part the key criteria for kings was to reward past service (chancellors were usually promoted to bishoprics) or as a recognition of expertise, such as the choice of Gilbert the Universal, a noted canon lawyer, as bishop of London by Henry I (see later in this volume). The episcopate was usually royalist and reluctant to oppose the king.

Bishops were summoned to meetings of the Anglo-Saxon witan, which evolved after 1066 into the king's council. They were the king's natural counsellors, though in practice their influence seems to have depended on their personal relationships with the king. Hagiographers naturally tended to talk up the influence of saintly ecclesiastics. Archbishop Dunstan was exiled twice in his career, but under Edgar, Edward the Martyr, and Æthelred he witnessed almost every royal charter issued before his death in 988.[59] Archbishop Wulfstan of York (d. 1023), homilist and legislator, played a key role in the reconciliation of Danes and English at the Council of Oxford in 1018, and was the architect of the great law code of 1020 or

---

[58] *English Historical Documents*, II, pp. 769–70.
[59] Michael Lapidge, 'Dunstan [St Dunstan] (*d.* 988)', *ODNB* www.oxforddnb.com/view /article/8288, accessed 20 May 2016.

1021.[60] Lanfranc was hand-picked by William the Conqueror to take over at Canterbury. He was the driving force behind the movement for reorganization in the English church. He was a trusted figure in the king's counsels, and is thought to have been responsible for articulating the idea that all land was to be held conditionally of the king.[61] Anselm by contrast, and setting on one side Eadmer's hagiographical account, seems to have had little influence over William Rufus or even Henry I. In fact, after Lanfranc's day it does not look as though any of the archbishops either of Canterbury or York were particularly influential at court. Archbishop Theobald's position was constrained by the prominence of the king's brother Henry of Blois, papal legate as well as bishop of Winchester. Theobald's resistance to Stephen's wishes over the succession, his defiance of the king's wishes over attendance at the papal council of Rheims, and then his difficult relations with Henry II clouded his final years.[62]

Individual bishops, too, had key roles in political society.[63] Archbishop Ealdred of York (d. 1069) was an envoy to the pope and to the emperor under Edward the Confessor. He may have crowned Harold Godwinson in 1066 and then William and later Matilda.[64] William Warelwast, bishop of Exeter, acted as an envoy to the pope under both Rufus and Henry I.[65] Roger bishop of Salisbury was King Henry's chief minister and presided over the exchequer. Ranulf Flambard built a strong base at Durham and a second castle at Norham, and established a network of under-tenants, some of whom were his own kin. Henry of Blois, bishop of Winchester, seems to have been responsible for securing his brother's accession to the throne, and in 1141 it was he who attempted to pave the way for a transfer of power to the empress.[66] Some bishops were royal justices, like Robert Bloet, bishop of Lincoln, Richard of Ilchester, bishop of Winchester, and Geoffrey Ridel, bishop of Ely.[67] What is difficult to discern is how much

[60] Patrick Wormald, 'Wulfstan (d. 1023)', *ODNB* www.oxforddnb.com/view/article/30098, accessed 20 May 2016.

[61] Garnett, *Conquered England*, p. 41.   [62] HH, p. 758.

[63] That is not to say that tenth- and eleventh-century bishops did not do so, merely that the evidence becomes stronger from the later eleventh century.

[64] M. K. Lawson, 'Ealdred (d. 1069)', rev. Vanessa King, *ODNB* www.oxforddnb.com /view/article/37382, accessed 20 May 2016.

[65] Frank Barlow, 'Warelwast, William de (d. 1137)', *ODNB* www.oxforddnb.com/view /article/28731, accessed 20 May 2016.

[66] Edmund King, 'Blois, Henry de (c.1096–1171)', *ODNB* www.oxforddnb.com/view /article/12968, accessed 20 May 2016.

[67] Dorothy M. Owen, 'Bloet, Robert (d. 1123)', *ODNB* www.oxforddnb.com/view/article /2660, accessed 20 May 2016; John Hudson, 'Ilchester, Richard of (d. 1188)', *ODNB* www.oxforddnb.com/view/article/23515, accessed 20 May 2016; A. J. Duggan, 'Ridel,

weight the bishops' advice carried in discussions about war and peace or the distribution of patronage.

Bishops had an important role as peacemakers. In 994 Ælfheah bishop of Winchester and Ealdorman Æthelweard were responsible for escorting English hostages to the Norwegian king Olaf, then escorting Olaf to Andover, where he was baptized and adopted by King Æthelred as his son.[68] Archbishop Stigand acted as an intermediary between Edward the Confessor and Harold Godwinson in 1051, but was unable to prevent the latter leaving the country.[69] Archbishop Ealdred of York is thought to have been sent to Hungary by Edward the Confessor to arrange for the return of Edward the Exile. He was received by Emperor Henry III and by the archbishop of Cologne and presented gifts.[70] He was also with the English leaders in 1066 after the Battle of Hastings, leading a party for Edgar Ætheling.[71] In 1120 Archbishop Thurstan of York was said to have brokered peace between Louis VI and Henry I.[72]

Bishops were responsible for reconciling feuds and administering ordeals.[73] Bishop Wulfstan was held to be remarkably effective in this respect, preaching peace so effectively on one occasion that even obdurate enemies were brought to reconciliation.[74] His contemporary Bishop Walcher of Durham was less fortunate, when trying to arrange a settlement following the killing of a man named Liulf.[75] He had knights in his household who were said to have been allowed to plunder locally, and he seems not to have taken any action in the face of the Scottish invasion of 1079.[76] However, it was the death of Liulf which led to the bishop's own death. Liulf was described by the Worcester chronicler as a noble thegn with many estates throughout England who, because of his love for St Cuthbert, had retired to Durham with his men in the face of the Normans.[77] He was married to a daughter of Earl Ealdred.[78] He fell foul of Leofwin, to whom Walcher had entrusted the spiritual affairs of the kingdom, who in turn spurred on Gilbert, the bishop's officer and his nephew, to have Liulf killed. The bishop sent messengers to say that he

Geoffrey (d. 1189)', *ODNB* www.oxforddnb.com/view/article/23618, accessed 20 May 2016.

[68] ASC, C, D, E, F, 994; JW, II, p. 444.

[69] *Life of King Edward Who Rests at Westminster*, p. 34.   [70] JW, II, pp. 574–6.

[71] ASC, D, 1066; JW, II, pp. 604–6.

[72] Hugh the Chanter, *History of the Church of York*, p. 160.

[73] Giandrea, *Episcopal Culture in Late Anglo-Saxon England*, pp. 108–9.

[74] WM, *Saints' Lives. Wulfstan*, pp. 90–3.   [75] *Libellus*, pp. 212–13.

[76] *Ibid.* For Malcolm's invasion, see ASC, D, 1079; JW, III, p. 30.   [77] *Ibid.*, p. 32.

[78] Symeon of Durham, *Historia Regum, Opera omnia*, II, p. 209.

had not known about the murder; and that he had outlawed Gilbert and his accomplices and was ready to clear himself of complicity. When the bishop arrived to try to make peace with Liulf's kin, he could not convince them that he had not ordered the killing. Moreover, Leofwin had received Gilbert on the night of the murder, and the bishop had continued to show him favour. The bishop realized that the kin were not going to be satisfied without Gilbert's head, and he sent him outside the church where they had taken refuge. Gilbert was killed, then the bishop, and finally Leofwin.[79]

The outbreak of civil war in England after the death of Henry I brought the role of bishops and abbots as peacemakers centre stage.[80] Henry bishop of Winchester was particularly important, especially between 1139 and 1141, when he sought to broker a peace between the two sides.[81] After the Battle of the Standard, a truce with the Scots was arranged through the papal legate, together with the bishop of Carlisle, the abbot of Fountains, and the bishop of Hereford.[82] The bishop of Lincoln was present when the earls of Chester and Leicester made their famous treaty.[83] New religious foundations could help to bind neighbours together in acts of patronage, or put disputed land outside a combat zone. Bishop Alexander of Lincoln, for example, instigated the foundation of Louth Park, and this brought two rival contenders for certain land into association as benefactors.[84] Newhouse was another Lincolnshire foundation which brought rivals together. The abbey was founded by Peter of Goxhill on land whose tenure was disputed by William de Roumare, who nevertheless confirmed land given to the new foundation.[85]

Ailred, the Cistercian abbot of Rievaulx, is seen as another particularly important figure, both through his role as a peacemaker and through his writings. His biographer wrote of the way he made Rievaulx the home of

---

[79] JW, III, pp. 32–7; WM, *Gesta Regum Anglorum*, I, pp. 488–501. Symeon of Durham was noticeably reticent, see *Libellus*, pp. 216–19. For comment, see Kapelle, *Norman Conquest of the North*, pp. 137–40.

[80] C. Holdsworth, 'War and Peace in the Twelfth Century: the Reign of Stephen Reconsidered', B. P. McGuire (ed.), *War and Peace in the Middle Ages* (Copenhagen: Reitzel, 1987), pp. 67–93; P. Dalton, 'Churchmen and the Promotion of Peace in King Stephen's Reign', *Viator*, 31 (2000), 79–120.

[81] Edmund King, 'Blois, Henry de (*c.*1096–1171)', *ODNB* www.oxforddnb.com/view/article/12968, accessed 20 May 2016.

[82] John of Hexham, continuation to *Historia Regum*, Symeon of Durham, *Opera omnia*, II, pp. 299–300.

[83] F. M. Stenton, *The First Century of English Feudalism*, 2nd edn (Oxford: Clarendon Press, 1961), pp. 286–8.

[84] Dalton, 'Churchmen and the Promotion of Peace', p. 97.   [85] *Ibid.*, pp. 97–103.

'piety and peace' through his personal leadership.[86] On a visit to the wilds of Galloway he was able to bring peace where the king of Scotland had failed to do so.[87] Through his writing and his letters he promoted Christian ideals of peace and love, in works such as *The Mirror of Charity*, and *On Spiritual Friendship*.[88] In his letter to Henry, the future Henry II, he wrote a lament for King David of Scots, 'a gentle king, a just king' who epitomized Christian kingship, who administered justice without cruelty. David's special care were the poor and widows, and he sought to prevent churchmen from public disagreement. Ailred continued with Henry's family tree back to Adam and then back to King Æthelwulf and his successors, highlighting examples of Christian kingship and demonstrating how success attended kings who followed God's laws.[89]

The role of bishops as military figures was not negligible. In the first place, their lands (and those of major Benedictine houses) owed military service.[90] This might involve sending contingents of armed men, funding ships, or providing financial support. After 1066 quotas of knight service were applied, the size of which varied, Canterbury owing sixty knights whilst York owed only two.[91] In the early days after 1066 some bishops, like Wulfstan of Worcester, kept knights in their households, but over time they were established on land.[92] William Rufus famously complained about the quality of the contingent Anselm sent when summoned in 1097.[93]

---

[86] Walter Daniel, *Life of Ailred*, p. 36.   [87] *Ibid.*, p. 18.   [88] *Ibid.*, pp. 45–6.

[89] Aelred of Rievaulx, *Historical Works*, pp. 41–122; Dalton, 'Churchmen and the Promotion of Peace', pp. 110–18.

[90] Abels, *Lordship and Military Obligation*, pp. 52–7; N. P. Brooks, 'The Archbishopric of Canterbury and the So-Called Introduction of Knight Service into England', *Anglo-Norman Studies*, 34 (2011), 41–62.

[91] *Ibid.*, pp. 46–7.   [92] WM, *Saints' Lives. Wulfstan*, pp. 108, 130.

[93] Eadmer, *The Life of St Anselm, Archbishop of Canterbury*, ed. and trans. R. W. Southern (Oxford: Clarendon Press, 1962), p. 88; *Historia Novorum*, p. 78; Stenton, *First Century of English Feudalism*, pp. 145–9. A letter by the Canterbury monks to Henry II explained that there had been no knights in England before the time of King William, who had ordered them to create knights for the defence of the land. They had given £200 worth of land to Lanfranc to acquit them of their obligation. Lanfranc had converted *threngs* into knights, *RRAN*, I, no. 264. This is obviously a much later account of the division of land between the archbishop and the monks, and of the process by which knights' fees were established on Canterbury lands. There was a dispute between William Rufus and Anselm about Canterbury land on which the king had enfeoffed knights after Lanfranc's death. As presented by Eadmer, this was about the king's right to create tenancies on the archbishop's land during a vacancy, as opposed to Anselm's stipulation that he should receive all the lands held by Lanfranc on the day of his death. Initially the king's response was to reserve judgement. The issue would certainly have fuelled his resentment over the

From time to time individual bishops and abbots were actively involved in war. Bishop Leofgar of Hereford was killed fighting the Welsh in 1056.[94] He had been Harold Godwinson's chaplain before his preferment, and was said to have kept his long moustaches even when bishop. Ælfwig abbot of New Minster was said to have died at Hastings, and Leofric abbot of Peterborough was also there.[95] In 1075 both Wulfstan of Worcester and Æthelwig abbot of Evesham took to the field against Earl Roger of Hereford.[96] Archbishop Anselm was with King Henry's army in 1101 and was said to have stiffened the resolve of the English troops.[97] In Stephen's reign the Scottish invasion of 1138 was countered by Archbishop Thurstan, who summoned local levies under the banners of their parish priests.[98] The author of the *Gesta Stephani* complained that the bishops, 'bent like a reed shaken in the wind', did not protect the church, but – if they took any action – passed sentences of excommunication which were speedily revoked. Many of them rode wearing armour and with swords, taking a share of the spoils of war by handing over captured knights. Amongst the worst offenders were the bishops of Winchester, Lincoln, and Chester.[99]

After 1066 some bishops had the custody of castles. The bishop of Durham held Durham and Norham.[100] From 1127 the archbishop of Canterbury had custody of Rochester.[101] Stephen grew especially concerned about the loyalty of his chief minister, Bishop Roger of Salisbury, who had custody of the royal castle at Salisbury and built castles at Sherborne, Malmesbury, and Devizes. His nephew Alexander of Lincoln had a fortified gate at Lincoln and built castles at Newark, Sleaford, and, later, Banbury, whilst Nigel, bishop of Ely, controlled the royal castle there.[102]

quality of the Canterbury contingent, *Historia Novorum*, p. 40. Given the size of the Canterbury quota (sixty knights), and the question of royal rights during ecclesiastical vacancies, the matter was not negligible.

[94] ASC, C, D, 1056; JW, II, p. 580.

[95] *Liber Vitae: Register and Martyrology of New Minster and Hyde Abbey, Winchester*, ed. W. de Gray Birch (London, Winchester, Simpkin and Co, Warren and Son, 1892), p. 35, as cited Knowles, *Monastic Order*, p. 103; ASC, E, 1066.

[96] JW, III, p. 24.   [97] Eadmer, *Historia Novorum*, pp. 127–8.

[98] John of Hexham, continuation to *Historia Regum*, Symeon of Durham, *Opera omnia*, II, pp. 292–3; Ailred of Rievaulx, *Relatio de Standardo, Chronicles of the Reigns of Stephen, Henry II and Richard I*, III, p. 182; trans. Freeland, pp. 247–8.

[99] *Gesta Stephani*, p. 156. S. Marritt, 'Reeds Shaken by the Wind? Bishops in Local and Regional Politics in King Stephen's Reign', Dalton and White (eds.), *King Stephen's Reign*, pp. 115–38.

[100] Symeon of Durham, *Libellus*, pp. 274–6.   [101] RRAN, II, nos. 1475, 1606.

[102] WM, *Historia Novella*, p. 46; Kealey, *Roger of Salisbury*, pp. 86–90; for Newark and Sleaford, WM, *Historia Novella*, pp. 48–9; for the Eastgate at Lincoln, RRAN, II, no

Their castles would be a valuable asset to the Angevins, and so the king decided on a pre-emptive strike in 1139, seeking to arrest them and to confiscate their castles.[103] Henry of Winchester was said to have built several castles: Farnham (Surrey), Merdon, Bishop's Waltham, and Downton (Hampshire), and after 1141 he had custody of the royal castle at Winchester.[104] The bishop of London did not control either of the castles in the city, but he did have a castle at Bishop's Stortford in Hertfordshire.[105]

BISHOPS AND THE LAW

Knowledge of law was crucial. We have already noted Archbishop Wulfstan's role as a legislator. He saw his central mission as bringing the English people into conformity with God's law. From his perspective, God's law was all inclusive: there was no distinction between sin and crime. Christians were to keep their oaths, to respect the rights of the church on matters such as tithes and sanctuary, and to repent of their sins.[106] Another theme was that of marriage, the situation of widows, and the need for clerical celibacy.[107] Archbishop Lanfranc was responsible for a collection of canon law, based on Pseudo-Isidore.[108] Ernulf, abbot of Peterborough and then bishop of Rochester, was an expert in canon law, composing a letter discussing the question whether an incestuous wife should be separated from her husband. Ernulf was probably the moving

---

1784; for Banbury, Oseney annals (Wykes), *Annales Monastici*, ed. H. R. Luard, 5 vols., RS (London: Longman, Green, Roberts, Longman and Green, 1864–9), IV, p. 18; *Liber Eliensis*, p. 328.

[103] WM, *Historia Novella*, pp. 46–60, 64–70; *Gesta Stephani*, pp. 72–80.

[104] *Annales Monasterii de Wintonia, Annales Monastici*, II, p. 51. For discussion of the sites mentioned in this annal, see N. Riall, 'The New Castles of Henry de Blois as Bishop of Winchester: the Case against Farnham, Surrey', *Medieval Archaeology*, 47 (2003), 115–29. The unidentified castle of *Lidelea* was mentioned in *Gesta Stephani*, pp. 208–9.

[105] Bates, *Acta of William I*, nos. 189–90.

[106] *Political Writings of Archbishop Wulfstan of York* (ed. Rabin), pp. 36–44; Wormald, *Making of English Law*, pp. 449–65.

[107] *Political Writings of Archbishop Wulfstan of York*, pp. 90, 157 (marriage) 121, 150 (widows), 99, 116–18, 148 (clerical celibacy).

[108] M. Philpott, 'Archbishop Lanfranc and Canon Law', D. Phil. thesis (Oxford, 1993); Gullick, 'Lanfranc and the Oldest Manuscript of the *Collectio Lanfranci*', Brasington and Cushing (eds.), *Bishops, Texts and the Use of Canon Law around 1100*, pp. 79–86; H. E. J. Cowdrey, *Lanfranc, Scholar, Monk, and Archbishop* (Cambridge: Cambridge University Press, 2003), pp. 139–43; M. Brett, 'The *Collectio Lanfranci* and Its Competitors', L. Smith and B. Ward (eds.), *Intellectual Life in the Middle Ages: Essays Presented to Margaret Gibson* (London: Hambledon Press, 1992), pp. 157–74.

spirit behind the *Textus Roffensis*, the first part of which was a compendium of early laws from the time of Æthelbert of Kent to Henry I.[109] Alexander bishop of Lincoln had an interest in Anglo-Saxon law, and is thought to have been responsible for a glossary of Old English terms.[110] Gilbert the Universal, bishop of London (1128–34) achieved fame for his knowledge of canon law and for his contribution to the *Glossa Ordinaria* commentary on the Bible.[111] Robert Pullen taught law at Exeter and Oxford. He was archdeacon of Rochester before 1137, lectured in the schools of Paris, and went to Rome, where he became the pope's chancellor between 1144 and 1146.[112]

The rise of men educated at the schools of advanced learning, or *magistri*, was the most significant development in bishops' households in the twelfth century. Some studied at English schools, at Oxford, Northampton, or Lincoln.[113] Others went to Bologna to study Roman civil law, others to northern France to study philosophy and theology, to Laon but above all to Paris, before returning to England.[114] They returned with sharpened wits and skills which could be employed by bishops and kings, and the ablest of them moved up the ladder of preferment. Theobald became archbishop of Canterbury at a time when it was particularly important for ecclesiastics to keep abreast of legal studies, and his household included several clerks who had studied canon and civil law abroad like Thomas Becket, John of Salisbury, Roger of Pont l'Evêque, and Bartholomew of Exeter. Vacarius of Bologna became a member of his household in about 1143, before moving to the service of Roger of Pont l'Evêque.[115] Hilary of Chichester and Roger of Worcester were also expert in the law of the church.[116]

---

[109] P. Cramer, 'Ernulf of Rochester and Early Anglo-Norman Canon Law', *Journal of Ecclesiastical History*, 40 (1989), 483–510.

[110] *Red Book of the Exchequer*, II, cclxii–cclxiii.

[111] Falko Neininger, 'Gilbert (*d.* 1134)', *ODNB* www.oxforddnb.com/view/article/10673, accessed 20 May 2016.

[112] David Luscombe, 'Pullen, Robert (*d.* in or after 1146)', *ODNB* www.oxforddnb.com /view/article/22877, accessed 20 May 2016.

[113] H. M. Thomas, *The Secular Clergy in England, 1066–1216* (Oxford: Oxford University Press, 2014), pp. 112–13, 135–9, 242–3.

[114] *Ibid.*, chapter 10.

[115] Peter Stein, 'Vacarius (*c.*1120–*c.*1200)', *ODNB* www.oxforddnb.com/view/article/28048, accessed 20 May 2016.

[116] H. Mayr-Harting, 'Hilary, Bishop of Chichester (1147–1169) and Henry II', *English Historical Review*, 78 (1963), 209–24; Frank Barlow, 'Bartholomew (*d.* 1184)', *ODNB* www.oxforddnb.com/view/article/1577, accessed 20 May 2016; A. Morey, *Bartholomew*

ABBOTS

Abbots clearly were powerful figures who meted out discipline in their own communities. Punishment could be draconian. In a story in the Selby Chronicle, two monks ran off with nearly eight pounds of silver which Abbot Benedict had collected. The abbot and a band of men caught up with the thieves near Northampton, injured, and finally castrated them.[117] Another case which became notorious because reported by Ailred of Rievaulx was that of the nun of the Gilbertine house of Watton in Yorkshire who became pregnant by a lay brother and gave birth. She was whipped and chained by the sisters, who took the extreme step of castrating the lay brother.[118] In less extreme cases, monks might be transferred to other houses for a time, for example, the troublesome monk of Westminster, Osbert of Clare, who was sent from Westminster to Ely.[119] Thurstan, abbot of Glastonbury, was sent back to his home monastery at Caen for a time after an incident in 1083 when his armed men shot and killed monks in the abbey church, though he eventually returned.[120]

Personal leadership was crucial, for it was charisma which attracted recruits and retained them, for example, Ailred, under whose abbacy the numbers of monks and lay brothers at Rievaulx greatly expanded, so that when he died there were 140 monks and 500 lay brothers and servants.[121] Abbots also needed to be able to establish and maintain friendships with local benefactors, so that gifts were renewed and augmented down the generations.

As well as spiritual qualities, abbots also needed the ability to manage estates in a way that could feed the community and provide finance for

---

of Exeter (Cambridge: Cambridge University Press, 1937); M. G. Cheney, *Roger, Bishop of Worcester, 1164–1179* (Oxford: Clarendon Press, 1980).

[117] *Historia Selebiensis Monasterii: the History of the Monastery of Selby*, ed. and trans. J. Burton with L. Lockyer (Oxford: Clarendon Press, 2013), p. 56.

[118] Ailred of Rievaulx, 'De Sanctimoniali de Wattun', Migne, *Patrologia Latina*, cxcv, cols. 789–95; 'A Certain Wonderful Miracle', *Lives of the Northern Saints*, pp. 109–22; G. Constable, 'Aelred of Rievaulx and the Nun of Watton: an Episode in the Early History of the Gilbertine Order', D. Baker (ed.), *Medieval Women: Dedicated and Presented to Professor Rosalind M. T. Hill on the Occasion of her Seventieth Birthday* (Oxford: Blackwell, 1978), pp. 205–26.

[119] Frank Barlow, 'Clare, Osbert of (*d.* in or after 1158)', *ODNB* www.oxforddnb.com /view/article/5442, accessed 20 May 2016.

[120] ASC, E, 1083; JW, III, pp. 38–40. Thurstan was restored under William Rufus. For trouble at St Augustine's Canterbury in 1087, see *Acta Lanfranci, English Historical Documents*, II, pp. 676–81.

[121] Walter Daniel, *Life of Ailred of Rievaulx*, p. 38.

building projects. Monastic chroniclers often reported adversely on abbots who established their kinsmen as permanent fixtures on abbey lands or who lacked a keen eye for business. A few abbots had wider reputations, such as Æthelwig, abbot of Evesham, who acted as a regional governor for William the Conqueror in the west for a few critical years after 1066.[122] Jocelin of Brakelond created a vivid picture of Abbot Samson of Bury (1182–1211). The abbot took over after a period of lax administration. He tackled debt by having the abbey's resources carefully surveyed, ending the practice of leasing demesne manors, imposing unpopular austerity measures on the monks whilst nevertheless continuing with building work. He was robust in his defence of the abbey's privileges, a respected papal judge delegate, and loyal to the Angevins. In 1193, wearing armour, he attended the siege of Windsor with the abbey's contingent of knights.[123] The office of abbot of Bury was exceptional in that the abbot was in effect lord of the western half of Suffolk. He had responsibilities in the region whether he wanted them or not, and Samson clearly was no shrinking violet. Yet by the late twelfth century it had become unusual for abbots, even those of the older and richer houses, to have much of a profile outside their own communities.

Over the best part of two centuries it was inevitable that the roles of archbishops, bishops, and, up to a point, abbots, had altered. Archbishops and bishops came to be at the head of a hierarchy of officials and lower clergy, and they themselves had to adjust to the reality both of papal and royal power in a way that necessitated new expertise. Most were men who, having become bishops, did their best to carry out their multifarious duties. Few were spontaneously venerated as saints in their own lifetimes or, in the case of Becket, soon after their deaths, but for these men, like their illustrious predecessors in the early medieval church, power was not confined to their lifetimes, but continued after death.

---

[122] Thomas of Marlborough, *History of the Abbey of Evesham*, ed. and trans. J. Sayers and L. Watkiss (Oxford: Clarendon Press, 2003), pp. 160–74.

[123] Jocelin of Brakelond, *Chronicle of the Abbey of Bury St Edmunds* (trans. Greenway and Sayers); Antonia Gransden, 'Samson (1135–1211)', *ODNB* www.oxforddnb.com/view /article/24601, accessed 20 May 2016.

6

Individuals, Communities, and Networks

To this point, this book has been concerned with individuals, the ways they exercised power sometimes collaboratively, sometimes competitively, and sometimes in confrontation: rights to use coercive force, to hunt on one's own land, and to exercise justice and jurisdiction were disputed areas. The emphasis has been on vertical relationships, on the obedience owed to kings and lords, to bishops and abbots. Here the focus switches to ties of family, occupation, and political allegiance. These were both vertical and lateral, shifting and overlapping, yet intrinsic to our understanding of medieval society. As Gerd Althoff argued in *Family, Friends and Followers: political and Social Bonds in Early Medieval Europe*, these social ties, sustained by ritual, were pervasive and important.[1] In recent years historians have emphasized the importance of ties of family and kindred, neighbourhood, that is, village and parish, voluntary associations such as gilds and fraternities, friendship networks, and a sense of community and identity in towns.[2] Susan Reynolds's *Kingdoms and Communities in Western Europe 900 to 1300* (1984) argued persuasively for the continuing importance of ties binding men together at the local and regional levels (she did not include family ties or religious communities). Furthermore, she argued that they should not be seen as declining in the face of the rising power of the modern

---

[1] G. Althoff, *Family, Friends and Followers. political and Social Bonds in Early Medieval Europe*, trans. C. Carroll (Cambridge: Cambridge University Press, 2004).

[2] S. Reynolds, *Kingdoms and Communities in Western Europe 900–1300* (Oxford: Clarendon Press, 1984). C. Clarke, too, has tackled the relationship between vertical pressures and what might be called horizontal associations, 'patterns of reciprocity and economies of mutual obligation' in her *Writing Power in Anglo-Saxon England* (Woodbridge: D. S. Brewer, 2012).

state as a kind of inevitable process.[3] The first part of this chapter explores different kinds of lateral and voluntary ties, including some such as family, kinship, and religious patronage not covered by Reynolds. It is argued, further, that it is the combination of vertical and lateral ties, overlapping and shifting, in the form of networks, spreading outward from the centre, which helps to explain how society worked. A brief discussion of towns in terms of communities and identities is included, but towns as nodes of power are discussed further in Chapters 7 and 8.

FAMILY AND KINSHIP

The most immediate ties were those of family and kinship. Throughout the period the closest personal ties were those of the nuclear family, father, mother, and children.[4] The term *familia*, though literally translated as 'family', in fact is closer to 'household'. *Familiae* included children being fostered, thegns, knights, and officers of the household. Within marriage the power of husbands over wives and fathers over children remained constant. Women passed from the households of their fathers or guardians to those of their husbands. Widows were to be remarried (though churchmen were ambivalent on this), but not too quickly, and not against their will. Their rights over land and property they had brought to the marriage, their marriage portion, and the dower bestowed on them by their husbands, were not absolute. Surviving wills by Anglo-Saxon women show them disposing of land, property, and personal possessions, and freeing slaves, and have in the past been taken as evidence of a relative independence which they lost after 1066.[5] It is clear, however, that many of the testators were widows, and that their wills should be seen in the context of family strategies involving men as well as women.[6] After 1066

---

[3] *Kingdoms and Communities*, pp. 337–9. Thus, for example, the first chapter of W. L. Warren's *Governance of Norman and Angevin England* (London: Edward Arnold, 1987) begins with a review of 'the bonds of society' viz. kindred, community, lordship, and kingship, but after a second chapter dealing with the 'Normanization of England' the book is organized round royal government, both strong and weak. Kindred and community in effect go underground.

[4] J. S. Moore, 'The Anglo-Norman Family: Size and Structure', *Anglo-Norman Studies*, 14 (1991), 153–96.

[5] For a critique, see P. Stafford, 'Women and the Norman Conquest', *Transactions of the Royal Historical Society*, 6th series, 4 (1994), 221–49 at p. 223; Tollerton, *Wills and Will-Making in Anglo-Saxon England*.

[6] J. Crick, 'Women, Posthumous Benefaction and Family Strategy in Pre-Conquest England', *Journal of British Studies*, 38 (1999), 399–422.

land held by knight service was not devisable, though movable property was, hence there are very few surviving wills.[7] By the twelfth century women were issuing charters relating to their marriage portions, and it became common to record the involvement of their husbands and heirs, presumably to head off any potential trouble.[8]

Marriage partners had to be sought outside the prohibited degrees of kinship. From the ninth century these were set at seven degrees, calculated according to descent from a common ancestor in a way that had the effect of reducing the available pool of marriage partners.[9] The prohibition extended to relationships established by godparenthood, or affinity. Not only that, but the church's insistence on the sacramental nature of marriage made it harder for marriages lawfully contracted to be dissolved. By the twelfth century marriage litigation could be brought before the church courts and then, as Duby pointed out, the discovery that marriage partners were too closely related offered an escape route from marriages which had proved unsuitable or barren.[10] The church's takeover of marriage, formerly an arrangement between families with perhaps a nuptial blessing, had important consequences for other heterosexual unions, and for their offspring: the status of concubines, clerical wives, and their children was downgraded, and only the children of legitimate marriage had claims on a family's land.

There is very little direct evidence about inheritance customs at the start of our period, and specifically how far they shaped provision for all the children of a marriage. Parents doubtless wished to make some provision for all children, but it seems likely that there was also concern to keep land together, possibly by designating one son as heir. Inherited land was subject to stronger expectations than land which had been acquired by other means. The various conquests (Vikings, Danes, and Normans) were another complicating factor, for fathers could only dispose of what was rightfully theirs. We never have the full picture. Moreover, the huge turnover of land in the upper levels of society and the changing role of documentation further complicates discussion. The consequences of defeat and dispossession could be mitigated by intermarriage. Elisabeth

---

[7] Tollerton, *Wills and Will-Making*, pp. 279–83; Hudson, *Oxford History of the Laws of England*, II, pp. 378–9.

[8] Green, *Aristocracy of Norman England*, pp. 364–83; Johns, *Noblewomen, Aristocracy and Power in the Twelfth-Century Anglo-Norman Realm*, part 2.

[9] C. B. Bouchard, 'Consanguinity and Noble Marriages in the Tenth and Eleventh Centuries', *Speculum*, 56 (1981), 268–87.

[10] G. Duby, *Medieval Marriage: Two Models from Twelfth-Century France* (Baltimore, MD, and London: Johns Hopkins University Press, 1975).

van Houts has studied the eleventh-century evidence, chiefly from names and from Domesday Book, which gives some clue at least about high-status men and women.[11] She has found eight examples of English women marrying Danes between 1017 and 1041, three more who married Frenchmen between 1041 and 1066, one man marrying a Dane between 1017 and 1041 and between 1041 and 1066 seven men, all but one of mixed race themselves, who married or were betrothed to women from Normandy or Flanders. There are more examples after 1066, not least because of Domesday evidence, but even so the numbers for both men and women are relatively small. Even with high-status individuals there are problems with this kind of evidence: names are not necessarily an accurate guide to ethnic identity, and relationships could vary from betrothals to unofficial but long-term relationships and Christian marriage. It is unlikely, however, that more than a fraction of land transferred to Danes or Normans passed via marriage, and therefore title depended to a greater or lesser degree on submission to a conqueror. In the first generation after such a submission, a new lord may have had more freedom to dispose of his land, though again the pressure to keep it together may have been strengthening lineage well before the coming of the Normans.

Again not much is known about Norman inheritance practice in the early eleventh century. What there is suggests that customs were broadly similar to those in England. As J. C. Holt pointed out, in the first generation after 1066 English estates represented acquisitions, of which their holders had some freedom to dispose.[12] However, a high proportion of the tenancies-in-chief recorded in Domesday Book passed without division to one son, usually the eldest. This may be due to a combination of factors, including the preference of king and aristocracy for unity over partition, and the format of the Domesday Inquest itself, which provided a record of landholders. In subsequent generations a clear preference for male primogeniture becomes apparent. Where there were no sons but several daughters, the norm was division. By the time of Glanvill, it was possible to outline norms for the proportion of land of which a lord could dispose, and to whom.[13] To sum up: whilst kinship ties did matter in

[11] 'Intermarriage in Eleventh-Century England', D. Crouch and K. Thompson (eds.), *Normandy and Its Neighbours 900–1250: Essays for David Bates* (Turnhout: Brepols, 2011), pp. 237–70.

[12] 'Politics and Property in Early Medieval England'.

[13] Glanvill, books vi (dower), vii (marriage-portions and other forms of alienation).

deciding how land was to be assigned, over time the degree of flexibility diminished and agnatic tendencies strengthened.

In the early Middle Ages kindreds provided security and redress for their members. At its most dramatic this was by banding together to avenge a kinsman who was killed or injured. More usually it was by acting as security for oaths, or as pledges for good behaviour. At the start of our period feud was clearly still very much in evidence. Earlier in the tenth century King Edmund's laws show the king seeking to regulate rather than eradicate feud.[14] Moreover, even in those regions which were organized in shires and hundreds, older loyalties remained potent. One's neighbours were likely to be kinsmen, and if oath helpers were needed, one's first port of call was likely to be one's kin. Equally it is clear that whilst criminal prosecution throughout our period relied heavily on personal accusation or appeal, then kin were directly involved in bringing wrongdoers to justice, and this remained true even as the procedures involved in bringing men to justice changed. The compensatory principle which had in theory provided an incentive for the kin to act as well as to secure redress may have been eroded by fines to the king and to the lord by the start of our period. Nevertheless, issues of honour and injury, as Paul Hyams has argued, did not simply disappear.[15] Rather they were submerged beneath the records of judicial process.

What happened in England north of the Humber and Mersey remains largely obscure, and what evidence there is comes from eleventh-century Durham. First there was the murder of Bishop Walcher in 1080 at Gateshead, which occurred when he sought to pacify a hostile crowd seeking vengeance for their kinsman, killed, they believed, with the involvement of the bishop's kinsman.[16] Secondly, there is the text relating the history of certain estates which Bishop Ealdhun (who died in 1018) had granted in marriage with his daughter, and which the monks clearly believed belonged to the patrimony of St Cuthbert. It was a story of death and vengeance, ending at Settrington in Yorkshire in 1073 with a final act of violence by Earl Waltheof.[17] The maintenance of law and order elsewhere in the north outside the shire regions must have continued to depend on communities of kin and neighbours, enforced as and when by lords, simply because of distance and the lack of sheriffs and of frankpledge, but once again, there are few details.

[14] Hudson, *Oxford History of the Laws of England*, II, pp. 171–5.
[15] Hyams, *Rancor and Reconciliation*, pp. 82–4.   [16] JW, III, pp. 32–6.
[17] *De Obsessione Dunelmi*, Symeon of Durham, *Opera omnia*, I, pp. 215–20.

The importance of ties of kinship as a mechanism for protection and support of its members did not disappear in face of the rising power of lordship and kingship, but rather was subsumed: depending on circumstance, family, neighbours, or lords might be called up in support. Similarly, ties of kinship as a determinant of political behaviour did not disappear, but were woven into the politics of the period, and came to the surface during succession crises. The period between the death of Cnut and that of Harold II saw high politics dominated by the rivalry between the Godwins and the Leofricsons, with the former so dominant that Harold was able to seize the throne in 1066, only to bring his whole family to destruction at Hastings. The Leofricsons, Edwin and Morcar, survived only a few years, their power and influence eroding before the Normans' advance.

The Normans who followed William to England were a small group which, related to each other and to the duke, had profited from his rule in Normandy and backed his invasion of England with their own kinsmen and followers. The first occasions when kinship determined political allegiance were in 1088 and 1101, when the sons of Roger of Montgomery acted in support of Duke Robert rather than, respectively, William Rufus and Henry I, and when the Beaumont brothers Henry earl of Warwick and Robert count of Meulan supported Henry I.[18] How important ties of kinship remained as members of the same family established different lordships has not been explored. The two branches of the Lacy family, for instance, or the different branches of the Clare family are possible case studies.[19]

There was undoubtedly a high rate of turnover in leading families due to war, politics, and the vicissitudes of hereditary succession, and this instability worked against long-lasting solidarities based on kinship ties. Sooner or later, lords were killed or died without heirs, and kings were able to profit by inserting their own men into lordships, especially through

[18] J. F. A. Mason, 'Roger of Montgomery and His Sons', *Transactions of the Royal Historical Society*, 5th series, 13 (1963), 1–28; David Crouch, 'Beaumont, Henry de, First Earl of Warwick (d. 1119)', *ODNB* www.oxforddnb.com/view/article/19984, accessed 20 May 2016; Crouch, 'Beaumont, Robert de, Count of Meulan and First Earl of Leicester (d. 1118)', *ODNB* www.oxforddnb.com/view/article/1881, accessed 20 May 2016.

[19] W. E. Wightman, *The Lacy Family in England and Normandy 1066–1194* (Oxford: Clarendon Press, 1966). The two main branches of the Clare family in England were descended from Richard FitzGilbert and Baldwin FitzGilbert, see R. Mortimer, 'Clare, Richard de (1030 x 1035–1087 x 1090)', Judith A. Green, 'Baldwin [Baldwin de Meulles] (d. 1086 x 90)', *ODNB* www.oxforddnb.com/view/article/1161, accessed 20 May 2016.

marriage. How far the newcomers were able to take over existing networks is a relatively neglected topic. Such transitions were not always peaceful: William Maltravers, lord of the Lacy honour of Pontefract in the later years of Henry I's reign, was murdered by a knight loyal to the Lacy family.[20]

ALEHOUSES, CHURCHES, AND MEETINGS

Beyond the confines of family and household, men were tied to their neighbours through frequenting alehouses and their local churches. Neither is easy to document for our period. Alehouses were numerous, since brewing was a household activity. Frequenting one might involve membership of a gild, especially in towns.[21] The proliferation of local churches provided meeting places and, even where built by lords, were a response to the needs of local communities.[22] In eastern England, and in towns, churches multiplied mightily. In London each neighbourhood, almost each street, had its own church, some of which were associated with particular occupations by the start of the twelfth century.[23] Some villages included several estates; others had only one, and in these the manorial court was a meeting place for all the (male) villagers for decisions about cooperative action and resources complementary to that of the church in village life. From these communities were drawn the representatives who would attend the courts of hundred or wapentake.

TOWNS

Towns and cities have not been given much attention in this book so far, and it is easy to underestimate their importance as nodes of power, different from, yet intertwined with, kings, lords, and churchmen. Most were in the south and midlands of England, and had been fortified – or used Roman walls – as bases, *burhs*, for defence against Viking attack in the ninth and tenth centuries.[24] Responsibility for maintaining the walls in good repair was apportioned on land, and the townsmen were expected to

[20] *RRAN*, III, no. 428.   [21] Blair, *Church in Anglo-Saxon Society*, pp. 453–4.
[22] *Ibid.*, pp. 498–500.
[23] J. Schofield, 'Saxon and Medieval Parish Churches in the City of London: a Review', *Transactions of the London and Middlesex Archaeological Society*, 45 (1994), 23–145 at p. 35.
[24] For a recent review, see Lavelle, *Alfred's Wars: Sources and Interpretations of Anglo-Saxon Warfare in the Viking Age*, chapter 6.

provide military service. In the Danelaw five towns, Leicester, Nottingham, Derby, Lincoln, and Stamford, were strongholds with territories dependent on them.[25] From the mid-eleventh century ports in the south-east were granted privileges in return for providing ships to the king. The original Cinque Ports were Hastings, Romney, Dover, Sandwich, and Hythe. It is thought that when Edward the Confessor disbanded his stipendiary fleet in 1049 or 1050, and abandoned the here-geld which formed their wages, he turned instead to the ports for ships in return for annual squadrons of ships, which supplemented the levies of ships levied through shires and ship-sokes.[26]

Towns were closely linked with rural lords, who often owned urban property.[27] Towns, though generally small by Italian standards, were centres of commerce and manufacture and both reflected and stimulated economic development. Many expanded into new suburbs, and many new towns were founded during our period by lay or ecclesiastical lords who benefitted from rents and from tolls taken there.[28] They housed mints, which gave kings another direct interest. Moneyers had to have considerable supplies of silver available to make coins of the current issue, in which payments to the king had to be made. At the start of our period minting was decentralized with many mints except in northern England but, as we have seen, by the end of our period it was much more centralized on London.

As towns became more important they needed to develop both agencies to regulate internal governance and to deal with their external relations, especially with kings, and the latter particularly helped to strengthen a sense of collective identity. We first hear of towns, the five boroughs mentioned previously, as being taken over by King Edmund in 942. They then seceded before being taken back into English control.[29] In 1013 they made a separate submission to King Swein, as did Oxford.[30] In 1066 the men of Winchester advised Queen Edith to submit to King William.[31]

---

[25] N. J. Higham, 'Five Boroughs', (Lapidge and others, eds.), *Blackwell Encyclopaedia of Anglo-Saxon England*, p. 186; P. Stafford, *The East Midlands in the Early Middle Ages* (Leicester: Leicester University Press, 1985), pp. 136–43.

[26] Hooper, 'Some Observations on the Navy in Late Anglo-Saxon England', Harper-Bill, Holdsworth, and Nelson (eds.), *Studies in Medieval History Presented to R. A. Brown*.

[27] R. Fleming, 'Rural Elites and Urban Communities in Late-Saxon England', *Past and Present*, 141 (1993), 3–37.

[28] R. Britnell, 'The Economy of British Towns 600–1300', D. M. Palliser (ed.), *Cambridge Urban History of Britain*, I (Cambridge: Cambridge University Press, 2008), pp. 105–26.

[29] ASC, A, D, 942.

[30] ASC, E, 1013; cf. the annal for 1015, which refers to seven boroughs.

[31] *Carmen de Hastingae Proelio*, pp. 36–8.

The men of London, Dover, and Canterbury similarly made separate submissions.[32] In 1068 the citizens of Exeter held the city against the Normans. The king himself was forced to besiege the city and, having gained the citizens' submission, he built a castle there.[33] These episodes occurred at times of crisis; more usually citizens negotiated with a new king to secure confirmation of their privileges. These came to be recorded in charters.[34]

Payments to the king over and above those from rents and tolls included in the sheriff's farm had to be negotiated, and this meant that townsmen had to be able to act as a group. By the later twelfth century, as reported in the *Dialogue of the Exchequer* when the amount had been negotiated, the townsmen organized how it was apportioned.[35] Freedom to detach the farm from the sheriff's county farm was a privilege for which citizens were prepared to pay: in 1130 the citizens of Lincoln had made a proffer to this end.[36] The Londoners were even more ambitious because they wanted the right to have sheriffs of their own choosing.[37] Not long afterwards, at the start of Stephen's reign, they are reported to have formed a sworn alliance, or commune.[38] Such associations had grown up in continental towns where they were associated with violence and threats to the established order, as at Le Mans and Laon.[39] In England, the essence of the matter was a desire for greater autonomy. The Londoners probably tried to use Stephen's difficulties to extract more privileges (see further in Chapter 8). There is a possibility, too, that a commune existed in Oxford in the 1140s.[40] There are reports of communes in Gloucester and York during the revolt of 1173–4.[41]

Secondly, towns needed councils and courts for the management of their affairs. London's court of husting is thought to have received its

---

[32] ASC, D, 1066; William of Poitiers, *Gesta Guillelmi*, pp. 142–4.

[33] OV, II, pp. 210–14.

[34] William the Conqueror's charter for the Londoners was an early example, Bates, *Acta of William I*, no. 180.

[35] *Dialogus de Scaccario*, p. 162.   [36] *Pipe Roll 31 Henry I*, p. 90.   [37] Ibid., p. 116.

[38] *Gesta Stephani*, pp. 6–7; WM, *Historia Novella*, pp. 94–5.

[39] Reynolds, *Kingdoms and Communities*, pp. 176–7.

[40] See earlier in this volume. The evidence comes from a charter in the Oseney cartulary whereby the island of Medley was confirmed to the abbey by the 'commune of the city and the gild of merchants', *Cartulary of Oseney Abbey*, ed. H. E. Salter, 6 vols., Oxford Historical Society, 89–91, 97–8, 101 (1929–36), IV, p. 86.

[41] *Pipe Roll 16 Henry II*, p. 79; *Pipe Roll 22 Henry II*, p. 106; J. Tait, *The Medieval English Borough: Studies on Its Origins and Constitutional History* (Manchester: Manchester University Press, 1936), pp. 176–7.

Danish name in the early eleventh century.[42] It comprised the aldermen or chief men of the wards, the city's subdivisions for policing. In Scandinavian-settled areas there were lawmen in boroughs who sat in judgement.[43] Gilds were an important feature of urban life. By the early twelfth century merchant gilds are mentioned in pipe rolls, because they were prepared to pay for recognition, and also there were gilds for individual crafts.[44] These regulated matters such as pricing and training through apprenticeships, but they were also associations for welfare, and were linked with particular churches and saints.[45]

Thirdly, by the twelfth century a developing sense of civic identity was reflected in legends about their foundation.[46] The association of Colchester with King Cole was known to Henry of Huntingdon and Geoffrey of Monmouth.[47] By the fourteenth century the townspeople of Grimsby believed that their founder was Grim, who appears as the foster father of Havelock the Dane in Gaimar's *Estoire des Engleis*.[48] According to Geoffrey of Monmouth, London was founded by Brutus as his capital city and named 'New Troy'. Later King Lud surrounded the city with walls and ordered it to be called after himself.[49] William FitzStephen in his famous description of London composed after the death of Thomas Becket, also believed that London was founded by Brutus before, therefore, Rome was founded by Romulus and Remus.[50] For Lucian, who composed a poem in praise of Chester between about 1195 and 1224, the city's main streets in the form of a cross meeting at the market place, 'mystically revealed the innate power' of God.[51] In this case, it was the symbolism of the city's urban geography, not its legendary past which mattered.

---

[42] P. Nightingale, 'The Origin of the Court of Husting and Danish Influence on London's Development into a Capital City', reprinted in *Trade, Money and Power in Medieval England*, pp. 559–78.

[43] Tait, *Medieval English Borough*, pp. 43–4.

[44] Reynolds, *Kingdoms and Communities*, pp. 67–78.

[45] In about 1100 two London churches were associated, respectively, with porters and seamen, Schofield, 'Saxon and Medieval Parish Churches in the City of London: a Review', p. 35, as cited Blair, *Church in Anglo-Saxon Society*, p. 501.

[46] G. Rosser, 'Myth, Image and Social Process in the English Medieval Town', *Urban History*, 23 (1996), 5–25.

[47] HH, pp. 60, 474; Geoffrey of Monmouth, *HKB*, Book V, para. 78 (ed. Reeve, pp. 94–7).

[48] *Lestoire des Engleis*, lines 332, 369.

[49] Geoffrey of Monmouth, *HKB*, Book II, para. 22 (ed. Reeve, pp. 28–31).

[50] *Materials for the History of Thomas Becket*, III, p. 8.

[51] K. D. Lilley, 'Imagining the City: Christian Symbolism and Chester's Medieval Urban Form', www.medievalchester.ac.uk/context/lilley.html.

A sense of identity could be reinforced by ritual. In larger cities, as noted previously, this was probably centred on small neighbourhood churches, but elsewhere celebrations for the local saint may have been the focus. Processions at the great festivals, or special ceremonies when saints were translated to new shrines, were attended by crowds. The arrival of the king may have been ceremonial. When Rufus's body was taken to Winchester after his death in the New Forest the clergy and poorer townspeople came out to meet the cortege.[52] The arrival of Becket in 1070 at London and Canterbury was reportedly attended by great crowds.[53]

By the later twelfth century towns possessed seals, on which were images representing their identity. The earliest impression of that of London showed the walled city with the Tower and the cathedral on one side with St Paul hovering overhead, and on the other Thomas Becket, who had become the second patron saint of the city.[54] Approaching urban history from the perspective of collective identities, whether in dealings with kings or lords, or internal cohesion through ties of neighbourhood, gild and church membership, could be misleading. Domestic politics in particular are likely to have seen contests rooted on family or occupational lines. Violence against different ethnic or religious groups happened from time to time: the Danes at Oxford were killed in 1002 on the orders of King Æthelred, for instance.[55] The Jews in Norwich came under suspicion in 1144 when the body of a murdered child was discovered.[56] Antagonism between rich and poor is harder to identify. There were rich neighbourhoods in London, for example, but presumably the rich in their stone houses were well protected.[57] Only in the late twelfth century do we hear of a revolt headed by William FitzOsbert in

[52] OV, V, p. 292.

[53] Herbert of Bosham, *Materials for the History of Thomas Becket*, III, pp. 478, 482–3.

[54] For a reproduction and discussion, see Keene, 'Text, Visualization and Politics: London, 1150–1250', p. 77.

[55] ASC, C, D, E, 1002 reports the king's order. For Æthelred's charter referring to the killing, S909, *English Historical Documents*, I, pp. 557–9. For the Oxford dig which uncovered skeletons thought to be those killed in 1002, Wallis, *Oxford Henge and Late Saxon Massacre*.

[56] M. D. Anderson, *A Saint at Stake: the Strange Death of William of Norwich* (London: Faber, 1964); S. Yarrow, *Saints and Their Communities: Miracle Stories in Twelfth-Century England* (Oxford: Clarendon Press, 2006), chapter 6.

[57] J. Schofield, *London 1100–1600. The Archaeology of a Capital City* (Sheffield: Equinox, 2011), p. 61.

London against the unequal burden of taxation carried by the poor.[58] There is little to be said of inter-family rivalries at this early date, though doubtless they existed.

FRIENDSHIP

To this point, we have been looking at ties that existed from birth, those voluntarily entered into such as godparenthood, marriage, gild member-ship, religious patronage, and those resulting from situation in villages, parishes, or towns. What, however, of friendship? Friendships then as now took many forms, ranging from those based purely on affection to those in which mutual interests were of primary importance.[59] Moreover, the term *amicitia* as used in monastic circles belonged to a specific literary genre. Letter collections, such as those of Archbishops Anselm and Thomas Becket or John of Salisbury, used the term in different ways. An influential model here was Cicero's *De Amicitia*.

In contrast with monastic or clerical friendships, the friendship circles recorded in letter collections, we are much less well informed about friendships of any kind in the secular world. Later tradition, for instance, ascribed to two Domesday lords in Oxfordshire, Roger d'Ivry and Robert d'Oilly, a brotherhood-in-arms which is not in itself improbable given their close association.[60] The Battle Chronicle refers to a pact of friendship between Reginald earl of Cornwall, uncle of Henry II, Richard du Hommet, his constable (mentioned earlier), Richard de Lucy the justiciar, and his brother, Walter, abbot of Battle.[61] The abbot was trying to secure a royal charter confirming the abbey's exemption from episcopal author-ity. Archbishop Theobald of Canterbury had got involved, and the king had countermanded the issue of a charter. The case had been heard and a decision deferred until more propitious circumstances. The king there-upon took advice, and amongst those who gave counsel were those bound in friendship to the abbot. The term 'friendship' is used here in a context in which 'alliance' might be more accurate. We learn quite by accident that

---

[58] Derek Keene, 'William fitz Osbert (*d.* 1196)', *ODNB* www.oxforddnb.com/view/article /9621, accessed 20 May 2016.

[59] J. Haseldine, 'Friendship and Rivalry: the Role of Amicitia in Twelfth-Century Monastic Relations', *Journal of Ecclesiastical History*, 44 (1993), 390–414; J. Haseldine, 'Understanding the Language of Amicitia: the Friendship Circle of Peter of Celle (*c.* 1115–1183)', *Journal of Medieval History*, 20 (1994), 237–60.

[60] *Cartulary of Oseney Abbey*, IV, p. 1.   [61] *Chronicle of Battle Abbey*, pp. 160–1.

three of the four knights who murdered Becket had previously been bound to him by oath, but there is no information about its meaning.[62]

NETWORKS

Networks naturally tended to form and dissolve over time. This was especially the case for those established by kings or great lords. Those based on ties of religious patronage were rather different, but even here communities had to work hard to sustain bonds with donor families. Continuing favour could not be taken for granted, particularly during political upheavals, or when there were new potential beneficiaries for patrons. One approach to English society in this era is thus through networks focussed on powerful men, who in turn were bound to the king.

Between the reigns of Edgar and Harold II political power was concentrated in very few hands, but it is only in the eleventh century that it is possible to identify the lesser thegns commended to the ealdormen and their successors, the earls. Stephen Baxter, for instance, was able to use Domesday evidence with a range of other sources to show how one Mercian family rose to prominence under King Æthelred, and circumnavigated the perils of politics under that king and his Danish successors to become the second most powerful family in the country in 1065: Edwin as earl of Mercia, their brother Morcar as earl of Northumbria, and their sister Ealdgyth as wife of Harold Godwinson, soon to be king. Their power rested on landed wealth, on the numbers of thegns commended to them, on their offices which brought more land and a stake in the boroughs, and on ties with local monasteries, Coventry, Evesham, Worcester, Burton, the minster churches of Leominster, Wenlock, St John's and St Werburgh's at Chester, and Stow in Lincolnshire.[63] Not only that, but Earl Leofric's nephew and namesake, Leofric, became abbot of Peterborough and was also said to have held the abbeys of Coventry, Burton, Crowland, and Thorney.[64] Yet even though Edwin and Morcar did not fight at Hastings and made their submission to King William, within five years or so of Hastings, their power had been destroyed. They

---

[62] N. Vincent, 'The Court of Henry II', Harper-Bill and Vincent (eds.), *Henry II. New Interpretations*, pp. 278–355, at p. 317, citing *Materials for History of Thomas Becket*, III, p. 135.
[63] Baxter, *Earls of Mercia*, chapter 5.
[64] ASC, E, 1066; *The Chronicle of Hugh Candidus, a Monk of Peterborough*, ed. W. T. Mellows (Oxford: Oxford University Press for the Friends of Peterborough Cathedral, 1949), pp. 66–7.

were unable to prevent the establishment of Normans on lands within their earldoms, and their ties with churchmen were broken. Pushed into rebellion, Edwin was killed by his own men and Morcar was captured by King William, being released only in 1087.[65]

The insertion of a new ruling elite after 1066 essentially destroyed most of the old networks of lordship and commendation, though not all. One very striking case where a new tenant-in-chief not only succeeded to the lands of a named pre-Conquest predecessor, but also to his commended men, who had been able to 'sell their land', is that of Geoffrey I de Mandeville. He succeeded, probably soon after the Battle of Hastings, to the lands of Ansger the Staller. By 1086 he was not only in possession of Ansger's estates, but also of many men and freemen who had held of Ansger. The terminology used in Circuit III of Domesday Book, which included Cambridgeshire, Hertfordshire, and Middlesex, where Geoffrey held land, makes clear which land had been held in dependent tenure before 1066, as Baxter pointed out.[66] Thus in Cambridgeshire in 1086 Geoffrey held land in ten places.[67] In four of these his tenant was Sigar, who had held under Ansger, and could grant or sell without Ansger's permission, though in two of them the soke remained with the lord.[68] Sigar had also held Sawston and Haslingfield, and could grant or sell, the soke remaining with the lord, but here he had been succeeded by a man named Roger, who held from (*de*) Geoffrey. In Fulbourn and Guilden Mordern the picture was the same: a man who could sell had held from Ansger, and by 1086 there were tenants with Norman names, whom, we must assume from later practice, would only have been able to alienate their land with the lord's permission. Chippenham was Geoffrey's largest manor, specifically said in 1086 to be held from the king. This had been held by Ordgar, King Edward's sheriff, who was later (perhaps after 1066) Ansger's man and possibly joined the rebellion of Hereward the Wake.[69]

The successors to the earls of Mercia in many respects were the Norman earls of Chester, and their strategies of lordship reveal points of continuity and also important changes. Chris Lewis demonstrated how the vast estates of Earl Hugh (who died in 1101) were accumulated in stages. Hugh acquired many estates formerly in the hands of Harold II and

---

[65] Baxter, *Earls of Mercia*, chapter 7.   [66] *Ibid.*, p. 225.   [67] DB, I, fol. 197r.

[68] Sigar was identified as a juror, former steward of Ansger, in the *Inquisitio Comitatus Cantabrigiensis*, ed. N. E. S. A. Hamilton (London: John Murray, 1876), pp. 43, 73.

[69] C. P. Lewis, 'Ordgar (*fl.* 1066)', *ODNB* www.oxforddnb.com/view/article/20814, accessed 20 May 2016.

other members of the Godwin family, with a further grant in 1070 or 1071 of a compact lordship centred on Cheshire to guard the frontier against the Welsh. Here he acquired all land not held by the church, including the estates of Earl Edwin, and he held the town of Chester. A few years later he benefited from the downfall of Earl Ralph and acquired the lands of many thegns in East Anglia.[70] He was a key figure under William Rufus, and that king granted him even more estates.[71]

Hugh's only son died in the wreck of the White Ship, and he was succeeded by a cousin, Ranulf I, whose marriage to Lucy had brought Lincolnshire estates into the family. Ranulf II and his half-brother William de Roumare shared Lucy's inheritance, and when war broke under Stephen the brothers worked to build up their power in Lincolnshire at Lincoln itself, by holding important manors with rights of jurisdiction attached, and by bringing local families into alliance.[72] Ranulf also fought to establish himself at Coventry, which brought him into conflict with Robert Marmion.[73] Ranulf's death in 1153 left a minor as his successor. Hugh II was married to Bertrada, daughter of Simon, count of Evreux and lord of Montfort, a Franco-Norman magnate whom Henry II wished to keep on side.[74] When Earl Hugh II attained his majority he was not included in the king's inner circle. It is not surprising, therefore, to see the earl on the side of the rebels in 1173–4, as a result of which he lost lands and castles.[75] He remained vastly rich in lands and castles, but the timing of his father's death and Henry II's determination to recover ground lost to the great magnates in the civil war, together, perhaps, with his own personality and temperament, meant that his political influence was far less than his father's had been.

Formal treaties between magnates were made, though not often recorded in writing unless land or property rights were involved. They emerge in the

---

[70] C. P. Lewis, 'The Formation of the Earldom of Chester, 1066–1100', *The Earldom of Chester and Its Charters. A Tribute to Geoffrey Barraclough*, ed. A. T. Thacker, *Journal of the Chester Archaeological Society*, 71 (1991), 37–68.

[71] W. Farrer, *Honors and Knights' Fees*, 3 vols. (Manchester: Manchester University Press, 1923–5), II, pp. 6–7.

[72] P. Dalton, 'Aiming at the Impossible: Ranulf II of Chester and Lincolnshire in the Reign of King Stephen', *Earldom of Chester and Its Charters*, pp. 109–34.

[73] HH, p. 744.

[74] D. J. Power, *The Norman Frontier in the Twelfth and Early Thirteenth Centuries* (Cambridge: Cambridge University Press, 2004), pp. 230–1.

[75] Vincent, 'Did Henry II Have a Policy towards the Earls?', Given-Wilson, Kettle, and Scales (eds.), *War, Government and Aristocracy in the British Isles c. 1150–1500: Essays in Honour of Michael Prestwich*, pp. 7, 10, 15.

written record in the early twelfth century. David Crouch has argued that the
key characteristic of the treaty 'is that it has to be a settlement reached
between independent and near-equal powers'.[76] They are most visible in
Stephen's reign. The *Gesta Stephani*, for instance, reported the kinsmen,
vassals, and neighbours of Richard FitzGilbert (Strongbow), who allied
with him by oaths and giving of hostages.[77] The term 'hostage' has of course
overtones of distrust. More positively men were prepared to pledge themselves to support treaties or act as witnesses. This was certainly the case for
the charters of two great magnates, Robert earl of Gloucester and Ranulf II
earl of Chester.[78] The former's charters included the earl's half-brother, Earl
Reginald, Humphrey de Bohun, Richard du Hommet, Stephen de
Mandeville, and William de Mountfitchet. The witness lists of the latter's
charters comprised Cadwaladr, brother of the king of Gwynedd, his own
brother-in-law Gilbert FitzRichard, and Walter FitzAlan. The witnesses to
a grant made at Wenlock in 1153 included Walter brother of the earl of
Hereford, Richard of Clare, Gilbert son of Baderon of Monmouth, and his
own kinsman, William FitzOtuel. Paul Dalton has argued that Ranulf and his
half-brother, William de Roumare, were particularly concerned to establish
regional domination over Lincolnshire lords.[79] David Crouch has drawn
attention to the affinity of Roger earl of Hereford in south Wales and the
borders.[80] Geoffrey de Mandeville at the height of his power was also able to
draw others into his orbit, for grants made to them were included in the first
charter granted to him by the empress.[81] The charters of Henry earl of
Northumberland, son of King David of Scots, were witnessed by local
lords.[82] At one level it may be argued that such alliances were a response to
the weakening of royal authority in the localities. As Crouch has pointed out,
the famous magnate treaties or *conventiones* made in Stephen's reign disappear within a year or two of the accession of Henry II.[83] Such alliances
were probably in part a reflection of the contested politics of Stephen's reign,
but not entirely so.

[76] D. Crouch, 'A Norman "*Conventio*" and Bonds of Lordship', G. Garnett and J. Hudson
(eds.), *Law and Government in Medieval England and Normandy: Essays in Honour of
Sir James Holt* (Cambridge: Cambridge University Press, 1994), pp. 299–324 at p. 309.
[77] *Gesta Stephani*, p. 16.   [78] Green, *Aristocracy of Norman England*, pp. 213–17.
[79] P. Dalton, 'Aiming at the Impossible: Ranulf II Earl of Chester and Lincolnshire in the
Reign of King Stephen', *Earldom of Chester and Its Charters*, Chester Archaeological
Society, 71 (1991), 109–34.
[80] Crouch, 'The March and the Welsh Kings', King (ed.), *Anarchy of King Stephen's Reign*,
pp. 281–3.
[81] Green, *Aristocracy of Norman England*, p. 217.   [82] *Charters of David I*, p. 20.
[83] Crouch, 'A Norman "*Conventio*"', pp. 315–16.

Of course, Domesday Book is not going to reveal anything about post-Conquest relationships which were not based on landholding, as the commissioners were most concerned about those responsible for dues owed to the king. Moreover, there are relatively few private charters dating from the early post-Conquest period. It could be argued that charters addressed to 'sworn men' and 'friends' as well as 'men' are an indication of different ties, even if the form of greeting was modelled on that of royal charters.

What we do find, as charters begin to survive in greater numbers from the 1140s, is the attestation of men who were not tenants or the grantors, but evidently allies. They were, in other words, part of a lord's affinity. Where royal justice provided an alternative avenue for conflict resolution, then formal alliances recorded in writing may have been less necessary. The changing role of charters, too, has to be borne in mind: witnesses may have been mainly drawn from a lord's tenants because this was all that was necessary for the ratification of a grant or confirmation. Even so, we need not suppose that affinities themselves, if we mean by that aristocratic groupings, disappeared: far from it. Marriages and grants of land remained the currency, and occasionally we catch glimpses of baronial strategies. Crouch drew attention to the enfeoffment in the late 1160s or 1170s by William earl of Gloucester of the chief justiciar, Richard de Lucy, a grant which was recorded in a charter.[84]

Some alliances rested on mutual interest and friendship, possibly cemented by marriage. The working partnership between Miles of Gloucester and Payn FitzJohn between about 1127 and 1137 when Payn died is a case in point.[85] Payn was active on the Marches by about 1119, having married Sybil Talbot, niece of Hugh de Lacy. He became sheriff of Herefordshire and then Shropshire. Miles had been married to the heiress of Brecon in 1121, and in 1126 or 1127 he succeeded his father as sheriff of Gloucester and a royal justice. His son Roger married Cecily, daughter of Payn FitzJohn. A similar partnership in the 1120s was formed in northern England between Walter Espec and Eustace FitzJohn.[86] Walter

---

[84] *Earldom of Gloucester Charters: the Charters and Scribes of the Earls and Countesses of Gloucester to A. D. 1217*, ed. R. B. Patterson (Oxford: Clarendon Press, 1973), no. 115; Crouch, 'A Norman "*Conventio*"', p. 317.

[85] J. F. A. Mason, 'Pain fitz John (*d.* 1137)', *ODNB* www.oxforddnb.com/view/article/9615, accessed 20 May 2016; David Walker, 'Gloucester, Miles of, Earl of Hereford (*d.* 1143)', *ODNB* www.oxforddnb.com/view/article/10820, accessed 20 May 2016.

[86] Paul Dalton, 'Espec, Walter (*d.* 1147 x 58)', *ODNB* www.oxforddnb.com/view/article /8885, accessed 20 May 2016; T. F. Tout, 'Eustace fitz John (*d.* 1157)', rev. Paul Dalton, *ODNB* www.oxforddnb.com/view/article/9614, accessed 20 May 2016.

had acquired land in Northumberland (Wark) and Yorkshire (Helmsley) before about 1120. Eustace similarly was granted land in both counties, at Alnwick (by his marriage to Beatrice de Vescy) and Malton, and he also had custody of the castle and honour of Tickhill. Both were royal justices and lavish patrons of the church. Each founded religious houses, Walter at Kirkham, Rievaulx, and Wardon, and Eustace at Alnwick, Old Malton, and Watton (both Gilbertine), as well as making gifts to Fountains.

Ties of friendship and neighbourhood could be strengthened by collaboration in the foundation and endowment of religious houses. Tenants might well follow their lord's lead. Earl Hugh of Chester's tenants, for example, made gifts to the Norman abbey of Saint-Evroul.[87] When he went on to re-endow St Werburgh's at Chester, his tenants lined up to make gifts to that house.[88] The tenants of Earl Roger similarly made gifts to Shrewsbury Abbey, established by the earl.[89] Henry de Ferrers founded a priory at Tutbury, and the confirmation charter issued by Robert II listed the donations of his tenants and of Henry's daughter and her husband, Nigel d'Aubigny.[90] Robert I de Brus established an Augustinian priory at Guisborough in 1119. He endowed the priory with land at Guisborough, Kirkleatham, Coatham and eight churches with their tithes.[91] Robert's tenants duly followed suit: Ernald de Percy of Kildale, William Ingram, Alvred, Roger de Rosel, Theobald of Lofthus, and Robert Esturmy made gifts at the priory's foundation.[92] Such collaboration was particularly striking in the case of northern houses. Whilst the initial endowment was the work of one individual or individuals, others chipped in. Walter Espec was the founder of Rievaulx, a house which attracted patronage from a handful of major families and many middling and lesser ones. Archbishop Thurstan was closely involved with the introduction of the Cistercians into Yorkshire. He was (by accident) the founder of Fountains; his assistance was sought by the monks of a struggling Savigniac community at Calder, and he was a point of contact with lay patrons. Patterns of

[87] *The Charters of the Anglo-Norman Earls of Chester c. 1071–1237*, ed. G. Barraclough, Record Society of Lancashire and Cheshire, 126 (1988), no. 1.

[88] *Ibid.*, nos. 3, 8, 13, 28: although the charters are spurious, the gifts they record are not.

[89] *The Cartulary of Shrewsbury Abbey*, ed. U. Rees, 2 vols. (Aberystwyth: National Library of Wales, 1975), I, no. 34: Henry I's confirmation of the abbey's endowments. The text as it stands is problematic, but not the endowments.

[90] *The Cartulary of Tutbury Priory*, ed. A. Saltman, Collections for a History of Staffordshire, 4th series, 4 (London, 1962), no. 52.

[91] *Cartularium Prioratus de Gyseburne*, I, ed. W. Brown, Surtees Society, 86 (1889), nos. 1, 2.

[92] R. Blakeley, *The Brus Family in England and Scotland 1100–1295* (Woodbridge: Boydell Press, 2005), pp. 131–2.

landholding meant that confirmation charters were solicited from over-lords, who thus renewed ties of association both with tenants and with the religious houses concerned. The Mowbray charters provide a number of examples here, not only of houses in Yorkshire, but also Durham, Revesby in Lincolnshire, Pipewell and Welford in Northamptonshire, Combe in Warwickshire, and Southwark in Surrey, as well as houses in Normandy.

The history of these networks have several common features: good luck in surviving long enough to leave adult sons, adroit political judgement, the importance of office and more generally royal patronage, the role of alli-ances with local families, and relations with religious houses. Yet there were changes over time. One is the declining influence of noble families over episcopal and abbatial appointments. The influence of Leofric earl of Mercia over the midland abbeys has been noted. Earl Godwin was even more ambitious. In 1051 his kinsman Æthelric was proposed as archbishop of Canterbury.[93] This nomination was vetoed in favour of the king's choice of Robert of Jumièges, bishop of London, but if it had succeeded the earl's position in Kent would have been greatly strengthened. After 1066 the most important houses were in the short term committed to Normans and then as time wore on, more likely to be filled internally or from another house, and only occasionally by men from noble families. A second change is the association of lineage with place, as centres of lordship acquired added prestige as family seats, embellished with stone castles (see later).

Although the upper clergy was less closely bound to the high nobility by the end of our period, there were nevertheless important networks *within* the church. Archbishop Dunstan was evidently very well connected. He is mentioned as the kinsman of Æthelhelm, bishop of Wells and archbishop of Canterbury, Ælfheah, bishop of Winchester, and Cynesige of Lichfield, as well, possibly, as a link with the royal family.[94] The family of Archbishop Stigand came from East Anglia. Stigand became bishop of North Elmham, and when he was appointed to Canterbury he was suc-ceeded there by his brother Æthelmaer.[95] The mother of Bishop Wulfstan II of Worcester is thought to have been a sister of Archbishop Wulfstan of York, and mother of Brihtheah bishop of Worcester.[96] Lanfranc's nephew

[93] *Life of King Edward Who Rests at Westminster*, p. 30.

[94] Michael Lapidge, 'Dunstan [St Dunstan] (d. 988)', *ODNB* www.oxforddnb.com/view/article/8288, accessed 20 May 2016.

[95] H. E. J. Cowdrey, 'Stigand (d. 1072)', *ODNB* www.oxforddnb.com/view/article/26523, accessed 20 May 2016.

[96] E. Mason, *St Wulfstan of Worcester c. 1008–1095* (Oxford: Blackwell, 1990), p. 32.

Paul became abbot of St Albans, and Anselm's became abbot of Bury.[97] Ansger, a married priest who became a canon of St Paul's, was the father of Thurstan, archbishop of York and Audoen bishop of Evreux. The Glanville family, which was later to produce the crusader Hervey and the chief justiciar Ranulf de Glanville, included Archdeacon Nicholas of Huntingdon and his son Henry, also archdeacon and better known as a historian.[98] Finally, the Percy family retained close links with Whitby Abbey. William de Percy had afforded protection to Reinfrid, leader of the hermits who settled there. Despite various vicissitudes, during which William fell out with some of the hermits, his brother Serlo became leader of the community which settled at Whitby, and was succeeded in his turn by their nephew William.[99]

Clerical families were particularly strong in the eleventh and twelfth centuries until the insistence on clerical celibacy finally began to take effect. Ranulf Flambard promoted the careers of his family at Durham, and tried to secure the Norman bishopric of Lisieux for his nephew.[100] Richard de Beaumais, bishop of London between 1108 and 1127, established several nephews as canons and, the family proved to have considerable staying power.[101] Richard appointed his nephew William de Mareni as dean. He was succeeded by Ralph of Langford, brother of Richard II de Beaumais, and the latter by Hugh de Mareni, and so on. Bishop Roger of Salisbury (1106–39) was a pluralist on a grand scale, and he also advanced the careers of members of his family. Particularly significant was the way his relatives were appointed archdeacons: Roger (Berkshire), Adelelm (Dorset), and dean of Lincoln, and Roger of Ramsbury (Wiltshire). In effect then Roger dominated justice in his diocese, whether administered in secular or ecclesiastical courts. Two of the archdeacons also held royal office, Roger as Stephen's chancellor, and Adelelm as treasurer. Alexander, Roger's nephew, was appointed bishop of Lincoln and his

[97] *Gesta Abbatum Sancti Albani a Thoma Walsingham, regnante Ricardo Secundo, ejusdem ecclesiae praecentore, compilata*, ed. H. T. Riley, 3 vols., RS (London: Longmans, Green, Reader and Dyer, 1867–9), I, p. 51; Eadmer, *Historia Novorum*, p. 15; G. R. Evans, 'Anselm (d. 1148)', *ODNB* www.oxforddnb.com/view/article/38778, accessed 20 May 2016.

[98] R. Mortimer, 'The Family of Ranulf de Glanville', *Historical Research*, 54 (1981), 1–16.

[99] *Cartularium Abbathiae de Whiteby*, ed. J. C. Atkinson, I, Surtees Society, 69 (1879), pp. 1–3.

[100] OV, V, pp. 320–3.

[101] C. N. L. Brooke and G. Keir, *London 800–1216: the Shaping of a City* (Berkeley, Los Angeles: University of California Press, 1975), pp. 345–7. As the authors point out, Gilbert Foliot also appointed his nephews as canons of St Paul's.

brother David became archdeacon in the see. Alexander's nephew in turn became archdeacon and was the father of another archdeacon. Roger's nephew Nigel was first treasurer and then bishop of Ely. He fathered at least three sons of whom one, Richard FitzNigel, archdeacon of Ely, became royal treasurer under Henry II.[102]

A different kind of network were those centred on monastic communities, which sought assiduously to sustain their links with benefactor families. Older communities had to be able to sustain their place in local communities in changing times. Andrew Wareham has shown how the monks of Ely Abbey had to adjust to the declining fortunes of the founding families and to build relationships with others.[103] The Norman Conquest proved a difficult era for the abbey. It took years to recover lost lands and rights, and a heavy burden of knight service was imposed by King William.[104] The community at Durham was at the heart of a strong network, for almost all the land in the county was held of the bishop. The community inscribed the names of benefactors in the *Liber Vitae* so that their names could be memorialized.[105]

The relationship between benefactor and monastery was of mutual importance. Monasteries needed endowments, whether of estates or, increasingly from the later eleventh century, of churches and tithes. They needed powerful protectors who would support them against their opponents. In return they offered prayers for the souls of deceased benefactors and, sometimes, burial within the monastic precincts. The *Liber Vitae* of the New Minster at Winchester, founded by King Alfred, survives, too, and shows how the names of English and Normans were added. Rochester was a small community of clerks in the late eleventh century when Gundulf of Bec was appointed as bishop, essentially to assist Archbishop Lanfranc, whose benefactions helped to set the see on its feet financially.[106] The cathedral was rebuilt and Benedictine monks introduced. Donors were encouraged to grant lands and particularly tithes. In return they were received into fraternity, as the *Textus Roffensis*

---

[102] Kealey, *Roger of Salisbury*, Appendix 3, pp. 272–6.

[103] A. Wareham, *Lords and Communities in Medieval East Anglia* (Woodbridge: Boydell Press, 2006), chapters 5, 9.

[104] *Liber Eliensis*, pp. 216–17. The original quota of knight service for Ely was forty.

[105] *The Durham Liber Vitae: London, British Library, MS Cotton Domitian A. VII: Edition and Digital Facsimile with Introduction*, ed. D. W. Rollason, L. Rollason, E. Briggs, A. J. Piper, 3 vols. (London: British Library, 2007).

[106] Martin Brett, 'Gundulf (1023/4–1108)', *ODNB* www.oxforddnb.com/view/article/11738, accessed 20 May 2016.

shows.[107] They included both Normans of the highest rank like Hugh de Port, possibly the first Norman sheriff of Kent, followers of Odo of Bayeux like Ansgot of Rochester who took the monastic habit at Rochester on his deathbed, William d'Aubigny, butler of Henry I, and men and women of both English and Norman descent. By bringing English and Normans together in this form of association, the community would help to establish a new political society in west Kent.

The interest of the Rochester material is that it relates to a relatively short period of time, when the community was being reorganized and its endowments augmented. Robin Fleming has argued that at Christ Church Canterbury lists of benefactors were revised from time to time, as, for instance, when the names of the Godwin family were quietly dropped from the lists of benefactors as embarrassing to the community.[108] The names of benefactors, whether of local or national importance, were only worth preserving as long as they could be useful.

In contrast to these older communities were those newly established in the twelfth century which had to build relations with benefactors from scratch. The Cistercians proved adept networkers, keeping up links with each other as well as with lay families. A detailed study by Emilia Jamroziak of the patrons of the Cistercian abbey of Rievaulx in Yorkshire has been particularly illuminating in this respect.[109] She pointed out that houses closely tied to one or two lay patrons might find their endowments in some jeopardy if that patron fell from grace, whereas a diversity of neighbours opened up the possibility of a range of lay benefactors.[110] Their motives for giving to this house rather than others were varied, as was the scale and character of gifts. However, it is clear that patrons valued their relationship with the abbey, not least through the possibilities of being remembered in the monks' prayers. The monks of Rievaulx had many contacts with other religious houses, especially Cistercians. They were also in contact with the canons of York, who frequently witnessed their charters. Their involvement with York peaked in the 1140s when they were embroiled in the contested election to the see. In 1141 Ailred and the archdeacon of York went to Rome to put the case against William

[107] H. Tsurushima, 'The Fraternity of Rochester Cathedral Priory about 1100', *Anglo-Norman Studies*, 14 (1991), 313–37.
[108] R. Fleming, 'History and Liturgy at Pre-Conquest Christ Church', *Haskins Society Journal*, 6 (1994), 67–83.
[109] E. Jamroziak, *Rievaulx Abbey and Its Social Context 1132–1300: Memory, Locality and Networks* (Turnhout: Brepols, 2005).
[110] *Ibid.*, p. 63.

FitzHerbert but their mission failed. A second two years later resulted in the case being referred to a judge delegate. FitzHerbert was consecrated in 1143 but two years later, with a Cistercian pope, his election was declared invalid. In 1147 Henry Murdac, a Cistercian from Fountains, was elected, and FitzHerbert retired, but was reinstated in 1153. Monastic houses were thus not only at the heart of a network of lay benefactors, but also linked with bishops and with other religious houses.

Networks were the glue binding together different elements in English society. The very fact that they were permeable and transient meant that new nodes of power could be established relatively quickly and as quickly superseded. Because they were shifting, it is hard to be categoric about change over time. The means by which the earls of Mercia built up their power in the early eleventh century do not seem to have been fundamentally different from those of the earls of Chester a century later, involving as it did land, lordship, and influence over courts and religious houses. The success or failure of dynastic strategies was critical, as well as successful negotiation of politics. The importance of grants of land in the exercise of lordship was doubtless at its height in the years after 1066, but the relationship between lords and men was about a set of values and a need for loyalty and service that remained unchanged.

Context was all important. In those regions where lordships were territorially compact and large, the relationship between lord and man was immediate and exclusive. In other regions, where men held of different lords, it was less so. This may have been a constant throughout our period. Certainly in Domesday Book there were many who held of more than one lord. The role of landholding in that relationship changed over time. In England after 1066 it was arguably more central to lordship than it had been before as a new elite distributed lands to its followers, but over time and generations loyalties had to be sustained in different ways and in a changing context. Historians in the past used to write in terms of the honour and of its decline, tracing through charter witness lists the way tenant families fell away from witnessing the charters of their lords.[111] It is very hard to generalize here: some honorial communities were evidently more cohesive than others; some lords were better able than others to forge extensive ties in their regions.

One dimension of this subject touched on in relation to urban communities is courts as a focus of community and identity, and linkages between centre and periphery. The establishment of shires, hundred, and wapentakes took place over a protracted period, and some had longer stable

[111] Thomas, *Vassals, Heiresses, Crusaders and Thugs*, introduction and chapter 1.

boundaries than others. Courts of shire and hundred gave kings crucial points of entry into the localities (see previously in this volume). Royal writs and writ-charters in the eleventh and twelfth centuries were regularly addressed to all the men of the shire.[112] Courts were the meeting places of bishops, ealdormen, or earls (or their representatives), and leading males of the community. The fact that they were supposed to meet at regular intervals, shire courts twice a year, and hundred courts once a month gave a measure of continuity. It has also been suggested that the origins of the later shire communities at least in some counties may be traced back to the tenth century. Ann Williams has argued from charter evidence that there was a shire community in Kent before 1066, and also in Herefordshire, Oxfordshire, and perhaps Buckinghamshire and the neighbouring counties.[113] Their composition obviously changed radically with the arrival of many new faces after 1066. The disappearance of earls from many counties between 1066 and 1135 also meant that the sheriffs for a time were in a particularly influential position. Written evidence of the work of shire courts in the Norman period is intermittent, but clearly from the accession of Henry II their role, and that of the local knights, was changing. On their shoulders rested much of the work of Angevin government, as members of juries, responsible for inquisitions and for supervising the collection of taxation. The king, it is argued, now communicated directly with the men of the shires, rather than indirectly through great magnates.[114] These were the kind of men who made use of the new forms of judicial action, or found themselves summoned to the exchequer having incurred debts to the king.

This chapter has focussed on the multifarious bonds of society which united families, neighbours, lords and men, bishops, monks, and clergy. The bonds were lateral and vertical, or a mixture of the two, between individuals or groups, variously determined by occupation, status, and location. Some were enduring, others less so. They intersected with membership of courts at every level, courts of hundreds and wapentakes, towns, shires, and the king's court, and it was through these courts that royal authority by the later twelfth century was penetrating ever more deeply into the localities.

---

[112] R. Sharpe, 'The Use of Writs in the Eleventh Century', *Anglo-Saxon England*, 32 (2003), 247–91.

[113] Williams, *World before Domesday*, chapter 3.

[114] W. L. Warren, 'The Myth of Norman Administrative Efficiency', *Transactions of the Royal Historical Society*, 6th Series, 34 (1984), 113–32, at p. 131.

7

Power and Place

Amongst the most dramatic changes in English society between the tenth and twelfth centuries are the shift in building from wood to stone, and a dramatic scaling up in size and grandeur of conception, reflecting the aims of their builders and patrons, and in the increased wealth expended on them. The cultural framework is important: were patrons influenced by the past, for example, the buildings of Imperial Rome, or were they aspiring to create something new and daring? Was display to be the order of the day, or was the intention something altogether simpler? Moreover, assemblages of buildings in their landscape setting are important: archaeologists have been increasingly emphasizing the importance of planned landscapes and the distant perspective. Then there is the whole area of form in relation to function. Were residential complexes designed to accommodate garrisons, great courts, or hunting parties? How were women and children, the sick, or servants to be housed? Internal arrangements involved questions of hierarchy, privacy, and gender. Externally social exclusion could be marked by burial outside churchyards.[1] Finally, archaeologists and landscape historians point out the antiquity of open-air meeting places for hundreds and wapentakes.[2] The links between power and place are thus multifarious, and the field of research vast.

Here the focus is on power as reflected and projected through buildings. The first part of this chapter sketches principal trends: the shift to stone,

[1] A. Reynolds, *Anglo-Saxon Deviant Burial Customs* (Oxford: Oxford University Press, 2009).
[2] S. Brookes and A. Reynolds, 'The Origins of Political Order and the Anglo-Saxon State', *Archaeology International*, 13 (2009), 84–93.

the size and splendour of the greater churches, castles and landscapes of power, and the internal arrangements of buildings. The second part considers examples of cities as nodes of power reflected in their great buildings: Winchester as a leading centre of the tenth-century monarchy, York developed as a northern capital under the Norman kings, Lincoln, a Roman city and Viking centre, dominated after 1066 by its cathedral and castle, and Oxford, developing by the later twelfth century as a centre for the royal court and for religious houses with schools. London is reserved for separate treatment in Chapter 8.

THE SHIFT TO STONE

At the start of our period, of the large buildings only churches tended to be built in stone. Timber was used for enclosures and the buildings within them, especially the halls. The buildings at the royal site of Cheddar in Somerset provide a good example of a high-status complex of buildings, and Goltho in Lincolnshire one of middling status.[3] After the millennium stone churches began to proliferate: as Ralph Glaber famously wrote, Europe was coming to be clothed in a mantle of white churches.[4] Many of those built in England from the eleventh century were small local churches. Stone was also increasingly used for residential complexes and was a mark of status. A good deal was imported from the quarries near Caen in Normandy and Purbeck stone from Dorset was also widely used in southern England.

THE GREATER CHURCHES

Relatively little is known about many of the cathedrals of mid-tenth-century England because they were largely swept away subsequently. One phase of construction was associated with the Benedictine reform of the later tenth century. At Winchester Bishop Æthelwold reformed the community at the Old Minster Winchester, and promoted the cult of St Swithun. A new cathedral was built, and the relics translated to a new location at the west end of the church in a splendid new

---

[3] P. Rahtz, *The Saxon and Medieval Palaces at Cheddar: an Interim Report of Excavations in 1960–1962*, British Archaeological Reports, British Series, 65 (1979); G. Beresford, *Goltho. The Development of an Early Medieval Manor c. 850–1150* (London: Historic Buildings and Monuments Commission for England, 1987).

[4] Rodulfus Glaber, *Historiarum Libri Quinque. The Five Books of the Histories*, ed. J. France (Oxford: Clarendon Press, 1989), pp. 114–16.

reliquary.[5] Then in the 1050s two major construction projects began, one at St Augustine's Canterbury, the other at Westminster. At St Augustine's Abbot Wulfric's plan to link two churches with a rotunda may either have been modelled on Charlemagne's palace at Aachen or on churches such as that at Charroux or Saint-Benigne at Dijon.[6] In fact Wulfric died in 1061, and his next but one successor, Abbot Scolland, pressed ahead with building, but on a different plan: a single very large church in the Romanesque style. In 1091 St Augustine's relics were translated to the new shrine, flanked by his successors, Mellitus and Lawrence, in great ceremonies lasting eight days.[7] At Westminster Edward the Confessor decided to restore a small monastic church dedicated to St Peter and endowed by Archbishop Dunstan, situated on a small island near the river Thames.[8] According to the *Life of King Edward*, the king was motivated in part by his devotion to St Peter, in part because of the location of the church near London and his plan to be buried there.[9] He seems to have preferred to live near the site of the new abbey buildings. These were also built in the Romanesque style, and were similar to the Norman abbey of Jumièges.[10]

The pace of change accelerated after 1066. The headquarters of some dioceses were relocated, necessitating new building, as at Lincoln (which had been moved from Dorchester), Norwich, Old Sarum, Bath, Lincoln, Chester (and Lichfield in the twelfth century), Chichester, and Exeter. Secondly, fires damaged existing cathedrals at Christ Church Canterbury (1067), York (1067, 1079), London (1087), and the abbey church at Gloucester (1088). Thirdly, some churches were overdue for renovation. Rochester, like Lichfield, for instance, was in a bad state of repair in 1066 with a very small community.[11] Fourthly, there was

---

[5] F. Barlow, M. Biddle, O. von Feilitzen, and D. J. Keene (eds.), *Winchester in the Early Middle Ages*, Winchester Studies, I (Oxford: Clarendon Press, 1976), pp. 306–8; Lapidge, *Anglo-Saxon Minsters of Winchester*, 4, part 2. *The Cult of St Swithun*; J. Crook, *English Medieval Shrines* (Woodbridge: Boydell Press, 2011), pp. 82–6.

[6] R. Gem, 'The Anglo-Saxon and Norman Churches', R. Gem (ed.), *The English Heritage Book of St Augustine's Abbey Canterbury* (London: English Heritage, 1997), pp. 90–122 at pp. 109–11.

[7] R. Sharpe, 'The Setting of St Augustine's Translation, 1091', R. Eales and R. Sharpe (eds.), *Canterbury and the Norman Conquest: Churches, Saints, and Scholars, 1066–1109* (London: Hambledon Press, 1995), pp. 1–13.

[8] *Early Lives of St Dunstan*, pp. xlvii–xlviii.

[9] *Life of King Edward Who Rests at Westminster*, pp. 66–70, 203–6.

[10] R. Gem, 'The Romanesque Rebuilding of Westminster Abbey (with a reconstruction by W. T. Ball)', *Anglo-Norman Studies*, 3 (1980), 33–60.

[11] Eadmer, *Historia Novorum*, p. 15; E. Fernie, *The Architecture of Norman England* (Oxford: Oxford University Press, 2000), pp. 115–17.

a need to provide for growing communities, not only by enlarging monastic buildings, but also by providing larger churches. Beyond these pragmatic considerations are others, less tangible, perhaps, but equally influential: cathedrals were deemed inadequate, either because they were in need of repair after fire damage, as at Canterbury and York, or they were too small, too old-fashioned, or seemed to give out the wrong message.

At St Albans there had been a plan to rebuild in the late tenth century, but it had not taken place, and it was Abbot Paul, Lanfranc's nephew, who undertook a great rebuilding programme. The new church was remarkable for its re-use of Roman material, and for the exceptional length of its eastern arm. As there was no crypt, it seems likely that the length was to be explained as a setting for a shrine.[12] According to Bede, Germanus, bishop of Auxerre, had visited Alban's grave, and placed there relics of other saints.[13] The monks celebrated the role of King Offa as the patron of the re-founded church, and by the early twelfth century they claimed that Germanus had given them relics of the twelve Apostles and of martyrs.[14] At Bury, where some building had taken place under Cnut, Abbot Baldwin began a great new church, modelled on Winchester Cathedral.[15] Before the church was completed, there was a change of plan, perhaps to ensure that the resulting building was longer than the new cathedral being built at Norwich.[16] Archbishop Lanfranc at Canterbury chose to pull down the old cathedral. His new church was broadly similar to the abbatial church of St Stephen at Caen, but with some differences, notably the raised crypt and the form of the western towers. On the towers there were golden cherubs, which could be seen from a considerable distance. Inside, whilst the tomb of St Dunstan was accorded a place of honour before the High Altar, the relics of other Anglo-Saxon saints were relocated to less prominent locations. For

[12] *Gesta Abbatum Monasterii Sancti Albani*, I, pp. 53–4; Fernie, *Architecture of Norman England*, pp. 111–15.
[13] *Bede's Ecclesiastical History of the English People*, ed. and trans. B. Colgrave and R. A. B. Mynors (Oxford: Clarendon Press, 1992 edn), book I, chapter 18, pp. 58–60.
[14] *Gesta Abbatum*, I, pp. 69–70.
[15] E. Fernie, 'Baldwin's Church and the Effects of the Conquest', T. Licence (ed.), *Bury St Edmunds and the Norman Conquest* (Woodbridge: Boydell Press, 2014), pp. 74–93; *Memorials of St Edmund's*, I, p. 85; Fernie, *Architecture of Norman England*, pp. 128–9.
[16] E. Fernie, 'The Romanesque Church of Bury St Edmunds Abbey', A. Gransden (ed.), *Bury St Edmunds. Medieval Art, Architecture, Archaeology, Economy*, British Archaeological Association (London, 1998), pp. 1–15.

Lanfranc, the aim of the new building was to refocus worship on Christ the Saviour.[17]

There were various forces driving the great building boom: the need to accommodate growing communities of monks and canons, to honour the great saints of the past with new shrines and, a factor often forgotten, because newly appointed bishops and abbots simply *could*: they had wealth from lands and churches to finance building programmes, and, if not, then new shrines would attract pilgrims with offerings. Even so, building went in fits and starts. Sometimes funds dried up, or there were hitches, like the fall of the central tower at Winchester in 1107. Yet what was remarkable about so many churches was their scale and ambition. Most striking was the size of the new churches. Even where sites were constrained by their urban location, as in London or Winchester, churches as large as possible for the site were built. One aim was to match the dimensions of churches like old St Peter's at Rome. The length of eight or nine churches built after 1066 was that of St Peter's: Winchester, York, Ely, Bury, Anselm's Canterbury, Durham, Norwich, Peterborough, and probably St Paul's London.[18] The round Church of the Holy Sepulchre at Jerusalem was copied at Northampton and Cambridge, and in churches built by the Templars and Hospitallers.[19] Size may have been an aesthetic aim (bigger means better), or there may have been a desire to build a church large enough for all the Christians of the diocese, or, in the case of shrines, to accommodate pilgrim traffic. Experimentation and inventiveness were also characteristic of the new buildings: the development of rib vaults, flying buttresses, the treatment of western facades, and the splendour of, for instance, the 'glorious choir' at Christ Church Canterbury may be cited.[20]

English churches were not only radically different from those which had gone before, but also from Norman churches. One of the most interesting aspects of that process of construction was the way it was

---

[17] Fernie, *Architecture of Norman England*, pp. 104–6; Gibson, *Lanfranc of Bec*, pp. 162–7; R. W. Southern, *St Anselm: a Portrait in a Landscape* (Cambridge: Cambridge University Press, 1990), pp. 326–7; J. Rubinstein, 'Liturgy against History: the Competing Visions of Lanfranc and Eadmer of Canterbury', *Speculum*, 74 (1999), 279–309.

[18] Fernie, *Architecture of Norman England*, p. 284.

[19] *Ibid.*; R. Griffith-Jones and D. Park (eds.), *The Temple Church in London* (Woodbridge: Boydell Press, 2010).

[20] Fernie, *Architecture of Norman England*, pp. 140–4. Fernie suggests that the choir may have been built to provide more space for the Anglo-Saxon saints, or for veneration of the Virgin Mary.

preceded by destruction of the old. William of Malmesbury famously wrote of Bishop Wulfstan's tears when he ordered Bishop Oswald's church at Worcester to be demolished at the point when the new building could be used: 'we miserable sinners destroy the works of the saints to win ourselves renown. That age of fortunate men never thought to raise grandiloquent edifices, but under whatever roof offered themselves to God and led all those about them by their example. We by contrast labour to pile up stones, neglecting our souls.'[21] He was chided by his friends, who pointed out that the increased number of monks necessitated new building, and the fact remains that he did go ahead with the building. The break with the past in this and other buildings is striking, in particular by contrast with today where the imperative is towards preservation of historic buildings rather than destruction.

Another key issue was the competing claims of elaboration and simplicity. Some features of Anglo-Saxon architecture were carried through into the new buildings, such as the love of decorated surfaces. Examples include Barnack and Earl's Barton in Northamptonshire, Bradford-on-Avon in Wiltshire, and Barton-on-Humber in Lincolnshire.[22] The use of architectural sculpture, rudimentary before the late eleventh century, became more widespread and more sophisticated, as at Lewes Priory and Reading Abbey in the early twelfth century. Great sculptured portals on the lines of French churches were rarely emulated: the great west door of the Rochester Cathedral priory is a rare example. Here Christ in Glory was flanked with Saints Justus and Ethelbert, angels, symbols of the four evangelists, the twelve Apostles beneath and figures, identified as Solomon and Sheba, on either side of the doorway.[23] Importance was attached to the west front of cathedrals. At Lincoln Bishop Alexander, who died in 1148, was probably the patron of a design with three great arches and a sculptured frieze. George Zarnecki argued that the inspiration was the three west doors at Saint-Denis and that instead of portals, for which there was little room in the recessed arches, a narrative frieze, with scenes from the Old and New Testaments, was used instead.[24]

[21] *Gesta Pontificum*, I, pp. 428–30.
[22] E. Fernie, *The Architecture of the Anglo-Saxons* (London: Batsford, 1983), chapter 9.
[23] D. Kahn, 'The West Doorway at Rochester Cathedral', in N. Stratford (ed.), *Romanesque and Gothic: Essays for George Zarnecki*, 2 vols. (Woodbridge: Boydell Press, 1987), I, pp. 129–34.
[24] G. Zarnecki, *Romanesque Lincoln. The Sculpture of the Frieze* (Lincoln: Honeywood Press, 1988).

The Cistercians of course rejected elaboration in architectural form and decoration. The buildings constructed in twelfth-century England reflected their ideals of simplicity, and the special characteristics of their communities: the need to accommodate lay brothers, and to house various craft activities on site. The Burgundian houses – austere, with flat east ends and little by way of decoration – provided a template for early houses. Then in the mid-twelfth century the English Cistercian houses adopted early Gothic, initially again as an import. Key houses here include Furness, Roche, Kirkstall, and Byland. English buildings which were not Cistercian may have been the critical influences, for example, Jervaulx Abbey in Yorkshire was influenced by Archbishop Roger's choir at York and his work at Ripon. The Cistercian order by this time may not have been able to influence specifically what the English communities were choosing to build.[25]

Certain features of churches were given special attention. One was obviously the principal doorways, whether on the south or west sides. The idea of a westwork was introduced into England from Germany. One example is that constructed at Durham under Bishop Hugh du Puiset, probably between 1170 and 1175.[26] Another earlier case is that at Winchester in the church built by Bishop Æthelwold (see later in this chapter). Within the church consideration was given to patterns of worship. How many altars were needed? Were monks and nuns to be kept separate from the laity? Where were shrines to be placed, or, in the case of earlier tombs, relocated? At Ely in about 1154 Prior Alexander translated into the cathedral the bones of Archbishop Wulfstan of York (who had expressed a wish to be buried at Ely), Ealdorman Beorhtnoth, and five early bishops. These were placed in niches along the north side of the wall at the rear of the choir stalls, each niche with an inscription.[27]

Often relics were placed in a place of honour in the apse behind the high altar. Where the whole body survived, as in the case of Cuthbert at Durham, the bones were encased in a wooden coffin. In other cases relics were placed in reliquaries of gold and silver, studded with gems.[28] One type of shrine took the form of a chest raised on pillars. Another form which became more fashionable in the twelfth century was the shrine over

[25] P. Fergusson, *The Architecture of Solitude. Cistercian Abbeys in Twelfth-Century England* (Princeton, NJ: Princeton University Press, 1984).

[26] S. A. Harrison, 'Observations on the Architecture of the Galilee Chapel', D. Rollason, M. Harvey, and M. Prestwich (eds.), *Anglo-Norman Durham* (Woodbridge: Boydell Press, 1994), pp. 213–34.

[27] Crook, *English Medieval Shrines*, pp. 178–9. [28] *Ibid.*, pp. 103–6.

a tomb slab with portholes in the sides for the faithful, the shrine with *foramina*, which is thought to have been inspired from the tomb of Christ in the Holy Land. This form may possibly have been used for the shrine of Edward the Confessor in 1163, and for that of Thomas Becket in 1170.[29]

RESIDENCES

Residential accommodation raises a number of interlocking considerations, reflected in a variety of building forms. One was protected space in a location of strategic importance. Form might be determined by the terrain and the purpose of the site: where sites were defended outposts, garrisons might be small; where relatively large numbers had to be accommodated at frequent intervals, larger spaces were needed. Another was comfort, even luxury. A third was privacy. Henry II's mistress Rosamund Clifford was provided for in a discreet villa at Everswell in the park at Woodstock, where there was a much-frequented royal residence. The form of Everswell, known from a seventeenth-century drawing by John Aubrey, had a fountain and pools, perhaps in the manner of Italian villas.[30] Personal tastes came into the equation, as well as cultural vocabulary, that is, building a stone castle in the twelfth century was a mark of status, distinguishing the holder from his neighbour with a more modest moated manor house. Bishops' palaces included halls, chambers, and chapels, but in the twelfth century these were sometimes arranged round courtyards, thus forming cloisters analogous to monastic cloisters. Roger of Salisbury's residence at Sherborne in Dorset and Henry of Blois' palace at Wolvesey are examples.[31] Then there is the landscape context, a topic to which archaeologists and historians have given increasing attention. Finally, there is the question of change over time: there was often continuity of occupation, but significant changes in design. Bamburgh in Northumberland, for instance, was a fortress which was taken over by Anglian kings of Northumbria. According to the (much later) Anglo-

[29] *Ibid.*, pp. 133–69.
[30] *Victoria County History, Oxfordshire*, XII, pp. 435–9; H. M. Colvin (general editor), *The History of the King's Works*, 6 vols. (London: HMSO, 1963–82), II, pp. 1010–16.
[31] B. K. Davison, *Sherborne Old Castle* (London: English Heritage, 2001); J. Wareham, *Three Palaces of the Bishops of Winchester Wolvesey (Old Bishop's Palace), Hampshire, Bishop's Waltham Palace Hampshire, Farnham Castle Keep Surrey* (London: English Heritage, 2000), pp. 17–24; R. A. Stalley, 'A Twelfth-Century Patron of Architecture: a Study of the Buildings Erected by Roger, Bishop of Salisbury, 1102–1139', *Journal of the British Archaeological Association*, 34 (1971), 62–83; M. W. Thompson, *Medieval Bishops' Houses in England and Wales* (Aldershot: Ashgate, 1998), pp. 68–9.

Saxon Chronicle, in the sixth century King Ida built Bamburgh, 'which was first enclosed with a hedge and afterwards with a wall'.[32] According to Bede, King Oswald's hand and arm were preserved there in the church of St Peter.[33] Excavations of the cemetery have revealed graves both of the British and Anglian periods. By 1095 it was in Norman hands, and then, probably in the twelfth century, a stone keep was built.[34] At Dover the defences evolved possibly from Iron Age times. According to William of Poitiers, Harold promised Duke William that Dover was to be fortified and garrisoned on the duke's behalf.[35] After Hastings the English gathered there in the castle.[36] If the Normans had a motte built, it seems to have been subsumed into the great stone keep on which Henry II lavished so much money in the 1180s.[37] One issue is that of terminology, which used to be highly contested. It used to be argued that pre-Conquest fortifications were primarily defended settlements (*burhs*), whilst post-Conquest buildings were castles (*castels* or *castella*) built by kings or lords. The implied contrast between as it were public defences for towns and private castles muddied the waters. Ann Williams pointed out that the word *burh* simply means a defended space.[38] In fact, many post-Conquest castles were built within the walls of *burhs*.

Most late tenth- and eleventh-century complexes are thought to have included halls, chambers, kitchens, and other domestic offices, enclosed by fenced ditches, with a defended gate.[39] The classic text is the early eleventh-century text *Geþyncðo*: 'And if a ceorl prospered so that he had fully five hides of his own land, church and kitchen, bell house and *burhgeat*, a seat and special office in the king's hall, then was he thenceforward entitled to the rank of a thegn.'[40] Examples have been excavated in different parts of the country: Raunds in Northamptonshire, Sulgrave in the same county, and Goltho in Lincolnshire.[41] These were similar in character to the

---

[32] ASC, E, 547.   [33] *Ecclesiastical History*, book III, chapter 6, p. 230.
[34] ASC, E, 1095.   [35] William of Poitiers, *Gesta Guillelmi*, p. 70.   [36] *Ibid.*, p. 144.
[37] R. Allen Brown, *Dover Castle* (London: HMSO, 1966); J. Gillingham, 'The King and His Castle: How Henry II Rebuilt His Reputation', *BBC History Magazine*, 3 March (2011).
[38] A. Williams, 'A Bell-House and a Burh-geat: Lordly Residences in England before the Norman Conquest', *Medieval Knighthood*, IV, C. Harper-Bill and R. Harvey (eds.) (Woodbridge: Boydell Press, 1992), pp. 221–40, reprinted in *Anglo-Norman Castles* (ed. Liddiard), pp. 23–40, at p. 24.
[39] *Ibid.*
[40] *Die Gesetze der Angelsachsen*, I, p. 456; *English Historical Documents*, I, pp. 431–2.
[41] A. Chapman, *West Cotton, Raunds: a Study of Medieval Settlement Dynamics AD 450–1450. Excavation of a Deserted Medieval Hamlet in Northamptonshire, 1985–1989* (Oxford, Oakville: Oxbow, 2010), p. 56; P. V. Addyman, 'The Anglo-Saxon House: a New

eleventh-century Norman site at Mirville in Normandy excavated by Jacques Le Maho.[42] Timber halls could be relatively large and comfortable. Several are mentioned in Domesday Book, such as Waltheof's hall at Hallam, and Edwin's at Laughton-en-le-Morthen, both in Yorkshire.[43] Halls were places for social gatherings, and also where ties of lordship could be formed and reformed, where dues were paid, and where discipline was exercised. Residential complexes were defended, though it is hard to be categoric about the *degree* of fortification.

Enclosure sites continued after 1066, either on existing or new sites. Sometimes walls and ditches were strengthened, perhaps with a stone perimeter wall, or gatehouses were built. At Sulgrave, for instance, the Norman lord simply moved into the Anglo-Saxon thegnly residence.[44] However, after 1066 the degree of fortification and the *number* of fortified sites increased. The vast majority were initially constructed in earth and timber, but in the twelfth century they were increasingly built or rebuilt in stone. The motte-and-bailey form proved particularly suitable in unsettled times and was used widely. Mounds were used as the bases of watchtowers, whilst the baileys housed halls, chambers, and domestic buildings. Both enclosure sites and mottes were functional, and in the case of mottes and baileys could be erected at speed if necessary.

However, almost from the beginning, other kinds of high-status residences were being built. A handful of castles were built in stone in the eleventh century. Most famous was the White Tower at London, begun on the orders of William the Conqueror.[45] Colchester was also begun in his reign. It was built over the top of the temple of the Emperor Claudius, which in turn may have been built over the palace of Cunobelinus, or Old King Cole, the pre-Roman ruler.[46] Both the White Tower and Colchester made a statement about royal power and its links with the Roman past. Richmond Castle, overlooking the river Swale at a crucial point, was a fortified enclosure with a stone hall and a mid-twelfth-century tower.[47] Chepstow dates from the time of William FitzOsbern, who left

---

Review', *Anglo-Saxon England*, 1 (1972), 273–307; Beresford, *Goltho. The Development of an Early Medieval Manor*, pp. 61–7.

[42] J. Le Maho, 'Note sur l'histoire d'un habitat seigneurial des XIe et XII siècles en Normandie: Mirville (S. Mme)', *Anglo-Norman Studies*, 7 (1984), 214–23.

[43] DB, I, fols. 320r, 319r.

[44] B. K. Davison, 'Excavations at Sulgrave, Northamptonshire, 1960–76: an Interim Report', *Archaeological Journal*, 134 (1977), 105–14.

[45] Fernie, *Architecture of Norman England*, pp. 55–61.   [46] *Ibid.*, pp. 61–7.

[47] *Ibid.*, pp. 68–72.

England in 1070 and died in the following year. The castle was probably built in stone from the first, and included a tower and a hall.[48] The site was halfway between Roman Caerleon and Gloucester, at the lowest bridging point and on the Welsh side of the river Wye.

Many new sites were fortified after 1066. In the North Riding of Yorkshire Count Alan chose to build at Richmond, overlooking the river Swale, instead of basing himself at Gilling on lower ground to the north.[49] In the West Riding Ilbert de Lacy built his castle at Pontefract rather than at Tanshelf.[50] Roger de Bully chose to build his at Tickhill rather than Dadsley.[51] Many castles were built close to Roman roads or to river crossings. Some were clearly intended as centres of lordship for the payment of dues and services. Others were sited as convenient lodges for hunting: the king's castle of Rockingham in Northamptonshire was a case in point.[52] Barnard Castle in county Durham took its name from Bernard de Balliol, son of the grantee of Gainford. Gainford and its constituent elements had belonged at different times to the bishop and to the earl of Northumbria, but it was in the king's hands when it was granted to Guy de Balliol, probably therefore between September 1093 and September 1094.[53] The grant seems to have been made with an eye to placing someone loyal to the king in Teesdale, in the context of incursions from the Scots and the potential disloyalty of the bishop, and of Robert de Mowbray, who in fact rebelled in 1095. The castle was placed not at the estate centre, but where the Roman road crossed the river Tees.[54]

Some castles were more obviously about social prestige. The great keep built at Castle Rising by William d'Aubigny II followed his marriage to Adeliza of Louvain, the queen dowager, in 1138.[55] As Robert Liddiard has argued, the decision to build in west Norfolk may have been because the land was available and there was no need to buy. The castle was sited

---

[48] J. C. Perks, *Chepstow Castle Gwent. Castell Cas-gwent*, 2nd edn, 6th impression (London: HMSO, 1978).

[49] DB, I, fols. 309r, 309v: Count Alan's manor was named *Hindrelag* in Domesday Book.

[50] DB, I, fol. 316v (Tanshelf); Wightman, *Lacy Family in England and Normandy 1066–1191*, pp. 24–7.

[51] *Ibid.*; DB, I, fol. 319r (Dadsley). The castle had been built by 1102, when Orderic Vitalis referred to it as Blyth, the name of the nearby village, OV, VI, p. 22.

[52] DB, I, fol. 220r.

[53] D. Austin, *Acts of Perception. A Study of Barnard Castle in Teesdale*, Antiquarian and Archaeological Society of Durham and Northumberland, Research Report, 2 vols. (Hassocks, 2007), I, p. 54.

[54] *Ibid.*, II, pp. 651–2.

[55] R. Allen Brown, *Castle Rising* (London: English Heritage, 1987), pp. 12, 45–6.

in a spot where it could be seen from the surrounding countryside, and a deer park and town were probably part of the original plan. Visitors entered via a grand staircase to first floor reception rooms.[56] A second castle, at New Buckenham, also built by William d'Aubigny II, takes the form of a circular tower within a ringwork.[57] The castle was not far from Old Buckenham, and the new site in an open location made it possible to lay out a borough alongside.[58] Hedingham Castle in Essex originally consisted of two grand reception rooms over basement storage. It was thought to have been built to celebrate Aubrey de Vere's elevation to the earldom of Oxford.[59] Orford, the first royal castle in Suffolk was built by Henry II, in the 1160s, with a view to coastal defence against a possible attack by King Louis VII of France.[60] The keep is polygonal outside and cylindrical inside. Three clasping towers and chambers in the thickness of the wall suggest that defensive considerations were not primarily upper- most in the mind of its designer. Rather, it has been suggested, it was designed to be different, perhaps to recall circular halls known in the east.[61] A little later Henry II's half-brother Hamelin, who married the Warenne heiress, built Conisbrough Castle around 1180. Its site once again was not chosen as the highest point in the locality. Its design, a circular tower with six clasping buttresses, was intended as a luxurious lodging for the lord and lady, and was apparently paralleled by the building of a similar castle at Mortemer, also held by the Warennes, in Normandy.[62]

Accommodation for large numbers of residents and visitors meant frequent rebuilding. If we are to believe the well-known letter of Peter of Blois complaining about Henry II's sudden decisions to move on, many

---

[56] R. Liddiard, 'Castle Rising Norfolk: a "Landscape of Lordship"?', *Anglo-Norman Studies*, 22 (1999), 169–86.

[57] Could this have been copied from Windsor? Henry I was responsible for some work there, including a stone hall. There could have been an early twelfth-century stone tower, preceding that built by Henry II. Henry and Adeliza had been married at Windsor.

[58] D. J. Cathcart King, *Castellarium Anglicanum*, 2 vols. (Milwood, London, Nendeln: Kraus, 1983), II, p. 308.

[59] P. Dixon and P. Marshall, 'The Great Tower at Hedingham Castle: a Reassessment', R. Liddiard (ed.) *Anglo-Norman Castles* (Woodbridge: Boydell Press, 2003), pp. 297–306.

[60] V. Potter, M. Poulter, and J. Allen, *The Building of Orford Castle: a Translation from the Pipe Rolls 1163–1178* (Orford: Orford Museum, 2002), pp. 36–7.

[61] T. A. Heslop, 'Orford Castle: Nostalgia and Sophisticated Living', Liddiard (ed.), *Anglo-Norman Castles*, pp. 273–96.

[62] H. Sands, H. Braun, and L. C. Loyd, 'Conisbrough and Mortemer', *Yorkshire Archaeological Journal*, 32 (1936), 147–59.

members of the court had to fend as best they could for lodgings.[63] Presumably many were accommodated in wooden buildings or tents, which have not survived. We hear only of the violence which sometimes accompanied the scramble for lodgings, as, for instance, when in 1051 Count Eustace's men in Dover killed one of the townsmen, and they retaliated.[64] In 1139 the men of Count Alan of Brittany brawled with those of Bishop Roger of Salisbury. The bishop's men won the battle, but the king intervened and arrested the bishop and his nephews.[65]

For monastic communities, stationary in one place, other solutions had to be found. The Benedictine obligation to provide hospitality was challenging when high-status visitors turned up in numbers and often.[66] Bermondsey Priory, for instance, was situated not far from the city of London, and hospitality for visitors and pilgrims must have been a considerable problem. Suitable accommodation reflecting the status of visitors had to be provided. If the visitor was the king, this might be the occasion for requesting a confirmation of lands and privileges, or for a grant of a fair or market, so for the community, this was a two-way process. However, it was important not to disrupt monastic life, and one solution for those communities which could afford it was to build suites of guest accommodation, including chambers, halls, and stables. Christ Church Canterbury, for instance, had to accommodate large numbers of visitors, and under Prior Wibert (*c.* 1154–67) in the mid-twelfth century undertook a major building programme to provide, *inter alia*, a suite of guest buildings ordered according to social status.[67] Romanesque in style, the buildings were characterized by high-quality sculpture, glittering polished marbles, and polychromy. A supply of piped water was provided, famously pictured in the map in the Eadwine Psalter; guest accommodation was built, an infirmary hall and almonry were built, as was a hall for the prior's court. Subsequently additions were made to the cathedral to take account of washing rituals and to store treasure and vestments.[68] Within a few years the splendour of all this work was eclipsed as a new cathedral, in the Gothic style, began to take shape following a fire in 1174.

---

[63] Letter no. 14, Migne, *Patrologia Latina*, ccvii, cols. 48–9; Warren, *Henry II*, pp. 209–10.
[64] ASC, D, 1051.   [65] WM, *Historia Novella*, pp. 46–8.
[66] J. Kerr, *Monastic Hospitality: the Benedictines in England, c. 1070-c. 1250* (Woodbridge: Boydell Press, 2007).
[67] P. Fergusson, *Canterbury Cathedral Priory in the Age of Becket* (New Haven, CT, and London: Yale University Press, 2011).
[68] *Ibid.*

Information about secular buildings in towns is particularly thin on the ground. That there was a guildhall in London by the early twelfth century is known, and the later building is thought to have been constructed on the same site.[69] Wealthier townsmen had stone houses, of which a few twelfth-century examples survive, but within the city walls there was obviously limited space.[70] The exceptions included episcopal palaces. As noted previously, they included the core elements of hall, chamber, and chapel, but were sometimes arranged round a courtyard. Once again, the archbishop's residence at Canterbury led the way in size and magnificence. Lanfranc was responsible for the building of a great hall, kitchen, and private chamber to the north-west of the cathedral. These were still in use a century later, at the time of Becket's murder.[71] Archbishop Hubert Walter (1193–1205) was responsible for building a much bigger hall there, as well as for a new complex at Lambeth.[72]

The topic of gendered space in castles and residences has been neglected until relatively recently.[73] Documentary evidence for women's lives in the residences of Anglo-Saxon and Norman lords is scanty.[74] It is reasonable to assume that great ladies and their attendants had their own apartments as well as access to the hall and chapel. By the mid-twelfth century at Westminster there were separate apartments for the king and the queen.[75]

LANDSCAPES OF POWER

It is now appreciated that lords gave much more attention to the context of their castles than used to be thought. The castle was but one element in a planned landscape. At Castleacre in Norfolk, for instance, William de Warenne built a defended country house adjacent to a Cluniac priory.[76] Robert Liddiard demonstrated how the approach road, the Peddars' Way, was diverted so that the traveller gained the fullest impression of the whole

---

[69] Schofield, *London 1100–1600*, pp. 23–4.   [70] *Ibid.*, p. 61.

[71] T. Tatton Brown, *Lambeth Palace* (London: SPCK, 2000), pp. 10–14.

[72] *Ibid.*, pp. 22–7.

[73] L. Hicks, 'Magnificent Entrances and Undignified Exits: the Symbolism of Castle Space in Normandy', *Journal of Medieval History*, 35 (2009), 52–69.

[74] R. Gilchrist, *Gender and Archaeology. Contesting the Past* (London: Routledge, 1999), pp. 109–45.

[75] A. Richardson, 'Gender and Space in English Royal Palaces c. 1160–c. 1547: a Study in Access Analysis and Imagery', *Medieval Archaeology*, 47 (2003), 131–65; Colvin (ed.), *History of the King's Works*, I, p. 492.

[76] J. Coad, *Castle Acre Castle, Norfolk* (London: Historic Buildings and Monuments Commission for England, 1984), p. 20.

complex.[77] A church or priory and a borough might be added as well. Geoffrey de Clinton, Henry I's chamberlain, sheriff of Warwickshire and a prominent royal justice, established a castle, priory, and borough at Kenilworth, not far from Warwick, the earl's principal castle, and thus perhaps a deliberate challenge to the earl's local pre-eminence.[78] A much smaller complex in Herefordshire was the work of Hugh FitzWilliam, lord of Kilpeck. In 1143 he gave the church of Kilpeck to Gloucester Abbey. The building has an elaborate decorated doorway with a tympanum and knights on the door jambs, corbels round the outside, and on the inside carving round the apse.[79] Adjacent to the church is the remains of a stone castle, with a small borough. Here again, then, we have the classic combination of the lord's castle, a church, and a borough, conceived as an entity.

Having looked at some of the main themes of architectural and landscape history in relation to power, we turn now to consider a selection of cities where great stone buildings, royal palaces and castles, cathedrals and monastic churches and, in a few cases, houses belonging to rich townsmen, were built. In these examples, open spaces were usually restricted, and relatively little is known for our period about precisely how outdoor processions were staged. The architectural context of ritual, whether religious, civic, or royal in inspiration, would obviously have underscored the messages conveyed by the great buildings.

WINCHESTER

For the kings of Wessex, Winchester was the closest to a capital city. In the tenth century the city included the cathedral, the Old Minster, buildings for the bishop and the community, and a royal palace. In addition there were two other major monastic foundations. The Old Minster had been founded by St Birinus in the seventh century, but it was under Bishop Æthelwold (963–84) that a great rebuilding took place. The relics of St Swithun were translated from their original position outside the west door into the church. The new church had a westwork over the shrine,

---

[77] R. Liddiard, *Landscapes of Lordship. Norman Castles and the Countryside in Medieval Norfolk, 1066–1200*, British Archaeological Reports, British Series, 309 (2000), pp. 60–2.

[78] D. Crouch, 'Geoffrey de Clinton and Roger Earl of Warwick: New Men and Magnates in the Reign of Henry I', *Bulletin of the Institute of Historical Research*, 55 (1982), 113–24.

[79] Fernie, *Architecture of Norman England*, pp. 222–3; *Historia et Cartularium Monasterii Gloucestriae*, ed. W. H. Hart, 3 vols., RS (London: Longman, Green, Longman, Roberts and Green, 1863–7), I, p. 16.

probably modelled on Rhineland examples. There has been some discussion about its function, and it may be, as Eric Fernie has suggested, that there was more than one: as a separate western sanctuary, a shrine for the saint, and, on occasion, a tribune for the king and his retinue.[80]

King Edgar provided a new reliquary made of gold, silver, and precious stones. The Old and New Minsters and the royal palace formed a ceremonial complex. It was here that Cnut, Emma, and their son Harthacnut were buried, and where Edward the Confessor was crowned in 1042. When the Norman Walkelin became bishop he began to rebuild the cathedral on a vast scale, longer at 162 metres than old St Peter's (120 metres). In 1093 the relics of St Swithun were translated once again, and the old church was demolished. Seven years later William Rufus, having died in the New Forest, was buried there.

The New Minster was first mentioned in 901.[81] In the tenth century a new church was built, and the citizens had the right of burial in its cemetery. It was or became the town church whereas the cathedral was the bishop's church.[82] King Alfred's body was moved there, and there were other royal burials, those of his wife, Ealswith, Edward the Elder and two of his sons, and finally King Eadwig.[83] The community was reformed under Bishop Æthelwold. It went from strength to strength under Æthelred, who paid for a new tower (in competition with that of the Old Minster), and Cnut, who gave it a great gold cross, whilst Queen Emma gave it a 'Greek shrine' with the head of St Valentine and other relics.[84] The timing of a fire in 1065 which destroyed the abbey buildings, followed soon after by William the Conqueror's enlargement of the royal palace, placed physical constraints on the site.[85] The building of a greatly enlarged Old Minster was an additional problem, and around 1111 the monks of the New Minster moved to Hyde, just outside the north gate of the city.[86] The New Minster burned down in the siege of 1141, and in the fire Cnut's cross was melted down.[87] The then bishop, Henry of Blois, had

[80] Fernie, *Architecture of the Anglo-Saxons*, pp. 117–21.   [81] ASC, F, 903.

[82] *Winchester Studies*, I, p. 314.

[83] *Liber Monasterii de Hyda*, ed. E. Edwards, RS (London: Longman, Green, Reader and Dyer, and Co, 1866), pp. 83, 116, 167.

[84] *Liber Vitae Hyde Abbey Winchester*, pp. lxiii–lxv, 151–3, 161–3; WM, *Historia Novella*, p. 104. There is an image of the cross in the portrait of Cnut and Emma in the *Liber Vitae* (ed. de Gray Birch, frontispiece). For Emma's gift of the head of St Valentine, ASC, F, 1042.

[85] *Liber Vitae*, p. 2.

[86] The move was recorded in a charter of Henry I, *RRAN*, II, no. 1070.

[87] *Gesta Stephani*, p. 130.

kept the abbacy vacant since the death of the previous abbot. He is thought to have tried, but failed, to have his see raised to metropolitan status, a project which inevitably complicated his relations with the cathedral chapter and the abbey.[88]

In contrast to the male houses, little is known about the Nunnaminster. Founded in 903 by Ealhswith, widow of King Alfred, it possessed the relics of St Eadburh, daughter of King Edward the Elder, who had been a nun there.[89] Bishop Æthelwold ordered her remains to be placed in a shrine, but the gold and silver was stripped off in the 980s to pay for the ransom of captives.[90] Her life was composed by Osbert of Clare in the twelfth century. The nunnery too suffered from fire in 1141.[91]

The creation of a residence for the bishops is thought to have dated from Bishop Æthelwold's time. Bishop William Giffard (1100–29) was responsible for building there, including laying on piped water.[92] His work, either a hall or a complete residence, was added to by Bishop Henry, who added an east hall. Henry also founded a hospital at St Cross in about 1136.[93]

By the 1140s Winchester had changed considerably since the mid-tenth century. Its role as an important royal centre continued under the first three Norman kings, and Henry I in particular found it a convenient point of transit en route to Normandy. However, its importance to the kings declined after the siege of 1141, and it was the bishop who was thereafter the dominant figure in the city.

YORK

This is an example of a town which had a distinguished history as the Roman capital of the northern province of Britain, and more recently in the Viking era had flourished as an important trading centre.[94] The Anglo-Saxon Minster, about which nothing is known, had been built over the *principium* of the Roman fortress, and there may have been a royal residence in the early Middle Ages on the west bank of the river Ouse.

---

[88] *Annales Monastici*, II, p. 53. [89] *Liber Vitae*, p. 5; *Winchester Studies*, I, pp. 321–3.
[90] Osbert of Clare, *Vita Edburge*, Ridyard, *The Royal Saints of Anglo-Saxon England*, pp. 19–20, 292–4.
[91] WM, *Historia Novella*, p. 102. [92] *Winchester Studies*, I, p. 324.
[93] *English Episcopal Acta*, VIII, *Winchester 1070–1204*, ed. M. J. Franklin (London: published for the British Academy by Oxford University Press, 1993), no. 134, pp. 99–100.
[94] D. M. Palliser, *Medieval York: 600–1540* (Oxford: Oxford University Press, 2014).

After the death of Eric Bloodaxe in 954 the southern kings appointed earls, and in the eleventh century the earls had a residence outside the city walls to the west.[95] As Sarah Rees Jones has pointed out, the kings do not seem to have had lands in the vicinity of the city.[96] Effectively, then, the archbishop and the earl were the key figures. York was sufficiently important to have moneyers, and the city had prospered under Viking rule.[97] The urban landscape was transformed after the Conquest, and it has been argued that the first three Norman kings decided to promote York as a northern capital.[98] Initially the Normans' position was insecure: there were risings in 1068 and 1069, and in the latter year the cathedral was burned.[99]

The Conqueror's response was to construct two motte-and-bailey castles to guard the approaches to the city by the rivers Ouse and Foss.[100] A new Norman archbishop, Thomas of Bayeux, was appointed in 1070 and during a long period as archbishop oversaw the building of a vast new cathedral, some 362 feet long. This was of an unusual design, being a long, aisleless nave with an apse, constructed with a lot of salvaged Roman stone, its external walls plastered and painted. It was very different from other churches built in England in the same period, presumably intentionally.[101] Towards the end of the Conqueror's reign a new abbey took shape on what had been the earl's land outside the city wall. Count Alan, who had taken over some of the estates of the pre-Conquest earls, made a start. Then William Rufus took charge, and rafts of grants from leading Normans followed.[102] The Conquest brought damage and destruction, as reported in the Domesday account, but new building followed as the Normans left their imprint.

Henry I visited the city on several occasions, and it is during his reign that the existence of a royal house, occupying part of the site of the Roman *colonia*, is reported.[103] The king did not have large estates in the vicinity, but royal forests were established, Galtres, Ainsty, and the forest between

---

95   S. Rees Jones, *York: the Making of a City 1068–1350* (Oxford: Oxford University Press, 2014), chapter 2.
96   *Ibid.*, p. 48.   97   *Ibid.*, pp. 10–13.   98   *Ibid.*, chapter 4.   99   ASC, D, 1068, 1069.
100   ASC, D, 1068.   101   Fernie, *Architecture of Norman England*, pp. 122–4.
102   Jones, *York: the Making of a City*, pp. 158–61.
103   *Ibid.*, pp. 91–3; for a visit to the city in 1105, see *RRAN*, II, nos. 713–15 issued there; for 1109, see *Ibid.*, nos. 925–7; for 1122, see Symeon of Durham, *Historia Regum, Opera omnia*, II, p. 267. He may also have been in Yorkshire in 1113, according to the story about an expedition to Scotland in the chronicle of the foundation of Nostell Priory. The evidence is discussed by Duncan, *Kingship of the Scots 842–1292. Succession and Independence*, p. 64.

the rivers Ouse and Derwent.[104] There was a larderer, David, who was the king's forester and also supervised meat sales in the city.[105] Stephen too visited York on several occasions, but his protracted struggles against the Angevins meant that his earl, William count of Aumale, assumed authority over the city.[106] A disputed archiepiscopal election following the death of Archbishop Thurstan in 1140 brought tension. The death in 1154 of William FitzHerbert, the king's nominee as archbishop, was attributed to poison, and miracles at his tomb followed.[107] His successor, Roger of Pont l'Evêque, was responsible for the reconstruction of the crypt and choir of the Minster, the latter one of the first Gothic buildings in northern England.[108]

Henry II also visited the city on several occasions, the most significant in 1175 when the Scottish bishops and abbots were in York Minster to witness their king, William the Lion, perform homage.[109] The financial burden of Henry's rule weighed heavily on the city, and it was not surprising that prominent citizens were involved in the rebellion of 1173–4. Thomas 'beyond the Ouse' and his son were fined 'for the commune they wanted to have': whether they represented the majority of the citizens or only a minority is unknown.[110] The citizens certainly wanted fiscal autonomy, and were to secure permission to pay their farm directly at the exchequer in 1189.[111] Tensions were running high in that year, leading to the attack on the Jewish community, one of the most important in England.[112]

---

[104] Jones, *York: the Making of a City*, p. 98.   [105] *Ibid.*, pp. 93–4.

[106] Stephen's presence in York was recorded in 1136, 1142, 1148, 1149, and 1154, *RRAN*, III, xxxix–xliv. For his relations with William count of Aumale, see P. Dalton, 'William Earl of York and Royal Authority in Yorkshire in the Reign of Stephen', *Haskins Society Journal*, 2 (1990), 155–65.

[107] Janet Burton, 'William of York (*d.* 1154)', *ODNB* www.oxforddnb.com/view/article /9606, accessed 20 May 2016.

[108] E. A. Gee, 'Architectural History until 1290', G. E. Aylmer and R. Cant (eds.), *A History of York Minster* (Oxford: Clarendon Press, 1977), pp. 111–48 at pp. 121–5; S. Brown, *'Our Magnificent Fabrick': York Minster an Architectural History c. 1220–1500* (Swindon: English Heritage, 2003), pp. 20–5.

[109] Howden, II, pp. 79–82.

[110] *Pipe Roll 21 Henry II*, p. 180; it is possible that this Thomas was the same person as Thomas son of Ulviet, whose fine to be an alderman in the merchant gild occurs in the 1130 pipe roll, *Pipe Roll 31 Henry I*, p. 27; Jones, *York: the Making of a City*, pp. 113–14, 192; Palliser, *Medieval York 600–1540*, pp. 111–12.

[111] *Pipe Roll 2 Richard I*, p. 59.

[112] S. Rees Jones and S. Watson (eds.), *Christians and Jews in Angevin England: the York Massacre of 1190, Narratives and Contexts* (Woodbridge: York Medieval Press, 2013); R. B. Dobson, *The Jews of York and the Massacre of March 1190*, University of York Borthwick Paper, 45 (1974).

York had changed very much during our period. In the mid-tenth century it was a flourishing trading centre and the seat of the northern archbishopric, and for more than a century after 954 the city and surrounding region were only loosely tied into southern affairs. The years after 1066 brought damage and destruction, but then a period when castles and a royal residence were built, together with the Minster and other churches which cumulatively transformed the urban landscape. Over time the density of settlement within the city increased. The surrounding villages supplied food and raw materials, but the city did not dominate the surrounding countryside politically in the way that Italian cities were able to do.[113]

LINCOLN

Like London and Winchester Lincoln was a walled Roman city on a Roman road, in this case Ermine Street. By the tenth century a mixed population of English and Danes had settled beyond the walls in suburbs, and the city was thriving.[114] However, from the perspective of the Normans, it lacked the presence of a royal stronghold and a cathedral church, both of which were being built soon after 1066 in the upper sector of the Roman city. This in effect became an elite space. Work on the castle began relatively early, in 1068, as the king retreated southwards, having gone to York to deal with rebellion.[115] It was sited in the south-west corner of the northern part of the city, taking advantage of the Roman wall on two sides. In 1086 some 1166 holdings are reported as having been destroyed on account of the castle.[116] By the early twelfth century there was a stone curtain wall, and two stone towers, one to the south-east and a larger to the west, which came to be associated with Countess Lucy of Chester.[117]

Nothing has survived of the minster church at Lincoln, but in the 1070s Bishop Remigius began work on a new cathedral, moving the headquarters of his see from Dorchester, at its southern extremity, to Lincoln in the north. The cathedral faced the castle across the main north–south street. Its most striking feature was the western façade. This gives the impression

---

[113] Jones, *York: the Making of a City*, pp. 238–54.
[114] F. Hill, *Medieval Lincoln* (reprinted edn, Stamford: Paul Watkins, 1990), chapter 2.
[115] OV, II, p. 218.   [116] DB, I, fol. 336v.
[117] Hill, *Medieval Lincoln*, chapter 5. A possible parallel here is Baynard's and Mountfitchet's towers, which seem to have been part of one fortification, in south-west London.

of a castle, like fortified cathedrals in France. Modelled once again on St Stephen's at Caen, it was substantially complete by 1093.[118] The sculptured portals and the frieze at the west end, the only one still *in situ* in England, have been attributed to Bishop Alexander 'the Magnificent' (1123–48). Possibly looking back to classical friezes, that at Lincoln instead had scenes from the Old and New Testaments.[119] A third element in the transformation of the upper city was the construction of a residence for the bishop. Henry I granted Bishop Robert permission to make an exit in the wall of the castle for the convenience of his house, and later granted the city's Eastgate with the tower over it as a lodging to Bishop Alexander.[120] Stephen then granted Alexander land between St Michael's Church and the city ditch.[121] Henry II granted all the land with the ditch from the wall of the king's bailey on the east side, round the church of St Michael to the cemetery of St Andrew's church, and thence to the city wall on the east.[122] Thus over two centuries the city had come to be dominated by twin powers, that of the king and of the bishop.

OXFORD: COURT, COMMERCE, AND CLERKS

The story of Oxford during these centuries is of a town growing from a walled *burh*, situated on the Mercian side of the border with Wessex, to that of a complex of royal, episcopal, and monastic buildings, a centre for teachers and students seeking to learn and to make their way in the world.[123] In the tenth century there was a thriving town, indicated by the presence of a mint.[124] It is likely that then as later the chief crafts were leatherworking and cloth production. There were several minster churches in the region, including that of St Frideswide, dedicated to a putative daughter of an early Mercian king, within the burh.[125] There were also several important royal centres nearby, some of which were conveniently situated for the hunting grounds mentioned in Domesday Book: Shotover, Stowford, Woodstock, Cornbury, and Wychwood.[126]

[118] Fernie, *Architecture of Norman England*, pp. 108–11.

[119] Zarnecki, *Romanesque Lincoln*.

[120] *Registrum Antiquissimum*, I, ed. C. W. Foster, Lincoln Record Society, 27 (1931), pp. 20, 34, 269.

[121] *Ibid.*, pp. 54–5.   [122] *Ibid.*, pp. 86–7.

[123] J. Blair, *Anglo-Saxon Oxfordshire* (Stroud: Alan Sutton, 1994), pp. 99–101, 145–52.

[124] *Ibid.*, pp. 152–3.

[125] J. Blair, 'St Frideswide's Monastery: problems and Possibilities', *Oxoniensia*, 53 (1998), 221–58.

[126] DB, I, fol. 154v; Blair, *Anglo-Saxon Oxfordshire*, pp. 108–11.

Æthelred II had issued two law codes at Woodstock.[127] There may also
have been a residence at the royal manor of Headington.[128] The town was
on the front line of the struggle between Æthelred and the Danes, and
there was also a Danish community. In 1002 the king ordered all the
Danes to be slaughtered, and those at Oxford took refuge in St
Frideswide's.[129] A few years later there seems to have been an administrative reorganization with Oxford as the head of a new county.[130]
The town was taken by Swein in 1013, and it was here, two years later
in Earl Eadric's chamber, that two leading thegns, Sigeferth and Morcar,
were murdered.[131]

Oxford retained its importance as a royal centre under the Danish
kings, and there may have been a garrison based at St Clement's outside
the East Gate.[132] An assembly was held between the English and the
Danes in 1018, at which Cnut agreed to abide by the laws of King
Edgar.[133] After Cnut's death a council was held at Oxford, where Earl
Leofric of Mercia, the thegns north of the Thames, and the shipmen of
London chose Harold Harefoot as king.[134] The earls of Mercia notionally
had charge of Oxfordshire, but Earl Harold held four manors there, three
of which were in the king's hands in 1086.[135]

Little is known about the fate of the town in the immediate aftermath of
the Battle of Hastings. Earl Edwin was not removed, and the English
sheriff Saewold was addressed in a royal writ concerning Oxfordshire of
around 1067.[136] However, a castle was soon built and, it was reported,
a new bridge, the Grandpont. Custody of the castle and the shrievalty
were entrusted to Robert d'Oilly, whose wife was English, the daughter of
Wigod of Wallingford.[137] In 1086 a remarkable number of houses in the

---

[127] Æthelred issued law codes (I Atr, IX Atr) at Woodstock, Liebermann, *Die Gesetze der Angelsachsen*, I, pp. 216–20, 269.

[128] Headington was a major royal estate in 1086 with the jurisdiction of two hundreds, DB, I, fol. 154v.

[129] A charter of King Æthelred for St Frideswide's mentions the order to kill the Danes, S909; *English Historical Documents*, I, no. 127, pp. 590–3.

[130] Blair, *Anglo-Saxon Oxfordshire*, pp. 102–5.   [131] JW, II, pp. 472, 478–80.

[132] Blair, *Anglo-Saxon Oxfordshire*, pp. 167–70.

[133] JW, II, p. 504. In 1065 Tostig Godwinson was outlawed there, *ibid.*, p. 598.

[134] ASC, E, F, 1035. ASC, E, 1040 says that Harold Harefoot died at Oxford, whereas John of Worcester gives the place as London, JW, II, p. 528.

[135] Harold held the royal manors of Bampton, Langford, and Shipton, plus Churchill, DB, I, fols. 154v, 157r, 160v. Tostig held Stoke Lyne, *ibid.*, fol. 157v.

[136] Bates, *Acta of William I*, no. 296.

[137] John Blair, 'D'Oilly, Robert (*d. c.*1092)', *ODNB* www.oxforddnb.com/view/article/23719, accessed 20 May 2016. For the castle, said to have been built in 1071, see *Annales*

town were reported to be 'waste' and not contributing to the geld.[138] Whether this reflects a real downturn in the town's fortunes or other factors is not clear.

By the early twelfth century, however, the town's fortunes were rising. Henry I enjoyed hunting in the forests of Oxfordshire, and had a favourite hunting lodge at Woodstock, where his famous menagerie was housed.[139] He also had a new hall built at Beaumont outside the walls.[140] The castle continued to be held by the d'Oilly family, and Robert II d'Oilly was married to one of the king's daughters. The town was a focus of literary and intellectual life. The church of St George within the castle was a collegiate church whose canons included Geoffrey of Monmouth, author of the *History of the Kings of Britain*, and Walter the archdeacon.[141] St Frideswide's was converted into an Augustinian priory under the aegis of Roger bishop of Salisbury.[142] By the 1130s Theobald d'Etampes and Robert Pullen were teaching there, indicating that there were students to be taught.[143] A glimpse of urban life is gained in the 1130 pipe roll, in which payments for gilds of weavers and cordwainers were recorded.[144]

Oxford's location made it of strategic importance to both sides in the civil war of Stephen's reign. In 1136 Stephen held his Easter court there, which was very well attended, and he and the queen were present at the foundation of Godstow nunnery three years later.[145] In 1140 the church of St George was converted into an Augustinian house at Oseney.[146] The castellan Robert II d'Oilly married, it must be remembered, to the empress's half-sister, delivered the castle to the empress, and she took refuge there but then fled in 1142.[147] Stephen's commander, William de Chesney, brother of the bishop of Lincoln, took command, and in 1147

Monastici, IV, p. 9; R. H. C. Davis, 'The Ford, the River and the City', *From Alfred the Great to Stephen* (London: Hambledon Press, 1991), pp. 281–91.

[138] DB, I, fol. 154r.   [139] *Gesta Stephani*, p. 138.   [140] HH, p. 488.

[141] Geoffrey of Monmouth, *HKB*, Book XI para. 177 (ed. Reeve, pp. 248–9); H. E. Salter, 'Geoffrey of Monmouth and Oxford', *English Historical Review*, 34 (1919), 382–5.

[142] Kealey, *Roger of Salisbury*, pp. 121–2.

[143] G. R. Evans, 'Étampes, Theobald d' (*c*.1060–*c*.1125)', *ODNB* www.oxforddnb.com /view/article/53483, accessed 20 May 2016; David Luscombe, 'Pullen, Robert (*d.* in or after 1146)', *ODNB* www.oxforddnb.com/view/article/22877, accessed 20 May 2016.

[144] *Pipe Roll 31 Henry I*, pp. 2, 4.

[145] RRAN, III, nos. 382, 31, 142, 271, 469–70, 616, 685–6, 784, 366. *The Latin Cartulary of Godstow Abbey*, ed. E. Amt (Oxford: published for the British Academy by Oxford University Press, 2014).

[146] D. Postles, 'The Foundation of Oseney Abbey', *Historical Research*, 53 (1980), 242–4.

[147] *Gesta Stephani*, pp. 116, 126, 138–44.

was described as 'alderman of the commune' through whom a grant was made to Oseney Abbey.[148] William and the burgesses of Oxford were able to reach terms with Henry II. The former seems to have retained much of his land, and the latter had their (generous) liberties confirmed by the king in 1156.[149]

It is not clear how far the conflict had led to a decline in the town's prosperity, but if so, it resumed its importance as a royal centre after 1154. Henry II frequently stayed at Oxford or Woodstock, as his itinerary shows.[150] Queen Eleanor gave birth to Richard at Beaumont Palace, Oxford.[151] It is striking that the visits of the court, especially in the later years of the reign, were clearly great council meetings where matters of moment such as the marriage of the king of Scots or the issue of new coinage (both in 1180) were discussed. The presence of the court, the flourishing churches, and the busy town were all potential draws for teachers and students. Oxford was on the way to being a powerhouse of a kind unique in England at this date.

CONCLUSION

The visible expression of power in the form of building and, even more, the concentration of stone buildings in cities and towns, was one of the most immediate ways in which messages about power and social order were conveyed. The transformation of the urban landscape during our period was profound, as stone buildings were erected, altered, and demolished at vast cost in terms of labour and expense. Within the walls space was zoned by status and by occupation: cathedrals, their closes, and castles closed off whole quarters for bishop, monks, and king. Arrivals and departures were great moments of theatre, none more so than Henry II's penance at Canterbury in 1172. The great churches housed the shrines of saints, places of special power. They were the setting for elaborate ceremonial, with their treasures in the form of books, vestments, and

[148] *Ibid.*, pp. 130, 180. *Cartulary of Oseney Abbey*, IV, pp. 86–8; Crouch, *Reign of King Stephen*, pp. 205, 217, 222–3, 239, 278, 326–7; Amt, *Accession of Henry II in England*, pp. 51–3; R. J. Ivens, 'Deddington Castle, Oxfordshire, and the English Honour of Odo of Bayeux', *Oxoniensia*, 49 (1984), 101–19.

[149] Amt, *Accession of Henry II in England*, pp. 60–1.

[150] R. W. Eyton, *Court, Household, and Itinerary of Henry II* (Dorchester: Foster, 1878), pp. 2–3, 58–9, 66, 88, 191, 214, 230, 268 (Oxford); 13–14, 30, 34, 63, 70, 73, 84, 91, 136, 191, 192, 199, 223, 244, 257, 268, 271, 272, 273 (Woodstock).

[151] Diceto, I, p. 302. John is often said to have been born at Beaumont, but there seems to be no corroborative evidence.

plate on display. The very size of the post-Conquest churches was testimony to the aspirations of their patrons: here were some of the largest churches in Christendom. Stone castles housed the armed men with whom coercive power ultimately rested. They dominated the landscape either through the choice of site, as at Richmond, or because they lay alongside a routeway. Again they were the setting for display, for ritual, and for assemblies in which social bonds were forged and discipline applied.

8

London: the Making of a Capital City

London's population, size, and wealth grew substantially between the late tenth and twelfth centuries, and by the late twelfth century it had become in effect a capital city. The first section of this chapter traces the relationship between the city and the monarchy, in terms of events and people, those who emerged as leaders and rulers of the Londoners. The second section is about building, looking at the relationship between power and place in this, the largest city in the kingdom. The walled city, Westminster, and Southwark formed three settlements which by the end of our period were linked by ribbon development on the interconnecting roads.[1] The walls, gates, and bridge separated the city from the suburbs and surrounding countryside. The townscape was dominated by the cathedral church and royal castles, especially the Tower, yet within its narrow streets nobles, churchmen, and merchants lived in close proximity. The power of wealth as opposed to social origin or occupation was based on a different set of values. At Westminster the royal residence with its great hall and the abbey church formed a focal point and, increasingly, central departments of government were stationed there. Southwark originated as a settlement south of the river near the bridgehead. Here the most prominent building was the Augustinian priory. Though there were impressive buildings, they were individual elements in what was an increasingly complex and densely populated townscape, not one of wide boulevards and open vistas.

---

[1] G. Rosser, *Medieval Westminster: the Vill and the Urban Community 1200–1540* (Oxford: Clarendon Press, 1989), chapter 7; M. Carlin, *Medieval Southwark* (London: Hambledon Press, 1986), chapter 4.

The third section is about identities. The growing evidence of awareness of the city as an entity is traced. Then attention is given to other solidarities, those focussed on saints, churches, and gilds, before, finally, looking at social tensions. On two occasions in the twelfth century, in 1141 and 1191, the Londoners banded together to form a commune, but, despite similarities with Italian cities, London ultimately did not break away politically, and it is worth asking why this was.[2]

The writing of London history draws on both narrative sources and archaeological investigations. Very few buildings from our period remain above ground. Although no one wrote a specific history of the city, several chroniclers noticeably commented on London matters, most famously William FitzStephen, who prefaced his biography of Becket with a description of the city in the 1170s.[3] There is an invaluable account from St Paul's dating from about 1127 about the chapter's urban properties which names many of the more prominent citizens.[4] A collection was made by an unknown author of legal and historical material relating to the city in the years leading up to the rebellion of 1215.[5] This not only included the texts of royal charters to the city, but materials relating to London customs and the history of one prominent London family, the Cornhills.[6] It also included an interpolated version of the *Leges Edwardi Confessoris* and a supposed letter from Pope Eleutherius, both of which reflected views about good kingship which were evidently circulating in John's reign.[7] Not only therefore does the manuscript demonstrate an interest in law as it affected the city, but also a concern that the king should abide by that law which, as Sir James Holt pointed out, reflected ideas which lay behind Magna Carta.[8] The chapter of St Paul's included at least one canon, Gervase of Howbridge, who opposed the king in 1215.[9] Archaeologists, especially in recent times, have done much to throw light

---

[2] D. Keene, 'Metropolitan Comparisons: London as a City-State', *Historical Research*, 77 (2004), 459–80.

[3] *Materials for the History of Thomas Becket*, III, pp. 1–13.

[4] London, London Metropolitan Archives, St Paul's Liber L, ff. 47r–50v; see H. W. C. Davis, 'London Lands and Liberties of St Paul's, 1066–1135', A. G. Little and F. M. Powicke (eds.), *Essays in Medieval History Presented to T. F. Tout* (Manchester: Manchester University Press, 1925), pp. 45–59, at pp. 55–9.

[5] See especially D. Keene, 'Text, Visualisation and Politics: London, 1150–1250', *Transactions of the Royal Historical Society*, 6th series, 18 (2008), 69–99.

[6] *Ibid.*, p. 89.   [7] O'Brien, *God's Peace and King's Peace*, pp. 118–19.

[8] J. C. Holt, *Magna Carta*, 3rd edn (Cambridge: Cambridge University Press, 2015), pp. 73–4.

[9] J. C. Holt, review of N. Fryde, *Why Magna Carta? Angevin England Revisited*, in *English Historical Review*, 118 (2003), 989; Holt, *Magna Carta*, p. 244.

both on long-vanished buildings and on the way of life of those who lived in them.[10] Study of the mint and the moneyers provides information both about its own importance and relative to other mints.[11]

London at the start of our period was already the largest city in the country, as it had been since Roman times. In middle Saxon times the trading area of Lundenwic had grown up to the west of the walled city along the Strand, but was later abandoned, perhaps because of the decline of continental emporia.[12] Earlier part of the Mercian kingdom, it had been taken over by King Alfred in 886. Its prosperity was rooted in location, as the point where goods were brought from the hinterland, and where seaborne traders landed luxury goods and, presumably, slaves.[13] Many merchants came from northern France, from Flanders, and from Norway. There were Normans, too, whose privileged position was reported in the record of customs of Æthelred's reign, and after 1066 more arrived, of whom one was Becket's father.[14]

Flemish merchants were probably already buying and exporting wool, and by 1130 it seems that they were active in the business of exchanging money.[15] In the mid-twelfth century William Cade of Saint-Omer had a spectacular career as a financier.[16] By the twelfth century German merchants from cities such as Cologne were also involved in trade.[17] Imports had to be paid for, and the city was already important for its moneyers and the mint, which provided a considerable proportion of the coins in circulation in late Anglo-Saxon England. It was here that kings, nobles, and churchmen could raise credit from Flemings, then from Jews, and, in the later twelfth century, from the Templars.[18] A rising population had to be fed, clothed, and housed: amongst the trades there were butchers, fishmongers, bakers, weavers, and builders.[19] In this respect

[10] Schofield, *London 1100–1600. The Archaeology of a Capital City.*

[11] R. Naismith, 'London and Its Mint, *c.* 880–1066: a Preliminary Survey', *British Numismatic Journal*, 83 (2013), 44–74; Nightingale, 'Some London Moneyers and Reflections on the Organization of English Mints in the Eleventh and Twelfth Centuries', reprinted in Nightingale, *Trade, Money and Power in Medieval England*, V.

[12] R. Cowie and R. Whythead, 'Lundenwic: the Archaeological Evidence for Middle Saxon London', *Antiquity*, 63 (1989), 706–18.

[13] J. Haslam, 'The Development of London by King Alfred: a Reassessment', *Transactions of the London and Middlesex Archaeological Society*, 61 (2010), 109–44.

[14] IVAtr a, Liebermann, *Die Gesetze der Angelsachsen*, I, pp. 232–6.

[15] Adelulf the Fleming, *Pipe Roll 31 Henry I*, p. 114.

[16] Edmund King, 'Cade, William (*d.* in or before 1166)', rev. *ODNB* www.oxforddnb.com /view/article/37255, accessed 20 May 2016.

[17] WM, *Gesta Pontificum*, p. 222.   [18] Amt, *Accession of Henry II in England*, chapter 6.

[19] Brooke and Keir, *London 800–1216*, chapter 10.

commercial and craft activity was unusual only in scale, which in turn meant that supplying the city had a major impact on the surrounding region.

LONDON AND THE MONARCHY

There is very little evidence about the governance of the city in the tenth century, and about those who negotiated with the king on behalf of the Londoners. The London peace gild of Athelstan's reign provides a brief glimpse, as it refers to the bishop and the reeves who belong to London who have agreed to the peace gild.[20] Within the city there were private properties, or *hagas*, and there were private jurisdictions, or *sokes*, for which courts were held.[21] At some stage internal divisions of the city within the walls, the wards, were created. Perhaps around the same time each was placed under an alderman.[22] Then by the eleventh century the Londoners' court came to be known as the *husting*.[23] Kings needed to be sure about the security of the city and its defences; they needed financial contributions to their coffers and access to the luxury goods brought to the London wharves. The Londoners, for their part, wanted to be able to rule their own affairs, and to have favourable trading conditions in the rest of the kingdom. Their success depended on the strength of their negotiating position at any given moment. Meanwhile key agencies, the court of husting, and, from the 1190s, the mayoralty were coming into being.

London and the Danes

When Scandinavian attacks resumed in the later tenth century the wealth of the city inevitably proved a magnet. These attacks were reported in graphic detail in versions C, D, E, and F of the Anglo-Saxon Chronicle. It seems that these entries were the work of a single author, probably based in London, and writing between 1016 and 1023.[24] A narrative of

---

[20] VIAs, Liebermann, *Die gesetze der Angelsachsen*, I, pp. 173–82; *English Historical Documents*, I, pp. 423–9.

[21] Brooke and Keir, *London 800–1216*, pp. 149–58; W. Page, *London: Its Origin and Early Development* (London: Constable, 1923), chapter 4.

[22] Brooke and Keir, *London 800–1216*, chapter 7.

[23] *Ibid.*, pp. 248–51. Reynolds points out that aldermen can only be linked with the husting in the twelfth century, S. Reynolds, 'The Rulers of London in the Twelfth Century', *History*, 57 (1972), 337–57, at p. 339.

[24] S. D. Keynes, 'The Declining Reputation of King Æthelred the Unready', in Hill (ed.), *Ethelred the Unready*, pp. 227–53.

dramatic events clearly illustrates the city's importance to both the Danes and to Æthelred, who made his headquarters there. In 994 a force led by Olaf Tryggvason king of Norway and Swein king of Denmark attacked the city, but was beaten off.[25] In 1009 the city was attacked repeatedly, and in the following year an army was mustered against the Danes at London.[26] In 1011 Canterbury was sacked and Archbishop Ælfheah was taken hostage by Thorkell the Tall and his forces.[27] Then at Easter in 1012 a great council of all the leading magnates, including Eadric Streona, was held at London. Tribute was paid to the Danes, but they were not satisfied, and, despite strenuous efforts by Thorkell the Tall, they killed the archbishop at Greenwich where the fleet was based. Thorkell subsequently decided to stay in England and joined Æthelred's forces.[28] In 1013 Swein advanced towards London. Many of his men were drowned in the Thames because they were unable to find a crossing. When he did arrive, the Londoners, with King Æthelred and his Viking ally Thorkell the Tall, resisted for a time, but later in the year, most regions of the country having submitted, the Londoners too gave in. They handed over hostages, fearful that they would be pushed by mutilation and confiscation of their property. Swein and Thorkell both demanded payment and provisions for their forces. Æthelred's position had become untenable, and he fled into exile.[29]

After Swein died, the fleet elected his son Cnut as king, but 'all the councillors who were in England' sent messages to Æthelred, offering their support in return for better government. Æthelred returned and initially was successful against Cnut. He ordered that a tribute be paid to the army (*here*) at Greenwich.[30] Cnut returned in the following year with a great fleet, and by 1016 with forces from Wessex and Eadric Streona, he was plundering Mercia. Æthelred's son Edmund mustered an army, but his Mercian forces refused to fight the men of Wessex and the Danes unless the king and the Londoners were present.[31] Then again Edmund mustered an army and sent messages to his father at London. The latter responded, but, on learning of the likelihood of treachery, he returned to London without offering battle. He died not long afterwards, and was buried in St Paul's.[32]

[25] Niels Lund, 'Óláf Tryggvason (d. 999)', *ODNB* www.oxforddnb.com/view/article/49266, accessed 20 May 2016.

[26] ASC, E, F, 1009; JW, II, p. 464.   [27] ASC, C, D, E, 1011.

[28] ASC, C, D, E, 1012; JW, II, p. 470.   [29] ASC, C, D, E, 1013; JW, II, pp. 472–6.

[30] ASC, C, D, E, 1014; JW, II, pp. 476–8.   [31] *Ibid.*, pp. 480–2.

[32] *Ibid.*, pp. 482–4; S. Keynes, 'The Burial of King Æthelred the Unready at St Paul's', D. Roffe (ed.), *The English and Their Legacy 900–1200: Essays in Honour of Ann Williams* (Woodbridge: Boydell Press, 2012), pp. 129–48.

Edmund was chosen as king by the counsellors who were in London, the first time such an election is mentioned as having been held there. Later the Londoners were to claim their right to make such an election.[33] Within weeks the Danes arrived at Greenwich and from there moved up the Thames to the Bridge. They dug a channel on the south bank and dragged their ships round to the west, blockaded the river, and launched attacks on the city.[34] Edmund, who had previously left the city, returned later in the year to relieve the garrison, driving the enemy to their ships, but not for long. The Danes returned and renewed the attack, but then departed for the river Orwell.[35] The Battle of *Assandun* followed not long afterwards.[36] Edmund and Cnut had come to terms at Alney dividing the country between them, and it seems that London was assigned to the former.[37] Edmund's death left the citizens with little alternative but to make their peace with Cnut.[38] Two points emerge: London was evidently Æthelred's headquarters and also the object of repeated attack, and the large sums which had to be raised in danegeld may have been one of the reasons the mint was so important at this time.

In 1017 Cnut summoned a council to London, when it was stated that Edmund had wished him to be protector of the realm; oaths of loyalty were taken from those present.[39] Later in the year he had Eadric Streona put to death at London, and his body thrown over the city wall.[40] In 1018 most of the Danish forces were paid off, the city contributing some £10,500 to the tribute raised in that year.[41] Cnut's relations with the Londoners were problematic. Pamela Nightingale has suggested that the city was effectively under military occupation, as there were lithsmen, professional warriors, stationed there.[42] The staller Osgod Clapa, whose name suggests he was of Danish extraction, seems to have been the man dealing with the city on Cnut's behalf.[43] Church dedications indicate the presence of Scandinavians. Of the churches dedicated to the Scandinavian St Olaf (killed in 1030), St Olave's Monkwell Street, St Olave's by the

[33] M. McKisack, 'London and the Succession to the Crown in the Middle Ages', R. W. Hunt, W. A. Pantin, and R. W. Southern (eds.), *Studies in Medieval History Presented to F. M. Powicke* (Oxford: Clarendon Press, 1948), pp. 76–89.

[34] ASC, C, D, E, 1016; JW, II, pp. 484–6.   [35] ASC, C, D, E, 1016; JW, II, pp. 484–90.

[36] ASC, C, D, E, 1016; JW, II, p. 490.   [37] *Ibid.*, pp. 492–3 and note.   [38] *Ibid.*, p. 492.

[39] *Ibid.*, pp. 494–6.   [40] *Ibid.*, 502–4.

[41] ASC, D, 1018. ASC, E gives a figure of £11,000.

[42] Nightingale, 'Origins of the Court of Husting', *Trade, Money and Power in Medieval England*, p. 567.

[43] Ann Williams, 'Osgod Clapa (*d.* 1054)', *ODNB* www.oxforddnb.com/view/article/20890, accessed 20 May 2016.

Tower (Hart Street), and perhaps St Olave's (Broad Street) were close to the city walls; St Nicholas Olave was near the then waterfront, whilst St Olave Tooley Street in Southwark was close to the bridgehead.[44] There were two churches dedicated to St Clement, another saint favoured in the Scandinavian world.[45] Nightingale suggested further that it may have been Cnut who established himself at Westminster, where he could be protected by his fleet, rather than within the walled city.[46] It seems likely it was his decision to have the remains of Archbishop Ælfheah moved from St Paul's to Canterbury, perhaps because popular veneration would be a recurring and unwelcome reminder of a Danish atrocity. The occasion was tense: guards were posted, and the cortege was accompanied by an armed escort.[47]

There are signs of a change of policy under Edward the Confessor. Osgod Clapa was exiled in 1046 and, though he returned three years later with a fleet, he was unable to recover his influence.[48] Edward dismissed some of the ships stationed at London in 1050 and the remainder in 1051, and he suspended the *heregeld*, the tax taken for their support, in the following year.[49] He also confirmed the customs 'and the good laws which they had in the days of King Edgar and of my father and of Cnut' to the gild of knights which had jurisdiction outside the city wall east of Aldgate. His writ was addressed to Ælfweard the bishop and Wulfgar the port-reeve, and perhaps the address to a port-reeve rather than a staller is significant.[50] Edward appointed a Norman, Robert of Jumièges, as bishop of London.

Edward was at London in 1051 when he brought the Godwinsons to book, and again in the following year when they returned, sailing up the Thames to Southwark. There they waited for the tide and came to an agreement with the citizens 'that they would fall in with his [Godwin's] wishes in almost everything'. They also had supporters on the city side of the river where the king's forces were stationed. Although the king was

[44] Nightingale, 'Origin of the Court of Husting', p. 567 and n.

[45] For the cult of St Clement in England, see B. Crawford, 'The Saint Clement Dedications at Clementhorpe and Pontefract Castle: Anglo-Scandinavian or Norman?', J. Barrow and A. Wareham (eds.), *Myth, Rulership, Church and Charters: Essays in Honour of Nicholas Brooks* (Aldershot: Ashgate, 2008), pp. 189–210.

[46] Nightingale, 'Origins of the Court of Husting', *Trade, Money and Power in Medieval England*, pp. 567–8.

[47] H. Wharton, *Anglia Sacra* etc., 2 vols. (London: Richard Chiswel, 1691), II, p. 146; *Osbern's Life of Alfege*, trans. F. Shaw (London: St Paul's Publishing, 1999), p. 90.

[48] ASC, C, D, E, 1046; C, D, 1049.   [49] ASC, E, 1050; D, 1051.

[50] Harmer, *Anglo-Saxon Writs*, pp. 231–5.

initially reluctant, it was agreed that the family should be restored. The earl cleared himself and his children of the charges brought against them. Robert of Jumièges, now archbishop of Canterbury, and William, his successor at London, fled, though the latter soon returned.[51] Edward died at Westminster and was buried in the new abbey church.

London under the Norman Kings

After the Battle of Hastings the Londoners, under the leadership of Ansger the staller who was ill and directed operations from a litter, were initially prepared to continue the struggle against William the Conqueror.[52] The archbishop of York, the earls Edwin and Morcar, and the Londoners proceeded to elect Edgar Ætheling as king, but then decided to change sides, and to submit to the Conqueror.[53] In return they received a writ, still surviving and in English, confirming their customs: William granted them all the laws of which they were worthy in King Edward's day, and that every child should be his father's heir after his father's death.[54] There was thus a clear commitment to continuity. The reference to King Edward's laws is significant, as this was to become a mantra later on.

The writ was addressed to Bishop William and to Geoffrey the port-reeve, probably Geoffrey de Mandeville.[55] Geoffrey at some stage was put in charge of the Tower, and he also succeeded to the lands and, unusually, to the commended men of Ansger the staller.[56] That he later became sheriff of Middlesex, Essex, and Hertfordshire may have been the result

---

[51] ASC, D, E, 1051, 1052.   [52] *Carmen de Hastingae Proelio*, p. 38.   [53] ASC, D, 1066.

[54] Bates, *Acta of William I*, no. 180.

[55] A man of this name placed a symbol of William FitzOsbern's gift of land at Abbeville-Saint-Lucien to Saint-Amand, Rouen, *Recueil des Actes des Ducs de Normandie de 911 à 1066* (ed. Fauroux), no. 182. He also witnessed the restitution of a butcher's to Saint Ouen, Rouen, *ibid.*, no. 204. The likeliest place of his origin is Magneville near Dieppe, L. C. Loyd, *Origins of Some Anglo-Norman Families*, ed. C. T. Clay and D. C. Douglas, Harleian Society, 103 (Leeds, 1951), p. 57.

[56] For the offices and titles ceded to the younger Geoffrey, see *RRAN*, III, nos. 273–6. For discussion, see C. Warren Hollister, 'The Misfortunes of the Mandevilles', *History*, 58 (1973), 18–28 reprinted in *Monarchy, Magnates, and Institutions in the Anglo-Norman World* (London: Hambledon Press, 1986), pp. 117–27. K. S. B. Keats-Rohan suggested that Geoffrey's first wife, Athelais, was a daughter of William count of Eu and Beatrice de Bully, 'The Prosopography of Post-Conquest England: Four Case Studies', *Medieval Prosopography*, 14 (1993), 1–52, at pp. 10–11. For the site of the Tower, see Haslam, 'Parishes, Churches, Wards and Gates in Eastern London', Blair (ed.), *Minsters and Parish Churches*, pp. 35–44, at p. 39.

of personal success and good fortune. At any rate, his career was one of the more remarkable success stories of the Conquest.

Castles were soon built because, as William of Poitiers put it, it was of the utmost importance to hold in check the numerous and fierce Londoners.[57] Bishop William of London seems to have done well out of the Conquest. Knight service was imposed on the bishopric, but he evidently had the resources to buy land to grant out as fees.[58] He was not entrusted with custody of a castle in the city, which perhaps might have been feared as a rival node of power. Instead he was granted (Bishop's) Stortford in Hertfordshire adjacent to the Roman road, Stane Street.[59]

The Norman kings had thus buttressed their influence over the city as far as they could by building castles, by appointing Norman sheriffs, and by the continuing importance of the palace-abbey complex at Westminster. From 1066 the Norman kings visited Westminster with increasing frequency.[60] William the Conqueror tended to spend either Whitsuntide or Christmas there when in England, as did William Rufus and Henry I until 1121. London was particularly important to Stephen: his presence there is recorded in all but three years of the reign. Henry II was absent for protracted periods, but when in England he spent time at Westminster in 1155, 1157, 1163, 1164, 1165, 1170, then there was a gap until 1175–8, 1185, and a last visit was in 1186.[61] Londoners were said to have been loyal to the king during the rebellion of 1173–4.[62] The presence there of the exchequer and then of the panel of royal justices led to a permanent presence of clerks and officials.[63]

London and the surrounding area must have been a building site for much of the period. That the building work imposed heavy burdens was noted in the Anglo-Saxon Chronicle in 1097: 'many shires whose labour was due at London were hard pressed because of the wall they built about

---

[57] *Gesta Guillelmi*, pp. 160–2. For Ralph Baynard and Robert Gernon, custodians of the castles in the west of the city, see K. S. B. Keats-Rohan, *Domesday People: a Prosopography of Persons Occurring in English Documents, 1066–1166*. I, *Domesday Book* (Woodbridge: Boydell Press, 1999), pp. 327, 388. The former came from Saint-Leger-des-Rôtes, dép. Eure, the latter possibly from Condé-sur-Noireau, dép. Calvados, arr. Vire.

[58] For analysis of the list, see P. Taylor, 'The Endowment and Military Obligations of the See of London: a Reassessment of Three Sources', *Anglo-Norman Studies*, 14 (1991), 287–312 at pp. 293–303.

[59] Bates, *Acta of William I*, nos. 189, 190.

[60] Biddle, 'Seasonal Festivals and Residences'.

[61] Based on the itinerary in Eyton, *Court, Itinerary and Household of Henry II*.

[62] Jordan Fantosme (ed. Johnston), para. 173, p. 121.

[63] Rosser, *Medieval Westminster*, pp. 28–9.

the Tower, and because of the bridge that was nearly all carried away by a flood, and because of the work on the king's hall, that was being built at Westminster, and men were oppressed thereby.' The great new hall, seventy-three by twenty metres, was the setting for a great crownwearing in 1099, memorably described by Gaimar.[64]

Royal writs and charters were addressed variously to castellans, sheriffs, reeves, or justices.[65] Geoffrey de Mandeville does not seem to have had an uninterrupted tenure as sheriff, and by 1100 he had been succeeded by William de Mandeville, who was constable of the Tower when the bishop of Durham made his daring escape from captivity.[66] William died probably leaving a son under age, the younger Geoffrey, and custody of the other castles passed to the heirs of the Domesday holders. One important change was the appearance of Hugh of Buckland early in Henry I's reign. He was a canon of St Paul's, not a magnate, and he was sheriff of several counties. His appointment indicates a change of policy towards the city, perhaps with a view to collecting more revenue.[67] It is not altogether clear if Hugh was a sheriff or justiciar, the man responsible for hearing crown pleas, about whom more is heard for a time in Stephen's reign.[68]

In 1130 the king conceded to the citizens the right to elect their own sheriffs.[69] In this case the outgoing sheriffs were offering payments to leave office which at a total of £48 was a considerably smaller sum than the balance of the farm for the current year.[70] The Londoners were said to have found King Henry's laws oppressive, a statement which could refer to his imposition of *misericordiae*, extremely heavy fines.[71] Free election was included in a list of privileges and customs in the text of the king's purported charter to the Londoners.[72] The text includes a grant of the farm of London at a reduced figure of £300, as well as a list of fiscal and judicial rights and privileges.[73] There has been much discussion of the authenticity of this text, which survives only in a late copy.[74] Whilst it may

---

[64] *Estoire des Engleis*, lines 5978–6110.
[65] Reynolds, 'Rulers of London in the Twelfth Century'; Brooke and Keir, *London 800–1216*, appendix 2.
[66] OV, V, pp. 310–12.   [67] Brooke and Keir, *London 800–1216*, pp. 203–6.
[68] Reynolds, 'Rulers of London in the Twelfth Century', table 1, p. 354. It is possible that a justiciar only became necessary when the citizens nominated the sheriffs.
[69] *Pipe Roll 31 Henry I*, p. 116.
[70] *Ibid.*; Green, *Government of England under Henry I*, pp. 67–8.   [71] JW, III, p. 296.
[72] *RRAN*, II, no. 1645; Brooke, Keir, Reynolds, 'Henry I's Charter for the City of London'.
[73] *English Historical Documents*, II, pp. 946–7.
[74] D. Keene, 'Text, Visualisation and Politics: London, 1150–1250'.

have been based on an authentic text, some of the concessions, particularly such a large reduction in the farm, stretch credulity.

It seems more likely that such a claim was advanced either at the accession of King Stephen, or in 1141 when the Londoners once again had an important part in national politics.[75] Stephen as count of Mortain had substantial property in London, and as count of Boulogne had cross-Channel interests.[76] In 1135 the Londoners were said to have greeted him warmly and elected him as king.[77] They also formed a sworn association, or commune, the first occasion that this had happened in England.[78] It would not have been surprising had he confirmed their liberties on that occasion, but at this early juncture he would not have needed to make major new concessions.

However, by February 1141 the situation had altered: Stephen was imprisoned, and the empress, whose case had been backed by the bishop of Winchester, was pitching for control of London. Advantageous terms were offered to Geoffrey de Mandeville, now earl of Essex, who by this time was in possession of the Tower. She confirmed his earldom, then added hereditary custody of the Tower, plus the shrievalty and justiciarship of Essex.[79] In a second charter she added the shrievalty of London at £300, the justiciarship of London (and Middlesex) and of Hertfordshire as hereditary grants.[80] Her grants in effect concentrated power in the hands of one man, and could be seen as recreating the role of Ansger the Staller. Not surprisingly, Geoffrey's relations with the Londoners were evidently far from harmonious given the empress promised in her second charter that she would not make peace with them 'because they were his [Geoffrey's] mortal enemies'.

Geoffrey's power did not last long, for he and the empress's supporters were driven out of London by a rising.[81] Although King Stephen when released confirmed the empress's grants to Geoffrey, the latter's downfall came in 1143 when the king took away his castles; Geoffrey went on the offensive and died of wounds. After his death relations between the city and the king seem to have been more peaceful. The names of those mentioned as sheriffs suggest that the citizens may have been allowed to nominate sheriffs. A solitary reference to Richard de Lucy as justice of

[75] C. N. L. Brooke, G. Keir, and S. Reynolds, 'Henry I's Charter for the City of London', *Journal of the Society of Archivists*, 4 (1972), 558–78, at pp. 570–1.
[76] J. H. Round, 'The Counts of Boulogne as English Lords', Round, *Studies in Peerage and Family History* (Westminster: Constable and Co, 1900), pp. 147–80.
[77] *Gesta Stephani*, pp. 4–6.   [78] *Ibid.*, p. 6.   [79] *RRAN*, III, no. 274.
[80] *Ibid.*, no. 275.   [81] *Gesta Stephani*, pp. 120–6.

London is significant, as he was one of Stephen's leading officers in the second half of the reign.[82] His base may already have been the Tower, custody of which was ceded to him in the peace of 1153.[83] Richard was one of the chief justiciars appointed by Henry II, whom he served loyally, though he may have lost the custody of the Tower.[84] Two of Richard's daughters married the then lords of Baynard's and Mountfitchet's.[85] He remained loyal in the great revolt of 1173, though his son-in-law Gilbert de Mountfitchet garrisoned his castle against the king.[86] The Londoners remained loyal to Henry II, and welcomed him on his return to England.[87]

London and Henry II

Henry II seems to have dealt with the Londoners circumspectly. As mentioned previously, the charter he granted the citizens listed their legal and fiscal privileges: citizens were not to plead outside the city except for external holdings, and pleas concerning moneyers and royal officials; they were quit of the murder fine and were not to be tried by battle; in respect of pleas of the crown they were to 'make their proof' according to the custom of the city. Fines were to revert to customary figures, not negotiable sums; pleas of miskenning (procedural errors) were not to be heard, and the husting courts were to be held only once a week; pleas of debts contracted in London were to be heard there; and the citizens were to be freed from toll and lastage throughout the country, and from various other imposts. They were to have their hunting rights wherever they had had them in Henry I's reign. Henry II's charter makes no mention of the Londoners' right to elect their own sheriffs and justiciar.[88] Susan

---

[82] *RRAN*, III, no. 534.

[83] *Ibid*, no. 272; Emilie Amt, 'Lucy, Richard de (d. 1179)', *ODNB* www.oxforddnb.com /view/article/17149, accessed 20 May 2016.

[84] Thomas Becket is said to have held the Tower, William FitzStephen, *Materials for the History of Thomas Becket*, III, p. 20.

[85] Aveline married Gilbert de Mountfichet, and Matilda married Walter FitzRobert de Clare.

[86] *Jordan Fantosme's Chronicle*, paras. 97, 173 (ed. Johnston, pp. 68, 120).

[87] *Ibid*., paras. 203–6 (ed. Johnston, pp. 142–4).

[88] Brooke and Keir, *London 800–1216*, p. 40 and plate no. 10; *English Historical Documents*, II, no. 271, pp. 1013–14; *Munimenta Gildhallae Londoniensis: Liber Albus, Liber Custumarum et Liber Horn Gildhallensis*, ed. H. T. Riley, 3 vols. in 4, RS (London: Longman, Brown, Green, Longmans and Roberts, 1849–62), II part 1, pp. 31–2; Brooke, Keir and Reynolds, 'Henry I's Charter for the City of London', appendix II.

Reynolds suggested that in practice those nominated by the king were little different from those who might have been nominated by the citizens.[89] References to justiciars disappear and, as the new itinerant justices did not sit in the city, we may only speculate as to who presided over crown pleas.[90]

London made a major contribution to royal finances throughout our period, and for this reason, if for no other, kings had to keep on reasonable terms with the Londoners. We know that in 1018 the city contributed no less than £10,500 to the geld imposed by Cnut, an astonishingly large figure.[91] Thereafter figures are lacking until the twelfth-century pipe rolls. The farm of London and Middlesex was fixed at £500 of assayed silver and £22 by number. In addition large sums were levied every few years as 'aids' or 'gifts'. In 1130 the figure was £120, which seems to have been an annual levy.[92] In 1156 the figure was again £120, but in 1159 it rose to the massive figure of £1,043. Thereafter the sum most commonly levied was 1,000 marks (£666 13s. 4d.).[93] Moreover, the London mint became even more important as the number of mints was radically reduced in 1180.[94]

From the 1180s the Londoners were able to use their wealth and bargaining power to extract further concessions.[95] Probably from 1189 they secured the lowering of the farm to £300, then two years later John, in opposition to his absent brother, granted a commune whilst Henry FitzAilwin was recognized as mayor.[96] On Richard's return from captivity, though no mention was made of the commune, the farm remained the same and Henry remained as mayor, in return for a massive payment of £1,000.[97] London's importance to politics under John remained central, and in 1215 it was arguably the rebels' capture of the city that forced the king, however reluctantly, to the negotiating table.

Internal Governance

In the previous section we have seen the emergence of key institutions, the wards, the husting, and, in the 1190s, the mayor. Keeping the walls in repair and organizing the defences of the city were probably organized

---

[89] Reynolds, 'Rulers of London', p. 341.   [90] *Ibid.*, pp. 354–6.   [91] ASC, C, D, E, 1018.
[92] *Pipe Roll 31 Henry I*, p. 118.   [93] Reynolds, 'Farm and Taxation of London', table 2.
[94] M. Allen, *Mints and Money in Medieval England* (Cambridge: Cambridge University Press, 2012), pp. 41–3, 48, 53.
[95] Reynolds, 'Rulers of London', p. 343.   [96] *Ibid.*, pp. 347–51.
[97] *Pipe Roll 6 Richard I*, p. 182.

through the wards and, within them, the parishes.[98] According to the 'London Collection', the militia was under the command of Robert FitzWalter as lord of Baynard's castle. He was to meet the mayor, sheriffs, and aldermen at the great gate of the Church of St Paul, where he was to take charge of a banner of St Paul and carry it as far as Aldgate.[99] William FitzStephen claimed the city had had 20,000 horsemen and 60,000 foot soldiers in arms in Stephen's reign.[100] Another possibility is that the *cnihtengild*, which survived until 1125 when its land was transferred to the priory of Holy Trinity Aldgate, had had a military function, perhaps to defend the east wall of the city, and it was disbanded as the Tower site was developed.[101]

London's internal governance was organized, like that of other towns and cities, on the basis of assemblies, which gradually developed into institutions with defined membership. The general assembly of citizens, the *folkmoot*, met in the churchyard of St Paul's three times a year.[102] The husting was the smaller council, which came to be composed of aldermen, with functions approximately equivalent to those of the shire court.[103] By the late twelfth century a single individual was recognized as mayor, again much like those appearing as mayors or *podestàs* in continental towns. Henry FitzAilwin is thought to have been from one of the important city families, though not demonstrably an alderman. The same families too came to supply the sheriffs.[104]

TRANSFORMATION OF THE URBAN LANDSCAPE

The population density, the size and grandeur of new buildings, and the spread of suburbs outside the walls combined to transform the landscape. As Brooke and Keir pointed out, a valuable clue about the configuration of

---

[98] J. Haslam, 'Parishes, Churches, Wards and Gates'; J. Haslam, 'King Alfred and the Development of London', *London Archaeologist* (Spring 2010), 208–12. For discussion of the Roman inheritance, see J. Schofield, *The Building of London from the Conquest to the Great Fire*, 3rd edn (Stroud: Sutton Publishing, 1999), chapter 1.

[99] Brooke and Keir, *London 800–1216*, p. 216.

[100] *Materials for the History of Thomas Becket*, III, p. 4; *Gesta Stephani*, pp. 124, 128–30, 226.

[101] Haslam, 'Parishes, Churches, Wards and Gates in Eastern London'.

[102] Brooke and Keir, *London 800–1216*, p. 249.

[103] For a reference to aldermen, see *Leges Edwardi Confessoris*, cap. 32, 3, O'Brien, *God's Peace and King's Peace*, p. 190; Liebermann, *Die Gesetze der Angelsachsen*, I, p. 655.

[104] Derek Keene, 'Henry fitz Ailwin (d. 1212)', *ODNB* www.oxforddnb.com/view/article /9526, accessed 20 May 2016.

streets and wards lies in the creation of the many small parishes of the
medieval city, a process which seems essentially to have taken shape in the
eleventh century.[105] By that time most of the area within the Roman walls
was evidently occupied and these and their six gates were kept in repair.[106]

The new church at Westminster, dedicated to St Peter, was probably
the earliest of the large new buildings in and around the city. There was
already a church there, and, according to the anonymous *Life of King
Edward*, Edward decided to rebuild the monastery because of his devotion
to St Peter, and because he intended to be buried there.[107] The new church
was very similar to that at Jumièges in Normandy, though very much
bigger, and it is not clear which if either predated the other: the presence at
Edward's court of Robert of Jumièges, bishop of London and briefly
archbishop of Canterbury, was the obvious point of contact.
The Romanesque style of Edward's church was a clear statement of intent
about his cultural preferences, and about his ambition, for this was one of
the longest churches in Europe: 98.2 metres, or 322 feet, long.

Building continued under the Norman and Angevin kings, for whom
the church assumed central importance as the coronation church.
According to Osbert of Clare, William the Conqueror had presented
a *capsa*, a kind of metal superstructure for the Confessor's tomb.[108]
Edward the Confessor spent increasing amounts of time near the site,
and it seems to have been at this time that the palace at Westminster
became the permanent royal residence. Nearby William Rufus had a great
hall constructed as a setting for grand occasions (73 metres by 20 metres).

As noted earlier, William the Conqueror ordered the construction of
fortifications in London soon after his coronation. Two abutted the city
walls in the west, Baynard's and Mountfitchet's, whilst the Tower dominated the south-east corner.[109] Both Baynard's and Mountfitchet's were
swept away in later rebuilding, but the former is thought to have occupied

[105] Brooke and Keir, *London 800–1216*, chapter 6.   [106] *Ibid.*, pp. 149–62.
[107] *Life of King Edward*, pp. 66–70. Sulcard reported a different version: that Edward had
      intended to go to Rome as a thanksgiving for the peace of his accession, but was
      dissuaded from doing so by the magnates and instead used the funds to restore the
      abbey. B. W. Scholz, 'Prologus de Construccione Westmonasterii', *Traditio*, 20 (1964),
      59–91; R. Gem, 'The Romanesque Rebuilding of Westminster Abbey'.
[108] Osbert of Clare, *Vita Edwardi*, cap. 29 (ed. Bloch, p. 120); for the translation in 1163,
      Richard of Cirencester, *Speculum Historiale de Gestis Regum Angliae*, ed.
      J. E. B. Mayor, 2 vols., RS (London: Longman, Green, Longman, Roberts and Green,
      1863–9), II, pp. 319–27; for discussion Crook, *English Medieval Shrines*, pp. 157–60,
      187–91.
[109] William FitzStephen, *Materials for the History of Thomas Becket*, III, p. 3.

the south-west corner of the Roman walls. The latter was on a site given to the Dominicans, inside the city wall, south of Ludgate and north of Baynard's.[110] The first fortification on the site of the Tower may have been the 'little castle' of Ravenger, mentioned in the charter of the empress to Geoffrey de Mandeville.[111] The White Tower was probably started between about 1075 and 1079, with a second stage between the late 1080s and 1100. Gundulf, bishop of Rochester, was credited with supervising its construction.[112] Built of Caen stone, it was of great size and strength, and included a hall as well as a chapel.[113]

St Paul's was the mother church of the city, occupying a prominent site in the north-west of the walled city.[114] Nothing is known about the pre-Conquest building. A church council was held at London in 1075, but in 1087 the church was destroyed in a great fire.[115] Bishop Maurice began a great new building soon afterwards, modelled on St Stephen's Caen, but considerably bigger, as big, indeed, as the site permitted. The relics of St Erkenwald, a seventh-century bishop of London renowned for his holiness, miraculously escaped the fire of 1087 and were translated to the crypt.[116] By the 1130s the shrine was the focus of miracles. After an attempt to steal the body in 1140, it was moved for safety to the chancel, and then in 1148 translated once again to a new shrine behind the high altar.[117]

Then the Augustinians arrived. Their first house in London was the priory of Holy Trinity Aldgate. This was established in 1108 at the behest of Queen Matilda on the site of a church dedicated to the Holy Cross and St Mary Magdalene.[118] Although wrecked at the Dissolution, it has been possible to reconstruct its size and layout, and it was clearly a building of impressive size and finish.[119] Matilda was credited with the endowment of

[110] B. Watson, 'The Excavation of a Norman Fortress on Ludgate Hill', *London Archaeologist*, 6 no. 14 (Spring, 1992), 371–7.

[111] *RRAN*, III, no. 274.   [112] *Textus Roffensis* (ed. Hearne), p. 212.

[113] *History of the King's Works*, I, pp. 29–31.

[114] See especially D. Keene, A. Burns, and A. Saint (eds.), *St Paul's. The Cathedral Church of London 604–1204* (New Haven, CT, and London: Yale University Press, 2004).

[115] ASC, E, 1087.

[116] E. Gordon Whatley, *The Saint of London. The Life and Miracles of St. Erkenwald*, Medieval and Renaissance Texts and Studies, 58 (Binghamton, 1989), p. 61.

[117] A. Thacker, 'The Cult of Saints and the Liturgy', Keene, Burns, Saint (eds.), *St Paul's*, pp. 113–22.

[118] The church seems to have belonged to the canons of Waltham, whom Queen Matilda compensated.

[119] Vince, *Building of London*, pp. 46, 48.

a bathhouse complex at Queenhithe.[120] Tradition also links her with bridges at Bow and at Cobham on the London–Portsmouth road.[121]

The most important secular building within the city walls was the Guildhall. This was sited, perhaps deliberately, on the site of a Roman amphitheatre, and may have incorporated standing masonry.[122] The grander houses within the walls were being built in stone by the eleventh and twelfth centuries. One example is the stone house of William de Pont de l'Arche, Henry I's chamberlain.[123] Some of the larger gilds and trading associations had stone halls. The Cologne merchants, for instance, established their headquarters at the Steelyard (now under Cannon Street station) with a stone hall by the twelfth century.[124]

London Bridge

Apart from the walls and gates of London, the other important development was the rebuilding in stone of the bridge across the Thames. The bridge had earlier been important in the struggle against Scandinavian attacks, especially in 1014 by Olaf Haraldsson, and again in 1016 when Cnut's forces dragged their ships overland on the Surrey side to enable them to continue upstream.[125] The bridge suffered damage in 1097.[126] It was repaired before 1130.[127] In the late twelfth century it was decided to replace the wooden bridge in stone. The work, which began in 1176, was overseen by Peter the priest of St Mary Colechurch.[128] This was the parish where Becket had been born, and a chapel dedicated to the saint was built on the bridge.

---

[120] Huneycutt, *Matilda of Scotland*, p. 114.   [121] *Ibid.*, pp. 114–15.

[122] Schofield, *London 1100–1600*, pp. 23–6; Brooke and Keir, *London 800–1216*, p. 281.

[123] *RRAN*, III, no. 829; for stone houses, see M. Wood, *The English Medieval House* (London: J. M. Dent and Sons, 1965), chapter 1.

[124] For the Steelyard, see D. Keene, 'New Discoveries at the Hanseatic Steelyard of London', *Hansische Geschichtsblatter. Herausgegeben vom Hansischen Geschichtsverein*, 107 (1989), 15–25.

[125] The timber for this bridge has been shown to date between *c.* 987 and 1032, J. R. Hagland and B. Watson, 'Fact or Folklore: the Viking attack on London Bridge', *London Archaeologist*, 12 (Spring 2005), 328–33. It was replaced by a second timber bridge *c.* 1056, B. Watson, T. Brigham, and T. Dyson, *London Bridge: 2000 Years of a River Crossing*, Museum of London Archaeological Service, Monograph 8 (2001), pp. 57, 75.

[126] *Annales de Waverleia, Annales Monastici*, II, p. 207.

[127] *Pipe Roll 31 Henry I*, p. 113; *Annales de Bermundesia, Annales Monastici*, III, p. 435.

[128] *Annales de Waverleia, Annales Monastici*, II, p. 240; Derek Keene, 'Colechurch, Peter of (d. 1205)', *ODNB* www.oxforddnb.com/view/article/5868, accessed 20 May 2016; Derek Keene, 'Colechurch, Peter of (d. 1205)', *ODNB* www.oxforddnb.com/view/article/5868, accessed 20 May 2016.

Outside the City

The earliest reference to Southwark occurs in the tenth-century text known as the *Burghal Hidage*, indicating that there was a settlement on the south bank of the river.[129] By the mid-eleventh century there was a monastery and a tidal waterway held by the king. The king had two-thirds of the revenue from the waterway and Earl Godwin one-third. After 1066 it had passed into the possession of Odo of Bayeux.[130] Two royal officials, the chamberlain William de Pont de l'Arche and the dispenser William d'Anisy, established an Augustinian priory there with the assistance of the bishop of Winchester.[131]

Lambeth was described in 1086 as a manor belonging to St Mary's Church, which had been built by Countess Godgifu, the king's sister.[132] In 1088 it was given by William Rufus to the bishop and monks of Rochester, and not long afterwards we hear of Anselm's presence there.[133] Over time it became the London residence of the archbishops of Canterbury, and Archbishop Hubert Walter built a grand residence there.[134]

At Bermondsey east of Lambeth there had been an Anglo-Saxon monastery.[135] According to the (late) Bermondsey annals, the first steps towards the new foundation were taken in 1082 by a London citizen, Ailwin (Ælfwin or Æthelwine *Cild*), who assigned to it certain rents in London.[136] In 1086 a fine new church was reported in Domesday Book.[137] Four Cluniac monks arrived from La Charité-sur-Loire, and William Rufus donated the manor of Bermondsey.[138] Further benefactions were made by Henry I, and his sister-in-law Mary, countess of

---

[129] For the text, see A. R. Rumble and D. Hill (eds.), *Defence of Wessex: Burghal Hidage and Anglo-Saxon Fortifications* (Manchester: Manchester University Press, 1996), pp. 24–9, and for a translation pp. 32–3. The Southwark entry is on p. 33.

[130] DB, I, fol. 32r. Carlin, *Medieval Southwark*, p. 9–15. Part of Southwark was held by the archbishop of Canterbury from the twelfth century.

[131] For discussion of the bishop of Winchester's role, see M. Franklin, 'The Bishops of Winchester and the Monastic Revolution', *Anglo-Norman Studies*, 12 (1990), 47–65 at p. 49.

[132] DB, I, fol. 34r.

[133] *Registrum Roffense etc*, ed. J. Thorpe (London: J. Thorpe, 1769), pp. 459–60.

[134] *Textus Roffensis*, pp. 213–14; Eadmer, *Historia Novorum*, p. 74; Tatton Brown, *Lambeth Palace*, pp. 9–20.

[135] T. Dyson, M. Samuel, A. Steele, and S. M. Wright, *The Cluniac Priory and Abbey of St Saviour Bermondsey, Surrey*, Museum of London Archaeology Monograph, 1 (2011), pp. 13–99.

[136] *Annales Monastici*, III, pp. 425–6.   [137] DB, I, fol. 30r.

[138] *Annales Monastici*, III, pp. 427–8; *RRAN*, I, no. 398.

Boulogne, who was buried there.[139] Count William of Mortain, long a prisoner of Henry I, was said to have become a monk and died there.[140] A crucifix was discovered in the Thames in 1117 and, believed to be a relic of the Holy Cross, became an object of veneration.[141] The priory's location made it a convenient stopping point for travellers, including the royal court at Christmas 1154.[142] The close proximity of churches at Lambeth, Southwark, and Bermondsey on the south bank is unlikely to have been coincidental: this created in effect a demilitarized zone opposite the fortified city to the north.

Solidarities and Social Tensions

How far was the growing wealth and importance of the city reflected in a sense of its own identity and history? Geoffrey of Monmouth's *History of the Kings of Britain* claimed that Brutus founded the city as the new Troy, which then became known as Trinovantum, and bestowed it on the citizens by right of inheritance, together with a code of laws. King Lud supplied the walls and towers, and gave his name to the city. King Uther Pendragon held his court there. A later king, Cadwallo, was embalmed and his body was encased in bronze and placed on a horse outside the west gate of the city. Geoffrey's version of the *Prophecies of Merlin* included the prophecy that a tree would spring up on the Tower, that 20,000 people would die, and that the river would run red with blood.[143] In the present context what is significant is the idea that the city's origins and its laws went back before those of Rome.[144]

Geoffrey of Monmouth's version of early British history was evidently known to William FitzStephen.[145] In the prologue to his description of London, William explained that he had been a clerk in Becket's household

[139] *Annales Monastici*, III, pp. 430–5.   [140] *Ibid.*, p. 436.   [141] *Ibid.*, p. 432.

[142] Dyson, Samuel, Steele, and Wright, *Cluniac Priory and Abbey of St Saviour Bermondsey*, p. 99. For Henry II at Bermondsey at Christmas 1154, see Gervase of Canterbury, I, p. 160.

[143] Geoffrey of Monmouth, *HKB*, Book I, para. 22; Book III, para. 53; *Prophecies of Merlin*, Book VIII, para. 115, 137; Book XII, para. 201 (ed. Reeve, pp. 28–31, 66–7, 148–51, 182–3, 276–7).

[144] The reference to the citizens being given the city by inheritance may be an allusion to the Conqueror's confirmation in which he granted the citizens their right to succeed their fathers, Bates, *Acta of William I*, no. 180.

[145] *Materials for the History of Thomas Becket*, III, pp. 1–154. The prefatory section on London is pp. 1–13. For a translation by H. E. Butler, see F. M. Stenton, *Norman London*, Historical Association, 38 (London, 1915), pp. 26–32. For William's knowledge of Geoffrey of Monmouth, see Brooke and Keir, *London 800–1216*, p. 119.

and that, like the archbishop, he was a Londoner. London was where the sun rose for the archbishop, and Canterbury was where it set. The author wanted to place Becket in the history of illustrious Londoners, amongst whom he included Brutus, the founder of the city, Emperor Constantine, and, in more recent times, Empress Matilda and the Young King. William managed to avoid exile with Becket and, as he explains, was reconciled to Henry II by the composition of a Latin prayer for him, but he was in Canterbury at the time of the murder. His general motives for writing were thus presumably much the same as the other biographers, but the emphasis on London is particularly striking. Perhaps it was in response to the rapid spread of the cult beyond Canterbury, especially to London, where Becket was soon venerated. The dean of St Paul's, Ralph de Diceto, established a chapel dedicated to the saint, and the chapel on London Bridge was also dedicated to him.[146] With St Paul, Becket was adopted as co-patron saint of the city on the city's seal.[147] This biography alone gave due credit to the saint's birth and upbringing in London. For the historian, William's description is invaluable, especially for the buildings, but also for the way of life of the students, for sports and pastimes, and for the militia. He too mentioned the ancient laws of the city, its division into wards like Rome, and its sheriffs like Rome's consuls. Once again, then, the emphasis is on the antiquity of the city and its laws.

Who, then, preserved the laws and customs of the city? As we have seen, bishops took a lead role in preserving and transmitting legal knowledge, but this was not necessarily about laws and customs pertaining to specific cities. One of the early twelfth-century manuscripts of Anglo-Saxon laws, now Corpus Christi College Cambridge MS 383, may have been compiled at St Paul's, though the evidence for this rests on the addition of a list of the shipmen of St. Paul's.[148] The cathedral community preserved its own records in the form of charters and memoranda like the shipmen list or the record of St Paul's property dating from the 1120s. When and where did the citizens start preserving their records? The text of the London peace-gild of the tenth century survives in the early twelfth-century collection the *Textus Roffensis*.[149] That of Edward the Confessor

---

[146] Thacker, 'The Cult of Saints and the Liturgy', Keene, Burns, and Saint (eds.), *St Paul's*, p. 118.

[147] Keene, 'Text, Visualisation and Politics', p. 77.

[148] Wormald, *Making of English Law*, pp. 228–36. See now T. J. Gobbitt, 'The Production and Use of MS Cambridge, Corpus Christi College 383 in the Late Eleventh and Early Twelfth Centuries', PhD thesis, Leeds University, 2010.

[149] *Die Gesetze der Angelsachsen*, I, pp. 173–82.

for the *cnihtengild*, confirming the laws they had had in the days of Kings Edgar, Æthelred, and Cnut, survived in the archive of Holy Trinity Aldgate.[150] William the Conqueror's notification to the Londoners survives in the original and has remained in the city's archives, now housed in the London Metropolitan Archives.[151] As noted previously, the focus of the 'London Collection' is on laws and customs as they pertained to the city.

To outsiders the Londoners could be seen as a distinct group, as, for instance, to the author of the *Gesta Stephani*.[152] William of Malmesbury attributed to Bishop Henry of Winchester the comment that the Londoners were 'as if nobles (*optimates*) because of the size of the city'.[153] William FitzStephen repeated the statement: 'the inhabitants of other cities are called citizens, but of this they are called barons'.[154] Jordan Fantosme, too, referred to the citizens as barons.[155] One question which has attracted discussion is how far the leading citizens formed an urban elite, whose interests lay primarily in commerce and trade, unlike those of nobles and churchmen. Through her work on twelfth-century Londoners, Susan Reynolds demonstrated how difficult it is to pigeonhole individuals, some of whom had rural estates and married into landed families, and others of whom, such as Gervase of Cornhill, worked in royal service and may have married into a London family rather than have been born into one.[156] What is clear is that here, as in other English towns and cities, men of English extraction remained important after the Norman Conquest: the coming of the Normans was not as disastrous for wealthy Londoners as for their rural equivalents. The composition of the city was already diverse with foreign traders. Normans like Gilbert Becket, father of the archbishop, were able to settle and prosper, and in the train of the Normans came Jews from Rouen.[157] Neighbourhoods were often populated according to occupation or ethnicity, worshipping in the numerous small churches being established in the tenth and eleventh centuries, some of which were associated with gilds. For many it was the ties based on family, occupation, and neighbourhood that were the most immediate and perhaps important.

---

[150] *Anglo-Saxon Writs* (ed. Harmer), pp. 234–5.
[151] London, London Metropolitan Archives, COL/CH/01.
[152] *Gesta Stephani*, pp. 122–4, 126, 226.   [153] *Historia Novella*, p. 94.
[154] *Materials for the History of Thomas Becket*, III, p. 4.
[155] *Jordan Fantosme's Chronicle*, para. 97 (ed. Johnston, p. 68).
[156] Reynolds, 'Rulers of London', pp. 346–7.
[157] WM, *Gesta Regum Anglorum*, I, p. 562.

Inevitably there were rivalries and clashes between different groups. One such incident had occurred before 1130, for in the pipe roll of that year the sheriffs were fined for 'an assault on the ships and houses of London'.[158] We hear incidentally of tensions between rich and poor. For example, when funds were being raised for a new shrine for St Erkenwald in the 1130s, the poor were said to have contributed more than the rich.[159] The rich Londoners evidently preferred to direct their patronage elsewhere.[160] The city was certainly a violent place. Aubrey II de Vere was killed in the London streets in 1141.[161] Later that year the Londoners rose at the sound of the bells being rung and ejected the empress and her retinue from the city.[162] Roger of Howden reported trouble in the 1170s, when the sons of noble citizens engaged in robbery and murder. A gang broke into the stone house of one of the rich Londoners. Forewarned, he had armed himself and attacked one of the robbers, Andrew Buccuinte, cut off his right hand, and sounded the alarm. Andrew, having been handed over to the king's justice, saved his own life by betraying his confederates. Even this fate did not bring peace to the streets, for three years later a brother of the earl of Derby was murdered and his body thrown into the street.[163]

More serious in their implications were clashes between Christians and Jews and between rich and poor in the later twelfth century. The Jewish community was attacked in 1199 at the time of King Richard's coronation. They had congregated outside the gates of Westminster Abbey where they were attacked. Some were killed, and when the king sent the justiciar Ranulf de Glanvill to restore order he was beaten back by the crowd.[164] The career of William FitzOsbert in the late twelfth century also exposed tensions. According to William of Newburgh, he was an articulate and educated man who had been on crusade. He won a large following amongst the poor, who were protesting against an unfair share of the tax burden on the city.[165] FitzOsbert may well have been right, given that

---

[158] *Pipe Roll 31 Henry I*, p. 115.
[159] Whatley, *The Saint of London. The Life and Miracles of St Erkenwald*, p. 62.
[160] E.g. St Bartholomew's Smithfield, Haliwell, Clerkenwell, Brooke, and Keir, *London 800–1216*, pp. 327, 329, 332. Westminster Abbey began to attract increasing numbers of donations from Londoners in the twelfth century, *Westminster Abbey Charters* (ed. Mason), pp. 19–20.
[161] Howden, I, p. 205. [162] *Gesta Stephani*, p. 124.
[163] *Gesta Regis Henrici Secundi*, I, p. 155; Howden, II, p. 131.
[164] William of Newburgh, *Historia Rerum Anglicarum, Chronicles of the Reigns of Stephen, Henry II and Richard I*, II, pp. 294–9.
[165] *Ibid.*, pp. 466–71.

the sheriffs and aldermen were a small and presumably self-interested group. In 1196 he and his followers collected arms and, although he went to Normandy to secure the king's protection, he had attracted the animosity of the justiciar, Hubert Walter, archbishop of Canterbury. FitzOsbert and his associates took sanctuary at St Mary le Bow, which belonged to the archbishopric of Canterbury, but on the archbishop's orders they were burned out, surrendered, and were put to death.

By the end of our period London had grown in size, population density, and wealth. The basic framework of its institutions had emerged into the written record, and its citizens were able to use their bargaining power to win concessions from the king. There are many common factors in the city's history and that of continental towns and cities, but evidently the city did not go far down the road of political independence. The usual answer to the question why London did not become a city-state is that the power of English kings was too great. An alternative answer is that there was no need to aim at independence. Their symbiotic relationship meant that the king and the citizens could each usually achieve their ends by negotiation. In this period the Londoners on the whole were successful: the one possible exception was under King Cnut when, if Pamela Nightingale is correct, the city may have been in effect under military occupation. The end of the Danish dynasty and the rise of Westminster demonstrated a different kind of relationship between the monarchy and the city, close but distinct, and, as argued at the start of this chapter, by the late twelfth century London with Westminster had become in effect the kingdom's capital.

9

A Patchwork Kingdom

In previous chapters it has been argued that the evolution of political society between the tenth and twelfth centuries has to take account of both vertical and lateral relationships, of networks, and of places, especially cities, as nodes of power. This chapter explores the ways these come together in the formation of identities and loyalties which were both constructed and shifting according to time and perspective. The development of the kingdom and its linking with national identity is certainly an important theme, and it has been given heavy emphasis by historians of the modern state. The reign of Henry II in particular was of critical importance in this regard, in developing the centralized machinery of governance and integrating regions into those agencies. Nevertheless, regional diversity, reflecting different identities and loyalties, remained important, and has perhaps been neglected in comparison with growing integration and a rise of national identity.

Royal authority gained ground as a result of the direct and indirect consequences of the two conquests of the eleventh century. Protracted pressures imposed by Danish attacks and conquest necessitated increasing demands for service and for tribute in southern and midland England. War was thus a primary driver of internal consolidation and intensification of those regions under the control of English kings. However, it was the Norman Conquest which led to a more radical imposition of royal authority in outlying regions, especially in the north, beginning in the late eleventh century and intensifying in the twelfth. Kings had increasing numbers of local agents, especially sheriffs, justices, and constables of castles, and by their increasing use of documents were able to issue orders to remote corners of their realms. The rise of writ-based royal justice, and

A Patchwork Kingdom

the local visitations of royal justices, overlay earlier regional customs. So far, then, it would appear that royal power was evolving along lines which would eventually lead to the modern state, with – to some extent or another – fixed boundaries, centralized government, a monopoly claimed or exercised of the use of violence, and increasing bureaucracy.

There is no doubt that the English kingdom in the late twelfth century was more unified than it had been in 973. The establishment of a single political elite with geographically dispersed estates, the development of diocesan infrastructure, the spread of new religious houses, complemented and strengthened the extension of royal administration, law, and justice. These trends were reflected in a sense of national identity, of Englishness, but they overlay rather than eradicated other loyalties, to older kingdoms and provinces, to counties, to lordships, and to cities, especially London. The first part of this chapter is devoted to such loyalties before turning to explore Englishness and national identity.

REGIONAL DIFFERENCES AND IDENTITIES

Such loyalties operated at different levels and in different contexts. There were first of all memories of older political entities which were subsumed into the tenth-century kingdom of the English. Kent, for instance, had a long history as an entity with distinctive legal customs and farming patterns. The strength of ecclesiastical landholding provided a degree of continuity across the two conquests of the eleventh century, though there was a great deal of change amongst secular landholders.[1] Thus, although there may have been a community of local thegns in the early eleventh century, the changes wrought by the coming of the Normans brought a raft of French-speaking newcomers into the shire.[2] The men of Kent were supposed to have voluntarily submitted to the Conqueror, who confirmed their customs.[3] Hence they were never conquered, and *invicta* came to be adopted as the motto of the county.

Cornwall was a county whose late takeover by the English, its surviving vernacular language, and its different ecclesiastical organization gave it a distinctive character. According to William of Malmesbury, it was

---

[1] Continuity was relative, for there were gains and losses in the late Anglo-Saxon period, R. Fleming, 'Monastic Lands and England's Defence in the Viking Age', *English Historical Review*, 100 (1985), 247–65 at pp. 261, 264–5.
[2] Williams, *World before Domesday*, pp. 39–61.
[3] For the submission of the men of Canterbury, see William of Poitiers, *Gesta Guillelmi*, p. 144.

Æthelstan who took decisive action against the 'western Britons who are called Cornishmen'. They were driven out of Exeter, where they had hitherto lived on equal terms with the English, and their boundary was fixed at the Tamar. Exeter was then surrounded with walls and towers.[4] The history of Cornwall in the tenth century is badly documented. Cornwall seems to have been regarded as an adjunct to the ealdormanry of Devon or *Dumnonia*.[5] A see for Devon and Cornwall was established at Crediton and then moved to Exeter in 1050 under Bishop Leofric.[6] There were also bishops at St Germans in Cornwall, some of whom in the tenth century may have been Cornish.[7] Links with Brittany remained strong. Edward the Confessor whilst in exile in Normandy may have given St Michael's Mount to the abbey of Mont-Saint-Michel, close to the border between Normandy and France.[8]

After the Norman Conquest almost all the land not held by the church in Cornwall was handed over to a Breton, Count Brian. By 1086 he had been succeeded by Count Robert of Mortain. His headquarters in the county were at Launceston.[9] The settlement of new Breton lords bears witness to continuing links between Brittany and south-west England. A stock of legends about Cornwall and Tintagel fed into the twelfth-century Arthurian world of Geoffrey of Monmouth.[10] The *Prophecies of Merlin* referred to a killing of 'the sons of Toki' by a group of men headed by a sheriff, Frawin, an event which can be correlated with an entry in the 1130 pipe roll.[11] Later in the twelfth century John of Cornwall

---

[4] WM, *Gesta Regum*, I, p. 216. For discussion, see C. Insley, 'Athelstan, Charters and the English in Cornwall', Flanagan and Green (eds.), *Charters and Charter Scholarship in Britain and Ireland*, pp. 15–31.

[5] H. P. R. Finberg, 'The Early History of Werrington', *English Historical Review*, 59 (1944), 237–51 at p. 238.

[6] WM, *Gesta Pontificum*, p. 314. For comment, see Insley, 'Athelstan, Charters and the English in Cornwall', pp. 21–2.

[7] *Ibid.*

[8] *The Cartulary of St Michael's Mount*, ed. P. L. Hull, Devon and Cornwall Record Society, new series, 5 (1962), p. 61 = S 1061. For discussion, see now Bates, *Acta of William I*, no. 213.

[9] B. Golding, 'Robert of Mortain', *Anglo-Norman Studies*, 13 (1990), 119–44. Golding points out (p. 126) that the reference to Count Brian holding Cornwall comes from a charter of Count Alan III of Brittany (1140); D. J. A. Matthew, *The Norman Monasteries and Their English Possessions* (London: Oxford University Press, 1962), pp. 36–7.

[10] Padel, 'Geoffrey of Monmouth and Cornwall'.

[11] Geoffrey of Monmouth, *HKB, Prophecies*, Book VIII, para. 113 (ed. Reeve, pp. 146–9). The name Frawin is found in Domesday Book in Cornwall, holding Tregony of Count Robert, DB, I, fol. 125r.

wrote of Frawin's accomplices as *ceteri Cornubienses*.[12] There was thus in
the late eleventh and early twelfth centuries a population of British and
Bretons, Anglo-Saxons, and Normans, whose cultural worlds inter-
meshed and fed into developing Arthurian histories. There were of course
changes in the ranks of landholders, the most important of which was an
earldom, held between 1140 and 1175 semi-autonomously by Earl
Reginald, one of Henry I's children.[13] Meanwhile the church was being
reorganized, some of the older centres such as Bodmin being converted
into Augustinian priories.[14] A sense of political community existed (or
was created) by the early thirteenth century, when the men of Cornwall
successfully petitioned King John not to have a sheriff other than a man
from the county.[15] Over the two centuries with which we are concerned,
then, Cornwall became more fully integrated into the kingdom but
remained distant from the centres of power.

The memory that there had been, for instance, a pre-Viking kingdom of
Lindsey, which survived as a region into the eleventh century, and which
became one of the administrative divisions of the county of Lincolnshire,
tells us little about its significance. Certain activities involved cooperative
activity: the adult male freeholders had common responsibilities for service in the *fyrd*, for geld, and for attendance at court. For a brief moment
in the early eleventh century the men of Lindsey enter the historical record.
In 1014 after the death of Swein at Gainsborough, Cnut made an agreement with them to supply him with horses and to join him in ravaging,
only for them to be left to the vengeance of Æthelred when Cnut put out to
sea.[16] Two years later the ealdorman of Lindsey, the otherwise unknown
Godwin, was present at the battle of *Assandun*.[17] We may surmise that
there had been sympathy for Cnut's Danes in a region where much of the
population was of Scandinavian descent. It may have resurfaced in 1069
when surviving members of the Scandinavian fleet who had escaped from
York took refuge in the marshes, only to be slaughtered when they
emerged to share in local feasting.[18]

[12] M. J. Curley, 'A New Edition of John of Cornwall's *Prophetia Merlini*', *Speculum*, 57 (1982), 217–49, at p. 238.
[13] Frank Barlow, 'Ranulf (d. 1123)', *ODNB* www.oxforddnb.com/view/article/23048, accessed 20 May 2016; David Crouch, 'Reginald, Earl of Cornwall (d. 1175)', *ODNB* www.oxforddnb.com/view/article/23319, accessed 20 May 2016.
[14] S. Turner, *Making a Christian Landscape: the Countryside in Early Medieval Cornwall, Devon, and Wessex* (Exeter: Exeter University Press, 2006). For the cult of St Petroc, see K. Jankulak, *The Medieval Cult of St Petroc* (Woodbridge: Boydell Press, 2000).
[15] *Pipe Roll 10 John*, p. 183; Holt, *Magna Carta*, p. 78.   [16] ASC, C, D, E, 1014.
[17] ASC, C, D, E, 1016.   [18] OV, II, pp. 226, 230.

The union of the Mercian kingdom with Wessex, and its division into 'English' and 'Danish' areas did not completely obliterate older identities. There were occasions, first of all, when the older entity re-emerged, as in 957 when Edgar was recognized as king there whilst his brother Eadwig succeeded to Wessex.[19] Older units, the *Magonsæte*, *Wreocensæte*, and *Pecsæste* occur in a group of Edgar's charters. Even allowing that this usage may reflect scribal preferences, it is possible that they were still regarded as functioning in the later tenth century.[20] The land of the *Hwicce*, another early medieval people, retained its identity in the form of the bishopric of Worcester.[21] In the east midlands the shires were created around the mid-tenth century. It has been argued that King Edgar created the wapentakes and hundreds of Nottinghamshire and Derbyshire to serve as a buffer with Northumbria and to integrate them more fully into the kingdom.[22] The county of Lincolnshire was organized on the same lines. First mentioned in 1016, it was formed by uniting Lindsey and the territory dependent on Stamford.[23] The frontier between Northumbria and Mercia, so important in the pre-Viking period, remained a sensitive zone after the death of Eric Bloodaxe.[24] It has been plausibly suggested that the family of Wulfric Spot may have been established in this region as a buffer zone, a marcher lordship, in effect.[25]

Midland regions of Scandinavian settlement, notably the East Midlands, retained distinctive legal practices. It has been pointed out that the law code

---

[19] ASC, B, C, 957; for discussion, see L. Abrams, 'King Edgar and the Men of the Danelaw', Scragg (ed.), *Edgar, King of the English*, pp. 171–91.

[20] *Ibid.*, p. 178; S 677, *English Historical Documents*, I, pp. 557–8; S 723; S 712a, N. Brooks, M. Gelling, and D. Johnson, 'A New charter of King Edgar', *Anglo-Saxon England*, 13 (1984), 137–55.

[21] D. Hooke, *The Anglo-Saxon Landscape: the Kingdom of the Hwicce* (Manchester: Manchester University Press, 1985). William of Malmesbury, for instance, referred to Dunstan's consecration both as bishop of Worcester and bishop of the *Hwicce*, *Gesta Pontificum*, p. 32.

[22] For King Edmund's recovery of the five boroughs, ASC, A, B, C, D, 942. Roffe, 'Nottinghamshire and the Five Boroughs'; D. Roffe, 'The Origins of Derbyshire', *Derbyshire Archaeological Journal*, 106 (1986), 102–22.

[23] C. Mahany and D. Roffe, 'Stamford: the Development of an Anglo-Scandinavian Borough', *Anglo-Norman Studies*, 5 (1982), 197–219, at pp. 211–19.

[24] N. Higham, 'Northumbria's Southern Frontier: a Review', *Early Medieval Europe*, 14 (2006), 391–418, reviews the evidence, arguing that the region between Ribble and Mersey probably was incorporated into the earldom of Mercia in the later tenth century, so that the Ribble became its northern limit.

[25] C. Insley, 'The Family of Wulfric Spott: an Anglo-Saxon Mercian Marcher Dynasty', Roffe (ed.), *The English and Their Legacy 900–1200: Essays in Honour of Ann Williams* (Woodbridge: Boydell Press, 2012), pp. 115–28.

King Edgar issued at *Wihtbordestan* recognized Danish custom: 'I will that such good laws be in force among the Danes as they best prefer.'[26] He was also well known for his tolerance of 'foreign customs and brought too firmly heathen manners within this land, and attracted hither foreigners'.[27] Edgar's laws were later seen as talismanic: in 1018 Cnut promised to return to the law of King Edgar, and in 1065 the Northumbrians' demand to King Edward was for the restoration of the laws of King Cnut.[28] Distinctive legal practices were reflected in the *lagemen*, lawmen, who occur at Cambridge, Lincoln, Stamford, York, and probably Norwich, Thetford, Ipswich, and Chester.[29] The lawmen seem to have been men of substance, sometimes holding in hereditary succession, and at Chester they may have evolved into the members of the borough court.[30]

Cheshire was another region far from the centres of royal power, looking in this case more towards Wales and to the Irish Sea. The city of Chester had been occupied by the Vikings in 893 and recovered by Æthelflaed in 907. It became a staging post on the route between Viking Dublin and York.[31] There was an active mint in the early tenth century, possibly turning silver from Ireland into coin, and by 958 there was a church dedicated to St Werburgh.[32] The county was part of the ealdordom of Eadric Streona, from whom it passed to Earl Leofwin of Mercia and his family. In 1066 Earl Edwin was the chief landholder in a county where the king held no demesne land.[33] Already, then, it was a cohesive entity before the change at the top brought about by the Normans.

William established Gerbod and, after the latter's return to Flanders, the Norman Hugh d'Avranches.[34] The heading in Domesday Book says succinctly: 'The Land of Earl Hugh and his men', that is, he was the only lay tenant-in-chief in the shire, and his major tenants owed him service and attended his courts.[35] The earl's chamberlain did not account at the

---

[26] IV Eg, *Die Gesetze der Angelsachsen*, I, pp. 206–15.   [27] ASC, D, E, F, 959.

[28] JW, II, p. 504; ASC, D, E, 1065.

[29] DB, I, fols. 189r (Cambridge), 336r (Lincoln), 336v (Stamford), 298r (York), 262v (Chester). The lawmen of York appear in an inquest of 1106, R. C. Van Caenegem, *English Lawsuits from William I to Richard I*, 2 vols., Selden Society (London, 1990, 1991), I, no. 172, pp. 138–44.

[30] *Victoria County History, Cheshire*, V part 1 *Chester*, p. 27.   [31] *Ibid.*, pp. 16–33.

[32] C. P. Lewis, 'Edgar, Chester, and the Kingdom of the Mercians', Scragg (ed.), *Edgar, King of the English*, pp. 104–16.

[33] Baxter, *Earls of Mercia*, pp. 23, 65.   [34] OV, II, p. 260.

[35] C. P. Lewis, 'Formation of the Honour of Chester, 1066–1100', *The Earldom of Chester and Its Charters*, ed. A. T. Thacker, *Journal of the Chester Archaeological Society*, 71 (1991), pp. 37–68.

exchequer, and the justiciar dealt with pleas.[36] In Norman times a castle and abbey dedicated to St Werburgh were built, and by the end of the twelfth century a monk could compare the city with Rome.[37] Earl Ranulf III issued his own Magna Carta for Cheshire, probably shortly after King John's charter. It was witnessed by his chief tenants and reflected their concerns, and was not identical to Magna Carta.[38]

The Marcher lordships came into being in the years after 1066, and they evolved in a way that made them very different from most English counties.[39] The Conqueror's initial plan for the defence of Shropshire and Herefordshire, like Cheshire, had been to appoint earls with far-ranging powers, but the early death of William FitzOsbern in 1071 and the removal of Robert de Bellême in 1102 changed the situation.[40] Medium-sized compact lordships, heavily castled, were established. As Normans moved further into Welsh territory, further land was parcelled out, until a great swathe of territory across south and east Wales came also to be held on terms which, as they were in effect removed from the interventions of justices and sheriffs, gave their lords a great deal of autonomy, increasingly precious in the face of burgeoning royal administration.

The special characteristics of regional society thus came about through a mix of history, geographical location, and land use, and these did not disappear with the formation of a united kingdom. Yet before we assume that regions could be incorporated for the most part without threatening political unity, the slowness of the coming together of Mercia and Wessex has to be borne in mind, and the even more protracted and complex story of the integration of England north of the Humber and Mersey.[41] It was

---

[36] D. Crouch, 'The Administration of the Norman Earldom', *Earldom of Chester and Its Charters* (ed. Thacker), pp. 69–95.

[37] For Lucian of Chester, see www.medievalchester.ac.uk/texts/reading/Lucian/html. For discussion, see R. W. Barrett Jr., *Against all England. Regional Identity and Cheshire Writing, 1195–1656* (Notre Dame, IN: University of Notre Dame Press, 2009).

[38] G. J. White and J. Pepler, *The Magna Carta of Cheshire*, Cheshire Local History Association (Chester, 2015).

[39] R. R. Davies, 'Kings, Lords and Liberties in the March of Wales, 1066–1272', *Transactions of the Royal Historical Society*, 6th series, 29 (1979), 41–61; Davies, *Age of Conquest*, pp. 82–114; M. Lieberman, 'The Medieval "Marches" of Normandy and Wales', *English Historical Review*, 125 (2010), 1357–81.

[40] Lewis, 'Early Earls of Norman England'.

[41] The trajectory of East Anglia's history was different. After the end of the kingdom and the killing of St Edmund, the region experienced a good deal of Scandinavian settlement, whilst continuing to thrive economically. It was part of the tenth-century kingdom, and a series of ealdormen and then earls was appointed. The foundation of the abbey of Bury St Edmunds and the abbot's role in west Suffolk from the time of King Cnut was another

possible to envisage divisions of the realm as a way of providing for more
than one son, as in 957, or as the basis of a peace, as in 1016, when Cnut
and Edmund Ironside agreed to divide England at the Treaty of Alney.
Edmund was to rule Wessex and Cnut, Mercia. This was a peace treaty,
possibly intended to be short-term though it was to be claimed that
Edmund had pledged that Cnut should be the protector of Edmund's
sons.[42] After 1066 the Anglo-Danish population round York might have
united with one of the Danish fleets to open up a second front against the
Normans; and the status of both Cumbria and Northumberland was
contested between the English and the Scots from the later eleventh
century until 1237. In other words, whilst older loyalties for the most
part co-existed with loyalty to the king, an identification with England,
the unity of the kingdom could not be taken for granted.

It was the full incorporation of northern England which was the most
protracted, and only partially achieved, process.[43] As seen in Chapter 2,
the north was made up of different regions, subject to attacks by
Scandinavian fleets and Scottish armies. After the death of Eric
Bloodaxe in 954, Northumbria was no longer an independent kingdom.
The southern kings appointed earls, but although their title was 'of
Northumbria', in fact the lords of Bamburgh remained *in situ* until the
later eleventh century.[44] Not only that, but that portion of the old kingdom which lay north of the Tweed, Lothian, passed to the Scots, probably
from the later tenth century.[45] Only Earl Siward, who died in 1055, may

---

important development. See L. Marten, 'The Shiring of East Anglia: an Alternative
Scenario', *Historical Research*, 81 (2008), 1–27.

[42] ASC, C, D, E, 1016. For the claim that Edmund had agreed that Cnut should act as
protector of his sons, see JW, II, p. 494.

[43] For discussion of the definition of the north, see H. M. Jewell, *The North-South Divide:
the Origins of Northern Consciousness in England* (Manchester: Manchester University
Press, 1994), pp. 8–27.

[44] The region north of the Mersey and west of the Pennines had not been a single kingdom.
From Domesday Book it seems that south Lancashire (the 'land between Ribble and
Mersey') had been part of the southern kingdom, at least in the recent past. North
Lancashire and the southern parts of what were to become Westmorland and
Cumberland were surveyed under Yorkshire, and much of the land had been held by
Earl Tostig, see *Domesday Book*, ed. J. Morris, 26, *Cheshire*, ed. P. Morgan (Chichester:
Phillimore, 1978), appendix.

[45] The timing of the Scots' takeover of Lothian has been debated because different dates are
mentioned in the sources. The likeliest is that the Scots' king was gaining influence there in
the later tenth century, even if the southern king only formally recognized the transfer
later. B. Meehan, 'The Siege of Durham, the Battle of Carham and the Cession of
Lothian', *Scottish Historical Review*, 55 (1976), 1–19, and A. A. M. Duncan,
'The Battle of Carham, 1018', *Scottish Historical Review*, 55 (1976), 20–8; for the

have had authority, or at least no opposition, north of the Tyne. Having killed Eadwulf of Bamburgh, he married Eadwulf's niece.[46] After 1066 the Conqueror appointed a succession of earls. Copsi, who had deputized for Tostig Godwinson, was murdered by Osulf of Bamburgh, who himself was murdered shortly afterwards. William then appointed Gospatric, who was related to the Bamburgh family, but he rebelled, surrendered, went into exile, and eventually was granted land in Scotland.[47] Robert de Commines was murdered at Durham by Northumbrians, presumably to prevent any intrusion north of the Tyne. His successor was Waltheof, Siward's son. After Waltheof's execution in 1076, Bishop Walcher was entrusted with governance north of the Tyne and, after Walcher's murder, by Aubrey de Coucy, who did not last long but surrendered his estates and departed.[48] The Norman Robert de Mowbray was then appointed, probably by William the Conqueror, and at this stage it seems that his earldom extended between the Tees and the Tweed.[49] Robert lost his earldom and lands as a result of his revolt in 1095 and no successor was appointed by Rufus or Henry I. In 1130 the heading on the pipe roll for the region was *Norhumberland*.[50] Henry, son of king David, received the earldom in 1139. On his seal his title is earl of *Norhumberlandia*, and in the documents themselves usually *Northumbria*.[51] The term 'Northumbria' continued to be used in a general sense, for example, by the chronicler Symeon of Durham. Doubtless Earl Henry had hopes of an earldom which included Durham as well as Northumberland. A key moment was when the old ruling family of Bamburgh was superseded by royal sheriffs. Two possible early candidates as sheriffs were Gilbert, who deputized for Bishop Walcher, and Morel, the kinsman of Robert de Mowbray.[52]

argument that Carham took place in 1018 after Uhtred's death, cf. Woolf, *From Pictland to Alba*, pp. 236–7.

[46] William M. Aird, 'Siward, Earl of Northumbria (*d.* 1055)', *ODNB* www.oxforddnb.com /view/article/25652, accessed 20 May 2016.

[47] For Copsi and Gospatric, see Symeon of Durham, *Libellus*, pp. 180, 192.

[48] For Waltheof and Walcher, see Symeon of Durham, *Libellus*, pp. 212, 234; *Historia Regum, Opera omnia*, II, pp. 186, (Robert de Commines), 186, 190, 194, 196, 198 (Gospatric, Waltheof, Walcher, and Aubrey).

[49] R. Sharpe, *Norman Rule in Cumbria, 1092–1136*, Cumberland and Westmorland Antiquarian and Archaeological Society Tract Series, 21 (2006), pp. 30–1; Aird, *St Cuthbert and the Normans*, pp. 162–3.

[50] *Pipe Roll 31 Henry I*, p. 27.

[51] *Charters of David I*, p. 12. Henry was succeeded by his son William, but in 1157 Henry II resumed the county.

[52] Symeon of Durham, *Historia Regum, Opera omnia*, II, pp. 209–10; Gilbert, nephew of the bishop, attested a charter of Bishop Walcher, *Durham Episcopal Charters*, ed.

Morel disappeared into exile after 1095, and a sheriff named Roger Picot appears, about whom nothing is known.[53] He was succeeded by a man named Aluric who was based at Corbridge, and Odard at Bamburgh.[54] Nothing is known about the former, whilst the latter seems to have been of native extraction, son of a man named Liulf.[55] It looks as though the old ruling family's tenure of Bamburgh had been broken with the death of Waltheof.[56] In the twelfth century Bamburgh became the royal centre in the north, and Newcastle in the south. Newcastle, strongly refortified by Henry II, was in the custody of Roger FitzRichard lord of Warkworth at the time of the revolt of 1173–4.[57] Odard of Bamburgh was succeeded as sheriff by his son Adam. In about 1157 Adam was succeeded first by William de Vescy lord of Alnwick, then in 1170 by Roger de Stuteville, William's brother-in-law and a prominent figure in Henry II's rule of the north, and finally by Roger de Glanville, a kinsman of the justice Ranulf.[58]

Meanwhile the boundaries of the diocese and county of Durham slowly took their final shape. As Bill Aird has shown, the bishops and the hereditary clerks who cherished the relics of St Cuthbert had had to negotiate with different powers at different times, and it was perhaps surprising that they survived and at times seem to have flourished rather than have been swept away.[59] He also made the point that Durham before the twelfth century cannot simply be seen as an English bishopric. It lay between two kingdoms, and the bishop and clerks were naturally concerned first and foremost with safeguarding their interests and protecting their estates which extended across the political frontier. In the later tenth century the bishops seem to have allied themselves more closely with the earls based at Bamburgh, and in turn with *their* allies, the southern

---

H. S. Offler, Surtees Society, 179 (1968), no. 5a, pp. 45–6. For Morel, see now D. X. Carpenter, 'Morel of Bamburgh, Archil Morel, and the Death of King Malcolm III: a Case of Mistaken Identity', *Northern History*, 52 (2015), 314–23.

[53] *RRAN*, I, no. 367 (as Robert); II, nos. 572, 589, 624, 671. It is possible that Roger was castellan of Newcastle, on the grounds that this was a royal castle, but this is purely speculative.

[54] Sharpe, *Norman Rule in Cumbria*, p. 31.   [55] *Ibid.*, pp. 31–2.

[56] Aird, *St Cuthbert and the Normans*, p. 86, figure 2. 1.

[57] Jordan Fantosme, *Chronicle*, paras. 60, 61 (ed. Johnston, pp. 42–3); C. T. Clay, 'The Ancestry of the Early Lords of Warkworth', *Archaeologia Aeliana*, 4th series, 32 (1954), 65–71; H. Doherty, 'Robert de Vaux and Roger de Stuteville, Sheriffs of Cumberland and Northumberland, 1170–1185', *Anglo-Norman Studies*, 28 (2005), 65–102, at p. 76.

[58] Green, *English Sheriffs*, pp. 65–6; Doherty, 'Robert de Vaux and Roger de Stuteville', *passim*.

[59] Aird, *St Cuthbert and the Normans*, chapter 1.

kings.[60] After the murder of Earl Uhtred, the community had little option but to align itself with King Cnut. The bishop and the clerks returned to Durham in 1006, but faced attack by the Scots at the time, and again in 1040.[61] Moreover, kings from the time of Cnut were involved in choosing bishops, presumably with the intention of bringing the see more closely under control from the south.[62] Walcher, the first bishop selected by the Conqueror, was a clerk from Lotharingia. After his murder the Conqueror chose instead a Benedictine monk, William of Saint-Calais, who with papal authorization decided to re-establish the community as a monastery.

Assessing the significance of 1083 in the history of Durham is compli-cated by the near-contemporary testimony of Symeon of Durham, who naturally wished to stress the importance of reform and the new beginning of that year, even if he allowed that there were indications of monastic life in the earlier eleventh century. It is telling that all but one of the clerks opted not to enter the monastery (and thus to lose their lands), and that many of the monks probably came from the south.[63] The visual impact of the new cathedral which replaced Ealdhun's church, together with the castle, monastic buildings, and bishop's residence, has also to be borne in mind. The bishops from William's time also began to grant out land to hold by knight service: Ranulf Flambard's episcopate was particularly important in this respect.[64] It was in his time, too, that a castle was built at Norham on the Tweed, underscoring the much stronger alignment of the bishopric with the English kingdom.[65]

There was an attempted *revanche* by the Scots after the death of Bishop Geoffrey Rufus in 1141: given a disputed election at York and Stephen's imprisonment William Cumin, the chancellor of King David of Scots, sought to establish himself and fought a tenacious battle until he lost the backing of David and Earl Henry. They backed off in the face of opposi-tion headed by the prior in alliance with the papal legate, Bishop Henry of Winchester.[66] The prior and monks seem to have secured first the election

---

[60] *Ibid.*, pp. 41–53.

[61] 'De Obsessione Dunelmi', Symeon of Durham, *Opera omnia*, I, p. 215 (1006), 218: Uhtred was murdered and Eadulf Cudel ceded Lothian; Symeon of Durham, *Libellus*, p. 168 (1040).

[62] Viz., Edmund, Æthelric and Æthelwine, Symeon of Durham, *Libellus*, pp. 158–74, 192–4; Aird, *St Cuthbert and the Normans*, pp. 49–59.

[63] Symeon of Durham, *Libellus*, pp. 224–33; cf. Aird, *St Cuthbert and the Normans*, chapter 3, who argues for gradual change over a twenty-year period.

[64] *Ibid.*, chapter 5.   [65] Symeon of Durham, *Historia Regum*, *Opera omnia*, II, p. 260.

[66] See especially Young, *William Cumin: Border Politics and the Bishopric of Durham 1141–1144*.

of William of St Barbe, and then Hugh du Puiset, a kinsman of King Stephen.

By this time the bishop was lord of almost all the land in the county except in the south, the wapentake of Sadberge, which comprised the lands of the Balliol and Brus families who had probably been established there in the late eleventh century.[67] He had extensive powers of jurisdiction and, as in the case of Cheshire and the marcher lordships, as royal justice became more powerful and pervasive, the right to issue judicial writs became ever more valuable.[68] There was also a mint at Durham, functioning intermittently from 1087.[69] Durham developed into a cohesive lordship, the land of St Cuthbert, or the *Haliwerfolc*, the 'people of the holy man' (that is, St Cuthbert).[70] Knightly families were established as the bishop's tenants. Some had Anglo-Norman names, others were clearly descended from native families. Older tenures, thegnages and drengages, remained, and were sometimes commuted for cash.[71]

West of the Pennines the starting point and timescale for the exercise of authority by English kings was different. At the start of our period Cumbria formed the southern portion of the Brittonic kingdom of Strathclyde. This had expanded southwards from its heartland in the Clyde valley, along Roman roads through Annandale, Carlisle, and the Eden valley as local lords gave their allegiance to the Strathclyde kings.[72] In the mid-tenth century the term 'Cumbria' rather than 'Strathclyde' came to be used to describe this larger unit, in which there were both Brittonic speakers and Scandinavian settlers.[73] The last king was killed at

[67] C. M. Fraser and K. Emsley, 'Durham and the Wapentake of Sadberge', *Transactions of the Architectural and Archaeological Society of Durham and Northumberland*, 2 (1970), 71–81; for Balliol at Gainford, see Austin, *Acts of Perception: a Study of Barnard Castle in Teesdale*. Robert de Brus could have been installed at Hart at roughly the same time. Blakely, *Brus Family*, p. 18, suggested that Flambard's exile was the likeliest timing.
[68] M. Holford, 'Durham: History, Culture, Identity', M. L. Holford and K. J. Stringer (eds.), *Border Liberties and Loyalties: North-East England, c. 1200–c. 1400* (Edinburgh: Edinburgh University Press, 2010), pp. 17–57.
[69] M. Allen, 'The Durham Mint before Boldon Book', Rollason, Harvey, Prestwich (eds.), *Anglo-Norman Durham*, pp. 381–98.
[70] Symeon of Durham, *Libellus*, pp. 132, 156, 196, 140, 144, 186; Holford, 'Durham: History, Culture, Identity', Holford and Stringer (eds.), *Border Liberties and Loyalties*, pp. 38–44.
[71] Aird, *St Cuthbert and the Normans*, pp. 223–4.
[72] F. Edmonds, 'The Expansion of the Kingdom of Strathclyde', *Early Medieval Europe*, 23 (2015), 43–66.
[73] F. Edmonds, 'The Emergence and Transformation of Medieval Cumbria', *Scottish Historical Review*, 93 (2014), 195–216.

the battle of Carham, and it seems that in the early eleventh century the Northumbrian earls, especially Siward, were exercising power west of the Pennines.[74] King Malcolm III of Scots in turn seems to have taken over after 1066, possibly until 1092 when William Rufus established a castle and colony at Carlisle, committing the new lordship to Ivo Taillebois who was succeeded in turn by Ranulf Meschin. A start was made in establishing Normans in lordships and in bringing men of native extraction like Forne son of Sigulf, but there was no clean sweep of native families.[75] Rather the reverse as newcomers married into native families, which over time built castles and established religious houses.[76] Initially ecclesiastical jurisdiction had been committed to the archbishop of York, and when a new diocese was founded at Carlisle, part of Cumbria continued to form part of the archdeaconry of Richmond in the diocese of York. Although Æthelwold was consecrated in 1133, King David's takeover of Carlisle in 1135 meant that Æthelwold had come to terms with the Scots. Then after his death in 1156 or 1157 the see was kept vacant until 1204.[77] The establishment of an ecclesiastical infrastructure was relatively late, and so was the appearance of new-style religious communities.[78] Crown pleas were initially dealt with by the sheriff of Northumberland.[79] Then late in Henry I's reign a sheriff was appointed for Carlisle, and a mint was established, which minted coins for David I and his son Earl Henry, and then for Henry II. Henry II established Robert de Vaux as sheriff and castellan of Carlisle, having taken back Cumbria from the Scots. Robert's father had been granted land in Cumberland, and thus he was a dominant figure locally. He was also an itinerant justice in the north until Henry II removed him in 1185, at the same time as Roger de Stuteville in Northumberland. Henry II was reasserting royal authority in the northern counties.[80]

---

[74] Siward's authority in Cumbria, specifically Allerdale, is indicated by the writ issued by Gospatric to Thorfynn mac Thore, which mentions Earl Siward, *Anglo-Saxon Writs* (ed. Harmer), pp. 419–24.

[75] *Early Yorkshire Charters*, II, pp. 505–6.

[76] P. Latimer, 'Assimilation in North-Western England from the Norman Conquest to the Early Thirteenth Century: the Kirkby, Pennington and Copeland Families', *Northern History*, 47 (2010), 49–66.

[77] *English Episcopal Acta*, XXX, *Carlisle 1133–1202*, ed. D. M. Smith (Oxford: Oxford University Press for the British Academy, 2005), pp. xxxv–xxxviii.

[78] Latimer, 'Assimilation in North-Western England', pp. 62–6.

[79] Sharpe, *Norman Rule in Cumbria*, p. 30.

[80] Doherty, 'Robert de Vaux and Robert de Stuteville', pp. 79–102.

Kendal and Appleby in Westmorland remained baronies rather than constituting a county.[81] As Sir James Holt pointed out, 'in the normal course of events, Westmorland was not a shire, had no sheriff, and no account for it was presented at the exchequer'.[82] In the twelfth century Kendal was held by William of Lancaster, who also held Lancashire north of the Ribble in succession to Stephen and David of Scots.[83] William was of mixed ancestry. His family may have been in the region before 1066, but he was also related to Ivo Taillebois. William married a niece of the wife of William of Blois, King Stephen's son, who received the lordship of Lancaster as part of a massive landed endowment in return for surrendering his claim to the throne.[84] What became east Lancashire, the honours of Whalley and Clitheroe, were surveyed under Cheshire at the time of Domesday Book.[85]

South of the Lakeland fells, the Furness peninsula retained links with the Irish Sea littoral. Here the population was a mix of Northumbrians, Norse, and Anglo-Saxons, and on the eve of the Conquest it was part of the earldom of Tostig Godwinson.[86] Subsequently most of the region, together with north Lancashire, passed in succession to Roger the Poitevin and Stephen of Blois.[87] The latter transferred a great tract of land to the new Savigniac community he had established, which moved to Furness in 1127. William of Lancaster held much of north Lancashire, whilst Blackburnshire passed to the Lacy family of Pontefract in Yorkshire.[88] By 1086 the land 'between Ribble and Mersey' was divided into six great estates with hides and hundreds. Normans had already been established, most through Roger the Poitevin.[89] William FitzNigel, a major tenant of

[81] Kendal was held by Ivo Taillebois, and then for a time by Nigel d'Aubigny, Sharpe, *Norman Rule in Cumbria*, pp. 38–43. Appleby was held by Ranulf Meschin, *ibid.*, p. 49. In 1130 Appleby was accounted for by Richard FitzGerard, *Pipe Roll 31 Henry I*, p. 112. In 1173–4 it was held by Gospatric son of Orm, Jordan Fantosme, *Chronicle*, paras. 150–3 (ed. Johnston, pp. 108–10).
[82] J. C. Holt, *The Northerners. A Study in the Reign of King John* (Oxford: Clarendon Press, 1961), p. 199.
[83] Sharpe, *Norman Rule in Cumbria*, p. 43 and notes.
[84] William married as her second husband Gundreda, daughter of William II de Warenne. William of Blois married her niece, Isabel de Warenne, daughter of William III de Warenne.
[85] DB, I, fol. 270r.
[86] DB, I, fols. 301v–302r; F. Edmonds, 'The Furness Peninsula and the Irish Sea Region: Cultural Interaction from the Seventh Century to the Twelfth', C. Downham (ed.), *Jocelin of Furness: Essays from the 2011 Conference* (Donington: Shaun Tyas, 2013), pp. 17–44.
[87] The exception was Aldingham held by Michael the Fleming.
[88] Wightman, *Lacy Family in England and Normandy*, pp. 36–7.
[89] DB, I, fols. 269v–270r.

Earl Hugh of Chester, was lord of Halton on the west bank of the Mersey, and by 1086 held Widnes on the right bank. As in Cumbria, there was to be no clean sweep of native families or old tenures: thegnages and drengages survived alongside tenancies by knight service.[90] Over time castles were built and religious houses established, but rather later than in the south. Only in Henry II's reign were the two parts of Lancashire coming to be seen as a county.[91]

Of all the regions north of the Humber and Mersey, it was Yorkshire where the bases of royal authority, and thus for further integration, were strongest. After 954 kings appointed ealdormen who were outsiders there, as were the archbishops.[92] Quite how widespread their influence was is unknown. Domesday Book reveals a number of great estates which had been held either by the king or by Edwin, Morcar, Waltheof, or Tostig. Many of the lesser thegns mentioned there may have been commended to the earls: the situation is not clear. The great estates had demesne centres and outlying sokes and berewicks, and they may not have been broken up because they were royal or comital. There were many Scandinavian settlers in the county, and under the Danish kings the Norwegian Eric took over (whether of the whole of the north or only part is unclear) then the Dane Siward. York prospered in the Viking era, and after initial devastation, developed by the Norman kings as a northern capital (see earlier in this volume).

Key estates which had been held by earls were handed over to an inner group after 1066. Compact lordships were established to defend strategically important areas: in south Yorkshire, Tickhill, Conisbrough, and Pontefract; in the north-west Gilling; and in the south-east Holderness. The count of Mortain's large lordship was constructed differently, on the basis of grants of all the land in two hundreds not in the hands of the king or the church.[93] New honours were constructed as some of the first generation of lords fell by the wayside. Nigel d'Aubigny and his successors Walter Espec and Eustace FitzJohn played a particularly important role

[90] J. E. A. Jolliffe, 'Northumbrian Institutions', *English Historical Review*, 41 (1926), 1–42; W. Farrer, 'Feudal Baronage', *Victoria County History, Lancashire*, I, pp. 291–375.
[91] J. Tait, *Medieval Manchester and the Beginnings of Lancashire* (Manchester: Manchester University Press, 1904), pp. 4–5.
[92] Molyneaux, *Formation of the English Kingdom*, pp. 177–9; D. Whitelock, 'The Dealings of the Kings of England with Northumbria in the Tenth and Eleventh Centuries', P. Clemoes (ed.), *The Anglo-Saxons: Studies in Some Aspects of Their History and Culture Presented to Bruce Dickins* (London: Bowes and Bowes, 1959), pp. 70–88.
[93] P. Dalton, *Conquest, Anarchy and Lordship: Yorkshire 1066–1154* (Cambridge, 1994), pp. 49–54.

under Henry I. The later eleventh and early twelfth centuries was a time when archbishops were developing the infrastructure of their diocese, when Benedictine monasticism revived, and new communities were founded. A succession of sheriffs was appointed, the earliest being William Malet.[94] Royal forests were created. The forest of Galtres was under the supervision of John the king's larderer, who was in office at the start of Stephen's reign.[95] The forest of Pickering was accounting at the exchequer in 1130.[96]

Yorkshire was a county affected by the civil war of Stephen's reign. Not only did one of the two pitched battles, that of the Standard in 1138, take place there, but there were also local conflicts. William count of Aumale was appointed as Stephen's earl; he also held the royal forests and the city of York. His ambitions brought him into conflicts with other magnates such as Count Alan of Richmond. The disputed archiepiscopal election at York was a further complication, and it has been argued that royal authority in the county declined between 1149 and 1151.[97]

Henry II reappointed his grandfather's sheriff, Bertram de Bulmer, who was followed in 1163 by Ranulf de Glanville. Ranulf was replaced for a time by Robert de Stuteville, but from 1175 he was sheriff again until the end of the reign. Ranulf was one of a handful of *curiales* who brought the full weight of royal authority to bear in northern England, as the pipe rolls bear witness. Yorkshire, Northumberland, Cumberland, and the two parts of Lancashire had not yielded much revenue to the exchequer in 1130. Northumberland and Cumberland were only resumed by the crown in 1157. By that time revenues were rising. In the 1160s there were rising levels from justice, from forest offences, from escheated honours, and from the vacant archbishopric of York. As well as large individual proffers there was a myriad of smaller sums as lesser folk were brought under the cosh. After the rebellion of 1173–4 there were further fines imposed on those who had been implicated in rebellion.[98] Through eyres the north was being brought to heel and, given that it had not been closely governed from the south before, the impact of Henry II's rule cannot be underestimated.

---

[94] Gamel son of Osbern was addressed after Earl Morcar in a royal notification of 1067 x 1069, but no office was specified, Bates, *Acta of William I*, no. 32. For successive sheriffs, see Green, *English Sheriffs*, pp. 89–90.

[95] *RRAN*, III, no. 433.   [96] *Pipe Roll 31 Henry I*, p. 20.

[97] Dalton, *Conquest, Anarchy and Lordship*, pp. 145–95.

[98] Holt, *Northerners*, pp. 200–4; Glanville's wife came from a family which held land of the earldom of Richmond.

LANGUAGE AND IDENTITIES

Language was another form of identification and of status. The spoken vernacular languages included English (especially, in our period, the West Saxon form), Cornish, Brittonic, Welsh, Northumbrian, old Norse, and old French. The West Saxon form of Old English was very much associated with King Alfred and his successors, both spoken and written, as the language of laws, writs, chronicles, homilies, biblical literature, and saints' lives. Scandinavian settlement in eastern England and along the western seaboard was reflected in place names.[99] It has been argued that the newcomers and the natives spoke a mutually intelligible language.[100] Language was a marker of social standing as well as, perhaps even more than, ethnic or geographical origin. Cnut and his warriors shared a Scandinavian cultural world, and the skalds at his court recounted the great tales from the north.[101]

One of the most dramatic changes in post-Conquest England was the takeover of Latin from Old English in royal documents, historiography, and law, whilst Old French was the spoken language of the new elite. The downgrading of English was a telling symbol of conquest. The change has been traced in naming practices, the way that in the midlands and the south Alfred and Ælfric soon gave way to William or Richard for boys. Changes in girls' names took longer, but during the twelfth century Edith and Ælfgifu were replaced by names such as Matilda and Adeliza.[102] Further north the situation was different and, as Paul Latimer has indicated, there was less pressure to adopt French names.[103] The spread of biblical names, too, disguised ethnic origins.

There is evidence of suspicion and antipathy towards outsiders, who could be identified, amongst other signifiers, by the languages they spoke. Scandinavian communities in towns, speaking their own language and with their own churches, must have been conspicuous, as were those who spoke French. The need to protect the followers of the Danish and Norman kings from secret slaying lay behind the introduction of the

---

[99] Hadley, *Vikings in England*, pp. 2, 97–104.
[100] M. Townend, *Language and History in Viking Age England: Linguistic Relations between Speakers of Old Norse and Old English* (Turnhout: Brepols, 2002), pp. 43–87.
[101] Townend, 'Cnut's Poets: an Old Norse Literary Community in Eleventh-Century England 800–1250'.
[102] C. Clark, 'English Personal Names ca. 650–1300: Some Prosopographical Bearings', *Medieval Prosopography*, 8 (1987), 31–60.
[103] Latimer, 'Assimilation in North-Western England from the Norman Conquest to the Early Thirteenth Century: the Kirkby, Pennington and Copeland Families'.

murder fine.[104] It was claimed after the event by Ailnoth of Canterbury, an English monk who had left for Denmark, that Cnut's invasion of 1085 was in order to free the English from the tyranny of Norman rule.[105] As late as 1135 it was apparently credible that all the Normans in England, still a small minority of the population, might be murdered.[106] Less deadly perhaps but no less deeply felt was the despair of monks like Eadmer who felt that only foreigners could secure preferment in the English church.[107] The interlinked processes of accommodation, acculturation, and assimilation were thus protracted, sometimes tense, and culturally enriching, and there was no simple correlation between language and identity.

NATIONAL IDENTITY

The nature and strength of national identity in this period has naturally been much discussed: the relationship between *gens* and *natio* and that between national identity and the country, and the nature of loyalty to the king and the kingdom. How did ideas about national identity change over time, and in the context of foreign conquest and shifting boundaries? How is English identity to be defined and its relative strength assessed? One criterion is that of self-identification, another that of other commentators. Over time, assimilation and intermarriage blurred ethnic differences, but how quickly? Is it possible to identify an English political elite by the later twelfth century? Most of the evidence comes from narrative sources, composed for different audiences, usually retrospectively, and at different dates, so personal perspective has to be taken into account. One general point is the mental framework of all writers, that whilst God rules over all, the king rules the earthly kingdom of the English: God intervenes to punish the people for their sins, sometimes by subjecting them to invasion and war, and the king's fortunes reflected his own sinfulness as well as that of his people.

The king was leader of the *gens*, and it was to be the *gens Anglorum* which served to identify all the peoples settled in England.[108] This was an

[104] O'Brien, 'From *Morðor* to *Murdrum*: the Pre-Conquest Origin and Norman Revival of the Murder Fine'.
[105] *Gesta Swenomagni Regis et Filiorvm Eivs et Passio Gloriosissimi Canuti Regis et Martyris*, M. Cl. Gertz (ed.), *Vitae Sanctorum Danorum* (København: G. E. C. Gad, 1908–12), pp. 97–8.
[106] OV, VI, p. 494. [107] *Historia Novorum*, p. 224.
[108] P. Wormald, '*Engla Lond*: the Making of an Allegiance', *Journal of Historical Sociology*, 7 (1994), 1–24, at pp. 10–14.

identity which owed much to Augustine's mission to the *Angli* dispatched by Pope Gregory, as reported by Bede, and it was strengthened in critical ways during the reign of King Alfred.[109] Æthelstan was the first king who could claim to be the king of all the English, but already the idea of the English people was in circulation. Allegiance was upheld by oath and sustained by the Christian identity of the people, who had been converted by Augustine. Enemies of the king were punished severely, and into that category fell those who had committed a range of offences.

A plurality of *gentes* in a single *regnum* was reflected in the form in which the king's authority was announced in Latin diplomas, for example, *'ego Knut omnipotentis Dei disponente clementia Angli[ge]narum omnium[que] gentium secus habitantium rex'*.[110] After the Conquest such grandiose titles tended to disappear along with the Latin diploma. The king's title was *Rex Angl'*, and the clauses of royal writs and writ-charters addressed to shire courts might include 'French and English' or even 'French, Flemish (or Welsh), and English' as appropriate to the context.[111] Claims to rule over lesser kings and princes in Britain, and even over the British Isles, could be accommodated within this framework, as could the backward projection of kingship to the days of Brutus, in the *History of the Kings of Britain* of Geoffrey of Monmouth.

The many narrative sources of our period illustrate how the identity of a kingdom could be adapted to meet changing circumstances, and only a select few can be discussed here. The Anglo-Saxon Chronicle is much the most important narrative for the century between Edgar's reign and the Norman Conquest and, though written up in retrospect, the annals were composed not long after the events being described, focussing on kings and on events. Edgar was described at his death in versions D and E as 'ruler of the Angles, friend of the West Saxons and protector of the Mercians'. The situation became complicated between 1013 and 1016 as previously noted. In 1013 of Swein we hear in C, D, and E, that 'all the nation was regarded him as full king', *before* recounting later in the same annal King Æthelred's departure to Normandy. In the following year Swein died and Cnut, we are told, was elected king, but then emissaries were sent to King Æthelred, who promised better governance. When

[109] S. Foot, 'The Making of *Angelcynn*: English Identity before the Norman Conquest', *Transactions of the Royal Historical Society*, 6th series, 100 (1996), 25–49.
[110] *Early Yorkshire Charters*, I, pp. 23–7 (from the *Registrum Magnum Album*).
[111] R. Sharpe, 'Peoples and Languages in Eleventh- and Twelfth-Century Britain and Ireland', http://poms.cch.kcl.ac.uk/redist/pdf/SharpeFinal.pdf, pp. 4–34.

negotiations with the returning king were successfully concluded, 'they pronounced every Danish king an outlaw from England for ever'. In 1016 after Æthelred's death, King Edmund 'for the fifth time collected all the English nation' and fought at *Assandun*, where Cnut 'had the victory and won for himself all the English people'.[112] The year 1066 brought further complications. The D chronicle for 1066 called Harold king and William count, even after the Battle of Hastings, but from 1067 William was styled 'King William'. William's followers, rarely referred to, were described as 'French' rather than 'Norman'.[113] In other words, the annals were composed from the perspective of the king.

Twelfth-century historians continued to write from the perspective of the king and the kingdom. William of Malmesbury wrote a history of the bishops of England and a separate history of her kings: in both cases, therefore, the kingdom was the organizing framework. His history of the kings covered the time of the first arrival of the English to the days of Henry I, the first historian since Bede so to do, as he himself said.[114] Edgar was singled out for praise: 'the honour and delight of Englishmen', and Æthelred for sloth, haunted by the ghost of his dead brother Edward.[115] Edmund Ironside was tricked into meeting Cnut in battle by the arch-traitor, Eadric Streona. At *Assandun* Cnut 'destroyed a kingdom, there England's glory fell, there the whole flower of our country withered'.[116] At Hastings Harold also chose to meet his rival in battle and, with only a few English with him, was defeated. It was God's hidden purpose that Englishmen would never again fight in defence of their liberties, as though the strength of England had fallen with Harold.[117] In the following book he returned to the 'day of destiny' comparing two races, English and Norman, the former having lost the practice of piety, the latter pious and moderate in their habits.[118] Hastings was thus not just a punishment for Harold's perjury, but also for the sins of the English people. William is quite consistent in his identification of outsiders, Danes in the late tenth century, Norwegians and Normans in 1066. Those who continued to fight against a crowned king, like Edwin and Morcar against William, were rebels.[119]

---

[112] For the representation of Cnut, see J. Hobson, 'National-Ethnic Narratives in Eleventh-Century Literary Representations of Cnut', *Anglo-Saxon England*, 43 (2014), 267–95.
[113] ASC, D, 1069, 1074; E, 1070, 1074, 1083, 1088, 1093, 1094, etc.
[114] WM, *Gesta Regum Anglorum*, I, p. 796.　　　[115] *Ibid.*, pp. 238, 272.
[116] *Ibid.*, p. 316.　　　[117] *Ibid.*, p. 422.　　　[118] *Ibid.*, p. 456.　　　[119] *Ibid.*, p. 468.

When Henry of Huntingdon came to write his 'history of the kingdom and of the origins of our people', that is, the English, he began by writing of the five 'plagues' of invaders sent by God, the Romans, the Picts and Scots, the English, the Danes, and the Normans.[120] The Danes he saw as more cruel than the others, swooping and rushing from all directions very frequently and over a long period. He then went on to further identify them as 'Danes, Goths, Norwegians, Swedes, Vandals, and Frisians'.[121] His narrative of events was closely based on the Chronicle, so he describes the Danes, then the 'pagan army'. Under Alfred we hear of Vikings as well as the Danes. At the Battle of *Brunanburh* we hear of the Scots and the 'Danes who were living in England' and 'Frodo the Norman leader'.[122] He later reported the death of William son of Rollo, 'from whom the Norman race took its origin' before telling how King Edmund retook the Five Boroughs and completely rooted out the Danes, 'who were also called *Normanni*'.[123] Of Edgar he said that he gave too much security to the pagans who were settled in his country.[124] The invaders of the late tenth century are once again described as Danes, and he reported of danegeld that 'it has lasted to the present day'.[125] He began book six on the Normans in the year 1000 with the marriage between Æthelred and Emma, from which marriage the Normans were justified according to the 'law of peoples' in claiming the kingdom, before turning to the Danish invasions once again, suggesting (uniquely) that the king had sent messengers to Duke Richard II to request help.[126] Of the massacre of the Danes Æthelred ordered on St Brice's Day in 1002 based on the Anglo-Saxon Chronicle, he added that as a child he heard old men say that the king had sent letters to every city ordering a simultaneous attack on the Danes.[127]

Henry's account of the later years of Æthelred's reign drew heavily on the Anglo-Saxon Chronicle. Thus, for instance, Edmund Ironside was treated as a hero and Eadric Streona as a traitor. However, Henry added details, such as the words Eadric addressed to the English at *Assandun*: 'Flet Engle, flet Engle, ded is Edmund.' He subverted the dignity of kings with anecdotes, such as the killing of Edmund over a latrine pit by the son of Eadric Streona and, subsequently, Cnut's unavailing attempt to command the waves.[128] Following the Anglo-Saxon Chronicle again, Henry described the election of Harthacnut as king by the English and the Danes.

---

[120] HH, p. 14.   [121] *Ibid.*, pp. 272, 274.   [122] *Ibid.*, pp. 310, 312.   [123] *Ibid.*, p. 314.
[124] *Ibid.*, p. 320.   [125] *Ibid.*, p. 328.   [126] *Ibid.*, p. 344.   [127] *Ibid.*, p. 340.
[128] *Ibid.*, pp. 358–66.

After his death the English, 'delighted to be free from Danish rule', sent for
Alfred son of Æthelred.[129] From 1016, then, his account of the history of
the English portrays Cnut and his sons as kings, interweaving the history
of Normandy into his story, and leading up to Hastings. In the speech he
invented for the Conqueror at Hastings, William the Conqueror challenged the English, 'whom our Danish and Norwegian ancestors have
conquered in a hundred battles' to come forward to meet the sons of
Rollo.[130] What is interesting about Henry's take on the Scandinavian
attacks is that he was of mixed Norman and English ancestry based in
a region where there must have been many families of Scandinavian or
part Scandinavian ancestry. Whilst he thought the attacks the worst to
have affected England, they were in the past. Henry's account of the battle
of the Standard in 1138 is an interesting illustration of the different labels
he gave to the combatants: the forces fighting for Stephen were addressed
as 'nobles of England, Norman by birth' by the bishop of the Orkneys, and
'the whole English people' responded to him. They were opposed by the
Scots, including the men of Lothian.[131] In fact, the Scottish army included
Normans and Galwegians as well as the men of Lothian and those whom
Richard of Hexham called Picts.[132]

Ailred of Rievaulx's historical writing also included an account of this
battle. Ailred's own background and early career show some of the cross-
currents of northern England in the early twelfth century. He came from
a family of married priests with land at Hexham. He spent some time at
Durham, and entered the household of King David. When he entered
religion, it was not at Benedictine Durham or Augustinian Hexham, but
at the Cistercian community at Rievaulx in Yorkshire. He remained
attached to King David, and wrote a prefatory letter addressed to Henry,
then duke of the Normans, in which he presented the king of Scots as
a model for the Young King to follow. He also composed a brief history of
Henry's ancestors, tracing them back via his mother and grandmother
through the Anglo-Saxon kings to Adam. Edgar was praised as a holy
king who travelled his kingdom, investigating whether the laws were being
kept, and working with Dunstan to reform the clergy. Edmund Ironside
met with Cnut in single combat, and his valour so impressed Cnut that he

---

[129] *Ibid.*, p. 370.   [130] *Ibid.*, pp. 390–2.   [131] *Ibid.*, pp. 714–18.
[132] Richard of Hexham, *De Gestis Regis Stephani et de Bello Standardii, Chronicles of the
Reigns of Stephen, Henry II and Richard I*, III, p. 152: Normans, Germans, English,
Northumbrians, Cumbrians, [men] of Tweeddale and Lothian, and the Picts, 'who are
called Galwegians'.

wished to rule with him, dividing the kingdom. Edward the Confessor was a gentle and devout man who protected the kingdom more by peace than by force of arms. Henry, son of the empress, was hailed as duke of the Normans, count of the Angevins and Aquitanians, and truly the heir of England.[133] By tracing Henry's ancestry back through the female line, Henry could be presented as a true king of the English.

Finally, Jordan Fantosme's account of the great rebellion of 1173–4, composed in French shortly after the event, is interesting in its use of ethnic labels. The retreating Scottish army inflicts damage on 'the English of England' (line 631), and the poem later refers to the 'great army of England' (line 765). The enemy are the Flemings, who claimed that they had not come to England to hang about, but to destroy King Henry.[134]

How did contemporaries come to terms with invasion and settlement by people from Scandinavia, France, and, to a lesser degree, Flanders? The questions of accommodation, acculturation, and assimilation by the Danes and then the Normans have attracted a good deal of attention in recent years.[135] National identity gains traction from a sense of belonging, and it is important to know how far the different groups of Scandinavian settlers saw themselves as strangers in a foreign land, as new lords loyal to their king, possibly with native wives, and children born in England.[136] Those closest to the Danish kings are likely to have a shared sense of values.[137] The lithsmen based at London equally shared a sense of solidarity as warriors.[138] Those who had settled in towns such as Lincoln and York would in their daily lives have had to deal with natives, with

---

[133] Aelred of Rievaulx, 'The Genealogy of the Kings of the English', *Historical Works* (Freeland and Dutton), pp. 41–70.

[134] *Chronicle*, lines 631, 765, 991–9.

[135] Hadley, *Vikings in England*, pp. 98, 127, 131, 179, 215; Williams, *English and the Norman Conquest*, chapters 4–6; H. M. Thomas, *The English and the Normans: Ethnic Hostility, Assimilation, and Identity, 1066–c.1220* (Oxford: Oxford University Press, 2003); J. Gillingham, 'Gaimar, the Prose *Brut* and the Making of English History', *The English in the Twelfth Century: Imperialism, National Identity and Political Values* (Woodbridge: Boydell Press, 2000), pp. 113–22, and the essay which follows, 'Henry of Huntingdon and the Twelfth-Century Revival of the English Nation', *ibid.*, pp. 123–44; Green, *Aristocracy of Norman England*, pp. 429–38.

[136] C. Downham, 'Viking Ethnicities: a Historiographic Overview', *History Compass*, 10 (2012), 1–12.

[137] M. Townend, 'Contextualizing the Knútsdrápur: Skaldic Praise-Poetry at the Court of Cnut'; R. Frank, 'King Cnut in the Verse of His Skalds', Rumble (ed.), *Reign of Cnut*, pp. 106–24.

[138] For the lithsmen, N. Hooper, 'Military Developments in the Reign of Cnut', *ibid.*, pp. 89–100, at pp. 97–100. Lavelle, *Alfred's Wars*, pp. 154–7.

merchants and traders from different regions of Scandinavia or, in the case of Chester and Bristol, from Scandinavian settlements in Ireland. In fact, the stages by which Scandinavian settlers merged into the wider population remain largely obscure. Place name evidence, which shows Scandinavian elements strongest in eastern England and in regions such as the Wirral peninsula, has proved contentious.[139] Sculpture, such as hog-backed tombs, is hard to date precisely, and other material remains are few.[140] The Danelaw retained its distinctive assessments, in plough lands (*carucates*) and wapentakes rather than hundreds. There have been different views about the significance of new arrivals in the early eleventh century.[141] The evidence of personal names, still evident in Domesday Book, is complicated by the consideration that some were equally used in eleventh-century Normandy. It is particularly difficult to disentangle 'older' from 'newer' settlers in a region like East Anglia, where they were relatively plentiful.[142] However, in the case of one family with an unusual name, 'Swart', Lucy Marten has traced their history. Having arrived, she suggested, in Cnut's wake, they survived and married into native families.[143]

When religious houses that had suffered from Viking attack came later to write their histories, again there were differing perspectives. Ely reported attacks, but the history of the abbey also expatiated on the benefactions of King Cnut.[144] The Evesham Chronicle mentions the plunder of the shrine of St Ecwine by Danes living locally.[145] Abingdon Abbey was destroyed by the Danes, and the later Version B of the *History* describes their depredations. The Danes were punished through an image on a cross kept in the abbey. Later the barbaric army of Swein was described.[146] The earlier Version C of the Abingdon Chronicle inserted passages based on the Anglo-Saxon Chronicle about the Danish incursions. The author wrote of the reminders even in his own day of the

---

[139] Hadley, *Vikings in England*, pp. 2–4, 99–104.   [140] *Ibid.*, pp. 214–23.

[141] K. Mack, 'Changing Thegns: Cnut's Conquest and the English Aristocracy', *Albion*, 16 (1984), 375–87; A. Williams, 'Cockles among the Wheat: Danes and English in the Western Midlands in the First Half of the Eleventh Century', *Midland History*, 11 (1986), 1–22.

[142] For the context, see R. H. C. Davis, 'East Anglia and the Danelaw', *Transactions of the Royal Historical Society*, 5th series, 5 (1955), 23–39; C. Hart, *The Danelaw* (London: Hambledon Press, 1992), pp. 25–113.

[143] L. Marten, 'Meet the Swarts: Tracing a Thegnly Family in Late Anglo-Saxon England', Roffe (ed.), *English and Their Legacy*, pp. 17–32.

[144] *Liber Eliensis*, pp. 52–7, 150–4.

[145] Thomas of Marlborough, *History of the Abbey of Evesham*, p. 72.

[146] *Historia Ecclesie Abbendonensis*, I, pp. 266–72, 354.

destruction they wrought, of the church's losses through the payment of tribute, and of everything being given over to 'booty, burning, and death' during Swein's invasion. Yet after 1066 there were other problems, as church lands were given to Norman knights.[147]

Links with Scandinavia were still very much alive at Crowland Abbey in the fens in the early twelfth century, and it was from this source that Orderic Vitalis picked up information and inserted it into his *Ecclesiastical History*.[148] Gaimar's *Lestoire des Engleis* was composed in the 1130s for an audience based in Lincolnshire. Like Henry, Gaimar had to rely on the Anglo-Saxon Chronicle for tenth-century history. At times the Danes appeared in the role of bad guys, but there are more positive representations of Danes in the story of Havelock the Dane and Buern Butsecarl.[149] The tale of Drogo the sheriff who was outlawed, went to Norway, and married the king's daughter, again shows continuing ties with Scandinavia.[150] Memories of Earl Siward of Northumbria were preserved and fed into the later 'Life' of his son Earl Waltheof.[151]

Finally, a different perspective comes from consideration of those perceived to have been martyred by the Danes, King Edmund of East Anglia and Archbishop Ælfheah of Canterbury. The earliest version of the life of St Edmund was composed by Abbo of Fleury, and in the later eleventh century the accounts of the saint's miracles by Herman and Goscelin of Saint-Bertin were composed as the community embarked on a major rebuilding programme.[152] The possibility of Danish attack was still a reality at the time, for Bury was attacked in 1080.[153] The authors' sympathies lay with the English rather than the Danes. King Swein figured as a villain who tried to tax the saint's lands and was killed by the saint as a result.[154] King Cnut, on the other hand, was portrayed as a good king who was generous to Bury.[155]

[147] *Ibid.*, pp. 28, 138–40, 172–4, 220.
[148] S. Marritt, 'Crowland Abbey and the Provenance of Orderic Vitalis's Scandinavian and Scottish Material', *Notes and Queries*, 53 (2006), 290–2.
[149] Gaimar, *Lestoire des Engleis*, pp. xli–xliv.
[150] Marritt, 'Drogo the Sheriff: a Neglected Lost Romance Tradition'.
[151] *Vita et Passio Waldevi Comitis, Chroniques Anglo-Normandes*, ed. F. Michel, 3 vols. (Rouen: E. Frère, 1836–40), II, pp. 104–11.
[152] T. Licence, 'History and Hagiography in the Late Eleventh Century: the Life and Work of Herman the Archdeacon', *English Historical Review*, 124 (2009), 516–44.
[153] *Ibid.*, p. 522, citing C. H. Talbot, 'The Liber Confortatorius of Goscelin of Saint-Bertin', *Analecta monastica: textes et études sur la vie des moines au moyen âge troisième siècle: Studia Anselmiana*, 3rd series, 37 (1955), 1–117, at pp. 67–8.
[154] *Miracles of St Edmund*, pp. 14–24 (Herman), 144–56 (Goscelin).
[155] *Ibid.*, pp. 40–2 ('good king Cnut'), 188–90 (Goscelin).

Archbishop Ælfheah was killed by the Danes in 1012, having refused to allow ransom to be paid for him. Although he was venerated at London and then at Canterbury, Archbishop Lanfranc was said to have had initial doubts about Ælfheah's sanctity, until persuaded by Anselm.[156] Lanfranc duly commissioned a life to be composed, by Osbern of Canterbury.[157] The Worcester chronicler described the events leading up to Ælfheah's death in greater detail: although the Danes were paid tribute, they did not desist from ravaging. They besieged and entered Canterbury, imprisoned many of the clergy plus the sheriff and lay men and women. They then put to death nine out of every ten, and kept the archbishop in prison for months. He refused to allow himself to be ransomed, and accordingly was beaten by drunken Danes with stones and bones, before being finished off with an axe. The murder of Ælfheah was thus portrayed as a horrible episode in a bad year, rather than as an occasion to denounce the whole Danish people.[158]

In disentangling these very different kinds of sources, we can see how views about the Scandinavian invaders changed over time and according to circumstance. The Latin chronicles, with the exception of Henry of Huntingdon, have relatively little to say that reflects awareness of settlers of Scandinavian descent, or of surviving ties with Scandinavia: their priorities in reporting lay elsewhere.

One of the problems in assessing the legacy of Scandinavian settlement is the change of dynasty in 1066. From that year on, 1066 was seen as a major turning point in the history of the English kingdom, but how quickly did the Normans in England come to identify with their new country? Our understanding of chronology and process is complicated by our own baggage about ways newcomers have settled in past and present societies, and about terminology: separate identities, interaction, assimilation, and identification are all possible and may have overlapped. There has been disagreement about the timing of different stages: some historians, going back to Edward Augustus Freeman, thought that 'England became England once again' under Henry I, born in England and married to a wife who carried the blood of the Old English ruling house.[159] Certainly the English throne was of primary importance to the

[156] Eadmer, *Vita Anselmi*, pp. 50–4; Cowdrey, *Lanfranc*, pp. 175–84.
[157] Wharton, *Anglia Sacra*, II, pp. 122–47; *Osbern's Life of Alfege* (ed. Shaw).
[158] JW, II, pp. 468–70.
[159] E. A. Freeman, *The History of the Norman Conquest of England*, first edn, 6 vols. (Oxford: Clarendon Press, 1867–79), I, p. 2.

Norman kings and their followers who had gained massive estates in England. They began to marry into other families settled there and established religious houses in which they were buried, but none of this means necessarily that they *identified* with the English.

Nevertheless, there were factors working towards assimilation. Many intermarriages in the second ranks of the newcomers are thought to have taken place. This was an obvious strategy for incomers, moving out from the protection of the main bases into the countryside, to adopt. Support for the new regime from the upper ranks of the clergy was an important factor. The acceptance of the Norman view that Harold had been condemned by his perjury meant that the Norman dynasty had powerful backers. Developments in law and justice soon eroded any distinction based on ethnicity, bar the murder fine. What came to matter was free status, and those Englishmen who sought after 1154 to use the new procedures to recover lost lands found themselves hemmed in by restrictions.[160]

None of this of course means that the Normans in England necessarily identified themselves as part of a political community based on the kingdom. Many had family members and landed interests in Normandy, even if their own lives were spent in England, and that is not taking into account those who migrated to Wales or Scotland. As Hugh Thomas has argued, the construction of a positive identification with England has to be seen as a different process from assimilation, though related. He argued that the role of English clergy, the idea of English law, the law of King Edward, and English coinage were all crucial, as was the rise of xenophobia towards non-English in the later twelfth century.[161] We know very little about attitudes in England to Normandy by the later twelfth century. We may surmise that ties were strongest at the royal court, and they did not necessarily conflict with ties to family settled in England.[162] It was only in 1204 that families were forced to make a *choice*. The year 1215 has of course been seen as another staging post in the creation of a political community in clause sixty-one's reference to the 'community of England',

[160] Garnett, *Conquered England*, pp. 348–50.   [161] *English and the Normans, passim.*
[162] The Battle Chronicle has Richard de Lucy referring to 'we Normans' in his address to the king and court during the dispute between Battle Abbey, whose abbot was Richard's brother, and the bishop of Chichester, in 1157, *Chronicle of Battle Abbey*, pp. 178, 182. Richard's family came from Lucé near Domfront in western Normandy, but his career, which took him to the heights of the chief justiciarship, was in England. The account of the lawsuit in the chronicle was *parti pris*, so how far the statement may be regarded as hard evidence of a widespread sentiment in the aristocracy of England is hard to know.

but this was a political statement which by articulation gained momentum.[163] Loyalty to and identity with the English kingdom both at the start and the end of our period intermingled with other identities.

A MEDIEVAL STATE?

There has been a lively debate in recent years about the applicability of the term 'state' to the English kingdom in this period. Some would argue that the term is not useful because too closely tied to nineteenth-century ideas of 'the nation-state', or because, so far as England is concerned, it is too king-centred.[164] The issue is inescapable in the present context because of an influential line of argument that the Anglo-Saxon monarchy, certainly from the tenth century, if not before, as some would argue, was a state.[165] The difficulty is partly of definition: as a state is defined, so it is perceived to have been present or absent. There is too a danger of reifying the state, and not doing justice to power and power relations very different from the modern state.[166]

In his British Academy lecture 'The Late Anglo-Saxon State: a Maximum View', James Campbell noted the 'powerful intricacy of the late Anglo-Saxon State, elaborately organized … using and creating the resources of a developed economy'. He went on 'Late Anglo-Saxon England was a nation state. It was an entity with an effective central authority, uniformly organized institutions, a national language, a national church, defined frontiers (admittedly with considerable fluidity in the north), and, above all, a strong sense of national identity.'[167] Campbell's views were echoed by Patrick Wormald, who shared much the same vision of an English state, making if anything a stronger case for English identity, loyalty to the king sustained through oaths and treason punished severely.[168]

Some statements here are less problematic than others: there was a single church, itself the guardian of the history of the *gens Anglorum*, there was a sense of Englishness, and known if not fixed boundaries. More problematic is the location of power: 'Campbell's kingdom' suggests

---

[163] Holt, *Magna Carta*, pp. 394–7.
[164] Davies, 'The Medieval State: the Tyranny of a Concept?', pp. 288–90; cf. Reynolds, 'There Were States in Medieval Europe', *ibid.*, 550–5; Foot, 'The Historiography of the Anglo-Saxon "Nation-State"'.
[165] Campbell, 'The Late Anglo-Saxon State: a Maximum View'.
[166] Davies, 'The Medieval State'.   [167] Campbell, 'The Late Anglo-Saxon State', pp. 2, 10.
[168] Wormald, '*Engla lond*: the Making of an Allegiance'.

channels of authority from the king and court through to shires and their subdivisions, and a relatively broad political community. Susan Reynolds – who has argued that the word state *is* useful for the Middle Ages – has nevertheless pointed out the danger of underestimating the plurality of power.[169]

Weber's definition of the state included the criterion of the monopoly of the legitimate use of violence, as well as fixed boundaries, central institutions, and a bureaucracy. The difficulty here is that the 'Anglo-Saxon statists' see political society very much from the king's point of view, which could mean that power exercised by nobles and churchmen is judged by loyalty or disloyalty to the king. It is highly unlikely that this was how nobles and churchmen viewed their role. Stephen Baxter and Ann Williams have argued individually for the great earls under Edward the Confessor as royal officials, removable by the king, and conscious of the danger that by quarrelling they might imperil the security of the realm.[170] Yet this view, reflected in the language of Anglo-Saxon Chronicle D for 1051, was not the way Godwin and his sons would have seen their situation at that time, but (presumably) as victims of the king's preference for 'Frenchmen', and their restoration in turn as a recognition of the king's failure to act justly.

What we lack for our period are sources sympathetic to the use of force by laymen. It is all too easy to see those who took up arms as rebels, inimical to peace and order. Yet kings, though anointed, could rule unjustly. As the great men had a duty to him, so he had a duty to them. This relationship, founded on his promise to rule justly and their oaths of allegiance, might break down. By the twelfth century we hear of a *diffidatio*, most famously when Robert earl of Gloucester renounced his fealty to King Stephen.[171] Divided loyalties, there certainly during the first century of our period, are more easily documented during the second century, and they remained personal.

Glanvill, for instance, included in his list of royal pleas the killing of the king or the betrayal of the realm or the army.[172] John of Salisbury

[169] Reynolds, 'There Were States in Medieval Europe'.
[170] Baxter, *Earls of Mercia*, p. 124; A. Williams, 'Regional Communities and Royal Authority in the Late Old English Kingdom: the Crisis of 1051–1052 Revisited', *History*, 98 (2013), 23–40.
[171] For a recent reappraisal, see K. Thompson, 'A Different *Diffidatio*: Violence, Litigation and the Lord of Courville from the Letters of Ivo of Chartres', Dalton and Luscombe (eds.), *Rulership and Rebellion in the Anglo-Norman World*, pp. 77–90.
[172] Glanvill, p. 3.

famously discussed the difference between a tyrant and a true prince.
The true prince fights for the laws and liberty of the people. The tyrant
brings the laws to nothing and the people to slavery. Hence the true prince
is in the likeness of God, and the tyrant that of the Devil. Tyrants rule so
that the wicked may be punished and the good chastised, and may be
killed if they can be restrained in no other way. As the book of Judges told,
the children of Israel suffered under tyrants. They cried aloud to God and
at the allotted time were allowed to throw off the tyrants. This passage
was immediately followed by the statement that no one should kill
a tyrant who is bound to him by fealty, which presumably precluded all
the king's subjects.[173] The significance of these passages has been much
discussed, especially whether John was thinking of Henry II specifically, or
whether this was intended to be a theoretical discussion.[174] Twelfth-
century writers used the term 'tyrants', not least in connection with King
Swein, who, as John himself related, was punished with death by St
Edmund for trying to exact tribute from Bury (see earlier in this chapter).

By the twelfth century commentators were beginning to draw
a distinction between the person of the king and the crown. Debate
about the respective roles of the pope and emperor, and the influence of
Roman law, provided stimuli.[175] Similarly it may be argued that the rise of
the idea of an 'undying king' was another step forward in distinguishing
between the king and his kingdom.[176] As Garnett has argued, after 1066
particularly the contractual relationship between the king and the great
men was personal and ended when either king or his tenant-in-chief died.
Thus on the king's death there was an interregnum, hence the need for
a speedy coronation of a successor. Only at the end of Stephen's reign,
when Henry FitzEmpress was accepted as Stephen's heir, was a solution
found to this problem.[177] Even then there was an element of luck in seeing
the arrangement hold: if Stephen's son Eustace had not died in 1153,
events might have turned out very differently.

Garnett has argued, further, that references to 'the crown' as opposed
to 'the king' were absent from Anglo-Saxon laws, but the term began to be
used after 1066 as grants in perpetuity of jurisdictional rights were

---

[173] *Policraticus*, Books IV, VIII.
[174] See most recently, D. Luscombe, 'John of Salisbury and Courtiers' Trifles', Dalton and
Luscombe (eds.), *Rulership and Rebellion in the Anglo-Norman World*, pp. 141–61.
[175] F. L. Cheyette, 'The Invention of the State', B. K. Ladner and K. R. Philp (eds.), *Essays on
Medieval Civilization* (Austin: University of Texas Press, 1978), pp. 143–78.
[176] Richardson and Sayles, *Governance of Mediaeval England*, chapter 7.
[177] Garnett, *Conquered England*, pp. 262–93.

granted first to churches and then to laymen, the empress's first charter to Geoffrey de Mandeville in 1141 being the earliest to survive.[178] The term was increasingly used as a logical response to an unprecedented situation after the conquest where the king's rights, enduring between the death of one king and the accession of another, needed to be distinguished from the break in lordship when a king died. It was, in other words, a logical outcome of the concept of the king as *dominus* as well as *rex*, rather than, in the twelfth century, an indication of the advance of an impersonal state.

If, then, there are problems in using the word *state* for England in our period, it is safe to say that the characteristics of English monarchy became more state-like. Frontiers were stabilized, there was a much greater degree of internal consolidation, common law penetrated the whole country, and the number of royal officials was increasing. Warfare was becoming more expensive, and thus the king was better placed to marshal armies than his subjects by the late twelfth century, but it is hard to see that he had a monopoly of the legitimate use of force. His subjects could wait for God to take action, or they could join together and resist, as they did in 1215, a crisis which brought these fundamental questions to the surface of English society.

[178] G. Garnett, 'The Origins of the Crown', J. Hudson (ed.), *The History of English Law: Centenary Essays on 'Pollock and Maitland', Proceedings of the British Academy*, 89 (1996), 171–214; *RRAN*, III, no. 274.

10

Conclusion

This book has been about social and political change within England, but that does not mean its history is regarded as detached from its neighbours, or from changes in the wider Western world, far from it. The need to resist predatory attacks by Danes, Scots, and Normans was a driver of change. War drove the ceaseless search for resources of men and money, and for the fortification of towns on whose commercial activity prosperity increasingly depended. Conquests brought changes of dynasty and ruling elite, particularly following 1066 when the upper echelons of the church as well as the lay nobility were replaced. Political and cultural reorientation occurred, and possibly, though harder to document, shifts in patterns of trade. It was striking that the English kingdom was not incorporated into the conglomerates ruled by Cnut, the Normans, or the Angevins, and in that sense it retained its own identity and history. Far from being part of an island on the edge of the civilized world, England shared in trends which were affecting Western European society in general, notably population growth and movements for reform in the Western church.

Kings, lords, and churchmen with power at the start of our period remained powerful at the end, but the range of their powers and the way they were exercised had altered. The king was in a strong position initially because of his landed wealth, control of the coinage and the towns, and his influence over episcopal appointments. He was the greatest of warlords, able to raise armed men and money against external enemies and internal resistance. He had the power to appoint and dismiss ealdormen and their successors, earls, though as we have seen, Edward the Confessor was politically constrained. The destruction of the Old English nobility and establishment of a new French elite bound to the Norman kings may have given the kings an advantage for a time, but a contractual relationship was a two-edged sword. The king had the power to intervene in the affairs of the elite, but in return they expected to be consulted and to advise. Stephen's need for support led to the creation of more earldoms, but Henry II allowed few of them to survive, and reined back their powers, so that the title was more a sign of rank than a substantive office.

Meanwhile warfare was becoming more expensive: the cost of professional warriors, the nature of their training and expertise, and the multiplication of stone castles which, in theory at least, were in the hands of the king, meant that only the richest had the resources to engage in war. There was no change in the idea of the aristocracy as the warrior class, but by the end of the period elite fighting had come to be associated with the heavily armed cavalryman, and fortifications were both elaborate and stone-built. From 1154, kings not only insisted on the theory that all castles had to be surrendered on demand, but also in practice they had a greater number of castles than their subjects.[1] Furthermore, the king's access to wealth put him at an advantage in recruiting and retaining soldiers, whether housecarls, lithsmen, knights, archers, or mercenaries. Increasingly, the costs of war could only be met through extraordinary sources of revenue, especially taxation, which could only be levied by consent.

The great Old English families had accumulated lands and networks of patronage, yet ultimately they had not been able to establish permanent principalities. Within their spheres of influence there were many other landholders, a situation that continued after 1066, however disruptive the installation of the Normans. This gave the public courts of shire and hundred a continuing importance for the settlement of disputes, and this in turn sustained the king's power in the localities. Equally, the assertion by the Norman kings of monopoly rights of hunting certain animals not just on their own lands, but also on those of others, was politically as well as financially very important. On the one hand, hunting rights were granted as privileges to lords who probably enjoyed them as of right on their Norman estates. On the other, the extension of the limits of royal forests was a source of aggravation both to lords and peasants. Given that hunting and the consumption of game were seen as a mark of high status, being dependent on royal permission either to hunt in royal forests or to

[1] R. A. Brown, 'Royal Castle-Building in England, 1154–1216', *English Historical Review*, 70 (1955), 353–98.

construct parks and warrens on one's own land must have been particularly galling.[2]

For lay lords, the period was one of a high turnover in the upper echelons. Fortunes were made and lost, most spectacularly in the case of Earl Godwin and his family. There were possibilities for further gains in northern England, Wales, and later Ireland, and cross-Channel estates continued to be important to many families. By the twelfth century, the expansion of royal agencies gave greater opportunities for social mobility in the king's service, so much so that complaints about 'new men, raised from the dust' began to be heard. The crown's control over great inheritances meant that few dared to stand aloof from the court, and for the fortunate few marriage to an heiress or wealthy widow transformed their prospects. War brought dislocation and disruption, but in peacetime lords were able to increase rents and services, to profit from increasing commerce through markets and boroughs, and to bring new land into cultivation. Were there any effective checks against oppressive lords? Henry II had intended to investigate the activities of baronial officials as well as his own in 1170, but it appears that this did not happen. Lords had access to public and royal courts to recover absconding peasants and, in theory, to enforce service, but conversely their power over their free tenants was being eroded by the way inheritance was strengthening, and by the new forms of legal action which offered redress against arbitrary disseisin. As more layers were inserted into the hierarchy of landholders, and thus greater distance between lords and those who provided rents and services, so it was harder for lords to control land which had been granted out by knight tenure.

If the core ideas about kingly power, encapsulated in the oath kings swore at their coronation, remained broadly constant, the reality of royal power and the way it was exercised inevitably changed over two centuries. The king's duty to keep the peace, seen in his attempts to regulate feud and to punish wrongdoers, relied on local pledging units, juries, and courts of hundred and shire, reinforced by his sheriffs. Peer pressure remained one of the chief ways of bringing suspects to court. Where the great expansion of intervention came in the twelfth century was in land law, where initially the king had had only a limited role. Royal writs, sheriffs, and juries were the key instruments.

---

[2] J. A. Green, 'Forest Laws in England and Normandy in the Twelfth Century', *Historical Research*, 86 (2013), 416–31.

Royal consecration buttressed kingly authority, and in return kings acted as protectors of the church. Although the relationship between the two was sometimes fractious and occasionally confrontational, the church benefited from that peace which strong kings imposed. Bishops remained important figures in English society, but their role changed with the development of diocesan administration and courts. A few curial bishops were influential at court; by the twelfth century only a few were of noble birth. Some abbots, usually of the older Benedictine houses, had responsibilities in local society, but in general the external influence of heads of religious houses had diminished.

A further fundamental change was the rise of the papacy over a much more clearly defined hierarchical Latin church. This affected both the external relations of the English church and its internal organization. Popes began to send legates to England and to require English bishops to attend papal councils. By the twelfth century the appointment of the archbishop of Canterbury or, in the case of Henry of Blois, the bishop of Winchester, as legates, and of individual bishops as judges delegate, meant that the papacy, instead of a distant if venerated authority, had increasingly to be reckoned with at every level of society. The law of the church was being defined and recorded, and English practices from Cornwall to Carlisle had to be brought into conformity.

A good deal of the impetus towards ecclesiastical reorganization had come from concern felt acutely around the year 1000 about the imminent end of the world. Calls for repentance and reform met with responses from every social group. Many chose to interpret Christ's call to evangelical poverty and mission literally, by divesting themselves of earthly wealth and devoting themselves to religion, either singly as hermits or anchorites, or in groups. As a result much wealth flowed into the hands of the church, and especially to monastic foundations, which best seemed to embody the ideal of a Christian way of life. Gifts of land, churches, and tithes to monasteries were often made from mixed motives: as a way of putting contested land beyond the reach of one's rivals, of divesting oneself of churches and tithes which reformers were arguing should not be held by the laity, or of providing for the many younger sons and daughters of noble families disadvantaged by the rise of primogeniture. In the process, of course, monastic communities themselves became rich, and by the end of our period the church's wealth had come to be a matter of debate.

Veneration of the saints retained its importance in devotion, but shifts in hagiography are revealing about the changing concerns of those who sponsored hagiographical texts. Beginning in the late tenth century and accelerating in the eleventh, there had been a remarkable upsurge in hagiography as communities sought to resist or to justify change, as a focus of veneration or, increasingly after 1066, to justify and to defend rights and privileges. Most were heroic figures, usually male and often monk-bishops from the distant past. In the twelfth century there were fewer new saints. Again they were usually male, including those whose sudden deaths sparked a flurry of interest, most sensationally in the case of Becket. From the mid-twelfth century the involvement of the papacy in declaring new saints tended to narrow the field of candidates, as dossiers now had to be prepared for submission to Rome. One cult dominated all others, that of the Virgin, whose powers of intercession were deemed superior to those of more obscure local figures.

Much of the wealth of the church, as in the case of lay nobles, had been used to build in stone, and the rise of stone buildings was one of the most striking changes of the period. Stone building was itself a language of power: it was a sign of both wealth and status. At the start of our period, most secular buildings, from royal palaces to manorial complexes, were built in wood and enclosed by timber or earth and timber defences. By the end the residences of the elite in the countryside and the towns included stone buildings. These paled into insignificance in comparison with stone churches which from the later eleventh century were adventurous in size, architecture, and decoration.

The language of the powerful changed: English, the language of the lay elite and also widely used in the upper echelons of the church before 1066, lost prestige at court and then in the church. Nevertheless, it remained the language of the mass of the population and continued to evolve. At court in the early eleventh century, the spoken language was presumably Old Norse, and under the Normans, Old French, reflecting the continuing importance to the elite of its cross-Channel connections, even whilst identifying with the English kingdom.

Population growth, though checked by war and disease, brought incentives to bring more land into cultivation, and to produce for the market. Small estates proliferated, and in many parts of the country were characterized by locally resident lords. The more successful constituted a lesser aristocracy, which by the late twelfth century was relatively numerous and relatively independent of the great lords. It was this class, rather than the high nobility, which arguably benefitted from new legal remedies and by participating in royal administration.

The other principal effect of rising population was the growing number and size of towns. Older settlements expanded and new ones were founded. Eastern England prospered particularly: holdings were divided and further subdivided; lordship was relatively weak; and towns like Stamford, Boston, Norwich, and Ipswich grew, profiting not only from local and regional trade, but also from that across the North Sea, especially to Flanders and Germany. New towns were founded, especially in the midlands and the north. Notwithstanding, it is the pre-eminence of London, so much larger and politically more important than other English cities, the only one comparable in size to those in Italy, that is striking. Its great wealth derived from its geographical location, with relatively speedy links to the continent and to the Thames valley region, the physical protection afforded by its walls, and the importance attached to its retention by successive kings. When faced first with the accession of Cnut and then by William the Conqueror, the Londoners negotiated a separate surrender in return for confirmation of their privileges, and successive disputed successions provided further opportunities, culminating in 1215 when the capture of London by the rebel barons was the trigger which impelled King John to begin serious negotiations.

More settled conditions in turn increased the possibility that conflicts would be peacefully resolved, and a marked feature of the period is the recourse to courts of every kind and in every context, the study of law, and the rising importance of precise definition of status and tenure. Proprietorship, whether ownership or, in England, tenure, was geographically and locally defined. Slowly the landscape of lordship changed from power over extensive areas to smaller units. Communities had assemblies in which disputes could be adjudicated. These tied in with larger units, especially the shires, which again had courts. The administrative infrastructure of shires, hundreds or wapentakes, and vills paralleled and drew strength from the settlement of boundaries for dioceses, archdeaconries, deaneries, and parishes. In the church there was a parallel hierarchy of synods, national councils, and diocesan and deanery synods. Until the late eleventh century, there was clearly a good deal of intermingling of different types of action at the level of hundred courts, so that William the Conqueror had felt the need to issue an ordinance detaching ecclesiastical pleas from the hundred courts.[3] The development of lay and ecclesiastical laws, the codification of secular customs and laws of the church, and an increasing use of documents

---

[3] Bates, *Acta of William I*, no. 128.

brought efforts at classifying and codifying law, as men sought to establish greater precision about how and where wrongs were to be dealt with. Skills in reading, writing, and numeracy were in demand in the service of the powerful, and offered new avenues for the social advancement of young men.

It was not only the way power and status were expressed that changed, but also the way power was experienced. It was the powerful who defined social categories and increasingly policed membership of social groups. The church's teachings on several topics had profound social consequences. Firstly, closer definition of the tenets of orthodox belief potentially isolated the unorthodox, the dissident, and the non-Christian. Belief in various forms of magic remained strong, but the church frowned on those practices which involved relations with the Devil. Heresy, as opposed to unorthodox beliefs and practices, remained an isolated occurrence in England, as the environment which was favouring its growth on the continent seems to have been lacking. On the other hand, there were famous outbreaks of antisemitism against the Jewish communities established in England after 1066, prompted by their wealth and protected status, as well as by contemporary religious teaching. Secondly, the priesthood was envisaged as uniquely capable of administering the sacraments. Priests were to be celibate and free from worldly entanglements such as marriage and family. It was thus important to establish those who were and were not of clerical status, as the church sought to discipline the clergy and to defend its privileges. Finally, the church's teachings on marriage impacted sexual unions. Clerical wives were put beyond the pale at least officially, and it was harder for children of unofficial relationships to inherit. Elite families on the whole accepted these teachings, not least because legitimate status strengthened the claims of any children as heirs. The church's proscription of marriage within seven degrees proved unduly restrictive, though annulment had been possible for the wealthy or determined. Concerns about clerical celibacy resulted in a heightening of fears about female sexuality, but did not shake what remained a fundamentally patriarchal view of society.

The drive to define the characteristics of different social groups affected everyone. How was a clerk to be identified? How was he to be distinguished from a layman? How was a Christian to be distinguished from a Jew? What were the ranks of laymen, and of clergy? The nobility had only one internal rank, the ealdorman, then eorl, and finally earl. At the start of our period their higher status, like that of bishops, was reflected in the great value attached to their wergeld, or bloodprice, but by the twelfth century little is heard of judicial privileges associated with rank. The critical distinction in law came to be free status. All of free status were entitled to participate in the courts of shire and hundred, and to use the new forms of action. Those of unfree status were subject to the jurisdiction of their lords. Status was defined according to birth. The unfree comprised the successors of the slaves reported in the tenth and eleventh centuries, and the *villani* who provided labour service on manorial estates. By the twelfth century the latter were tied to the land more strictly than they had been, and were identified by the dues they owed their lords. An important staging post was the legal innovations of Henry II's reign which threw a spotlight on status.

One of the aims of this book was to challenge the periodization of English history, especially a preoccupation with 1066 as a caesura. Even if a slightly different date, 1075 or 1100 is chosen, the focus inevitably is on the Norman Conquest either as the end of Anglo-Saxon England or the start of an era of Norman and Angevin rule. Instead a date was chosen here, 973, when the imperial and sacramental kingship of King Edgar was displayed, and when the country was at peace. The end of Edgar's reign was the calm before the storm, but royal power was to survive, and eleventh- and twelfth-century kings were able to build on foundations laid in the tenth century and earlier, most notably in justice and taxation. At the end of the upheavals of the eleventh century there was a new ruling elite in church and state, but it was in the twelfth century that the pace of change accelerated.

Only in the later twelfth century (though a final peace settlement had to wait until 1237) did it become clear that the northern frontier of the English kingdom was going to stay at the rivers Solway and Tweed. The integration of the north, however belatedly and incompletely, was only finally achieved through the intensification of settlement, the building of castles, churches, and religious houses, in which the cooperation between the sons of Malcolm III of Scots and the Norman kings had played an important part. Under the assertive rule of Henry II, royal justice became more pervasive, and the political community was as yet prepared to contribute to the king's wars in forms of taxation which were better able to tap the country's wealth than the old danegeld. Finally, London had become uncontestably the capital of the kingdom.

Bibliography

1 MANUSCRIPT SOURCES

London, British Library, MS Stowe, 944.
London, London Metropolitan Archives, COL/CH/01.
London, London Metropolitan Archives, St Paul's Liber L.

2 PRINTED PRIMARY SOURCES

Aelfric: *Ælfric's Catholic Homilies: Introduction, Commentary, and Glossary*, ed. M. Godden, Early English Text Society (2001).
   Aelfric's Catholic Homilies, Second Series, ed. M. Godden, Early English Text Society (1979).
Ailred of Rievaulx: *Battle of the Standard, Chronicles of the Reigns of Stephen, Henry II and Richard I*, ed. R. Howlett, 4 vols., RS (London: Longman and Co 1884–9), III, pp. 181–200.
   'De Sanctimoniali de Wattun', Migne, *Patrologia Latina*, cxcv, cols. 789–95.
   Aelred of Rievaulx: the Historical Works, translated Jane Patricia Freeland, ed. M. L. Dutton (Kalamazoo, MI: Cistercian Publications, 2005).
Anglo-Saxon Chronicle: MS C: *The Anglo-Saxon Chronicle: a Collaborative Edition. Volume 5*, ed. K. O'B. Keeffe (Cambridge: D. S. Brewer, 2001).
   MS D: *The Anglo-Saxon Chronicle: a Collaborative Edition. Volume 6*, ed. G. P. Cubbin (Cambridge: D. S. Brewer, 1996).
   MS E: *The Anglo-Saxon Chronicle: a Collaborative Edition. Volume 7*, ed. S. Irvine (Cambridge: D. S. Brewer, 2004).
   MS F: *The Anglo-Saxon Chronicle: a Collaborative Edition. Volume 8*, ed. P. S. Baker (Cambridge: D. S. Brewer, 2000).
   The Anglo-Saxon Chronicle: a Revised Translation, trans. D. Whitelock, D. C. Douglas, and S. I. Tucker (London: Eyre and Spottiswoode, 1961).
   The Anglo-Saxon Chronicle, trans. M. Swanton (London: Dent, 1996).

Anglo-Saxon Writs, ed. F. E. Harmer (reprinted edition, Stamford: Paul Watkins, 1989).

Annales Monastici, ed. H. R. Luard, 5 vols., RS (London: Longman, Green, Roberts, Longman, Green, 1864–9).

Anselm: *Opera omnia*, ed. F. S. Schmitt, 6 vols. (I, Seckau: Office of the Abbot of Seckau, 1938), II–VI, Edinburgh: Thomas Nelson, 1938–61).

  The Letters of Saint Anselm of Canterbury, trans. W. Fröhlich, 3 vols. (Kalamazoo, MI: Cistercian Publications, 1990–4).

Bede's Ecclesiastical History of the English People, ed. and trans. B. Colgrave and R. A. B. Mynors (Oxford: Clarendon Press, 1992 edn).

Bloch, M. 'La vie de S. Edouard le Confesseur par Osbert de Clare', *Analecta Bollandiana*, 41 (1923), 5–131.

Brut y Tywysogion or the Chronicle of the Princes. Red Book of Hergest Version, ed. and trans. T. Jones (Cardiff: University of Wales Press, 1955).

Brut y Tywysogion or the Chronicle of the Princes. Peniarth MS 20 Version, ed. and trans. T. Jones (Cardiff: University of Wales Press, 1952).

Byrhtferth of Ramsey: *The Lives of St Oswald and St Ecgwine*, ed. and trans. M. Lapidge (Oxford: Clarendon Press, 2012).

Carmen de Hastingae Proelio, ed. and trans. F. Barlow, 2nd edn (Oxford: Clarendon Press, 1999).

Cartularium Abbathiae de Whiteby, ed. J. C. Atkinson, I, Surtees Society, 69 (1879).

Cartularium Prioratus de Gyseburne, I, ed. W. Brown, Surtees Society, 86 (1889).

Cartulary of Eynsham Abbey, ed. H. E. Salter, 2 vols., Oxfordshire Historical Society, 49, 51 (1907, 1909).

Cartulary of Oseney Abbey, ed. H. E. Salter, 6 vols., Oxford Historical Society, 89–91, 97–8, 101 (1929–36).

The Cartulary of St Michael's Mount, ed. P. L. Hull, Devon and Cornwall Record Society, New Series, 5 (1962).

The Cartulary of Shrewsbury Abbey, ed. U. Rees, 2 vols. (Aberystwyth: National Library of Wales, 1975).

The Cartulary of Tutbury Priory, ed. A. Saltman, Collections for a History of Staffordshire, 4th Series, 4 (London, 1962).

The Charters of King David I: the Written Acts of David I, King of Scots, 1124–1153 and of His Son Henry Earl of Northumberland, 1139–1152, ed. G. W. S. Barrow (Woodbridge: Boydell Press, 1999).

The Charters of the Anglo-Norman Earls of Chester c. 1071–1237, ed. G. Barraclough, Record Society of Lancashire and Cheshire, 126 (1988).

The Chronicle of Battle Abbey, ed. and trans. E. Searle (Oxford, 1980).

The Chronicle of Hugh Candidus, a Monk of Peterborough, ed. W. T. Mellows (Oxford: Oxford University Press for the Friends of Peterborough Cathedral, 1949).

Chronicle of Melrose: a Stratigraphic Edition, 1: Introduction and Facsimile Edition, ed. D. Broun and J. Harrison (Aberdeen: Scottish Historical Society, 2007).

Chronicle of Melrose, Early Sources of Scottish History, trans. A. O. Anderson, 2 vols. (Stamford: Paul Watkins, 1990).

Chronicon Petroburgense, ed. T. Stapleton, Camden Society, 48 (1849).
Councils and Synods with Other Documents Relating to the English Church, I A. D. 871–1204, Part I, 871–1066 (Oxford: Clarendon Press, 1981); Part 2, 1066–1204, ed. D. Whitelock, M. Brett, and C. N. L. Brooke (Oxford: Clarendon Press, 1986).
The Cistercian World. Monastic Writings of the Twelfth Century, ed. and trans. P. Matarasso (London: Penguin, 1993).
Dialogus de Scaccario: the Dialogue of the Exchequer, ed. and trans. E. Amt; *Constitutio Domus Regis: Disposition of the King's Household*, ed. and trans. S. D. Church (Oxford: Clarendon Press, 2007).
Die Gesetze der Angelsachsen, ed. F. Liebermann, 3 vols. in 4 (Halle: Niemayer, 1898–1916).
Domesday Book, seu liber censualis Willelmi primi Regis Angliae inter archivos regni in domo capitulari Westmonasterii asservatus. Jubente Regi Augustissimo Georgio Tertio praelo mandatus typis, ed. A. Farley, 4 vols. (London, 1783–1816).
Domesday Book, ed. J. Morris, 38 vols. (Chichester: Phillimore, 1975–92).
Durham Episcopal Charters, ed. H. S. Offler, Surtees Society, 179 (1968).
The Durham Liber Vitae: London, British Library, MS Cotton Domitian A. VII: Edition and Digital Facsimile with Introduction, ed. D. W. Rollason, L. Rollason, E. Briggs, and A. J. Piper, 3 vols. (London: British Library, 2007).
Eadmer: *Historia Novorum*, ed. M. Rule, RS (London: Longman and Co, 1884).
  The Life of St Anselm, Archbishop of Canterbury, ed. and trans. R. W. Southern (Oxford: Clarendon Press, 1962).
  Lives and Miracles of Saints Oda, Dunstan, and Oswald, ed. and trans. A. J. Turner and B. J. Muir (Oxford: Clarendon Press, 2006), pp. 41–159.
Earldom of Gloucester Charters: the Charters and Scribes of the Earls and Countesses of Gloucester to A. D. 1217, ed. R. B. Patterson (Oxford: Clarendon Press, 1973).
Early Charters of the Cathedral Church of St Paul, London, ed. M. Gibbs, Camden Society 3rd Series, 58 (1939).
The Early Lives of Dunstan, ed. and trans. M. Winterbottom and M. L. Lapidge (Oxford: Clarendon Press, 2012).
Early Yorkshire Charters, I–III, ed. W. Farrer (Edinburgh: Ballantyne, Hanson, 1914–16); IV–XII, ed. C. T. Clay, Yorkshire Archaeological Society, Record Series, Extra Series, I–III, V–X, 1913–65. Extra Series vol. IV is Index to first three vols., C. T. Clay and E. M. Clay (eds.), 1942.
Encomium Emmae Reginae, ed. A. Campbell (reprinted Cambridge: Cambridge University Press, 1998).
English Episcopal Acta, VIII, Winchester 1070–1204, ed. M. J. Franklin (London: published for the British Academy by Oxford University Press, 1993).
English Episcopal Acta, XXX, Carlisle 1133–1202, ed. D. M. Smith (Oxford: Oxford University Press for the British Academy, 2005).
English Historical Documents I, ed. D. Whitelock, 2nd edn (London: Eyre Methuen, 1979).
English Historical Documents II, ed. D. C. Douglas and G. W. Greenaway, 2nd edn (London: Eyre and Spottiswoode, 1981).

Fell, C. *Edward King and Martyr* (Leeds: University of Leeds, School of English, 1971).

Galbert of Bruges: *The Murder of Charles the Good Count of Flanders*, trans. and ed. J. B. Ross (New York: Harper, 1967).

Garnier de Pont-Sainte-Maxence: *La Vie de Thomas Becket*, ed. E. Walberg (Lund: C. W. K. Gleerup, 1952).

Geffrei Gaimar: *Estoire des Engleis. History of the English*, ed. and trans. I. Short (Oxford: Oxford University Press, 2009).

Geoffrey of Burton: *Life and Miracles of St Modwenna*, ed. R. Bartlett (Oxford: Clarendon Press, 2002).

Geoffrey of Monmouth: *The History of the Kings of Britain*, trans. L. Thorpe (Harmondsworth: Penguin, 1966).

Gerald of Wales: *De Principis Instructione Liber, Opera*, ed. J. S. Brewer, J. F. Dimock, and G. F. Warner, 8 vols., RS (London: Longman, Green, Longman and Roberts, 1861–91), VIII (London: Eyre and Spottiswoode, 1891), pp. 1–329.

Gervase of Canterbury: *The Historical Works of Gervase of Canterbury*, ed. W. Stubbs, 2 vols., RS (London: Longman and Co, 1879–80).

Gesta Abbatum Sancti Albani a Thoma Walsingham, regnante Ricardo Secundo, ejusdem ecclesiae praecentore, compilata, ed. H. T. Riley, 3 vols., RS (London: Longmans, Green, Reader and Dyer, 1867–9).

Gesta Regis Henrici Secundi Benedicti Abbatis: the Chronicle of the Reign of Henry II and Richard I, A. D. 1169–1192, ed. W. Stubbs, 2 vols., RS (London: Longman and Co, 1867).

Gesta Stephani, ed. and trans. K. R. Potter with a new introduction and notes by R. H. C. Davis (Oxford: Clarendon Press, 1976).

Gesta Swenomagni Regis et Filiorvm Eivs et Passio Gloriosissimi Canuti Regis et Martyris, M. Cl. Gertz (ed.), *Vitae Sanctorum Danorum* (København: G. E. C. Gad, 1908–12).

Gilbert of Limerick: 'De Statu Ecclesiae' Migne, *Patrologia Latina*, clix, cols. 997a–1004a.

Goscelin: *Translatio Sancte Mildrethe Virginis*, ed. D. Rollason, *Medieval Studies*, 48 (1986), 139–210.

The Liber Confortatorius of Goscelin of Saint-Bertin', ed. C. H. Talbot, *Analecta monastica: textes et études sur la vie des moines au moyen âge troisième siècle: Studia Anselmiana*, 3rd series, 37 (1955), 1–117.

Hemingi Chartularium Ecclesiae Wigorniensis, ed. T. Hearne, 2 vols. (Oxford: e Theatro Sheldoniano, 1723).

Henry of Huntingdon, *Historia Anglorum*, ed. and trans. D. Greenway (Oxford: Clarendon Press, 1996).

Historia Ecclesie Abbendonensis. The History of the Church of Abingdon, ed. and trans. J. Hudson, 2 vols. (Oxford: Clarendon Press, 2002, 2007).

Historia et Cartularium Monasterii Gloucestriae, ed. W. H. Hart, 3 vols., RS (London: Longman, Green, Longman, Roberts and Green, 1863–7).

Historia Selebiensis Monasterii: the History of the Monastery of Selby, ed. and trans. J. Burton with L. Lockyer (Oxford: Clarendon Press, 2013).

The History of the Kings of Britain, ed. M. D. Reeve, trans. N. Wright (Woodbridge: Boydell Press, 2007).

History of William Marshal, ed. A. J. Holden, trans. S. Gregory, notes D. Crouch, 3 vols., Anglo-Norman Text Society, Occasional Publications Series, 4–6 (London, 2002, 2004, 2006).

Hugh the Chanter: *History of the Church of York, 1066–1127*, ed. and trans. C. Johnson, new edn, revised M. Brett, C. N. L. Brooke, and M. Winterbottom (Oxford: Clarendon Press, 1990).

Inquisitio Comitatus Cantabrigiensis, ed. N. E. S. A. Hamilton (London: John Murray, 1876).

Jocelin of Brakelond: *Chronicle of the Abbey of Bury St Edmunds*, trans. D. Greenway and J. Sayers (Oxford: Oxford University Press, 1989).

John of Hexham: Continuation of the *Historia Regum*, Symeon of Durham, *Opera omnia*, ed. T. Arnold, 2 vols., RS (London: Longman and Co, 1882–5), II, pp. 284–332.

John of Salisbury: *Historia Pontificalis*, ed. M. Chibnall (London, Edinburgh, Paris, Melbourne, Toronto: Thomas Nelson, 1956).

Policraticus sive De Nugis Cvrialium et Vestigiis Philosophorum Libri VIII, ed. C. C. Webb, 2 vols. (Oxford: Clarendon Press, 1909).

Policraticus, Books I–IV, ed. K. S. B. Keats-Rohan (Turnhout: Brepols, 1993).

John of Worcester: *The Chronicle of John of Worcester*, II, ed. R. R. Darlington and P. McGurk, trans. J. Bray and P. McGurk (Oxford: Clarendon Press, 1995); III, ed. and trans. P. McGurk (Oxford: Clarendon Press, 1998).

Jordan Fantosme: *Jordan Fantosme's Chronicle*, ed. and trans. R. C. Johnston (Oxford: Clarendon Press, 1981).

The Latin Cartulary of Godstow Abbey, ed. E. Amt (Oxford: published for the British Academy by Oxford University Press, 2014).

Leges Henrici Primi, ed. L. J. Downer (Oxford: Clarendon Press, 1972).

Letters of Lanfranc, Archbishop of Canterbury, ed. and trans. H. Clover and M. Gibson (Oxford: Clarendon Press, 1979).

Liber Eliensis, ed. E. O. Blake, Camden Society, 3rd Series, 92 (1962).

Liber Eliensis: a History of the Isle of Ely from the Seventh Century to the Twelfth, Compiled by a Monk of Ely in the Twelfth Century, trans. J. Fairweather (Woodbridge: Boydell Press, 2005).

Liber Monasterii de Hyda, ed. E. Edwards, RS (London: Longman, Green, Reader and Dyer, 1866).

The Liber Vitae of the New Minster and Hyde Abbey, Winchester, ed. S. Keynes (Copenhagen: Roskilde and Bagge, 1996).

Liber Vitae: Register and Martyrology of New Minster and Hyde Abbey, Winchester, ed. W. de Gray Birch (London and Winchester: Simpkin and Co, Warren and Son, 1892).

The Life of Christina of Markyate, trans. C. H. Talbot, revised with an introduction and notes by S. Fanous and H. Leyser (Oxford: Oxford University Press, 2008).

The Life of King Edward Who Rests at Westminster, ed. and trans. F. Barlow (Oxford: Clarendon Press, 1992).

Materials for the History of Thomas Becket, Archbishop of Canterbury, ed. J. C. Robertson and J. B. Sheppard, 7 vols., RS (London: Longman and Co, 1875–85).

Memorials of St Edmund's Abbey, ed. T. Arnold, 3 vols., RS (London: HMSO, 1890–6).

Miracles of St Edmund, ed. T. Licence (Oxford: Clarendon Press, 2014).

Munimenta Gildhallae Londonensis; Liber Albus, Liber Custumarum et Liber Horn, ed. H. T. Riley, 3 vols. in 4, RS (London: Longman, Brown, Green, Longmans and Roberts, 1849–62).

Orderic Vitalis: *The Ecclesiastical History of Orderic Vitalis*, ed. M. Chibnall, 6 vols. (Oxford: Clarendon Press, 1969–80).

Osbern's Life of Alfege, trans. F. Shaw (London: St Paul's Publishing, 1999).

Patrologia Latina, ed. J.-P. Migne, 221 vols. (Paris: Garnier and J.-P. Migne's successors, 1844–64).

Pipe Rolls: Pipe Roll 31 Henry I, ed. J. A. Green, Pipe Roll Society, 57 (2012); *Pipe Rolls 2–4 Henry II* were edited by J. Hunter for the Record Commission; subsequent rolls were edited on behalf of the Pipe Roll Society.

The Political Writings of Archbishop Wulfstan, ed. A. Rabin (Manchester: Manchester University Press, 2015).

Ralph of Diceto: *Radulfi de Diceto decani Londoniensis opera historica*, ed. W. Stubbs, 2 vols., RS (London: Longman and Co, 1876).

Recueil des Actes des ducs de Normandie 911 à 1066, ed. M. Fauroux (Caen: Caron, 1961).

Red Book of the Exchequer, ed. H. Hall, 3 vols., RS (London: printed for HMSO by Eyre and Spottiswoode, 1896).

Regesta Regum Anglo-Normannorum. The Acta of William I (1066–1087), ed. D. Bates (Oxford: Clarendon Press, 1998).

Regesta Regum Anglo-Normannorum 1066–1154, 4 vols., I, ed. H. W. C. Davis, II, ed. C. Johnson and H. A. Cronne, III and IV, ed. H. A. Cronne and R. H. C. Davis (Oxford: Clarendon Press, 1923–69).

Reginald of Durham: *Vita Sancti Oswaldi Regis et Martyris*, in Symeon of Durham, *Opera omnia*, ed. T. Arnold, 2 vols., RS (London: Longman and Co, 1882–5), I, pp. 326–85.

Registrum Antiquissimum, I, ed. C. W. Foster, Lincoln Record Society, 27 (1931).

Registrum Roffense etc, ed. J. Thorpe (London: J. Thorpe, 1769).

Richard of Cirencester: *Speculum Historiale de Gestis Regum Angliae*, ed. J. E. B. Mayor, 2 vols., RS (London: Longman, Green, Longman, Roberts and Green, 1863–9).

Richard of Hexham: *De Gestis Regis Stephani et de Bello Standardo*, in *Chronicles of the Reigns of Stephen, Henry II and Richard I*, ed. R. Howlett, 4 vols., RS (London: Longman and Co, 1884–9), III, pp. 139–78.

Robert of Torigny: *Chronicles of the Reigns of Stephen, Henry II and Richard I*, ed. R. Howlett, 4 vols., RS (London: Longman and Co, 1884–9), 4, 3–316.

Rodulfus Glaber: *Historiarum Libri Quinque. The Five Books of the Histories*, ed. J. France (Oxford: Clarendon Press, 1989).

Roger of Howden: *Chronica Magistri Rogeri de Houedene*, ed. W. Stubbs, 4 vols., RS (London: Longmans, Green, Reader and Dyer, 1868–71).

Rotuli de Dominabus et Pueris et Puellis de XII Comitatibus 1185, ed. J. H. Round, Pipe Roll Society, 35 (1913).

Rotuli Hundredorum, ed. W. Illingworth and J. Caley, 2 vols. (London: Record Commissioners, 1812–18).

Snorri Sturluson, *Heimskringla. History of the Kings of Norway*, trans. L. M. Hollander (Austin: University of Texas Press, 1964).

Stubbs, W. *Select Charters*, 9th edn, revised H. W. C. Davis (Oxford: Clarendon Press, 1913).

Sulcard: B. W. Scholz, 'Prologus de Construccione Westmonasterii', *Traditio*, 20 (1964), 59–91.

Symeon of Durham: *Opera omnia*, ed. T. Arnold, 2 vols., RS (London: Longman and Co, 1882–5).

  Libellus de Exordio atque Procursu istius hoc est Dunhelmensis Ecclesie, ed. and trans. D. Rollason (Oxford: Clarendon Press, 2000).

Textus Roffensis, ed. T. Hearne (Oxford: e Theatro Sheldoniano, 1720).

Thomas of Marlborough: *History of the Abbey of Evesham*, ed. and trans. J. Sayers and L. Watkiss (Oxford: Clarendon Press, 2003).

Tractatus de legibus et consuetudinibus regni Anglie qui Glanvilla vocatur: the Treatise on the Laws and Customs of the Realm of England Commonly Called Glanvill, ed. G. D. G. Hall with further reading by M. T. Clanchy (Oxford: Clarendon Press, 1993).

Twelfth-Century English Archidiaconal and Vice-Archidiaconal Acta, ed. B. R. Kemp, Canterbury and York Society, 92 (2001).

Ungedruckte Anglo-Normannische Geschichtsquellen, ed. F. Liebermann (Strassburg: K. J. Trübner, 1879).

Van Caenegem, R. C. *English Lawsuits from William I to Richard I*, 2 vols., Selden Society (London, 1990, 1991).

Vita et Passio Waldevi Comitis, Chroniques Anglo-Normandes, ed. F. Michel, 3 vols. (Rouen: E. Frère, 1836–40), II, pp. 104–11.

Walter Daniel: *The Life of Ailred of Rievaulx*, ed. and trans. F. M. Powicke (London: Thomas Nelson, 1950).

Walter Map: *De Nugis Curialium. Courtiers' Trifles*, ed. and trans. M. R. James, revised edn, C. N. L. Brooke and R. A. B. Mynors (Oxford: Clarendon Press, 1983).

The Waltham Chronicle, ed. and trans. L. Watkiss and M. Chibnall (Oxford: Clarendon Press, 1994).

Wharton, H. *Anglia Sacra etc*, 2 vols. (London: Richard Chiswel, 1691).

Whatley, E. Gordon. *The Saint of London. The Life and Miracles of St. Erkenwald*, Medieval and Renaissance Texts and Studies, 58 (Binghamton, 1989).

Westminster Abbey Charters, ed. E. Mason, London Record Society, 25 (1988).

William of Jumièges: *Gesta Normannorum Ducum*, ed. and trans. E. M. C. Van Houts, 2 vols. (Oxford: Clarendon Press, 1992, 1995).

William of Malmesbury: *Gesta Pontificum Anglorum*, I, ed. and trans. M. Winterbottom, II, Introduction and Commentary, R. M. Thomson (Oxford: Clarendon Press, 2007).

Gesta Regum Anglorum, I, ed. and trans. R. A. B. Mynors, R. M. Thomson, and M. Winterbottom. II, *General Introduction and Commentary*, R. M. Thomson (Oxford: Clarendon Press, 1999).

Historia Novella, ed. E. King, trans. K. R. Potter (Oxford: Clarendon Press, 1998).

Saints' Lives: Lives of Saints Wulfstan, Dunstan, Patrick, Benignus and Indract, ed. and trans. M. Winterbottom and R. M. Thomson (Oxford: Clarendon Press, 2002).

William of Newburgh: *Historia Rerum Anglicarum, Chronicles of the Reigns of Stephen, Henry II and Richard I*, ed. R. Howlett, 4 vols., RS (London: Longman and Co, 1884–9), I, II, pp. 1–584.

William of Poitiers: *Gesta Guillelmi*, ed. and trans. R. H. C. Davis and M. Chibnall (Oxford: Clarendon Press, 1998).

Wulfstan: *Die 'Institutes of Polity, civil and ecclesiastical': ein Werk Erzbischof Wulfstans von York*, ed. and trans. K. Von Jost (Bern: Francke, 1959).

3 SECONDARY SOURCES

Abels, R. P. *Lordship and Military Obligation in Anglo-Saxon England* (Berkeley, Los Angeles, London: University of California Press, 1988).

Abrams, L. 'Conversion and Assimilation', *Cultures in Contact: Scandinavian Settlement in England in the Ninth and Tenth Centuries*, ed. D. M. Hadley and J. D. Richards (Turnhout: Brepols, 2000), pp. 135–53.

'King Edgar and the Men of the Danelaw', *Edgar King of the English, 959–975: New Interpretations*, ed. D. Scragg (Woodbridge: Boydell Press, 2008), pp. 171–91.

'Diaspora and Identity in the Viking Age', *Early Medieval Europe*, 20 (2012), 17–38.

Adams, C. Phythian. *Land of the Cumbrians* (Aldershot, Brookfield: Scolar Press, Ashgate, 1996).

Addyman, P. V. 'The Anglo-Saxon House: a New Review', *Anglo-Saxon England*, 1 (1972), 273–307.

Aird, W. M. *St Cuthbert and the Normans: the Church of Durham 1071–1153* (Woodbridge: Boydell Press, 1998).

Allen, M. 'The Durham Mint before Boldon Book', *Anglo-Norman Durham*, ed. D. Rollason, D. Harvey, and M. Prestwich (Woodbridge: Boydell Press, 1994), pp. 381–98.

'Henry II and the English Coinage', *Henry II. New Interpretations*, ed. C. Harper-Bill and N. Vincent (Woodbridge: Boydell Press, 2007), pp. 257–77.

Mints and Money in Medieval England (Cambridge: Cambridge University Press, 2012).

Althoff, G. *Family, Friends and Followers. Political and Social Bonds in Early Medieval Europe*, trans. C. Carroll (Cambridge: Cambridge University Press, 2004).

Amt, E. 'The Forest Regard of 1155', *Haskins Society Journal*, 2 (1990), 189–95.

The Accession of Henry II in England. Royal Government Restored 1149–1159
(Woodbridge: Boydell Press, 1993).

Anderson, M. D. *A Saint at Stake: the Strange Death of William of Norwich*
(London: Faber, 1964).

Aurell, M. *L'empire des Plantagenêts 1154–1224* (Paris: Perrin, 2003).

Austin, D. *Acts of Perception. A Study of Barnard Castle in Teesdale*, Antiquarian
and Archaeological Society of Durham and Northumberland, Research
Report, 2 vols. (Hassocks, 2007).

Babcock, R. S. 'The Irish Sea Province and the Accession of Henry I', *Haskins
Society Journal*, 17 (2006), 39–62.

Banham D. and Faith, R. *Anglo-Saxon Farms and Farming* (Oxford: Oxford
University Press, 2014).

Barlow, F. *Edward the Confessor* (London: Eyre Methuen, 1970).
  The English Church 1000–1066, 2nd edn (London: Longman, 1979).
  The English Church 1066–1154 (London, New York: Longman, 1979).
  William Rufus (London: Methuen, 1983).
  Thomas Becket (London: Weidenfeld and Nicolson, 1986).
  The Godwins: the Rise and Fall of a Noble Dynasty (Harlow Pearson, 2002).

Barlow, F., Biddle, M. Von Feilitzen, O, and Keene, D. J. (eds.), *Winchester in the
Early Middle Ages*, Winchester Studies, I (Oxford: Clarendon Press, 1976).

Barrett, R. W. Jr. *Against all England. Regional Identity and Cheshire Writing,
1195–1656* (Notre Dame, IN: University of Notre Dame Press, 2009).

Barrow, G. W. S. 'King David I, Earl Henry and Cumbria', *Transactions of the
Cumberland and Westmorland Antiquarian and Archaeological Society*, 99
(1999), 117–27.

Barrow, J. 'Chester's Earliest Regatta? Edgar's Dee-Rowing Revisited', *Early
Medieval Europe*, 10 (2001), 81–93.

Bartlett, R. *Trial by Fire and Water: the Medieval Judicial Ordeal* (Oxford:
Clarendon Press, 1986).
  'Symbolic Meanings of Hair in the Middle Ages', *Transactions of the Royal
Historical Society*, 6th Series, 4 (1994), 43–60.
  England under the Norman and Angevin Kings 1075–1225 (Oxford: Clarendon
Press, 2000).

Bates, D. 'The Origins of the Justiciarship', *[Transactions of the Battle Conference
on] Anglo-Norman Studies*, 4 (1981), 1–12.
  'The Conqueror's Earliest Historians and the Writing of his Biography', *Writing
Medieval Biography 750–1250: Essays in Honour of Professor Frank
Barlow*, ed. D. Bates, J. Crick, and S. Hamilton (Woodbridge: Boydell
Press, 2006), pp. 129–41.
  The Normans and Empire (Oxford: Oxford University Press, 2013).

Baxter, S. *The Earls of Mercia: Lordship and Power in Anglo-Saxon England*
(Oxford: Oxford University Press, 2007).

Beresford, G. *Goltho. The Development of an Early Medieval Manor c. 850–1150*
(London: Historic Buildings and Monuments Commission for England,
1987).

Beresford, M. *New Towns of the Middle Ages* (London: Lutterworth Press, 1967).

Beresford, M. W. and St Joseph, J. K. S. *Medieval England* (Cambridge: Cambridge University Press, 2009 edn).

Biancalana, J. 'For Want of Justice: Legal Reforms of Henry II', *Columbia Law Review*, 88 (1988), 433–536.

Biddle, M. 'Seasonal Festivals and Residence: Winchester, Westminster and Gloucester in the Tenth to Twelfth Centuries', *Anglo-Norman Studies*, 8 (1985), 51–72.

Bishop, T. A. M. 'Monastic Granges in Yorkshire', *English Historical Review*, 51 (1936), 193–214.

Bisson, T. N. (ed.), *Cultures of Power: Lordship, Status and Process in Twelfth-Century Europe* (Philadelphia: University of Pennsylvania Press, 1995).

'The Lure of Stephen's England: *Tenserie*, Flemings and a Crisis of Circumstance', *King Stephen's Reign 1135–1154*, ed. P. Dalton, P. and G. J. White (Woodbridge: Boydell Press, 2008), pp. 171–81.

The Crisis of the Twelfth Century: Power, Lordship, and the Origins of European Government (Princeton, NJ: Woodstock, 2009).

Blackburn, M. 'Coinage and Currency under Henry I: a Review', *Anglo-Norman Studies*, 13 (1990), 49–81.

'Coinage and Currency', *The Anarchy of King Stephen's Reign*, ed. E. King (Oxford: Oxford University Press, 1994), pp. 145–205.

'Æthelred's Coinage and the Payment of Tribute', *The Battle of Maldon in AD 991*, ed. D. Scragg (Oxford: Blackwell, 1991), pp. 156–69.

Blair, J. (ed.), *Minsters and Parish Churches: the Local Church in Transition, 950–1200* (Oxford: Oxford University Committee for Archaeology, 1988).

Anglo-Saxon Oxfordshire (Stroud: Alan Sutton, 1994).

'St Frideswide's Monastery: Problems and Possibilities', *Oxoniensia*, 53 (1998), 221–58.

The Church in Anglo-Saxon Society (Oxford: Oxford University Press, 2005).

Bolton, T. *The Empire of Cnut the Great: Conquest and the Consolidation of Power in Northern Europe in the Early Eleventh Century* (Leiden, Boston: Brill, 2009).

Bonner, G., Rollason, D., and Stancliffe, C. (eds.), *St Cuthbert, His Cult and Community*, (Woodbridge: Boydell, 1989).

Bouchard, C. B. 'Consanguinity and Noble Marriages in the Tenth and Eleventh Centuries', *Speculum*, 56 (1981), 268–87.

Brand, P. '"Multis vigiliis excogitatam et inventam": Henry II and the Creation of the English Common Law', reprinted in *Making of the Common Law* (London: Hambledon Press, 1992), pp. 77–102.

Brett, M. *The English Church under Henry I* (Oxford: Oxford University Press, 1975).

'The *Collectio Lanfranci* and Its Competitors', *Intellectual Life in the Middle Ages: Essays Presented to Margaret Gibson*, ed. L. Smith and B. Ward (London: Hambledon Press, 1992), pp. 157–74.

Britnell, R. 'The Economy of British Towns 600–1300', *Cambridge Urban History of Britain*, I, ed. D. M. Palliser (Cambridge: Cambridge University Press, 2008), pp. 105–26.

Britnell, R. and Campbell, B. M. S. (eds.), *A Commercialising Economy: England 1086 to c. 1300* (Manchester: Manchester University Press, 1995).

Brooke, C. N. L. and Keir, G. *London 800–1216: the Shaping of a City* (Berkeley, Los Angeles: University of California Press, 1975).

Brooke, C. N. L., Keir, G., and Reynolds, S. 'Henry I's Charter for the City of London', *Journal of the Society of Archivists*, 4 (1972), 558–78.

Brookes S. and Reynolds, A. 'The Origins of Political Order and the Anglo-Saxon State', *Archaeology International*, 13 (2009), 84–93.

Brooks, N. P. 'Arms, Status and Warfare in Late-Saxon England', *Ethelred the Unready*, ed. D. Hill, *British Archaeological Reports, British Series*, 59 (1978), pp. 81–103.

   The Early History of the Church of Canterbury: Christ Church from 597 to 1066 (London: Leicester University Press, 1984).

   'The Archbishopric of Canterbury and the So-Called Introduction of Knight Service into England', *Anglo-Norman Studies*, 34 (2011), 41–62.

Brooks, N. and Cubitt, C. (eds.), *St Oswald of Worcester: Life and Influence* (London: Leicester University Press, 1996).

Brooks, N. Gelling, M., and Johnson, D. 'A New Charter of King Edgar', *Anglo-Saxon England*, 13 (1984), 137–55.

Brown, R. A. 'Royal Castle-Building in England, 1154–1216', *English Historical Review*, 70 (1955), 353–98.

   Dover Castle (London: HMSO, 1966).

   Castle Rising (London: English Heritage, 1987).

Brown, S. *'Our Magnificent Fabrick': York Minster an Architectural History c. 1220–1500* (Swindon: English Heritage, 2003).

Brown, T. Tatton. *Lambeth Palace* (London: SPCK, 2000).

Burrow, J. W. *A Liberal Descent: Victorian Historians and the English Past* (Cambridge: Cambridge University Press, 1981).

Burton, J. *The Monastic Order in Yorkshire 1069–1215* (Cambridge: Cambridge University Press, 1999).

Callahan, D. F. 'The Cult of St Michael the Archangel and the "Terrors of the Year 1000"', *The Apocalyptic Year 1000: Religious Expectation and Social Change, 950–1050*, ed. R. Landes, A. Gow, and D. C. Van Meter (Oxford: Oxford University Press, 2003), pp. 181–204.

Campbell, J. (ed.), *The Anglo-Saxons* (Oxford: Phaidon, 1982).

   Essays in Anglo-Saxon History (London: Hambledon Press, 1986).

   'Was It Infancy in England? Some Questions of Comparison', *England and Her Neighbours 1066–1453: Essays in Honour of Pierre Chaplais*, ed. M. Jones and M. Vale (London: Hambledon Press, 1989).

   The Anglo-Saxon State (London: Hambledon and London, 2000).

Carlin, M. *Medieval Southwark* (London: Hambledon Press, 1986).

Carpenter, D. *The Struggle for Mastery: Britain 1066–1284* (Oxford, New York: Oxford University Press, 2003).

Carpenter, D. X. 'Morel of Bamburgh, Archil Morel, and the Death of King Malcolm III: a Case of Mistaken Identity', *Northern History*, 52 (2015), 314–23.

Chapman, A. *West Cotton, Raunds: a Study of Medieval Settlement Dynamics AD 450–1450. Excavation of a Deserted Medieval Hamlet in Northamptonshire, 1985–1989* (Oxford, Oakville: Oxbow, 2010).

Cheney, C. R. *From Becket to Langton: English Church Government 1170–1213* (Manchester: Manchester University Press, 1956).

Cheney, M. G. *Roger, Bishop of Worcester, 1164–1179* (Oxford: Clarendon Press, 1980).

Cheyette, F. L. 'The Invention of the State', *Essays on Medieval Civilization*, ed. B. K. Ladner and K. R. Philp (Austin: University of Texas Press, 1978), pp. 143–78.

Chibnall, M. *The Debate on the Norman Conquest* (Manchester: Manchester University Press, 1999).

Clanchy, M. T. *From Memory to Written Record*, 3rd edn (Oxford: Wiley-Blackwell, 2013).

Clark, C. 'English Personal Names ca. 650–1300: some Prosopographical Bearings', *Medieval Prosopography*, 8 (1987), 31–60.

Clarke, C. *Writing Power in Anglo-Saxon England* (Woodbridge: D. S. Brewer, 2012).

Clarke, H. B. 'Domesday Slavery (adjusted for slaves)', *Midland History*, 1 (1972), 37–46.

Clay, C. T. 'The Ancestry of the Early Lords of Warkworth', *Archaeologia Aeliana*, 4th Series, 32 (1954), 65–71.

Clayton, M. 'The Old English *Promissio Regis*', *Anglo-Saxon England*, 37 (2008), 91–150.

Coad, J. *Castle Acre Castle, Norfolk* (London: Historic Buildings and Monuments Commission for England, 1984).

Colvin, H. M. (general editor), *The History of the King's Works*, 6 vols. (London: HMSO, 1963–82).

Condon, A. 'Muirchertach ua Briain, Politics and Naval Activity in the Irish Sea, 1075 to 1119', *Keimelia: studies in Medieval History and Archaeology in Memory of Tom Delaney*, ed. G. MacNiocaill and P. F. Wallace (Galway: University of Galway Press, 1979), pp. 397–415.

Constable, G. 'Aelred of Rievaulx and the Nun of Watton: an Episode in the Early History of the Gilbertine Order', *Medieval Women: Dedicated and Presented to Professor Rosalind M. T. Hill on the Occasion of Her Seventieth Birthday*, ed. D. Baker (Oxford: Blackwell, 1978), pp. 205–26.

Coss, P. *The Origins of the English Gentry* (Cambridge: Cambridge University Press, 2003).

Coulson, C. 'Castles of the Anarchy', *The Anarchy of King Stephen's Reign*, ed. E. King (Oxford: Oxford University Press, 1994), pp. 67–92.

Cowdrey, H. E. J. 'Bishop Ermenfrid of Sion and the Penitential Ordinance Following the Battle of Hastings', *Journal of Ecclesiastical History*, 20 (1969), 225–42.

'The Anglo-Norman Laudes Regiae', *Viator*, 12 (1981), 37–78.

Lanfranc, Scholar, Monk, and Archbishop (Cambridge: Cambridge University Press, 2003).

Cowie, R. and Whythead, R. 'Lundenwic: the Archaeological Evidence for Middle Saxon London', *Antiquity*, 63 (1989), 706–18.

Cramer, P. 'Ernulf of Rochester and Early Anglo-Norman Canon Law', *Journal of Ecclesiastical History*, 40 (1989), 483–510.

Crawford, B. 'The Saint Clement Dedications at Clementhorpe and Pontefract Castle: Anglo-Scandinavian or Norman?', *Myth, Rulership, Church and Charters: Essays in Honour of Nicholas Brooks*, ed. J. Barrow and A. Wareham (Aldershot: Ashgate, 2008), pp. 189–210.

Creighton, O. *Castles and Landscapes* (London, New York: Continuum, 2002).

Crick, J. 'Women, Posthumous Benefaction and Family Strategy in Pre-Conquest England', *Journal of British Studies*, 38 (1999), 399–422.

Crick, J. and Van Houts, E. (eds.), *A Social History of England 900–1200* (Cambridge: Cambridge University Press, 2011).

Cronne, H. A. 'The Office of Local Justiciar in England under the Norman Kings', *University of Birmingham Historical Journal*, 6 (1958), 18–38.

Crook, J. *English Medieval Shrines* (Woodbridge: Boydell Press, 2011).

Crosby, E. U. *Bishop and Chapter in Twelfth-Century England, a study of the Mensa Episcopalis* (Cambridge: Cambridge University Press, 1994).

Crouch, D. 'Geoffrey de Clinton and Roger Earl of Warwick: New Men and Magnates in the Reign of Henry I', *Bulletin of the Institute of Historical Research*, 55 (1982), 113–24.

William Marshal: Court, Career and Chivalry in the Angevin Empire, 1147–1219 (Harlow: Longman, 1990).

'The Administration of the Norman Earldom', *The Earldom of Chester and Its Charters*, ed. A. Thacker, *Journal of the Chester Archaeological Society*, 71 (1991), 69–95.

The Image of Aristocracy in Britain 1000–1300 (London: Routledge, 1992).

'A Norman "Conventio" and Bonds of Lordship', *Law and Government in Medieval England and Normandy: Essays in Honour of Sir James Holt*, ed. G. Garnett and J. Hudson (Cambridge: Cambridge University Press, 1994), pp. 299–324.

'The March and the Welsh Kings', *The Anarchy of King Stephen's Reign*, ed. E. King (Oxford: Oxford University Press, 1994), pp. 255–89.

The Reign of King Stephen 1135–1154 (Harlow: Longman, 2000).

'The Troubled Deathbeds of Henry I's Servants: Death, Confession, and Secular Conduct in the Twelfth Century', *Albion*, 34 (2002), 24–36.

The Birth of Nobility: Social Change in England and France: 900–1300 (Harlow: Pearson Longman, 2005).

Tournament (London: Hambledon Press and London, 2005).

The English Aristocracy 1070–1272: a Social Transformation (New Haven, CT, London: Yale University Press, 2011).

Cubitt, C. 'The Tenth-Century Benedictine Reform in England', *Early Medieval Europe*, 6 (1997), 77–94.

'The Politics of Remorse: Penance and Royal Piety in the Reign of Æthelred the Unready', *Historical Research*, 85 (2012), 179–92.

'Apocalyptic and Eschatological Thought in England around the Year 1000', *Transactions of the Royal Historical Society*, 6th Series, 25 (2015), 27–52.

Curley, M. J. 'A New Edition of John of Cornwall's *Prophetia Merlini*', *Speculum*, 57 (1982), 217–49.

Dalton, P. 'William Earl of York and Royal Authority in Yorkshire in the Reign of Stephen', *Haskins Society Journal*, 2 (1990), 155–65.

'Aiming at the Impossible: Ranulf II Earl of Chester and Lincolnshire in the Reign of King Stephen', *The Earldom of Chester and Its Charters*, ed. A. Thacker, *Journal of the Chester Archaeological Society*, 71 (1991), 109–34.

Conquest, Anarchy and Lordship: Yorkshire 1066–1154 (Cambridge: Cambridge University Press, 1994).

'Churchmen and the Promotion of Peace in King Stephen's Reign', *Viator*, 31 (2000), 79–120.

Dalton, P. and Luscombe, D. (eds.), *Rulership and Rebellion in the Anglo-Norman World, c. 1066–c. 1216* (Farnham: Ashgate, 2015).

Dalton, P. and White, G. J. (eds.), *King Stephen's Reign 1135–1154* (Woodbridge: Boydell Press, 2008).

Danelt, B. and Bogoch, B. 'Whoever Alters This, May God Turn His Face from Him on the Day of Judgment', *Journal of American Folklore*, 105 (1992), 132–65.

Davies, R. R. 'Kings, Lords and Liberties in the March of Wales, 1066–1272', *Transactions of the Royal Historical Society*, 6th Series, 29 (1979), 41–61.

The Age of Conquest. Wales 1063–1415 (Oxford: Oxford University Press, 1987).

The First English Empire: Power and Identities in the British Isles, 1093–1343 (Oxford: Oxford University Press, 2000).

'The Medieval State: the Tyranny of a Concept?', *Journal of Historical Sociology*, 16 (2003), 280–300.

Davis, H. W. C. 'London Lands and Liberties of St Paul's, 1066–1135', *Essays in Medieval History Presented to T. F. Tout*, ed. A. G. Little and F. M. Powicke (Manchester: Manchester University Press, 1925), pp. 45–59.

Davis, R. H. C. 'East Anglia and the Danelaw', *Transactions of the Royal Historical Society*, 5th Series, 5 (1955), 23–39.

'The Ford, the River and the City', *From Alfred the Great to Stephen* (London: Hambledon Press, 1991), pp. 281–91.

Davison, B. K. 'Excavations at Sulgrave, Northamptonshire, 1960–76: an Interim Report', *Archaeological Journal*, 134 (1977), 105–14.

Sherborne Old Castle (London: English Heritage, 2001).

Denton, J. H. *English Royal Free Chapels 1100–1300* (Manchester: Manchester University Press, 1970).

Dixon P. and Marshall, P. 'The Great Tower at Hedingham Castle: a Reassessment', *Anglo-Norman Castles*, ed. R. Liddiard (Woodbridge: Boydell Press, 2003), pp. 297–306.

Dobson, R. B., *The Jews of Medieval York and the Massacre of March 1190*, University of York Borthwick Paper, 45 (1974).

Doherty, H. 'Robert de Vaux and Roger de Stuteville, Sheriffs of Cumberland and Northumberland, 1170–1185', *Anglo-Norman Studies*, 28 (2005), 65–102.

Dolley, R. H. M. and Metcalf, D. M. 'The Reform of the English Coinage under Eadgar', *Anglo-Saxon Coins: Studies Presented to F. M. Stenton on the*

Occasion of his 8oth Birthday, ed. R. H. M. Dolley (London: Methuen, 1961), pp. 136–68.

Downham, C. *Viking Kings of Britain and Ireland. The Dynasty of Ivarr to A. D. 1014* (Edinburgh: Edinburgh University Press, 2007).

Downham, C. 'Viking Ethnicities: a Historiographic Overview', *History Compass*, 10 (2012), 1–12.

Duby, G. *Medieval Marriage: Two Models from Twelfth-Century France* (Baltimore, MD, London: Johns Hopkins University Press, 1978).

Duggan, A. *Thomas Becket (Reputations)* (London: Arnold, 2004).

'Henry II, the English Church and the Papacy, 1154–76', *Henry II. New Interpretations*, ed. C. Harper-Bill and N. Vincent (Woodbridge: Boydell Press, 2007), pp. 154–83.

'Roman, Canon and Common Law in Twelfth-Century England: the Council of Northampton (1164) Re-examined', *Historical Research*, 83 (2010), 379–408.

Duggan, C. 'Papal Judges Delegate and the Making of the "New Law" in the Twelfth Century', *Cultures of Power: Lordship, Status and Process in Twelfth-Century Europe*, ed. T. N. Bisson (Philadelphia: University of Pennsylvania Press, 1995), pp. 172–99.

Duncan, A. A. M. 'The Battle of Carham, 1018', *Scottish Historical Review*, 55 (1976), 20–8.

Kingship of the Scots 842–1292. Succession and Independence (Edinburgh: Edinburgh University Press, 2002).

Dyer, C. *Making a Living in the Middle Ages. The People of Britain 850–1520* (London: Penguin, 2003).

Dyson, T., Samuel, M., Steele, A., and Wright, S. M. *The Cluniac Priory and Abbey of St Saviour Bermondsey, Surrey*, Museum of London Archaeology Monograph, l (2011).

Edmonds, F. 'The Furness Peninsula and the Irish Sea Region: Cultural Interaction from the Seventh Century to the Twelfth', *Jocelin of Furness: Essays from the 2011 Conference*, ed. C. Downham (Donington: Shaun Tyas, 2013), pp. 17–44.

'The Emergence and Transformation of Medieval Cumbria', *Scottish Historical Review*, 93 (2014), 195–216.

'The Expansion of the Kingdom of Strathclyde', *Early Medieval Europe*, 23 (2015), 43–66.

Elkins, S. *Holy Women of Twelfth-Century England* (Chapel Hill: University of North Carolina Press, 1988).

Eyton, R. W. *Court, Household, and Itinerary of Henry II* (Dorchester: Foster, 1878).

Faith, R. *The English Peasantry and the Growth of Lordship* (Leicester: Leicester University Press, 1997).

Fanger, C. 'Christian Ritual Magic in the Middle Ages', *History Compass*, 11/8 (2013), 610–18.

Farrer, W. *Honors and Knights' Fees*, 3 vols. (Manchester: Manchester University Press, 1923–5).

Fergusson, P. *The Architecture of Solitude. Cistercian Abbeys in Twelfth-Century England* (Princeton, NJ: Princeton University Press, 1984).

Canterbury Cathedral Priory in the Age of Becket (New Haven, CT, London: Yale University Press, 2011).

Fernie, E. *The Architecture of the Anglo-Saxons* (London: Batsford, 1983).

'The Romanesque Church of Bury St Edmunds Abbey', *Bury St Edmunds. Medieval Art, Architecture, Archaeology, Economy*, ed. A. Gransden, British Archaeological Association (London, 1998), pp. 1–15.

The Architecture of Norman England (Oxford: Oxford University Press, 2000).

'Baldwin's Church and the Effects of the Conquest', *Bury St Edmunds and the Norman Conquest*, ed. T. Licence (Woodbridge: Boydell Press, 2014), pp. 74–93.

Finberg, H. P. R. 'The Early History of Werrington', *English Historical Review*, 59 (1944), 237–51.

Flanagan, M. T. *Irish Society, Anglo-Norman Settlers, Angevin Kingship: Interactions in Ireland in the Late Twelfth Century* (Oxford: Clarendon Press, 1989).

Flanagan, M. T. and Green, J. A. (eds.), *Charter and Charter Scholarship in Britain and Ireland* (Houndmills: Palgrave, 2005).

Fleming, J. *Gille of Limerick (c. 1070–1145): Architect of a Medieval Church* (Dublin: Four Courts Press, 2001).

Fleming, R. 'Monastic Lands and England's Defence in the Viking Age', *English Historical Review*, 100 (1985), 247–65.

Kings and Lords in Conquest England (Cambridge: Cambridge University Press, 1991).

'Rural Elites and Urban Communities in Late-Saxon England', *Past and Present*, 141 (1993), 3–37.

'History and Liturgy at Pre-Conquest Christ Church', *Haskins Society Journal*, 6 (1994), 67–83.

Domesday Book and the Law: Society and Legal Custom in Early Medieval England (Cambridge: Cambridge University Press, 1998).

Britain after Rome: the Fall and Rise 400–1070 (London, New York: Allen Lane, 2010).

Fleming, D. and Pope, J. M. (eds.), *Henry I and the Anglo-Norman World. Studies in Memory of C. Warren Hollister, Haskins Society Journal*, 17 (2006).

Fletcher, R. *Bloodfeud. Murder and Revenge in Anglo-Saxon England* (London: Allen Lane The Penguin Press, 2002).

Flint, V. I. J. *The Rise of Magic in Early Medieval Europe* (Oxford: Oxford University Press, 1991).

Foot, S. 'The Making of *Angelcynn*: English Identity before the Norman Conquest', *Transactions of the Royal Historical Society*, 6th Series, 100 (1996), 25–49.

'The Historiography of the Anglo-Saxon "Nation-State"', *Power and the Nation in European History*, ed. L. Scales, L. and O. Zimmer (Cambridge: Cambridge University Press, 2005), pp. 125–42.

Æthelstan: the First King of England (New Haven, CT, London: Yale University Press, 2011).

Frank, R. 'King Cnut in the Verse of His Skalds', *The Reign of Cnut. King of England, Denmark and Norway*, ed. A. Rumble (London, New York: Leicester University Press, 1994), pp. 106–24.

Franklin, M. 'The Bishops of Winchester and the Monastic Revolution', *Anglo-Norman Studies*, 12 (1990), 47–65.

Fraser, C. M. and Emsley, K. 'Durham and the Wapentake of Sadberge', *Transactions of the Architectural and Archaeological Society of Durham and Northumberland*, 2 (1970), 71–81.

Freeman, E. A. *The History of the Norman Conquest of England*, first edn, 6 vols. (Oxford: Clarendon Press, 1867–79).

Frost, J. A. *The Foundation of Nostell Priory 1109–1153*, University of York Borthwick Paper, no. 111 (2007).

Galloway, A. (ed.), *Cambridge Companion to Medieval English Culture* (Cambridge: Cambridge University Press, 2011).

Gardiner, M. 'Late Saxon Settlements', *Oxford Handbook of Anglo-Saxon Archaeology* ed. D. A. Hinton, S. Crawford, and H. Hamerow (Oxford: Oxford University Press, 2011), pp. 198–217.

Garnett, G. 'Coronation and Propaganda: Some Implications of the Norman Claim to the Throne in 1066', *Transactions of the Royal Historical Society*, 5th Series, 36 (1986), 91–116.

'The Origins of the Crown', *The History of English Law: Centenary Essays on 'Pollock and Maitland', Proceedings of the British Academy*, ed. J. Hudson, 89 (1996), 171–214.

'The Third Recension of the English Coronation *ordo*: the Manuscripts', *Haskins Society Journal*, 11 (1998), 43–71.

Conquered England: Kingship, Succession, and Tenure 1066–1166 (Oxford: Oxford University Press, 2007).

Garnett G. and Hudson, J. (eds.), *Law and Government in Medieval England and Normandy: Essays in Honour of Sir James Holt* (Cambridge: Cambridge University Press, 1994).

Gee, E. A. 'Architectural History until 1290', *A History of York Minster*, ed. G. E. Aylmer and R. Cant (Oxford: Clarendon Press, 1977), pp. 111–48.

Gem, R. 'The Romanesque Rebuilding of Westminster Abbey (with a reconstruction by W. T. Ball)', *Anglo-Norman Studies*, 3 (1980), 33–60.

Gem, R. (ed.), *The English Heritage Book of St Augustine's Abbey Canterbury* (London: English Heritage, 1997).

Giandrea, M. *Episcopal Culture in Late Anglo-Saxon England* (Woodbridge: Boydell Press, 2007).

Gibson, M. *Lanfranc of Bec* (Oxford: Clarendon Press, 1978).

Gilchrist, R. *Gender and Archaeology. Contesting the Past* (London: Routledge, 1999).

Gillingham, J. '1066 and the Introduction of Chivalry into England', *Law and Government in Medieval England and Normandy: Essays in Honour of Sir James Holt*, ed. G. Garnett and J. Hudson (Cambridge: Cambridge University Press, 1994), pp. 31–55.

'Thegns and Knights in Eleventh-Century England: Who was then the Gentleman?', *Transactions of the Royal Historical Society*, 6th series, 5 (1995), 129–53.

'Kingship, Chivalry and Love. Political and Cultural Values in the Earliest History Written in French: Geoffrey Gaimar's *Estoire des Engleis*', *Anglo-Norman Political Culture and the Twelfth-Century Renaissance*, ed. C. Warren Hollister (Woodbridge: Boydell Press, 1997), pp. 37–58.

The English in the Twelfth Century: imperialism, National Identity and Political Values (Woodbridge: Boydell Press, 2000).

The Angevin Empire, 2nd edn (London: Arnold, 2001).

'Henry of Huntingdon in His Time (1135) and Place (between England and the royal court)', *Gallus Anonymous and His Chronicle in the Perspective of the Latest Research*, ed. K. Stopka (Krakow: Polish Academy of Arts and Sciences, 2010), pp. 157–72.

'The King and His Castle: How Henry II Rebuilt his Reputation', *BBC History Magazine*, 3 March (2011).

Conquest, Catastrophe and Recovery: Britain and Ireland 1066–1485 (London: Vintage, 2014).

Ginther, J. 'Between *Plena Caritas* and *Plenitudo Legis*: the Ecclesiology of the Norman Anonymous', *Haskins Society Journal*, 22 (2010), 141–62.

Godden, M. and Lapidge, M. (eds.), *Cambridge Companion to Old English Literature* (Cambridge: Cambridge University Press, 2013).

Goebel, J. *Felony and Misdemeanor: a Study in the History of English Criminal Procedure* (New York: the Commonwealth Fund, 1937).

Golding, B. 'Robert of Mortain', *Anglo-Norman Studies*, 13 (1990), 119–44.

Gilbert of Sempringham and the Gilbertine Order (Oxford: Clarendon Press, 1995).

Green, J. A. 'William Rufus, Henry I and the Royal Demesne', *History*, 64 (1979), 337–52.

'The Last Century of Danegeld', *English Historical Review*, 96 (1981), 241–58.

'The Sheriffs of William the Conqueror', *Anglo-Norman Studies*, 5 (1982), 129–45.

The Government of England under Henry I (Cambridge: Cambridge University Press, 1986).

'Anglo–Scottish Relations, 1066–1174', *England and Her Neighbours 1066–1453: Essays in Honour of Pierre Chaplais*, ed. M. Jones and M. Vale (London: Hambledon Press, 1989), pp. 53–73.

English Sheriffs to 1154 (London: Her Majesty's Stationery Office, 1990).

The Aristocracy of Norman England (Cambridge: Cambridge University Press, 1997).

'The Charter of Liberties of Henry I', *Charter and Charter Scholarship in Britain and Ireland*, ed. M. T. Flanagan and J. A. Green (Houndmills: Palgrave, 2005), pp. 53–69.

Henry I: King of England and Duke of Normandy (Cambridge: Cambridge University Press, 2006).

'Duchesses of Normandy in the Eleventh and Twelfth Centuries', *Normandy and Its Neighbours 900–1250: Essays for David Bates*, ed. D. Crouch and K. Thompson (Turnhout: Brepols, 2011), pp. 43–59.

'Forest Laws in England and Normandy in the Twelfth Century', *Historical Research*, 86 (2013), 416–31.

'The Charters of Geoffrey de Mandeville', *Rulership and Rebellion in the Anglo-Norman World, c. 1066–c. 1216*, ed. P. Dalton and D. Luscombe (Farnham: Ashgate, 2015), pp. 91–110.

Grellard, C. and Lachaud, F. (eds.), *A Companion to John of Salisbury* (Leiden, Boston: Brill, 2015).

Grierson, P. 'Domesday Book: the Geld *de moneta* and *monetagium*: a Forgotten Minting Reform', *British Numismatic Journal*, 55 (1985), 84–94.

Griffith-Jones, R. and Park, D. (eds.), *The Temple Church in London* (Woodbridge: Boydell Press, 2010).

Gullick, M. 'Lanfranc and the Oldest Manuscript of the Collectio Lanfranci', *Bishops, Texts and the Use of Canon Law around 1100: Essays in Honour of Martin Brett*, ed. B. C. Brasington and K. G. Cushing (Aldershot: Ashgate, 2008), pp. 79–90.

Hadley, D. M. *The Northern Danelaw: Its Social Structure, c. 800–1100* (London: Leicester University Press, 2000).

'Viking and Native: Rethinking Identity in the Danelaw', *Early Medieval Europe*, 11 (2002), 45–70.

Vikings in England: Settlement, Society and Culture (Manchester: Manchester University Press, 2006).

Hagland, J. R. and Watson, B. 'Fact or Folklore: the Viking attack on London Bridge', *London Archaeologist*, 12 (Spring 2005), 328–33.

Hall, D. *The Open Fields of England* (Oxford: Oxford University Press, 2014).

Hallam, E. *Capetian France 987–1328* (Harlow: Longman, 1980).

Hallam, H. (ed.) *Agrarian History of England and Wales*, II, *1042–1350* (Cambridge: Cambridge University Press, 1988).

Harper-Bill, C. and Vincent, N. (eds.), *Henry II. New Interpretations* (Woodbridge: Boydell Press, 2007).

Harrison, S. A. 'Observations on the Architecture of the Galilee Chapel', *Anglo-Norman Durham*, ed. D. Rollason, D. Harvey, and M. Prestwich (Woodbridge: Boydell Press, 1994), pp. 213–34.

Hart, C. 'Athelstan "Half King" and His Family', *Anglo-Saxon England*, 2 (1973), 115–44.

The Danelaw (London: Hambledon Press, 1992).

Harvey, S. P. J. 'The Knight and the Knight's Fee in England', *Past and Present*, 49 (1970), 1–43.

'Domesday Book and Anglo-Norman Governance', *Transactions of the Royal Historical Society*, 5th Series, 25 (1975), 175–93.

'The Extent and Profitability of Demesne Agriculture in England in the Later Eleventh Century', *Social Relations and Ideas: Essays in Honour of R. H. Hilton*, ed. T. H. Aston, P. R. Coss, C. Dyer, and J. Thirsk (Cambridge: Cambridge University Press, 1983), pp. 45–72.

'Domesday England', *Agrarian History of England and Wales*, II, *1042–1350* (Cambridge: Cambridge University Press, 1988), 45–136.

Domesday: Book of Judgement (Oxford: Oxford University Press, 2014).

Haseldine, J. 'Friendship and Rivalry: the Role of Amicitia in Twelfth-Century Monastic Relations', *Journal of Ecclesiastical History*, 44 (1993), 390–414.

'Understanding the Language of Amicitia: the Friendship Circle of Peter of Celle (*c.* 1115–1183)', *Journal of Medieval History*, 20 (1994), 237–60.

Haslam, J. 'Parishes, Churches, Wards and Gates', *Minsters and Parish Churches: the Local Church in Transition, 950–1200* (Oxford: Oxford University Committee for Archaeology, 1988), pp. 35–43.

'King Alfred and the Development of London', *London Archaeologist* (Spring 2010), 208–12.

'The Development of London by King Alfred: a Reassessment', *Transactions of the London and Middlesex Archaeological Society*, 61 (2010), 109–44.

Hayward, P. 'The Importance of Being Ambiguous: Innuendo and Legerdemain in William of Malmesbury's *Gesta regum* and *Gesta pontificum Anglorum*', *Anglo-Norman Studies*, 33 (2010), 75–102.

'Saints and Cults', *A Social History of England 900–1200*, ed. J. Crick and E. Van Houts (Cambridge: Cambridge University Press, 2011), pp. 309–20.

Helmholz, R. 'Excommunication in Twelfth-Century England', *Journal of Law and Religion*, 11 (1994), 235–53.

'Excommunication and the Angevin Leap Forward', *Haskins Society Journal*, 7 (1995), 133–49.

Oxford History of the Laws of England. I. The Canon Law and Ecclesiastical Jurisdiction from 597 to the 1640s (Oxford: Oxford University Press, 2004).

Herbert, J. 'The Transformation of Hermitages into Augustinian Priories in Twelfth-Century England', *Monks, Hermits and the Ascetic Tradition: Papers Read at the 1984 Summer Meeting and 1985 Winter Meeting at the Ecclesiastical History Society*, ed. W. Sheils, Studies in Church History, 22 (1985), 131–45.

Heslin, A. 'The Coronation of the Young King', *Studies in Church History*, ed. G. J. Cuming, II (1965), pp. 165–78.

Hicks, L. 'Magnificent Entrances and Undignified Exits: the Symbolism of Castle Space in Normandy', *Journal of Medieval History*, 35 (2009), 52–69.

Higham, N. 'Northumbria's Southern Frontier: a Review', *Early Medieval Europe*, 14 (2006), 391–418.

Hill, D. (ed.), *Ethelred the Unready*, British Archaeological Reports, British Series, 59 (1978).

An Atlas of Anglo-Saxon England (Oxford: Blackwell, 1981).

Hill, F. *Medieval Lincoln* (reprinted edn, Stamford: Paul Watkins, 1990).

Hinton, D. A., Crawford S., and Hamerow, H. (eds.), *Oxford Handbook of Anglo-Saxon Archaeology* (Oxford: Oxford University Press, 2011).

Hobson, J. 'National-Ethnic Narratives in Eleventh Century Literary Representations of Cnut', *Anglo-Saxon England*, 43 (2014), 267–95.

Hodges, R. *Dark Age Economics: the Origins of Towns and Trade A. D. 600–1000* (London: Duckworth, 1982).

Hollis, S. '"The Protection of God and the King": Wulfstan's Legislation on Widows', *Wulfstan, Archbishop of York. The Proceedings of the Second Alcuin Conference*, ed. M. Townend (Turnhout: Brepols, 2004), pp. 443–60.

Holdsworth, C. 'War and Peace in the Twelfth Century: the Reign of Stephen Reconsidered', *War and Peace in the Middle Ages*, ed. B. P. McGuire (Copenhagen: Reitzel, 1987), pp. 67–93.

Holford, M. L. and Stringer, K. J. (eds.), *Border Liberties and Loyalties: north-East England, c. 1200-c. 1400* (Edinburgh: Edinburgh University Press, 2010).

Hollister, C. W. *Anglo-Saxon Military Institutions on the Eve of the Norman Conquest* (Oxford: Clarendon Press, 1962).

Monarchy, Magnates, and Institutions in the Anglo-Norman World (London: Hambledon Press, 1986), pp. 97–115.

'The Greater Domesday Tenants-in-Chief', *Domesday Studies*, ed. J. C. Holt (Woodbridge: Boydell Press, 1987), pp. 219–48.

Holt, J. C. *The Northerners. A Study in the Reign of King John* (Oxford: Clarendon Press, 1961).

What's in a Name? Family Nomenclature and the Norman Conquest, Stenton Lecture 1981 (Reading, 1982).

'The Introduction of Knight Service into England', *Anglo-Norman Studies*, 6 (1983), 89–106.

'1153', *The Anarchy of King Stephen's Reign*, ed. E. King (Oxford: Oxford University Press, 1994), pp. 291–316.

Colonial England (London: Hambledon Press, 1997).

Review of N. Fryde, *Why Magna Carta? Angevin England Revisited,* in *English Historical Review*, 118 (2003), 989.

Magna Carta, 3rd edn (Cambridge: Cambridge University Press, 2015).

Holt, J. C. (ed.), *Domesday Studies* (Woodbridge: Boydell Press, 1987).

Hooke, D. *The Anglo-Saxon Landscape: the Kingdom of the Hwicce* (Manchester: Manchester University Press, 1985).

Hooper, N. 'The Housecarls in England in the Eleventh Century', *Anglo-Norman Studies*, 7 (1985), 161–76.

'Some Observations on the Navy in Late Anglo-Saxon England', *Studies in Medieval History Presented to R. Allen Brown*, ed. C. Harper-Bill, C. Holdsworth, and J. L. Nelson (Woodbridge: Boydell Press, 1989), pp. 203–13.

'Military Developments in the Reign of Cnut', *The Reign of Cnut. King of England, Denmark and Norway*, ed. A. Rumble (London, New York: Leicester University Press, 1994), pp. 89–100.

Howard, I. *Swein Forkbeard's Invasions and the Danish Conquest of England, 991–1007* (Woodbridge: Boydell Press, 2003).

Hudson, J. *The Oxford History of the Laws of England. II, 871–1216* (Oxford, 2012).

'The Fate of Waltheof and the Idea of Personal Law in England after 1066', *Normandy and England 900–1250: Essays for David Bates*, ed. D. Crouch and K. Thompson (Turnhout: Brepols, 2013), pp. 223–35.

Huneycutt, L. L. *Matilda of Scotland. A Study in Medieval Queenship* (Woodbridge: Boydell Press, 2003).

Hyams, P. R. *Kings, Lords and Peasants in Medieval England: the Common Law of Villeinage in the Twelfth and Thirteenth Centuries* (Oxford: Oxford University Press, 1980).

Rancor and Reconciliation in Medieval England (Ithaca, NY, London: Cornell University Press, 2003).

Insley, C. 'Athelstan, Charters and the English in Cornwall', *Charter and Charter Scholarship in Britain and Ireland*, ed. M. T. Flanagan and J. A. Green (Houndmills: Palgrave, 2005), pp. 15–31.

'The Family of Wulfric Spott: an Anglo-Saxon Mercian Marcher Dynasty', *The English and Their Legacy 900–1200: Essays in Honour of Ann Williams*, ed. D. Roffe (Woodbridge: Boydell Press, 2012), pp. 115–28.

Ivens, R. J. 'Deddington Castle, Oxfordshire, and the English Honour of Odo of Bayeux', *Oxoniensia*, 49 (1984), 101–19.

Jamroziak, E. *Rievaulx Abbey and Its Social Context 1132–1300: memory, Locality and Networks* (Turnhout: Brepols, 2005).

Jankulak, K. *The Medieval Cult of St Petroc* (Woodbridge: Boydell Press, 2000).

Jewell, H. M. *The North-South Divide: the Origins of Northern Consciousness in England* (Manchester: Manchester University Press, 1994).

John, E. 'The Litigation of an Exempt House, St Augustine's, Canterbury, 1182–1237', *Bulletin of the John Rylands Library*, 39 (1957), 390–415.

Johns, S. M. *Noblewomen, Aristocracy and Power in the Twelfth-Century Anglo-Norman Realm* (Manchester: Manchester University Press, 2003).

Jolliffe, J. E. A. 'Northumbrian Institutions', *English Historical Review*, 41 (1926), 1–42.

Angevin Kingship (London: A. and C. Black, 1955).

Jones, M. and Vale, M. (eds.), *England and Her Neighbours 1066–1453: Essays in Honour of Pierre Chaplais* (London: Hambledon Press, 1989).

Jones, S. Rees, *York: the Making of a City 1068–1350* (Oxford: Oxford University Press, 2014).

Jones, S. Rees and Watson, S. (eds.), *Christians and Jews in Angevin England: the York Massacre of 1190* (Woodbridge: York Medieval Press, 2013).

Jonsson, K. *The New Era: the Reformation of the Late Anglo-Saxon Coinage* (Stockholm, London: Kungl. Myntkabinett, Kungl. Vitterhets, historie och Antikvitets Akademien, Spink and Sons, 1987).

'The Post-reform Coinage of Edgar – the Legacy of the Anglo-Saxon Kingdoms', *Coinage and History in the North Sea World c. 500–1250. essays in Honour of Marion Archibald*, ed. B. Cook and G. Williams (Leiden, Boston: Brill, 2006), pp. 325–46.

Kahn, D. 'The West Doorway at Rochester Cathedral', *Romanesque and Gothic: Essays for George Zarnecki*, ed. N. Stratford (Woodbridge: Boydell Press, 1987), pp. 129–34.

Kantorowicz, E. *The King's Two Bodies. A Study in Medieval Political Theology* (Princeton, NJ: Princeton University Press, 1957).

Kapelle, W. E. *The Norman Conquest of the North: the Region and Its Transformation, 1000–1135* (London: Croom Helm, 1979).

Karkov, C. E. *The Ruler Portraits of Anglo-Saxon England* (Woodbridge: Boydell Press, 2004).

Kealey, E. J. *Roger of Salisbury. Viceroy of England* (Berkeley, Los Angeles: University of California Press, 1972).

Keats-Rohan, K. S. B. 'The Prosopography of Post-Conquest England: Four Case Studies', *Medieval Prosopography*, 14 (1993), 1–50.

Domesday People: a Prosopography of Persons Occurring in English Documents, 1066–1166. I, Domesday Book (Woodbridge: Boydell Press, 1999): II, *Domesday Descendants. Pipe Rolls to Cartae Baronum* (Woodbridge: Boydell Press, 2002).

Keefe, T. K. 'Shrine Time: King Henry II's Visits to Thomas Becket's Tomb', *Haskins Society Journal*, 11 (1998), 115–22.

Keen, L. *Studies in the Early History of Shaftesbury Abbey* (Dorchester: Dorset County Council, 1999).

Keene, D. 'New Discoveries at the Hanseatic Steelyard of London', *Hansische Geschichtsblatter. Herausgegeben vom Hansischen Geschichtsverein*, 107 (1989) 15–25.

'Metropolitan Comparisons: London as a City-State', *Historical Research*, 77 (2004), 459–80.

'Text, Visualisation and Politics: London, 1150–1250', *Transactions of the Royal Historical Society*, 6th Series, 18 (2008), 69–99.

Keene, D., Burns, A., and Saint, A. (eds.), *St Paul's. The Cathedral Church of London 604–1204* (New Haven, CT, London: Yale University Press, 2004).

Kemp, B. 'Informing the Archdeacon on Ecclesiastical Matters in Twelfth-Century England', *Medieval Ecclesiastical Studies in Honour of Dorothy M. Owen*, ed. M. J. Franklin and C. Harper-Bill (Woodbridge: Boydell Press, 1995), pp. 131–49.

'The Acta of English Rural Deans in the Later Twelfth and Early Thirteenth Centuries', *The Foundations of Medieval Ecclesiastical History. Studies Presented to David Smith*, ed. P. Hoskin, C. Brooke, and B. Dobson (Woodbridge: Boydell Press, 2005), pp. 139–58.

Kerr, J. *Monastic Hospitality: the Benedictines in England, c. 1070–c. 1250* (Woodbridge: Boydell Press, 2007).

Keynes, S. D. 'The Declining Reputation of King Æthelred the Unready', *Ethelred the Unready*, ed. D. Hill, British Archaeological Reports, British Series, 59 (1978), pp. 227–53.

The Diplomas of King Æthelred 'the Unready', 978–1016: a Study in Their Use as Historical Evidence (Cambridge: Cambridge University Press, 1986).

'Cnut's Earls', *The Reign of Cnut. King of England, Denmark and Norway*, ed. A. Rumble (London, New York: Leicester University Press, 1994), pp. 43–88.

'The Burial of King Æthelred the Unready at St Paul's', *The English and Their Legacy 900–1200: Essays in Honour of Ann Williams*, ed. D. Roffe (Woodbridge: Boydell Press, 2012), pp. 129–48.

King, D. J. Cathcart, *Castellarium Anglicanum*, 2 vols. (Milwood, London, Nendeln: Kraus, 1983).

King, E. *Peterborough Abbey 1086–1310* (Cambridge: Cambridge University Press, 1973).

King, E. (ed.), *The Anarchy of King Stephen's Reign* (Oxford: Oxford University Press, 1994).

King Stephen (New Haven, CT, London: Yale University Press, 2010).

Knowles, D. *The Monastic Order in England. From the Times of St Dunstan to the Fourth Lateran Council*, 2nd edn (Cambridge: Cambridge University Press, 1963).

Koziol, G. 'England, France, and the Problem of Sacrality in Twelfth-Century Ritual', *Cultures of Power: Lordship, Status and Process in Twelfth-Century Europe*, ed. T. N. Bisson (Philadelphia: University of Pennsylvania Press, 1995), pp. 124–48.

Kuttner S. and Rathbone, E. 'Anglo-Norman Canonists of the Twelfth Century: an Introductory Study', *Traditio*, 7 (1949–51), 279–358.

Lamb, H. H. *Climate, History and the Modern World* (London: Methuen, 1982).

Lapidge, M. *Anglo-Saxon Minsters of Winchester*, 4 part 2. *The Cult of St Swithun* (Oxford: Clarendon Press, 2002).

Lapidge, M., Blair, J., Keynes, S., and Scragg, D. (eds.), *Blackwell Encyclopaedia of Anglo-Saxon England* (Oxford: Blackwell, 1999).

Larson, L. M. *Canute the Great (circ.) 995–1035 and the Rise of Danish Imperialism during the Viking Age* (New York: Putnam, 1912).

Latimer, P. 'Henry II's Campaign against the Welsh in 1165', *Welsh Historical Review*, 14 (1989), 523–52.

'Assimilation in North-Western England from the Norman Conquest to the Early Thirteenth Century: the Kirkby, Pennington and Copeland Families', *Northern History*, 47 (2010), 49–66.

Lavelle, R. *Æthelred II King of the English 978–1016* (Stroud: Tempus, 2002).

Alfred's Wars: Sources and Interpretation of Anglo-Saxon Warfare in the Viking Age (Woodbridge: Boydell Press, 2010).

Lawrence-Mathers, A. *The True History of Merlin the Magician* (New Haven, CT, London: Yale University Press, 2012).

'John of Worcester and the Science of History', *Journal of Medieval History*, 39 (2013), 255–74.

Lawson, M. K. *Cnut: the Danes in England in the Eleventh Century* (Harlow: Longman, 1993).

Legg, L. G. Wickham (ed.), *English Coronation Records* (Westminster: Constable, 1901).

Le Maho, J. 'Note sur l'histoire d'un habitat seigneurial des XIe et XII siècles en Normandie: Mirville (S. Mme)', *Anglo-Norman Studies*, 7 (1984), 214–23.

Le Patourel, J. *The Norman Empire* (Oxford: Clarendon Press, 1976)

Lewis, C. P. 'The Norman Settlement of Hereford under William I', *Anglo-Norman Studies*, 7 (1984), 195–213.

'The Formation of the Earldom of Chester, 1066–1100', *The Earldom of Chester and Its Charters*, ed. A. Thacker, *Journal of the Chester Archaeological Society*, 71 (1991), pp. 37–68.

'The Early Earls of Norman England', *Anglo-Norman Studies*, 13 (1991), 207–23.

'Edgar, Chester, and the Kingdom of the Mercians', *Edgar King of the English, 959–975: New Interpretations*, ed. D. Scragg (Woodbridge: Boydell Press, 2008), pp. 104–23.

Licence, T. 'History and Hagiography in the Late Eleventh Century: the Life and Work of Herman the Archdeacon', *English Historical Review*, 124 (2009), 516–44.

Hermits and Recluses in English Society 950–1200 (Oxford: Oxford University Press, 2011).

Licence, T. (ed.), *Bury St Edmunds and the Norman Conquest* (Woodbridge: Boydell Press, 2014).

Liddiard, R. 'Castle Rising Norfolk: a "Landscape of Lordship"?', *Anglo-Norman Studies*, 22 (1999), 169–86.

   Landscapes of Lordship. Norman Castles and the Countryside in Medieval Norfolk, 1066–1200, British Archaeological Reports, British Series, 309 (2000).

Liddiard, R. (ed.), *Anglo-Norman Castles* (Woodbridge: Boydell Press, 2002).

Lieberman, M. *The March of Wales 1067–1300: a Borderland of Medieval Britain* (Cardiff: University of Wales Press, 2008).

   'The Medieval "Marches" of Normandy and Wales', *English Historical Review*, 125 (2010), 1357–81.

   'A New Approach to the Knighting Ritual', *Speculum*, 90 (2015), 391–423.

Lionarons, J. T. *The Homiletic Writings of Archbishop Wulfstan: a Critical Study* (Woodbridge: D. S. Brewer, 2010).

Little, L. K. *Benedictine Maledictions: Liturgical Cursing in Romanesque France* (Ithaca, NY, London: Cornell University Press, 1993).

Lukes, S. (ed.), *Power* (New York: New York University Press, 1986).

Lund, N. 'The Armies of Swein Forkbeard and Cnut: *leding* or *lið*?', *Anglo-Saxon England*, 15 (1986), 105–18.

Luscombe, D. 'John of Salisbury and Courtiers' Trifles', *Rulership and Rebellion in the Anglo-Norman World, c. 1066–c. 1216*, ed. P. Dalton and D. Luscombe (Farnham: Ashgate, 2015), pp. 141–61.

Mack, K. 'Changing Thegns: Cnut's Conquest and the English Aristocracy', *Albion*, 16 (1984), 375–87.

Maddicott, J. R. 'Edward the Confessor's Return to England in 1041', *English Historical Review*, 119 (2004), 650–66.

   The Origins of the English Parliament 924–1327 (Oxford: Oxford University Press, 2010).

Madox, T. *The History and Antiquities of the Exchequer of England*, 2nd edn (London: W. Owen and B. White, 1769).

Mahany C. and Roffe, D. 'Stamford: the Development of an Anglo-Scandinavian Borough', *Anglo-Norman Studies*, 5 (1982), 197–219.

Mann, M. *The Sources of Social Power*, 4 vols. (Cambridge: Cambridge University Press, 1986–2012).

Marritt, S. 'Crowland Abbey and the Provenance of Orderic Vitalis's Scandinavian and Scottish Material', *Notes and Queries*, 53 (2006), 290–2.

   'Drogo the Sheriff: a Neglected Lost Romance Tradition and Anglo-Norwegian Relations in the Twelfth Century', *Historical Research*, 80 (2007), 157–84.

   'Reeds Shaken by the Wind? Bishops in Local and Regional Politics in King Stephen's Reign', *King Stephen's Reign 1135–1154*, ed. P. Dalton and G. White (Woodbridge: Boydell Press, 2008), pp. 115–38.

Marten, L. 'The Shiring of East Anglia: an Alternative Scenario', *Historical Research*, 81 (2008), 1–27.

'Meet the Swarts: Tracing a Thegnly Family in Late Anglo-Saxon England', *The English and Their Legacy 900–1200: essays in Honour of Ann Williams*, ed. D. Roffe (Woodbridge: Boydell Press, 2012), pp. 17–32.

Mason, E. *St Wulfstan of Worcester c. 1008–1095* (Oxford: Blackwell, 1990).

Mason, J. F. A. 'Roger of Montgomery and His Sons', *Transactions of the Royal Historical Society*, 5th Series, 13 (1963), 1–28.

Matthew, D. J. A. *The Norman Monasteries and Their English Possessions* (London: Oxford University Press, 1962).

Matthew, H. C. G. and B. Harrison (eds.), *Oxford Dictionary of National Biography*, 61 vols. (Oxford: Oxford University Press in association with the British Academy, 2004).

Mayr-Harting, H. 'Hilary, Bishop of Chichester (1147–1169) and Henry II', *English Historical Review*, 78 (1963), 209–24.

Religion, Politics and Society in Britain 1066–1272 (Harlow: Pearson Education, 2011).

McKisack, M. 'London and the Succession to the Crown in the Middle Ages', *Studies in Medieval History Presented to F. M. Powicke*, ed. R. W. Hunt, W. A. Pantin, and R. W. Southern (Oxford: Clarendon Press, 1948), pp. 76–89.

McNamara, J. A. 'The *Herrenfrage*: the Restructuring of the Gender System, 1050–1150', *Medieval Masculinities: Regarding Men in the Middle Ages*, ed. C. A. Lees (Minneapolis: University of Minnesota Press, 1994), pp. 3–29.

Meehan, B. 'The Siege of Durham, the Battle of Carham and the Cession of Lothian', *Scottish Historical Review*, 55 (1976), 1–19.

Metcalf, D. M. 'The Taxation of Moneyers under Edward the Confessor and in 1086', *Domesday Studies*, ed. J. C. Holt (Woodbridge: Boydell Press, 1987), pp. 279–93.

Miller, E. *The Abbey and Bishopric of Ely* (Cambridge: Cambridge University Press, 1951).

Miller, E. and Hatcher, J. *Medieval England. Rural Society and Economic Change 1086–1348* (London: Longman, 1978).

Medieval England. Towns, Commerce and Crafts (London: Longman, 1995).

Mitchell, S. K. *Taxation in Medieval England* (New Haven, CT: Yale University Press, 1971 reprint).

Molyneaux, G. 'Why were some Tenth-century English Kings presented as Rulers of Britain?' *Transactions of the Royal Historical Society*, 6th Series, 21 (2011), 59–91.

The Formation of the English Kingdom in the Tenth Century (Oxford: Oxford University Press, 2015).

Moore, J. S. 'Domesday Slavery', *Anglo-Norman Studies*, 11 (1988), 191–220.

'The Anglo-Norman Family: size and Structure', *Anglo-Norman Studies*, 14 (1991), 153–96.

'Quot Homines? The Population of Domesday England', *Anglo-Norman Studies*, 19 (1996), 307–34.

Morey, A. *Bartholomew of Exeter* (Cambridge: Cambridge University Press, 1937).

Gilbert Foliot and His Letters (Cambridge: Cambridge University Press, 1965).

Morillo, S. *Warfare under the Anglo-Norman Kings 1066–1135* (Woodbridge: Boydell Press, 1994).

Morris, C. J. *Marriage and Murder in Eleventh-Century Northumbria: a Study of the 'De Obsessione Dunelmi'*, University of York Borthwick Paper, 72 (1992).

Morris, W. A. *The Medieval English Sheriff to 1300* (Manchester: Manchester University Press, 1927).

Mortimer, R. 'The Family of Ranulf de Glanville', *Historical Research*, 54 (1981), 1–16.

Naismith, R. 'London and Its Mint, *c.* 880–1066: a Preliminary Survey', *British Numismatic Journal*, 83 (2013), 44–74.

Nelson, J. L. 'The Rites of the Conqueror', *Anglo-Norman Studies*, 4 (1981), 117–32, 210–21.

'Inauguration Rituals', *Politics and Ritual in Early Medieval Europe* (London: Hambledon Press, 1986), pp. 283–307.

Nicholl, D. *Thurstan Archbishop of York (1114–40)* (York: Stonegate Press, 1964).

Nightingale, P. *Trade, Money and Power in Medieval England* (Aldershot: Ashgate, 2007).

O'Brien, B. 'From *Morðor* to *Murdrum*: the Preconquest Origin and Norman Revival of the Murder Fine', *Speculum*, 71 (1996), 321–57.

God's Peace and King's Peace. The Laws of Edward the Confessor (Philadelphia: University of Philadelphia Press, 1999).

Oosthuizen, S. 'The Emperor's Old Clothes: the Origins of Medieval Nucleated Settlements and Their Open fields', *Medieval Settlement Research*, 28 (2013), 96–8.

Owen, D. 'Bishop's Lynn: the First Century of a New Town?', *[Proceedings of the Battle Conference on] Anglo-Norman Studies*, 2 (1979), 141–53, 196–7.

Padel, O. 'Geoffrey of Monmouth and Cornwall', *Cambridge Medieval Celtic Studies*, 8 (1984), 1–27.

Page, W. *London: Its Origin and Early Development* (London: Constable, 1923).

Palliser, D. M. *Medieval York: 600–1540* (Oxford: Oxford University Press, 2014).

Pedersen, A. 'Power and Aristocracy', *Vikings. Life and Legend*, ed. G. Williams, P. Pentz, and M. Wemhoff (London: British Museum Press, 2014), pp. 122–55.

Perks, J. C. *Chepstow Castle Gwent. Castell Cas-gwent*, 2nd edn, 6th impression (London: HMSO, 1978).

Postles, D. 'The Foundation of Oseney Abbey', *Historical Research*, 53 (1980), 242–4.

Potter, V., Poulter, M., and Allen, J. *The Building of Orford Castle: a Translation from the Pipe Rolls 1163–1178* (Orford: Orford Museum, 2002).

Power, D. J. *The Norman Frontier in the Twelfth and Early Thirteenth Centuries* (Cambridge: Cambridge University Press, 2004).

Power, R. 'Magnus Barelegs' Expeditions to the West', *Scottish Historical Review*, 65 (1986), 107–32.

Pratt, D. 'Demesne Exemptions from Royal Taxation in Anglo-Norman England', *English Historical Review*, 128 (2013), 1–34.

Pryce, H. 'British or Welsh? National Identity in Twelfth-Century Wales', *English Historical Review*, 116 (2001), 775–801.

Rahtz, P. *The Saxon and Medieval Palaces at Cheddar: an Interim Report of Excavations in 1960–1962*, British Archaeological Reports, British Series, 65 (1979).

Ramsay, N., Sparks, M., and Brown, T. Tatton (eds.), *St Dunstan: His Life, Times and Cult* (Woodbridge: Boydell Press, 1992).

Reedy, W. T. 'The Origin of the General Eyre in the Reign of Henry I', *Speculum*, 41 (1966), 688–724.

Reynolds, A. *Anglo-Saxon Deviant Burial Customs* (Oxford: Oxford University Press, 2009).

Reynolds, S. 'The Rulers of London in the Twelfth Century', *History*, 57 (1972), 337–57.

Kingdoms and Communities in Western Europe 900–1300 (Oxford: Clarendon Press, 1984).

'There Were States in Medieval Europe: a Response to Rees Davies', *Journal of Historical Sociology*, 16 (2003), 550–5.

Riall, N. 'The New Castles of Henry de Blois as Bishop of Winchester: the Case against Farnham, Surrey', *Medieval Archaeology*, 47 (2003), 115–29.

Richardson, A. 'Gender and Space in English Royal Palaces c. 1160–c. 1547: a Study in Access Analysis and Imagery', *Medieval Archaeology*, 47 (2003), 131–65.

Richardson, H. G. and Sayles, G. O. *The Governance of Mediaeval England* (Edinburgh: Edinburgh University Press, 1963).

Ridyard, S. *The Royal Saints of Anglo-Saxon England* (Cambridge: Cambridge University Press, 1988).

Roach, L. *Kingship and Consent in Anglo-Saxon England 871–978: Assemblies and the State in the Early Middle Ages* (Cambridge: Cambridge University Press, 2013).

'Law Codes and Legal Norms in Later Anglo-Saxon England', *Historical Research*, 86 (2013), 465–86.

Roffe, D. 'The Lincolnshire Hundred', *Landscape History*, 3 (1981), 27–36.

'The Origins of Derbyshire', *Derbyshire Archaeological Journal*, 106 (1986), 102–22.

'Nottinghamshire and the Five Boroughs', *History in the Making, 1986: Papers from a Seminar of Recent Historical Research on Nottingham and Nottinghamshire 6 September 1986*, ed. S. N. Mastoris (Nottingham: Nottingham Museums, 1987), pp. 7–11.

'From Thegnage to Barony: Sake and Soke, Title and Tenants-in-Chief', *Anglo-Norman Studies*, 12 (1989), 157–76.

Roffe, D. (ed.), *The English and Their Legacy 900–1200: Essays in Honour of Ann Williams* (Woodbridge: Boydell Press, 2012).

Rollason, D., Harvey, M., and Prestwich, M. (eds.), *Anglo-Norman Durham* (Woodbridge: Boydell Press, 1994).

Rosser, G. *Medieval Westminster: the Vill and the Community 1200–1540* (Oxford: Clarendon Press, 1989).

'Myth, Image and Social Process in the English Medieval Town', *Urban History*, 23 (1996), 5–25.

Round, J. H. *Geoffrey de Mandeville* (London: Longmans, Green, 1892).

Studies in Peerage and Family History (Westminster: Constable and Co, 1900).

King's Serjeants and Officers of State with Their Coronation Services (London: Nisbet and Co, 1911).

Rubinstein, J. 'Liturgy against History: the Competing Visions of Lanfranc and Eadmer of Canterbury', *Speculum*, 74 (1999), 279–309.

Rumble A. (ed.), *The Reign of Cnut. King of England, Denmark and Norway* (London and New York: Leicester University Press, 1994).

Rumble, A. R. and Hill, D. (eds.), *Defence of Wessex: Burghal Hidage and Anglo-Saxon Fortifications* (Manchester: Manchester University Press, 1996).

Salter, H. E. 'Geoffrey of Monmouth and Oxford', *English Historical Review*, 34 (1919), 382–5.

Sanders, I. J. *English Baronies* (Oxford: Oxford University Press, 1960).

Sands, H., Braun, H., and Loyd, L. C. 'Conisbrough and Mortemer', *Yorkshire Archaeological Journal*, 32 (1936), 147–59.

Saunders, C. J. *Rape and Ravishment in the Literature of Medieval England* (Cambridge: Cambridge University Press, 2001).

Sawyer, P. H. *The Wealth of Anglo-Saxon England* (Oxford: Oxford University Press, 2013).

Scales, L. and Zimmer, O. (eds.), *Power and the Nation in European History* (Cambridge: Cambridge University Press, 2005).

Schofield, J. *The Building of London from the Conquest to the Great Fire*, 3rd edn (Stroud: Sutton Publishing, 1999).

'Saxon and Medieval Parish Churches in the City of London: a Review', *Transactions of the London and Middlesex Archaeological Society*, 45 (1994), 23–145.

London 1100–1600. The Archaeology of a Capital City (Sheffield: Equinox, 2011).

Scragg, D. (ed.), *The Battle of Maldon* (Manchester: Manchester University Press, 1981).

Edgar King of the English, 959–975: New Interpretations (Woodbridge: Boydell Press, 2008).

Searle, E. *Lordship and Community. Battle Abbey and Its Banlieu* (Toronto: Pontifical Institute of Medieval Studies, 1974).

Sharpe, R. 'The Setting of St Augustine's Translation, 1091', *Canterbury and the Norman Conquest: Churches, Saints, and Scholars, 1066–1109*, ed. R. Eales and R. Sharpe (London: Hambledon Press, 1995), pp. 1–13.

'1088: William II and the Rebels', *Anglo-Norman Studies*, 26 (2003), 139–57.

'The Use of Writs in the Eleventh Century', *Anglo-Saxon England*, 32 (2003), 247–91.

Norman Rule in Cumbria, 1092–1136, Cumberland and Westmorland Antiquarian and Archaeological Society Tract Series, 21 (2006).

Sheppard, J. 'Medieval Village Planning in Northern England', *Journal of Historical Geography*, 2 (1976), 3–20.

Short, I. 'Patrons and Polyglots: French Literature in Twelfth- and Thirteenth-Century England', *Anglo-Norman Studies*, 14 (1991), 229–49.

Smyth, A. *Scandinavian York and Dublin. The History and Archaeology of Two Related Viking Kingdoms*, 2 vols. (Dublin: Templekieran Press, 1975–9).

Sønnesyn, S. O. *William of Malmesbury and the Ethics of History* (Woodbridge: Boydell Press, 2012).

Southern, R. W. 'Ranulf Flambard', Alexander Prize Essay, first published in *Transactions of the* Royal *Historical Society*, 4th Series, 16 (1933), 95–128, reprinted in Southern, *Medieval Humanism.*

'The Place of Henry I in English History', *Proceedings of the British Academy*, 47 (1962), 127–69, reprinted in Southern, *Medieval Humanism.*

Medieval Humanism and Other Studies (Oxford: Blackwell Press, 1970).

St Anselm: a Portrait in a Landscape (Cambridge: Cambridge University Press, 1990).

Stafford, P. 'The Reign of Æthelred II: a Study in the Limitations on Royal Policy and Action', *Ethelred the Unready*, ed. D. Hill, British Archaeological Reports, British Series, 59 (1978), pp. 15–46.

'The Laws of Cnut and the History of Anglo-Saxon Royal Promises', *Anglo-Saxon England*, 10 (1981), 173–90.

The East Midlands in the Early Middle Ages (Leicester: Leicester University Press, 1985).

Unification and Conquest: a Political and Social History of England in the Tenth and Eleventh Centuries (London: Edward Arnold, 1989).

'Women and the Norman Conquest', *Transactions of the Royal Historical Society*, 6th Series, 4 (1994), 221–49.

Queen Emma and Queen Edith: Queenship and Women's Power in Eleventh-Century England (Oxford: Blackwell, 1997).

'Cherchez la Femme: Queens, Queens' Lands and Nunneries: Missing Links in the Foundation of Reading Abbey', *History*, 85 (2000), 4–27.

Stalley, R. A. 'A Twelfth-Century Patron of Architecture: a Study of the Buildings Erected by Roger, Bishop of Salisbury, 1102–1139', *Journal of the British Archaeological Association*, 34 (1971), 62–83.

Stancliffe, C. and Cambridge, E. (eds.), *Oswald: Northumbrian King to European Saint* (Stamford: Paul Watkins, 1995).

Stenton, F. M. *The First Century of English Feudalism*, 2nd edn (Oxford: Clarendon Press, 1961).

Stewart, I. 'Coinage and Recoinage after Edgar's Reforms', *Studies in Anglo-Saxon Coinage*, ed. K. Jonsson, Numismatiska Meddelanden, 35 (Stockholm 1990), 455–85.

Stratford, N. (ed.), *Romanesque and Gothic: Essays for George Zarnecki*, 2 vols. (Woodbridge: Boydell Press, 1987).

Strevett, N. 'The Anglo-Norman Civil War of 1101 Reconsidered', *Anglo-Norman Studies*, 26 (2003), 159–75.

Strickland, M. 'On the Instruction of a Prince: the Upbringing of Henry, the Young King', *Henry II. New Interpretations*, ed. C. Harper-Bill and N. Vincent (Woodbridge: Boydell Press, 2007), pp. 184–214.

Strong, R. *Coronation. From the 8th to the 21st Century* (London: Harper Perennial, 2006).

Tait, J. *Medieval Manchester and the Beginnings of Manchester* (Manchester: Manchester University Press, 1904).

The Medieval English Borough: Studies on Its Origins and Constitutional History (Manchester: Manchester University Press, 1936).

Taylor, P. 'The Endowment and Military Obligations of the See of London: a Reassessment of Three Sources', *Anglo-Norman Studies*, 14 (1991), 287–312.

Thacker, A. 'The Cult of Saints and the Liturgy', *St Paul's. The Cathedral Church of London 604–1204*, ed. D. Keene, A. Burns, and A. Saint (New Haven, CT, London: Yale University Press, 2004), pp. 113–22.

Thacker, A. (ed.), *The Earldom of Chester and Its Charters, Journal of the Chester Archaeological Society*, 71 (1991).

Thomas, H. M. *Vassals, Heiresses, Crusaders and Thugs: the Knightly Class of Angevin Yorkshire, 1154–1216* (Philadelphia: University of Pennsylvania Press, 1993).

The English and the Normans: Ethnic Hostility, Assimilation, and Identity, 1066–c.1220 (Oxford: Oxford University Press, 2003).

'Violent Disorder in England: a Maximum Argument', *King Stephen's Reign 1135–1154*, ed. P. Dalton and G. J. White (Woodbridge: Boydell Press, 2008), pp. 139–70.

The Secular Clergy in England, 1066–1216 (Oxford: Oxford University Press, 2014).

Thompson, K. 'A Different *Diffidatio*: Violence, Litigation and the Lord of Courville from the Letters of Ivo of Chartres', *Rulership and Rebellion in the Anglo-Norman World, c. 1066–c. 1216*, ed. P. Dalton and D. Luscombe (Farnham: Ashgate, 2015), pp. 77–90.

Thompson, M. W. *Medieval Bishops' Houses in England and Wales* (Aldershot: Ashgate, 1998).

Tillmann, H. *Die Päpstlichen Legaten in England bis zur beendigung der Legation Gualas (1218)* (Bonn: H. Ludwig, 1926).

Tollerton, L. *Wills and Will-Making in Anglo-Saxon England* (York: York Medieval Press, 2005).

Townend, M. 'Contextualizing the Knútsdrápur: Skaldic Praise-Poetry at the Court of Cnut', *Anglo-Saxon England*, 30 (2001), 145–79.

Language and History in Viking Age England: Linguistic Relations between Speakers of Old Norse and Old English (Turnhout: Brepols, 2002).

'Cnut's Poets: an Old Norse Literary Community in Eleventh-Century England', *Conceptualizing Multilingualism in Medieval England, 800–1250*, ed. E. M. Tyler (Turnhout: Brepols, 2011), pp. 197–215.

Townend, M. (ed.), *Wulfstan, Archbishop of York. The Proceedings of the Second Alcuin Conference* (Turnhout: Brepols, 2004).

Treharne, E. *Living through Conquest. The Politics of Early English 1020–1220* (Oxford: Oxford University Press, 2012).

Tsurushima, H. 'The Fraternity of Rochester Cathedral Priory about 1100', *Anglo-Norman Studies*, 14 (1991), 313–37.

Tudor, V. 'The Cult of St Cuthbert in the Twelfth Century: the Evidence of Reginald of Durham', *St Cuthbert, His Cult and Community*, ed. Bonner, Rollason, and Stancliffe, pp. 447–67.

Turner, R. V. *Men Raised from the Dust: Administrative Service and Upward Mobility in Angevin England* (Philadelphia: University of Pennsylvania Press, 1988).

Eleanor of Aquitaine (New Haven, CT, London: Yale University Press, 2009).

Turner, S. *Making a Christian Landscape: the Countryside in Early Medieval Cornwall, Devon, and Wessex* (Exeter: Exeter University Press, 2006).

Tyerman, C. *England and the Crusades 1095–1588* (Chicago, London: University of Chicago Press, 1988).

Tyler, E. M. *Conceptualizing Multilingualism in Medieval England, 800–1250* (Turnhout: Brepols, 2011).

Van Caenegem, R. C. *Royal Writs in England from the Conquest to Glanvill*, Selden Society, 77 (1959).

'Public prosecution in Twelfth-Century England', *Church and Government in the Middle Ages: Essays presented to C. R. Cheney on His Seventieth Birthday*, ed. C. N. L. Brooke, D. E. Luscombe, G. H. Martin, and D. Owen (Cambridge: Cambridge University Press, 1976), pp. 41–76.

Van Houts, E. 'Intermarriage in Eleventh-Century England', *Normandy and Its Neighbours 900–1250: Essays for David Bates*, ed. D. Crouch and K. Thompson (Turnhout: Brepols, 2011), pp. 237–70.

Vaughn, S. *The Abbey of Bec and the Anglo-Norman State 1034–1136* (Woodbridge: Boydell Press, 1981).

Vincent, N. 'Henry II and the Monks of Battle: the Battle Chronicle Unmasked', *Belief and Culture in the Middle Ages: Studies Presented to Henry Mayr-Harting*, ed. R. Gameson and H. Leyser (Oxford: Oxford University Press, 2001), pp. 264–86.

'The Pilgrimages of the Angevin Kings of England', *Pilgrimage: the English Experience from Becket to Bunyan*, ed. C. Morris and P. Roberts (Cambridge: Cambridge University Press, 2002), pp. 12–45.

'The Court of Henry II', *Henry II. New Interpretations*, ed. C. Harper-Bill and N. Vincent (Woodbridge: Boydell Press, 2007), pp. 278–334.

'Did Henry II Have a Policy towards the Earls?', *War, Government and Aristocracy in the British Isles c. 1150–1500: Essays in Honour of Michael Prestwich*, ed. C. Given-Wilson, A. Kettle, and L. Scales (Woodbridge: Boydell Press, 2008), pp. 1–25.

Vinogradoff, P. *Villainage in England: Essays in English Medieval History* (Oxford: Clarendon Press, 1892).

Vroom, W. *Financing Cathedral Building in the Middle Ages: the Generosity of the Faithful* (Amsterdam: Amsterdam University Press, 2010).

Wallis, S. *The Oxford Henge and Late Saxon Massacre with Medieval and Later Occupation at St John's College Oxford*, Thames Valley Archaeological Service Monograph, 17 (2014).

Wareham, A. 'The "Feudal Revolution" in Eleventh-Century East Anglia', *Anglo-Norman Studies*, 22 (1999), 293–321.

  Lords and Communities in Medieval East Anglia (Woodbridge: Boydell Press, 2006).

Wareham, J. *Three Palaces of the Bishops of Winchester Wolvesey (Old Bishop's Palace), Hampshire, Bishop's Waltham Palace Hampshire, Farnham Castle Keep Surrey* (London: English Heritage, 2000).

Warren, W. L. 'The Myth of Norman Administrative Efficiency', *Transactions of the Royal Historical Society*, 6th Series, 34 (1984), 113–32.

  Governance of Norman and Angevin England (London: Edward Arnold, 1987).

  Henry II, revised edn (New Haven, CT, London: Yale University Press, 2000).

Watkins, C. *History and the Supernatural in Medieval England* (Cambridge: Cambridge University Press, 2008).

Watson, B. 'The Excavation of a Norman Fortress on Ludgate Hill', *London Archaeologist*, 6 no. 14 (Spring 1992), 371–7.

Watson, B., Brigham, T., and Dyson, T. *London Bridge: 2000 Years of a River Crossing*, Museum of London Archaeological Service, Monograph 8 (2001).

Weber, M. *Economy and Society. An Outline of Interpretive Sociology*, ed. G. Roth and C. Wittich, I (Berkeley, London: University of California Press, 1978).

Weiler, B. 'William of Malmesbury on Kingship', *History*, 90 (2005), 3–22.

  'William of Malmesbury, King Henry I, and the *Gesta Regum Anglorum*', *Anglo-Norman Studies*, 31 (2008), 157–76.

West, F. J. *The Justiciarship in England 1066–1232* (Cambridge: Cambridge University Press, 1966).

White, G. J. *Restoration and Reform, 1153–1165: Recovery from Civil War in England* (Cambridge: Cambridge University Press, 2000).

White, G. J. and Pepler, J. *The Magna Carta of Cheshire*, Cheshire Local History Association (Chester, 2015).

Whitelock, D. 'The Dealings of the Kings of England with Northumbria in the Tenth and Eleventh Centuries', *The Anglo-Saxons: Studies in Some Aspects of Their History and Culture Presented to Bruce Dickins*, ed. P. Clemoes (London: Bowes and Bowes, 1959), pp. 70–88.

Wightman, W. E. *The Lacy Family in England and Normandy 1066–1194* (Oxford: Clarendon Press, 1966).

Williams, A. 'Some Notes and Considerations Connected with the English Royal Succession, 860–1066', *[Proceedings of the Battle Conference on] Anglo-Norman Studies*, 1 (1978), 144–67, 225–33.

  '*Princeps Merciorum Gentis*: the Family, Career and Connections of Ælfhere, ealdorman of Mercia', *Anglo-Saxon England*, 10 (1981), 143–72.

  'Cockles among the Wheat: Danes and English in the Western Midlands in the First Half of the Eleventh Century', *Midland History*, 11 (1986), 1–22.

'A Bell-House and a Burh-geat: Lordly Residences in England before the Norman Conquest', *Medieval Knighthood*, IV, ed. C. Harper-Bill and R. Harvey (Woodbridge: Boydell Press, 1992), pp. 221–40, reprinted in *Anglo-Norman Castles* (ed. Liddiard), pp. 23–40.

Kingship and Government in Pre-Conquest England, c. 500–1066 (Houndmills: Macmillan, 1999).

Æthelred the Unready: the Ill-Counselled King (London: Hambledon Press and London, 2003).

The World before Domesday: the English Aristocracy 871–1066 (London: Hambledon Press Continuum, 2008).

'Regional Communities and Royal Authority in the late Old English Kingdom: the Crisis of 1051–1052 Revisited', *History*, 98 (2013), 23–40.

Williamson, T. *Shaping Medieval Landscapes. Settlement, Society, Environment* (Macclesfield: Windgather Press, 2003).

Winchester, A. J. L. *Landscape and Society in Medieval Cumbria* (Edinburgh: Edinburgh University Press, 1987).

Wood, M. *The English Medieval House* (London: J. M. Dent and Sons, 1965).

Woolf, A. *From Pictland to Alba 789–1070*, New Edinburgh History of Scotland, 2 (Edinburgh: Edinburgh University Press, 2007).

Wormald, P. '*Engla Lond*: the Making of an Allegiance', *Journal of Historical Sociology*, 7 (1994), 1–24.

The Making of English Law: King Alfred to the Twelfth Century. I, *Legislation and Lawsuits* (Oxford: Blackwell, 1999).

'Germanic Power Structures: the Early English Experience', *Power and the Nation in European History*, ed. L. Scales and O. Zimmer (Cambridge: Cambridge University Press, 2005), pp. 105–24.

Wyatt, D. *Slaves and Warriors in Medieval Britain and Ireland, 800–1200* (Leiden, Boston: Brill, 2009).

Yarrow, S. *Saints and Their Communities: Miracle Stories in Twelfth-Century England* (Oxford: Clarendon Press, 2006).

Young, A. *William Cumin: Border Politics and the Bishopric of Durham 1141–1144*, University of York Borthwick Paper, 52 (1978).

Zarnecki, G. *Romanesque Lincoln. The Sculpture of the Frieze* (Lincoln: Honeywood Press, 1988).

4 UNPUBLISHED THESES

T. J. Gobbitt, 'The Production and Use of MS Cambridge, Corpus Christi College 383 in the Late Eleventh and Early Twelfth Centuries', PhD thesis, Leeds University, 2010.

M. Philpott, 'Archbishop Lanfranc and Canon Law', D. Phil. thesis (Oxford, 1993).

5 ONLINE SOURCES

Anglo-Norman Anonymous http://normananonymous.org/ENAP/ToC.jsp

Annals of Inisfallen www.ucc.ie/celt/published/T100004/

Annals of the Four Masters www.ucc.ie/celt/published/T100005a/

K. D. Lilley, 'Imagining the City: Christian Symbolism and Chester's Medieval Urban Form', www.medievalchester.ac.uk/context/lilley.html

For Lucian of Chester, see www.medievalchester.ac.uk/texts/reading/Lucian/html

R. Sharpe, 'Peoples and Languages in Eleventh- and Twelfth-Century Britain and Ireland', http://poms.cch.kcl.ac.uk/redist/pdf/SharpeFinal.pdf, pp. 4–34.

Textus Roffensis: http://enriqueta.man.ac.uk/luna/servlet/detail/Man4Medieval VC~4~4~990378~142729.

Index

abbeys: Benedictine, 1, 3, 17, 23, 26, 54, 77, 78, 84, 128, 129, 135, 137, 143, 169, 174, 185, 236, 242, 255; Cistercian, 26, 47, 133, 137, 166, 170, 171, 179, 242

abbots, 16, 19, 26, 50, 53, 56, 57, 86, 87, 90, 125, 126, 132, 142, 144, 147–8, 177, 191, 255; see also Ælfric of Eynsham, Ælfwig of New Minster, Winchester, Æthelwig of Evesham, Ailred of Rievaulx, Baldwin of Bury, Benedict of Selby, Leofric of Peterborough, Paul of St Albans, Samson of Bury, Scolland of St Augustine's, Serlo de Percy of Whitby, Spearhafoc of Abingdon, Wulfric of St Augustine's

Aberdeen, 34

Abernethy, 43

Abingdon Abbey, 244

Adelelm, treasurer of King Stephen, 168

Adeliza, queen, 97, 183

Ælfgar, earl of Mercia, 33, 38

Ælfgifu, consort of King Cnut, 95, 113, 118

Ælfheah, bishop of Winchester, archbishop of Canterbury, saint, 32, 141, 167, 202, 204, 245, 246

Ælfhelm, ealdorman of Northumbria, 55

Ælfhere, ealdorman of Mercia, 55

Ælfric, abbot of Eynsham, 27, 125

Ælfthryth, queen, 55, 95

Ælfwig, abbot of New Minster, 144

Æthelflaed, lady of the Mercians, 226

Æthelred, king, 27, 31, 32, 34, 35, 37, 50, 52, 55, 59, 63, 79, 81, 84, 92, 95, 104, 113, 118, 120, 141, 159, 161, 188, 194, 202, 203, 218, 224, 239, 240, 241

Æthelstan, king, 53, 223, 239

Æthelwig, abbot of Evesham, 144, 148

Æthelwine, bishop of Durham, 138

Æthelwine ealdorman of East Anglia, 55

Æthelwold, bishop of Carlisle, 233

Æthelwold, bishop of Winchester, saint, 23, 55, 135, 137, 174, 179, 187, 188, 189

Æthelwulf, king of Wessex, 143

Ailred, abbot of Rievaulx, saint, 17, 26, 143, 147, 170, 242

Alan, count, of Richmond, 62, 183, 185, 190, 236

Alan de Neville, 99

Albion, 38, 53

Aldhelm of Malmesbury, saint, 24

alehouses, 155

Alexander, bishop of Lincoln, 25, 110, 142, 144, 146, 168, 169, 178, 193

Alexander, king of Scots, 44

Alexander III, pope, 90, 127

Alfred, king, 2, 70, 169, 188, 189, 200, 237, 239, 241

Alfred the Ætheling, 35, 77, 95, 108, 118, 122, 242

Alney, treaty of, 203, 228

Alnwick, 45, 166, 230

Andover, 141

Andrew Buccuinte, 219

Angles, 53, 239

Anglo-Norman Anonymous, 19, 21, 125

Roger, bishop of Salisbury, 25, 97, 98, 110, 140, 144, 168, 169, 180, 185, 195
Roger, bishop of Worcester, 138, 146
Roger, earl of Hereford, 144, 164
Roger de Glanville, sheriff of Northumberland, 230
Roger de Stuteville, sheriff of Northumberland, 230, 233
Roger d'Ivry, 160
Roger FitzRichard, 230
Roger of Howden, 219
Roger of Montgomery, 39, 154, 166
Roger of Ramsbury, 168
Roger Picot, sheriff of Northumberland, 230
Roger the Poitevin, 109, 234
Rome, 14, 42, 50, 53, 54, 85, 87, 126, 127, 129, 130, 132, 146, 158, 170, 173, 216, 217, 227, 256; St Peter's, 177, 188; *see also* appeals
Romney, 156
Rosamund Clifford, 180
Rouen, 79, 218

Saewold, sheriff of Oxfordshire, 194
saints, 7, 9, 11, 12, 18, 20, 22, 23, 24, 25, 29, 80, 126, 136–7, 148, 158, 159, 176–8, 196, 199, 237, 255, 256; *see also* Ailred, Ælfheah, Æthelwold, Aldhelm, Anselm, Augustine, Birinus, Cuthbert, Dunstan, Eadburh, Edith, Edmund, Edward the Martyr, Erkenwald, Etheldreda, Frideswide, Michael, Modwenna, Olaf, Oswald, Swithun, Thomas Becket, Valentine, Virgin Mary, Wilfrid
Salisbury, 57, 99; bishop of, *see* Roger; castle, 144
Samson, abbot of Bury St Edmunds, 26, 148
sanctuary, 14, 145, 188, 220
Sandwich, 32, 156
Scandinavia, 6, 33, 34, 71, 91, 102, 158, 243, 244, 245, 246
Scandinavians, 4, 30, 37, 41, 51, 106, 121, 122, 158, 201, 203, 204, 214, 224, 225, 228, 232, 235, 237, 242, 243, 244, 246
schools, 6, 22, 50, 146, 174
Scolland, abbot of St Augustine's Canterbury, 175
Scotland, 16, 34, 40, 54, 130, 143, 229, 247
Scots, 4, 11, 17, 28, 29, 34, 37, 38, 40–5, 54, 86, 92, 110, 120, 121, 122, 141, 142, 144,

164, 183, 191, 196, 228, 231, 233, 234, 241, 242, 243, 252, 259
seals, 54, 88, 90, 93, 94, 159, 217, 229
Selby Abbey, 147
serfs, 8, 11, 121, 122, 124
serjeanty, 106
sermons, 18, 27, 108, 121, 126
Settrington, 153
Shaftesbury, 77, 79
Sherborne castle, 144, 180
sheriffs, 2, 17, 38, 39, 52, 57, 62, 63, 64, 66, 69, 74, 75, 76, 97, 98, 99, 101, 103, 115, 128, 129, 131, 153, 157, 162, 165, 170, 172, 187, 194, 205–6, 207, 208, 209, 211, 217, 219, 220, 221, 223, 224, 227, 229, 230, 233, 234, 236, 245, 246, 254
Shetland, 34
ship-sokes, 156
shires, 52, 62, 63, 64, 98, 103, 116, 153, 156, 171, 172, 206, 225, 249, 257
Shrewsbury, 54, 110; Abbey, 166
shrines, 11, 23, 24, 80, 86, 135, 136, 137, 159, 175, 176, 177, 179, 180, 187, 188, 189, 196, 213, 219, 244
Shropshire, 165, 227
Simon Bloet, dean of Lincoln, 132
simony, 25, 50, 131, 134, 139
Siward, earl of Northumbria, 42, 55, 56, 137, 228, 229, 233, 235, 245
slavery, 11, 22, 75, 109, 121, 122, 250
slaves, 8, 28, 42, 48, 120, 121, 122, 124, 150, 200, 259
slave trade, 122, 131
Sleaford castle, 144
soke, 66, 114, 162, 201, 235
Somerset, 30, 174
Song of the Battle of Hastings, 82
Southwark, 167, 198, 204, 215, 216
Spearhafoc, abbot of Abingdon, 138
St Albans Abbey, 168, 176
St Andrews, archbishopric, 130
St Davids, 54, 130
St Germans, diocese, 128, 223
St Ives, 48
St Michael's Mount, 223
Staffordshire, 46
Stamford, 156, 225, 257; lawmen, 226
state, 3, 4, 5, 9, 10, 22, 70, 149–50, 221, 222, 248–51
Stephen, king, 2, 13, 40, 50, 52, 60–1, 62, 66, 69, 70, 72, 75, 78, 79, 83, 85, 87, 91,